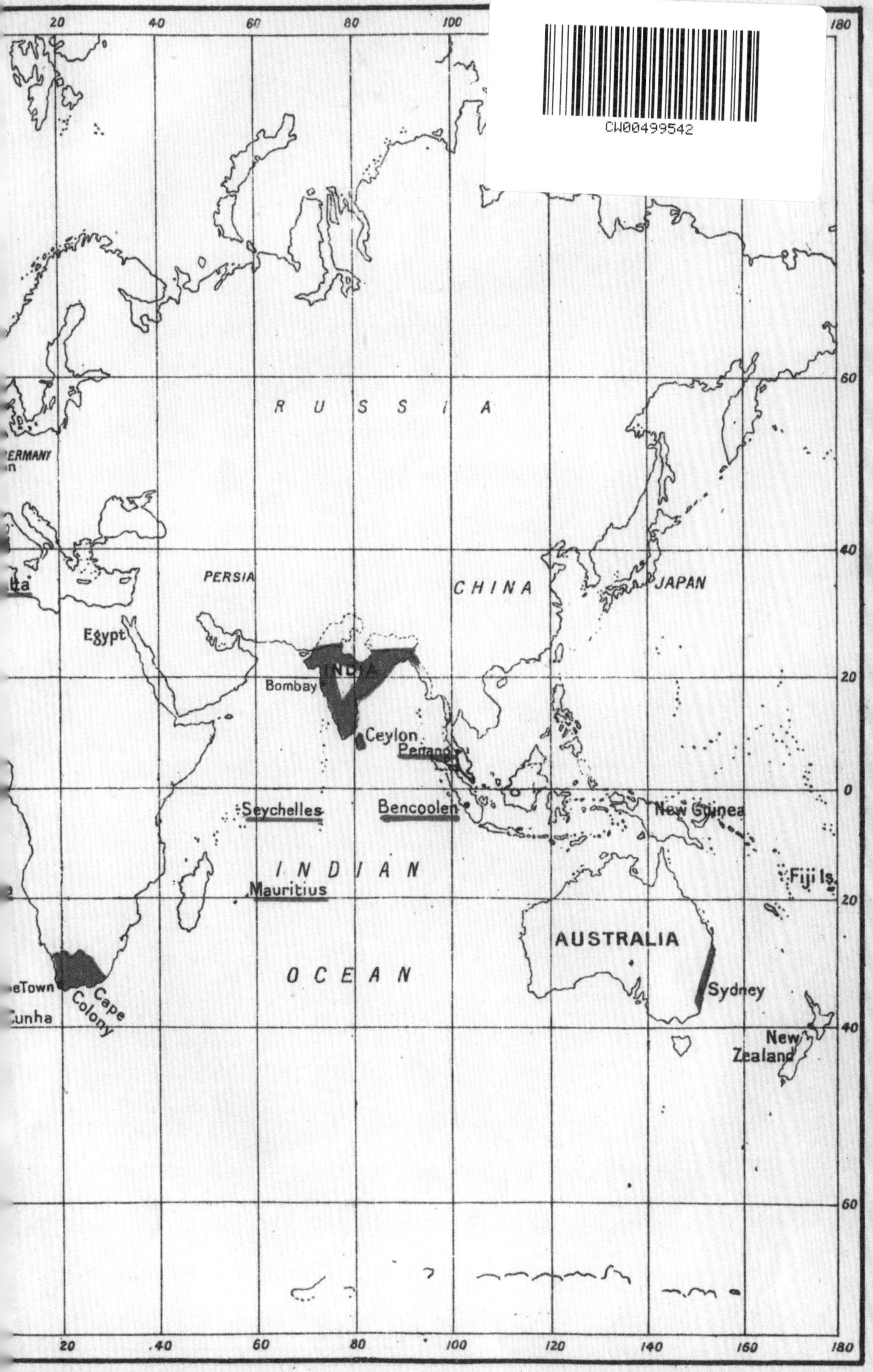
RUSSIA
PERSIA
CHINA
JAPAN
Egypt
INDIA
Bombay
Ceylon
Penang
Seychelles
Bencoolen
New Guinea
INDIAN
Mauritius
Fiji Is.
AUSTRALIA
OCEAN
Sydney
Cape Colony
New Zealand
20
40
60
80
100
120
140
160
180
0

Nicholas [illegible]

All Souls Coll. Oxon.

BRITAIN AND THE WORLD

Edited by The British Scholar Society

Editors:
James Onley, University of Exeter, UK
A. G. Hopkins, University of Cambridge
Gregory Barton, University of Western Sydney, Australia
Bryan Glass, Texas State University, USA

Other titles in the *Britain and the World* series include:

IMPERIAL ENDGAME
Britain's Dirty Wars and the End of Empire
Benjamin Grob-Fitzgibbon

SCIENCE AND EMPIRE
Knowledge and Networks of Science in the British Empire, 1850–1970
Brett Bennett and Joseph M. Hodge (editors)

BRITISH DIPLOMACY AND THE DESCENT INTO CHAOS
The Career of Jack Garnett, 1902–1919
John Fisher

ORDERING INDEPENDENCE
The End of Empire in the Anglophone Caribbean 1947–1967
Spencer Mawby

BRITISH IMAGES OF GERMANY
Admiration, Antagonism and Ambivalence, 1860–1914
Richard Scully

THE ANGLO-AMERICAN PAPER WAR
Debates about the New Republic, 1800–1825
Joe Eaton

BRITISH POLICY IN THE PERSIAN GULF, 1961–1968
Conceptions of Informal Empire
Helene von Bismarck

CINEMA AND SOCIETY IN THE BRITISH EMPIRE, 1895–1940
James Burns

THE BRITISH ABROAD SINCE THE EIGHTEENTH CENTURY
Vol. 1: *Travellers and Tourists*
Vol. 2: *Experiencing Imperialism*
Martin Farr and Xavier Guégan (editors)

IMPERIAL CULTURE IN ANTIPODEAN CITIES, 1880–1939
John Griffiths

SPORT AND THE BRITISH WORLD, 1900–1930
Amateurism and National Identity in Australasia and Beyond
Erik Nielsen

PAX BRITANNICA
Ruling the Waves and Keeping the Peace before Armageddon
Barry Gough

Forthcoming titles include:

BRITISH IMPERIALISM AND INDIA'S AFGHAN FRONTIER, 1918–1948
Brandon Marsh

NEW DELHI: THE LAST IMPERIAL CITY
David Johnson

Britain and the World
Series Standing Order ISBN 978–0–230–24650–8 hardcover
Series Standing Order ISBN 978–0–230–24651–5s paperback
(*outside North America only*)

You can receive future titles in this series as they are published by placing a standing order. Please contact your bookseller or, in case of difficulty, write to us at the address below with your name and address, the title of the series and one of the ISBNs quoted above.

Customer Services Department, Macmillan Distribution Ltd, Houndmills, Basingstoke, Hampshire RG21 6XS, England

---

Also by Barry Gough

THE ROYAL NAVY AND THE NORTHWEST COAST OF NORTH AMERICA, 1810–1914

THE NORTHWEST COAST: British Navigation, Trade and Discoveries to 1812

GUNBOAT FRONTIER: British Maritime Authority and Northwest Coast Indians

THE FALKLAND ISLANDS/MALVINAS: The Contest for Empire in the South Atlantic

BRITAIN, CANADA AND THE NORTH PACIFIC: Maritime Enterprise and Dominion, 1778–1914

FIRST ACROSS THE CONTINENT: Sir Alexander Mackenzie

FORTUNE'S A RIVER: The Collision of Empires in Northwest America

THE HISTORICAL DICTIONARY OF CANADA

JUAN DE FUCA'S STRAIT: Voyages in the Waterway of Forgotten Dreams

HISTORICAL DREADNOUGHTS: Arthur Marder, Stephen Roskill and Battles for Naval History

Pax Britannica

Ruling the Waves and Keeping the Peace before Armageddon

Barry Gough

palgrave
macmillan

First published 2014 by
PALGRAVE MACMILLAN

Palgrave Macmillan in the UK is an imprint of Macmillan Publishers Limited, registered in England, company number 785998, of Houndmills, Basingstoke, Hampshire RG21 6XS.

Palgrave Macmillan in the US is a division of St Martin's Press LLC, 175 Fifth Avenue, New York, NY 10010.

Palgrave Macmillan is the global academic imprint of the above companies and has companies and representatives throughout the world.

Palgrave® and Macmillan® are registered trademarks in the United States, the United Kingdom, Europe and other countries.

ISBN 978–0–230–35430–2

This book is printed on paper suitable for recycling and made from fully managed and sustained forest sources. Logging, pulping and manufacturing processes are expected to conform to the environmental regulations of the country of origin.

A catalogue record for this book is available from the British Library.

Library of Congress Cataloging-in-Publication Data
Gough, Barry M.
Pax Britannica : ruling the waves and keeping the peace before armageddon / Barry Gough, Independent Scholar, Canada.
pages cm. — (Britain and the world ; volume 14)
Includes bibliographical references and index.
ISBN 978–0–230–35430–2 (alk. paper)
1. Great Britain—History—19th century. 2. Great Britain—History—20th century. 3. Great Britain. Royal Navy—History. 4. Civilization, Modern—British influences. 5. Peace—History–19th century. 6. Peace—History—20th century. I. Title.
DA530.G66 2014
359.00941′09034—dc23 2014019988

To Wm. Roger Louis and to the memory of Gerald S. Graham

Now the old ships and their men are gone; the new ships and the new men, many of them bearing the old, auspicious names, have taken up their watch on the stern and impartial sea, which offers no opportunities but to those who know how to grasp them with a ready hand and undaunted heart.

Joseph Conrad, *The Mirror of the Sea*

England is mistress of the seas, not by virtue of any arrogant or aggressive pretensions, but by virtue of her history, of her geographical situation, of her economic antecedents and conditions, of her Imperial position and expansion. These conditions have given the dominion of the seas to her, not by any prescriptive right, but by a normal and almost natural process of evolution; and, so long as they subsist and she is true to herself, they will retain it for her.

The Times, 3 February 1902

Query by the Navy League: Does Britannia rule the waves, or does she mean to waive her rule?

Mr Punch on the Warpath

A heaving unsettled sea, and away over to the western horizon an angry yellow sun is setting clearly below a forbidding bank of the blackest of wind-charged clouds. In the centre of the picture lies an immense solitary cruiser with a flag... at her masthead blowing out broad and clear from the first rude kiss given by the fast-rising breeze. Then, away from half the points of a compass, are seen the swift ships of a cruiser squadron all drawing in to join their flagship. Some are close, others far distant and hull down, with nothing but their fitful smoke against the fast-fading lighted sky to mark their whereabouts; but like wild ducks at evening flighting home to some well-known spot, so are they, with one desire, hurrying back at the behest of their mother-ship to gather round her for the night.

Christopher Cradock, *Whispers from the Fleet*

Contents

Series Editors' Preface

From the sixteenth century onwards, Britain's influence on the world became progressively more profound and far-reaching, in time touching every continent and subject, from Europe to Australasia and archaeology to zoology. Although the histories of Britain and the world became increasingly intertwined, mainstream British history still neglects the world's influence upon domestic developments, and Britain's overseas history remains largely confined to the study of the British Empire. This series takes a broader approach to British history, seeking to investigate the full extent of the world's influence on Britain and Britain's influence on the world. *Pax Britannica* is published as the 14th volume in the British Scholar Society's *Britain and the World* series from Palgrave Macmillan.

Barry Gough's *magnum opus* investigates the century of British peace from 1815, with the final defeat of Napoleon at Waterloo, to 1914, with the outbreak of the First World War. Gough demonstrates that the long nineteenth century was dominated by Britain because the country controlled the most important military positions around the world. These allowed Britain to defend the empire, which would continue to grow throughout the century if, often, reluctantly. At the heart of *Pax Britannica* was the Royal Navy, the world's preeminent fleet, and its governance of the world's oceans. This unparalleled level of control also provided Britain with the opportunity to spread Christianity, commerce and civilization to all corners of the globe. According to Gough, '*Pax* was an exercise in self-disciplining statecraft where higher principles operated side by side with the pursuit of profit and the protection of power'. This British world peace would end with the outbreak of the First World War. The war signalled that the British were no longer powerful enough to control rising rivals such as imperial Germany and the United States. *Pax Britannica* is a systematic look at how Britain, a tiny archipelago off the northwest coast of Europe, moulded Europe and the world between 1815 and 1914.

Editors, *Britain and the World*:
James Onley, American University of Sharjah
A. G. Hopkins, Pembroke College, Cambridge
Gregory A. Barton, the Australian National University
Bryan S. Glass, Texas State University

Preface

This book's subject concerns a state of affairs that might never have existed, though it lived long in the hearts and minds of its practitioners that is, its policy-makers, its administrators, its viceroys and governors, its commissioners, and its guardians, both military and naval. It is, in essence, a biography of an idea possessed in the minds of men who fervently sought to implement it and to ensure its continuance.

Pax Britannica has been a subject of incomplete historical inquiry. Attempts to bring the whole into a reasonable compass have proved to be elusive. The reasons are obvious because the lines of inquiry were as imaginative as they were suggestive. Students of the history of British foreign policy have understandably defined *Pax* as an extension of British diplomatic and consular thinking, and they have connected it to a unique period of British predominance, with the statesman Palmerston as its archetypal practitioner. At the time of its flowering, the Roman model suggested itself to the Victorians and Edwardians and, indeed, to all of those who did its bidding. The economic underpinnings of *Pax* are likewise of significance, because at a time when Britain was the "workshop of the world" free trade was in the ascendant, a state of affairs that many hoped would long endure but in the end, like much else, came to an abrupt end with the intense international rivalries that characterized the late nineteenth century and brought on the deluge of 1914. But before this fateful catastrophe, lawful trade was seen as beneficial to European civilization, with Britain as example, progenitor and leader. The empire's expansion was largely motivated by the energies of the mercantile class. The commercial community created the conditions upon which British imperial policy was shaped. *Pax* rested on fiscal strength, banking acumen and techniques of state management. It also required the friendship, or at least forbearance, of European powers. British naval power made it possible. Technological change and innovation speeded its possibilities and centralized the means of command. It was also an idea with export value. Students of the history of colonial policy and colonial expansion, as well as of the history of the British dominions during this period, have seen the ideas of *Pax* echoed in local circumstances.

Above all, *Pax Britannica* was an achievement of a maritime power fresh from victory over a prodigious Continental power, France. Upon this state of affairs Britain was able to influence those places around the globe that fronted onto the oceans, seas and annexes. *Pax Britannica*'s progression and achievement was essentially a maritime one and chiefly a naval success story. It also required the deployment of armies and other military forces, including the Royal Marines and the East India Company Army, to exercise authority and secure interests ashore as required. These military units were guardians of *Pax*. Exercising *Pax* involved the extension and protection of legal trade, the putting-down of piracy and stamping out of the slave trade. It also involved other pursuits of a humanitarian nature: ending the blackbirding (or kidnapped labour) traffic in the South Pacific, outlawing cannibalism and propping up missionary endeavours. The whole had been realized and tied together by naval global influence and even dominance, and it is these matters that the present investigation uses as its basis of inquiry.

This book is mainly concerned with naval matters, principally the part played by the Royal Navy, but as we will see, naval operations and strategy cannot be separated from diplomacy and politics. This work is not about policy-making, and it is not a study of the Admiralty at work. Rather it is a pursuit of how the Navy influenced the wider world. In all of these things, *Pax* was an idea, even a state of mind; it was never an actual state of affairs. As an era in time, *Pax* was riddled with small wars. Many historians proclaim it as an illusion, and rightly so if they assume that an absolute peace was established. They perhaps misunderstand that it really was a hoped-for state of affairs – or a justification for actions taken. It was a powerful argument of those who aspired to bring law, justice and liberty to the empire and the wider world. It was global in its influence, and it was based on an assumption that law and justice, as developed by the British peoples and their institutions, was worthy of application to the wider world. It thus carried cultural assumptions, one might say even of superiority. It held within it no apologies. But when abuses occurred, as they were bound to, then the critics were anxious to point out how the concept, and the ideal, was violating the principles and the intentions of *Pax*.

British statesmen preferred to speak of British "interests", a term that was sufficiently broad in scope (and often open to discussion and debate). These interests were usually of enough importance to require protection. Long before the term "imperialism" entered the decades of its greatest use, the 1880s and 1890s, British "interests" were what concerned those who cared about the strength and vitality, as well as the future, of the nation, its trade and the empire. Although the historian Sir Keith Hancock warned that "imperialism" was no word for practitioners of the craft, inflamed as it was with rhetoric and imbalanced in its intentions, the fact of the matter is that it has entered our common vocabulary. *Pax Britannica* was a subset of the generality known as "imperialism", and it was often the stated means – or purpose – for which imperial growth and attendant imperial management was advanced. Just as statesmen would talk about British interests, so they would speak of the British Empire – as a territorial fact but also as a collectivity of territories overseas under the Union Flag. The British thought globally in this regard. And everywhere where the flag flew, so, too, was trade to be legal and peace to be established and reinforced. This was the *leitmotif* of *Pax Britannica*. Peace, order and good government were companions to legal trade, and law and justice. The humanitarian and philanthropic missions that were part of the general obligation of those pursuing *Pax* during this age proved to be a consuming and necessarily expensive feature. The Navy carried the burden and in so doing wrote one of the more virtuous chapters in its history, or indeed that of any navy.

Pax began in 1815, with the close of the wars with France and the United States. The peace arrangements ushered in a period of peace that lasted, for all intents and purposes, for a century.

If there is no quarrel with the beginning date of *Pax*, there is some argument about that of its termination. I am confirmed in my contention that *Pax* ended in 1914, for Gerald Graham and John Bach, examiners of the phenomenon, have concluded similarly in their respective books, *The Empire of the North Atlantic* and *The Australia Station*. The present study contends that 1914 marked the end of the unique epoch in history known as *Pax Britannica*. Could it be that certain British voices denied the early demise of *Pax*, thinking that it had a longer lease on life than it really did? Some adherents to *Pax* as an historical fact believe it to have had a longer period of extension. A revival of British imperial interests and obligations in the interwar period of 1919–1939 was no illusion, but the old order based on the older intentions of the nineteenth and early twentieth centuries had passed and given way to newer realities. That remarkable observer of the era, Lord Beloff, told me that he considered *Pax* to extend to the early years of the Second World War, the loss of HMS *Prince of Wales* and HMS *Repulse* in December 1941 in the South China Sea, with the fall of Singapore the following February marking its end. He even indicated that the Suez crisis of 1956 might be another possible closing date. I do not subscribe to this because it seems to me that the circumstances that brought Britain to war in 1914 marked the end of the period of isolation and freedom of action that was the hallmark of *Pax*. "We are fish, and we should think like fish," is the way the statesman Lord Salisbury had put it. But once constraints on British independence of action presented themselves, a unique period of independent, wide-ranging economic and political control came to an end. *Pax Britannica* as an idea died with the Continental Commitment, with the last death throes exhibited at the Dardanelles and particularly the Somme.

This book looks at the roles of the Royal Navy during *Pax Britannica*. In answer to the old question "Does trade follow the flag or the flag trade?", that question is the wrong one to ask. What needs exploring, as this book seeks to do, is an analysis of how naval power aided both the expansion of the empire ("formal empire") and the growth of trade, which would occur almost everywhere and most certainly in zones or areas of influence known as "informal empire". This book is not a history of the Royal Navy of the period, though it seeks to place the Navy at the centre of events and as the focal point of analysis. Students of naval history are aware that, unfortunately, the subject tends to live for itself, and to stand in isolation from those aspects of change that are actually tied to its own story – foreign affairs, imperial rivalry, and colonial and dominion territories. Sadly, attempts to interlock naval with British imperial history are not now as fashionable as they used to be, when practitioners of the art, such as James A. Williamson and Gerald Graham, ranked among the premier historians in this line of work. Here in these pages an attempt has been made to revisit some of the developments of the age, with the Navy at the centre and the empire as a field, or fields, of influence. A fundamental problem with R.E. Robinson and J. Gallagher's "The Imperialism of Free Trade", which upon its publication in 1953 revolutionized our general understanding of how the British Empire grew in a time of anti-imperial sentiment and free trade, is that the naval story seems completely left out. As these pages show, territorial growth of empire in the period 1815–1914 often featured springboards or locales of benefit to the Navy and to the growth of British influence, including trade protection, overseas. Similarly, the more recent overarching theory of British imperialism of the age, dubbed "Gentlemanly Capitalism" by Peter Cain and Anthony Hopkins, avoids the naval dimension. My therefore necessary contribution to the discussion of Cain and Hopkins appears in the collection of critiques edited by Raymond E. Dumett, *Gentlemanly Capitalism and British Imperialism: The New Debate on Empire* (1999). Echoes of it will be found in these pages. The energies of the mercantile class were largely responsible for British imperial expansion. The vast numbers in the commercial community, most of them unknown to history, created the conditions upon which British imperial policy was shaped by secretaries and undersecretaries of state.

Part of the problem is that naval historians in general have neglected to tell the linking story between naval power, and imperial strength and aggrandizement; or, more likely (and here I disclose my bias on this), perhaps it is the generality of historians who have failed to look at the naval and maritime underpinnings of the stories that they tell. It could be that both interpretations are correct. One of naval history's problems is that it seems to stand alone as a topic. With all of its fascinating dimensions, this is understandably the case. But by isolating itself from the problems ashore and neglecting the view from the quarterdeck (or, for that matter, from the Admiralty boardroom) concerning the imperial and colonial aspects of the widening world, naval history steers a narrow channel. In any event, this book seeks to widen the scope of naval studies – to explore the maritime foundations of imperial history. And, if it seems as if the pattern of analysis is a little disjointed – here West Africa, there the South Pacific, or here India and there British Columbia – it will be appreciated (and that is my hoped-for intent) that these events were happening simultaneously in various parts of the world. That the British were able to manage this whole scheme of global growth and control is a tribute to their administrative acumen and techniques. The Admiralty and the system that ran and directed the affairs of the Navy were uniquely centralized, unusually compact in size in comparison to the extent of the duties, and based on a tight system of interlocking responsibilities in which the individual – including the "man on the spot" – was always the key.

I am aware that the thrust of this work runs counter to the image of empire and British imperialism that is so widely accepted these days. I do not see that experience as one great mistake for which apologies must necessarily be made. But my intention is to reposition and recentre the Navy and sea power in imperial and indeed world history. Undoubtedly, critics who generally accept "post-colonial" postulations, including literary theory, deconstruction, subaltern studies, area studies, gender studies and discourse analysis, will say that my account of naval actions and influence is proof positive of imperialism at work. I have taken care to note benefits bestowed, and I fully accept the view, as I have developed in several chapters, that such actions brought physical and cultural traumas to those colonies or the indigenous peoples coerced under the guns of British warships. I cannot reverse what is now a general tendency in the historical profession, but I can maintain, and I do, that naval power and influence is a subject worth studying in its own right, warts and all. The Royal Navy was the first instrument of worldwide influence. The British Empire was the first effective global empire. As a neglected subject in world or global history, the naval and maritime dimensions of British hegemony merit consideration. Empires are built on power; Britain's was built on sea power. The instrument of this influence, in both the ships and the officers and men, was unique in human history, and we will not see its like again. In this work we are drawn back to an earlier age – one before that of the twentieth century's age of total war. At the centre of this influence lay the policies developed in offices in Whitehall and guided or directed by the will of a changing Parliament – policies influenced, too, by commercial interests and philanthropic organizations. It may seem odd to the reader that minimal intervention was the policy pursued. It may also seem odd that acquisitions of imperial real estate came with reluctance, often as a last resort. The evidence presented lends weight to the arguments that those who directed policies at home and abroad were answering the requirements posed by turbulent, threatening frontiers. Far from being a system directed from London, the empire grew in response to chaotic influences on the margins.

That having been said, metropolitan requirements dictated the Navy's commitments on distant seas. This was especially so in fighting the slave trade in foreign hands. A powerful segment of the British political elite, with broad national backing, demanded the Navy's intervention to stamp out the trade. Backed by the will of Parliament, the Foreign Office and Admiralty responded; they were answerable to the new mandate, the most altruistic as well as the most problematic of the Navy's efforts of the era. Coupled with anti-slavery was anti-piracy. The ongoing "war" against piracy, noted in these pages, receives broader coverage in a companion volume co-authored with Charles Borras. That volume focuses on British and American means and methods (sometimes in concert) in Caribbean waters from 1815 to 1860.

Among the greatest places of imperial influence in the *Pax Britannica* age was the Western Hemisphere. Latin America exhibited the greatest rate of increase in commercial growth, but the real source of wealth by foreign trade was that with the United States. The growth or consolidation of formal empire in the Western Hemisphere was, similarly, a remarkable imperial enterprise, Canada being a premier example. Maple-leaf-sporting Canadians may not think themselves inheritors of empire but they are indeed the new practitioners in the current age. On the British Columbia coast, many challenges presented to the Navy in establishing *Pax* and the voices of the aggrieved echo still, down to our own times. Gunboats have left a chill in the air. The growth of reassertion of British formal power in the nineteenth century also occurred in Honduras and the Falkland Islands. Bermuda was elevated as a naval base and the key of influence in the Americas. In the Caribbean, the British continued their influence on a multitude of islands, and they withstood challenges on the Nicaraguan and Panama coasts from the United States Government as well as American freebooters or filibusterers. In all of these Western Hemisphere locations, or areas of influence, the British expanded or consolidated their trade and empire. They did so at a time of the rise of the United States to global reach. For these several reasons, this book places a heavier emphasis on the Americas than do many histories of the British Empire.

As will become obvious, the practitioners of and believers in *Pax Britannica* saw in the United States the new trident-bearers and keepers of the flame. The United States came suddenly to this but was forced by circumstances to begin an imperial and global reach that continues to this day, though is sorely tested as to its strength and viability.

That *Pax Americana* derived from *Pax Britannica* will be made apparent here. I have made it one of the central purposes of this book to explain how it was that the British built up their global system. I have done so with the intent that those interested in American global power and influence in the future will see how bases and instruments of war are only as good as statecraft, and financial acumen and prudence at home. Like *Pax Britannica, Pax Americana* may come to an end. It may dissolve. It may be replaced by something else. We do not know the end result. From my perspective it was the shift of affairs in the Americas that provided the crossover between *Pax Britannica* and *Pax Americana*. The pivotal date is 1898. Two critical episodes or developments in this were the Spanish-American War and the resolution of the difficulties attendant to proceeding to construct the Panama Canal. It is true that the rise of imperial Germany, and to a lesser extent imperial Japan, changed strategic realities in Europe and East Asia, respectively, in the late nineteenth century but they seem less influential in the ending of *Pax* than the rise of the United States to global reach by war and victory over Spain in 1898. The process of succession dates from this time, and for these reasons the reader will perhaps find more on the history of the Americas in this book than they might expect.

The transference of authority, made more agreeable to the Americans whom the British had fought in the War of Independence and again in the War of 1812, allowed the British to prop up their endangered position of imperial and maritime supremacy as imperial Germany, in particular, came forward to exert world authority and vainly try to seize the trident of Neptune. The Germans did not succeed; *weltpolitik* lay beyond their ambitions. But the British and their newly acquired American ally in global reach and authority extended the old system that had been put in place in 1815. The Third Reich would make a similar challenge, one denied by sea power. The Soviet Union would do so similarly. In the end, however, and even until the present time, those who control the seas, who have bases of authority for extending the reach of the heartland empire to the distant places of need, who have the financial authority and acumen to keep the fiscal and economic basis upon which power alone can be sustained, and who have the diplomatic and military knowledge and systems to have the ability to enforce a state of peace, will possess the fundamental means of security and influence. Technical advantage will be of utmost importance, but it will be equivalent to nothing unless political will backed by financial strength exist in due proportion. The lessons that Alfred Thayer Mahan, naval officer, historian and strategist, taught so long ago about national stability speak down to us through the years.

Here I have not concerned myself with the shrinking of the empire. Many works have addressed that theme, notably on decolonization. But, for the age of *Pax Britannica* specifically, it will become clear in the reading of this book that many territorial acquisitions of empire during this unusual epoch were those that were for strategic advantage – Aden, Singapore, the Falkland Islands and even the development of Bermuda as a bulwark of empire. I am led to believe that many imperial historians have concentrated too much on colonial development along the lines of settlement, which, as important as it is, was only one component of expansion – and one of great financial expense. Other imperial historians have been preoccupied with issues of "imperial defence" and its imponderables. My concerns, however, are seagoing ones, those of command and of control, and of influence attained on and over the seas – and how to sustain such influence in trying conditions. Whereas various warships would age and outlive their usefulness, the bases formed the ongoing cement of empire. With regard to "imperialism", it will be seen that the pursuit of *Pax* was part of the search for law and peace on the international stage, as well as in colonial locales and in the dominions. This was the essential argument of the powerful and long-time MP William Ewart Gladstone, and it had many adherents. It might be imagined that the prophets of *Pax* were also acolytes of empire and of imperialism, and there is no way for precise differentiations on these terms. They obviously overlap. But my main concern has been to address the matter, or anatomy, of *Pax* – what it was, how it was effected and how it was maintained.

A few words are needed here as to how this book is organized. I have introduced the definition of *Pax Britannica* at the outset (Chapter 1) so that the reader might gain an appreciation of the concept and how it came to be called such. Then follows (Chapter 2) an examination of the nature of worldwide responsibilities in 1815 and how this afforded the dominant state of affairs for the balance of the 100 years of *Pax*. Next (Chapter 3) I look at naval bases, chiefly Bermuda, the bulwark of British Empire in the Americas and the means of exerting influence in the Western Hemisphere. Positioned on a crossroads of the American seas, it has enjoyed a powerful position in modern history that has seldom been appreciated, while the story of the construction of that base and the massive work overseas of British strategists has no equal in the nineteenth century (and foreshadows British plans for Singapore after 1919). Bermuda's naval history also opens a window on a human world hitherto unexamined – of how ex-slaves and convicts built a naval bulwark of empire. Some social aspects are introduced here, bearing on labour – free, slave and even convict. The whole forms a microcosm of the difficulties of constructing and maintaining a base far from home islands. At the same time as Britain was bringing forward Bermuda as a formidable base, the Navy was undertaking hydrographical surveys and, in parallel to this mission, supporting the investigations of British and European science on a global scale. Formidable results devolved from these parallel missions that are a central feature of *Pax Britannica*. Next (Chapter 5) I extend the discussion to fields of informal empire in the Americas, notably Brazil and the former Spanish American colonies (now new nations under British protection). Here the underlying theme is the relation of the City of London's influence to that of Westminster and Whitehall, a subject addressed by Cain and Hopkins (and their critics) in their discussion of "Gentlemanly Capitalism", with the Royal Navy the tool of the influence of protecting British interests, political and commercial. Our attention is drawn to Brazil, notably Río de Janeiro, and to Valparaiso, Chile, as informal anchors of empire – and springboards for British naval influence in distant waters. Herein, too, I discuss the Falkland Islands, where authority that was first exhibited in the 1760s was proclaimed once again in 1833. I move into European statecraft and to problems in the Mediterranean (Chapter 6). Then I deal with eastern seas, mainly Singapore and China, with side glances at Borneo and

Japan (Chapter 7). Next (Chapter 8) I show how the British wove, very reluctantly, a web of authority over the Pacific Islands. I use the British Columbia experience as an example of the dimensions and dilemmas of forceful policing measures – and the costs to the Navy and to British honour (Chapter 9). Then I address fighting the slave trade, first in West Africa waters of the American seas (Chapter 10), and second, dealing in turn with anti-piracy and anti-slavery duties from the Red Sea south to the Cape of Good Hope, and with the bold and gallant, if impossible, attempt to throttle the Arab-dominated slave trade of East Africa, centred on Zanzibar. The next three chapters re-examine the naval and strategic dynamics that constitute both the crises and the demise of *Pax* (Chapters 12–14). The war that Britain, the empire and their armed forces, including the Navy, faced was not one of their choice or of their doing. Rather, a web of rivals and a set of changing circumstances engulfed the practitioners and defenders of *Pax*, bringing down the curtain on one of the most remarkable and indeed promising experiments in the history of nations and international affairs. The rise of the German Empire was the principal cause of the end of *Pax Britannica*. Finally (Chapter 15) I provides a retrospective on the epoch and its transition to modern times. I have drawn conclusions at the close of this chapter. They are reflections on the central features of the epoch from the British standpoint.

It will be seen that this book makes no apology for British power at its supreme moment. Sordid examples could have filled our pages, had I gone seeking instances of the worst uses of British power. The world's history is replete with them. However, I have chosen to devote my space here to a different theme, and I am rather of the opinion that if history is a long chronology of human crime then the era of *Pax Britannica* is indubitably one of its most virtuous chapters.

The First World War was the ruination of many empires and the transformation of the British Empire. The year 1914 cast a long and terrible shadow on what had preceded it. Many an historian has wrung their hands about the subject of explaining the causes of the war. The British have taken their share of the blame, and President Woodrow Wilson classified "navalism" as one of the cardinal causes. Those who have decried the British Empire and the British imperial experience, as a wise historian said so long ago, had better take into account what transpired in their place, for it has yet to be demonstrated that the world, and the condition of mankind, is better in this age than it was in that particular epoch of the past that forms the subject of this book. The end of peace in August 1914 marked the biggest tragedy of a long era of global change in which the British were at the centre.

Just as *Pax* had been proclaimed after defeating France and Napoleon's pretensions to command the Continent, so did it end in the fateful struggle to contain imperial Germany and the Kaiser's desires for dominance on the Continent and overseas in rivalry to the British Empire.

This work on *Pax* is one attempt (there will be others) to try to provide a synthesis of an aspect of British influence – in this case on and over the seas at a critical period of modern history. Constraints of space alone have prevented an examination of many of the themes or treatments of subjects that are mentioned herein. I have undoubtedly failed in my attempt to cite every historical source and study worthy of notice, but I am reminded of the fact that I have been a witness to the shifts and changes of the historical profession, its passions and preoccupations, over nearly a half century, and I hope I have given balance and eschewed prejudice in this attempt to explain one aspect of the imperial moment.

I have not had the pleasure of visiting all of the imperial ports of call and beachheads written about in this book – Gibraltar, Malta and Aden have escaped me – for time and money are in short supply, but still I would like to think that having visited the strong "old dominions" of yesterday and many of their nearby islands and places of influence, I have had a good taste of empire overseas. Had I done the customary Grand Tour and then the route through Suez that was the hallmark of Victorian-day authors, I would have reflected on the age-old perspective of the route to the East, the importance of the Asian subcontinent and the sea road to Cathay. Rather, I think it is in the Western, or American, Hemisphere that the world's shift has occurred, and this may explain my preoccupation with the sources that reveal this aspect of the imperial story. This is not to say that the experience of the Asian subcontinent is not fundamental to the story, or that of Africa and its numerous peoples, but the pivot of the world's history has turned on the history of the Atlantic and notably the Pacific oceans. As a generality, the British, in so long thinking of India as "the jewel in the crown", have been the last and the most reluctant to recognize this shift, and I hope this book will broaden the scope of the post-imperial viewpoint and provoke some thinking about why Asia and Africa are the inveterate preoccupations.

A work such as this, a chapter in world history really, depends on a range of documents and historical studies. The "Notes on the Historical Materials" section contains the principal monographic works and general surveys that I have used. As to general works of travel and experience, I have experienced what Jan Morris confessed in writing her trilogy, confining my research to the wanderer's eye. If I have given a sense of what that era of *Pax Britannica* was like in all its splendour but also with all its difficulties, I shall be glad.

Barry Gough
Victoria, British Columbia, Canada

Acknowledgements

For guidance in the gestation and making of this book, thanks go to the late Gerald S. Graham, Rhodes Professor of Imperial History at the University of London, who crafted interpretations of *Pax* with admirable inclusions on aspects of the history of the North Atlantic, the Indian Ocean and the China seas. An invitation from the University of Nottingham to give the Cust Foundation Lecture allowed me to develop the themes of this work, a preliminary version of which appeared in *Round Table*, 314 (1990). I thank Prof. William Doyle and colleagues for their hospitality. The guidance of A.P. Thornton is appreciated. Raymond E. Dumett helped to sharpen my analysis of the Cain and Hopkins thesis "Gentlemanly Capitalism" and I am obliged to the authors for their remarks in return. I have leaned heavily on Sir John Manning Ward, W.P. Morrell and John Bach, who wrote about the extension of authority in Australasian and Pacific waters. I have benefited from the writings of many historians with regard to areas of influence: Grace Fox on naval influence in Chinese and Japanese waters; John Brookes in the search for authority among the Pacific Islands, notably Hawaii, and Iain Hamilton, familiar with the themes of this book, has made contributions to it, with comparisons to the French experience. Rebecca Berens Matzke's *Deterrence Through Strength: British Naval Power and European Policy under Pax Britannnica* (2011) provides detailed discussion of North American border disputes, Syria, and the First China War, all in 1835–1845. Daniel Baugh, with global sympathies that transcend the centuries of modern historical inquiry, has provided encouragement. Eugene Rasor answered questions about punishment, the manning of the fleet, and naval reforms of the Victorian era, plus bibliographical matters of which he is master. Wilfrid Laurier University awarded leaves for research in the National Archives, Kew, the Scott Polar Research Institute in Cambridge, the National Maritime Museum, Greenwich, where I was Caird Fellow, and the British Library Manuscripts Division, London, and to examine sources upon which this book is based. My appetite for world history was whetted in the old library of the Royal Commonwealth Society (the holdings are now housed in the Cambridge University Library) when as a postgraduate student at King's College London I had the run of the stacks, and I thank the late Donald Simpson and Terry Barrenger for guidance. Senate House Library, Institute of Historical Research of London University, Rhodes House, the Athenaeum and London Library have yielded treasures. The British Council made possible interviews with Sir Harry Hinsley, David Fieldhouse and Ronald Hyam. R.E. Robinson led me to the thesis of R. Gavin. A NATO research fellowship spurred recent studies.

The Archives Centre, Churchill College Cambridge, yielded many gems. The Sea Power Centre Australia (Naval History Section) in Canberra, the National University of Singapore, the Archives of Bermuda, the National Museum Bermuda and Bermuda Maritime Museum, Malta Maritime Museum, Heritage Malta, the Archives of British Columbia in Victoria, Naval and Military Museum, Canadian Forces Base Esquimalt, the Maritime Museum of British Columbia, Victoria, and the Maritime Command Museum, Halifax, Nova Scotia, provided many golden nuggets. Additional materials came from Library and Archives Canada, the Directorate of History, Department of National Defence, Ottawa, Special Collections of the Royal Military College of Canada, and the Public Archives of Nova Scotia.

I must particularly thank Captain Michael Barritt, John Bosher, James A. Boutilier, the late Charles Boxer, Peter Cain, John Darwin, the late John S. Galbraith, Liam Gauci, Edward Harris and Jane Downing, Anthony Hopkins, Robert Kubicek, Joseph Lenarcik, Antony Low, Charles Maier, Malcolm Murfett, James Onley, the late R.E. Robinson, Clare Sharpe, Bryan Smith, David Stevens and the late Robin W. Winks. Taking a cue from Frances Parkman, travel has been my great teacher, and my knowledge of imperial affairs has benefited from excursions to faraway places hitherto undreamed of before the advent of the jet age. I went to New Zealand courtesy of the William Evans Professorship, which I held at the University of Otago. Repeated visits to Australia have been made but none so significant as that when I was Commonwealth Scholar at the Australian National University, Canberra, holding the Thomas H.B. Symons Commonwealth Distinguished Fellowship. I ventured to South Africa, principally ZwaZulu Natal, under joint sponsorship of Wilfrid Laurier University and the University of Natal, an opportunity that allowed me to see at first hand the difficulties of South African harbours, the great Karoo and spacious veldt, and those remarkable drifts and escarpments of the Drakensberg which were the tragic sites of so many imperial wars. Fiji and Tahiti I visited on my South Pacific adventures. As a scholarly guest of the National University of Singapore, I had the opportunity to ransack the University Library for its strong holdings on the history of Southeast Asia and Anglo-Dutch rivalry. En route to Johannesburg I visited Río de Janeiro, that port of informal British Empire where British sea power indubitably played such an important role in the independence and young life of Brazil. On the way home a call to Buenos Aires highlighted other connections in the imperial story, more particularly about the Falkland Islands (Malvinas), about which I had contributed a book to the historical literature. Visits to Bermuda have been undertaken under my own steam, as it were, and each time I look at the buildings of empire there on Ireland Island with a gasp of memory: of how convicts could have built such a monument to an empire of yesteryear. Hong Kong, left surprisingly till last in my travels, turned out to be a fundamental explanation of British enterprises in

Far Eastern seas; and even today one senses in viewing the islands and waters from a distant overlooking peak the ghostly presence of a British man-of-war steaming up the long and crowded approach opposite the customs house, then coming smartly to anchor, a single representative of a country and crown so far away and of a mighty marine constabulary that was the arbiter of the world's affairs in the century after Waterloo. The Hong Kong Central Library and the Hong Kong Club offered many literary pearls that enriched imperial vistas and memories. For assistance with illustrations I thank the staff of the Naval and Military Museum, Canadian Forces Base Esquimalt, the Maritime Museum of British Columbia in Victoria, the Bermuda Maritime Museum, and the School of Oriental and African Studies. Unpublished Crown copyright material is published by permission of the Controller of Her Majesty's Stationery Office. Every effort has been made to contact all copyright holders. The publishers will be pleased to make good in future editions any errors or omissions brought to their attention.

I thank the editors of this series for embracing the topic, and the editors and the staff of Palgrave Macmillan for bringing the work into its final state. Charles Borras and Christopher Hagerman provided much useful commentary, for which thanks are due. Although I have benefited from the advice of many who have assisted me, and in some cases read sections of the manuscript, I alone am responsible for the use of the evidence and interpretations contained herein.

About the Author

Barry Gough received his PhD in imperial and commonwealth history from the University of London. A student under Gerald Graham, Rhodes Professor of Imperial History, King's College, London, he is now a retired scholar living in Victoria, British Columbia, Canada. He is past president of the North American Society for Oceanic History and also the Canadian Nautical Research Society. He has been an academic advisor to the International Churchill Society and twice has been a research by-fellow, Churchill College, Cambridge. The University of London awarded him a DLit for his distinguished contributions to imperial and commonwealth historical literature. He has toured and lectured in South Africa, New Zealand, Australia, Singapore and the United States. He is Professor Emeritus of Wilfrid Laurier University, Waterloo, Ontario. Among his publications are contributions to the *Oxford History of the British Empire*, the *Oxford Dictionary of National Biography* and a series of studies of British maritime ascendancy and sea power in action: *The Royal Navy and the Northwest Coast of North America*, *Gunboat Frontier* and *The Falkland Islands/Malvinas: The Contest for Empire in the South Atlantic*. Of recent note is his *Historical Dreadnoughts: Arthur Marder, Stephen Roskill and Battles for Naval History*. His books have won numerous prizes, not least the Clio Prize of the Canadian Historical Association.

Prologue

Westminster, Whitehall and the City of London lie in close proximity on the banks of the River Thames. They form a unique nexus of power built up over centuries, beginning at least in the sixteenth. From this stream in the days of imperial power and global maritime reach flowed the power of the metropolis. To this same waterway arrived the treasures of the wider world and the throbbing commerce of the globe. The might of empire was centred here – the governing bodies, as it were. The Church of England and other religious organizations had their heart here. So did the medical and legal professions and various seats of learning – all adjacent to the tidal waterway and its influences. The publishing and print media industries had concentrated nodes of global reach. Within the bounds of the City of London lay the hub of the maritime world – the Bank of England, the Royal Exchange, Lloyd's of London, the shipping companies and marine contractors, the railway and engineering firms, and others besides, plus the offices of the concerns of corporate empire, some of them ancient firms, including the East India Company and the Hudson's Bay Company. Altogether in this contracted geographical space, adjacent to and spanning the river, was formed a powerful nexus of financial and political technique quite unlike any other in the world. If Rome had dominated the Mediterranean and outlying ramparts, London had come to hold the world in its fee. This was the essence of it in 1815. All of the ancient controls of the mediaeval world had passed, save for ceremonial matters skilfully adhered to, and the commercial revolution had swept through this port. Calculated risk now was the feature of London's commercial intentions, and it held Parliament and successive ministries to the task of protecting the long-distance trades that brought Britain such wealth and influence.

London was the port of the world. Trade brought England its liquid wealth, and Daniel Defoe in 1724 spoke of the "silver Thames" because of the revenue that the river generated.[1] Downstream from this pulsating centre lay a hard and crowded workaday world with other naval and mercantile purposes. Its docks, wharves and factories were the great machinery of empire, and its mercantile history was of an ancient order. The Pool of London was as far as oceangoing vessels could navigate, and mainly below it was the vast conglomeration of docks and warehouses on either side of the river. Between London Bridge and Deptford, forests of masts could be seen. Here was a testament to Britain's wealth and power. At Deptford, Henry VIII had ordered a naval yard to be built. At Greenwich there was a naval hospital and later Royal Naval College, an establishment built on majestic proportions. High on the hill to the south, exactly on the zero meridian, the Royal Observatory marked the global imperial measurement that the British had negotiated with continental partners. The time machine there and the red ball that without fail descended from its mast at precisely one o'clock every afternoon set the standard to be observed by the clocks of the world. At Blackwall the East India Dock had been built and at Rotherhithe the Surrey Dock had been constructed. The massive Victoria Dock and Millwall Dock were designed to accommodate steamers, and below yet again Tilbury for still larger ones, the liners of the world capable of navigating that far upstream. It was a smoky, noisy and smelly world where human senses reacted keenly, and it was a world of steam, too, with tugs and ferryboats, railways, pumping stations, electronic generators, bridges and tunnels. The narrow river seemed to churn and vibrate with each passing of a paddlewheel steamer or propeller-driven vessel, the whole stream a pulsating force of imperial trade and purpose. The East End of London and Docklands – dark, dingy and often sinister – housed a crowded humanity that served the imperial commercial purpose. The growth of the docks and the changing of the ancient buildings into the new edifices of industry and mercantile exchange made hard pressed the locations of dire living that the working poor and the destitute endured of necessity. To the visitor, all seemed in motion. Here was the great artery of England, though the docks with their grey stone walls seemed to have been thrown up without any general plan. Each had a romantic connection with the river that they served, and each, as Joseph Conrad said, was unique "by the long chain of adventurous enterprises that had been their inception in the town and floated out into the world again on the waters of the river".[2] Below, yet again, the river opens to a broad estuary with its remote and flat marshes. Beyond once more, buoyed sands mark where the Straits of Dover begin. Here at last is found the English Channel leading to the oceanic world and the uttermost ends of the earth.

Mariners, self-employed or working for companies, sailed into many a heart of darkness. They returned as changed persons, for they had encountered many other societies in their voyages near and far. They carried their cultural baggage with them, and they formed views of foreign and non-Caucasian peoples that were often far short of anthropological or ethnological reporting on a scientific scale. They returned as global citizens, and probably a little wiser and better informed than when they had left the kingdom's shores. Inured to the rigours of the sea, they were harder bitten than landsmen, far less likely to espouse democratic causes, rather the opposite. The era of the yachtsman had not yet come, and those who sailed the seven seas did so for reasons of commerce. But sailors in the Royal Navy, officers and men alike, worked within a special legal world mandated by the state and enforced by the regulations of the King as directed by the lords commissioners of the Admiralty.

While the Thames, or the London River as it is also called, is a link to the watery wastes that rim the globe, it is also an important place of ingress and egress of the shipping of the British Isles. In these classic days of influence, this coastal trade had links to London, while highroads and railways plus the internal waterways of England, notably the canals, linked the industrial cities and the places of manufacture for the world. H.G. Wells thought Charing Cross Station "the heart of the world".[3] With ports on the Irish Sea, the North Sea and the English Channel, British traders were well positioned to exploit the ocean environments that began at their very doorstep. But the greatest of these was London, and it grew even greater as an imperial capital with the passage of this same period, 1815–1914, the years of *Pax Britannica.*

The Thames waterway, novelist Joseph Conrad wrote in the evocative, brilliant images in the opening scene of *Heart of Darkness*, leads "to the uttermost ends of the earth". "The tidal current," he continued,

> runs to and fro in its unceasing service, crowded with memories of men and ships it had borne to the rest of home or to the battles of the sea. It has known and served all the men of whom the nation is proud, from Sir Francis Drake to Sir John Franklin, knights all, titled and untitled....

And so many great ships had known that river too: *Golden Hind*, returning with her "flanks full of treasure," and *Erebus* and *Terror*, which never returned. To all seas the river had given men and ships to a variety of imperial ventures and colonial projects.

> Hunters for gold and pursuers of fame, they all had gone out on that stream, bearing the sword, and often the torch, messengers of the might within the land, bearers of a spark from the sacred fire. What greatness had not floated on the ebb of that river into the mystery of an unknown earth!... The dreams of men, the seed of commonwealths, the germs of empire.[4]

Often it has been said, and not without exaggeration, that the British Empire owed its existence to the sea. The outlying ramparts of British influence and obligation were established by the use and control of the sea. Whether it was trade or colonization, the British imperial ethos was a seaborne matter. This was as true in the early gropings for overseas influence dating from Tudor times as it was in the latter days of shrinking commitments, of which we are yet to see the sundown – Bermuda, Pitcairn and the Falklands Islands still imperial, the "limpet colonies", hanging on for dear life. And it was as true of the eighteenth century and the great wars for empire that marked that century as it was of the nineteenth century, that peculiar period, *Pax Britannica.* British power and influence rested on seaborne power – the means of making wealth and the ways of exercising power. The era of *Pax Britannica* was coincident with the great age of British maritime ascendancy.

Naturally endowed with an insular position athwart the continent of Europe and in proximity to favourable trade routes leading to the Baltic, the Mediterranean and the North Atlantic, Britain of the early modern era also possessed a society that was no longer feudal and was already showing early industrialization of the workforce. The supremacy of Parliament had triumphed as a result of the English Civil War and the subsequent evolution of constitutional monarchy. The founding of the Bank of England had given stability to the nation and its investors, and even adventurers. Long-term insurance favoured the shipping interests and the merchant traders by sea. The Agricultural Revolution expanded the capacity to produce food, in turn encouraging population growth and self-sufficiency. To this benefit was added the steady accumulation of skills – mercantile and financial – to manage and insure a global commerce. And if that were not enough, the commercial and shipping sectors of the economy received strong, consistent support from the state, a state dominated by perceptive aristocrats and agreeable gentry who embraced the global expansion, its obligations and its profits. It was an age of remarkable human movement, particularly across seas and oceans, and the British, like many European peoples, were populating the wider margins, notably in the early and mid-eighteenth century, and then again, in even greater numbers, during the near 100 years after 1815.[5] This diaspora, too, rested on the fruits of British sea power and naval hegemony.

Even so, the British had invariably preferred trade to dominion, noted statesman Lord Shelburne at the close of the War of American Independence. Then, as before and later still, Board of Trade decisions favoured commercial pursuits over territorial acquisition, and the monarchy and its attendant councils zealously regulated policies of trade in such a way as to give assurances to investors and facilitate economic change and expansion.[6] Circumstances, however, often denied the makers of strategy the ability to stick to such an axiom. From the days of the Restoration through those of Queen Anne and after, foreign rivals compelled the British to respond. When France rose with overreaching ambition (as the British saw it in Marlborough's day), that claim to continental dominance had to be checked by actions of fleets and amphibious responses. Allies were essential in order to defeat the continental aspirant. Much the same occurred in Wellington's day, when Emperor Napoleon surged forward in what proved to be a vain attempt to dominate Europe, the Mediterranean and points east. Between 1688 and 1815, no fewer than seven large European wars had steeled British resolve, failure and success alike strengthening the sinews of state. France regularly proved to be Britain's most formidable enemy. Canada was a spectacular addition to the imperial estate, with important commercial and strategic benefits over the duration of *Pax Britannica* and after. The Thirteen

Colonies broke from the fold in an equally spectacular revolutionary war. This was at once a reverse of British fortunes but strangely, as we will see, it created a parallel English-speaking and quasi-Britannic force that was to prove that blood was thicker than water in the imperial stakes of the late nineteenth century and its aftermath. British merchant mariners, traders and investors, exploiting the advantages that a gun-carrying merchant ship could wield, soon made the waters of the globe their hunting ground. The profits exceeded the risks. Patterns of migration by sea led to the planting of offshoots of the British peoples in distant lands, notably America and the West Indies. Religion was a powerful motive in overseas expansion as well. Early industrialization of the British workforce was a feature of Britain's rise to trading greatness. So, too, was the steady accumulation of mercantile and financial skills needed to manage a worldwide commerce. Backing from an effective fiscal state that had a powerful and perceptive aristocracy on side in its endeavours made for a powerful combination heretofore unseen on the world stage.[7]

From about 1651 onwards, England enshrined the policy of mercantilism to secure the means of its maritime and naval security, and thereby to create a merchant navy that would in time of war be a nursery of seamen. Defence and opulence went hand in hand. Sir Josiah Child, seventeenth-century scion of the East India Company, charged all who would read his tract on the future of British trade and dominion to be mindful of his maxim that "In all things, profit and power ought jointly to be considered."[8] By the late eighteenth century, and on the eve of the war with France, which began in 1793, British statesmen were well aware that commerce was the prime driver behind British foreign policy. The spirit of merchant enterprise was unbounded, said Henry Dundas, in charge of British trade policy at the time of the Nootka Sound crisis with Spain, and the pressures of the merchant community could not be denied. Parliament would demand redress of grievances and compensation for damages. Global thinking was a characteristic of this British age, and it is not too hard to comprehend that the ultimate step of this eastwards swing was to bring the influence of trade and empire to Peking and so reap the benefits. To some degree the subsequent and long war with France deferred or hampered British merchant enterprises (though war was good for commerce in other ways). Thus, when peace descended in 1815, older ambitions for dominance in eastern seas reasserted themselves. Simultaneously, new outlets for venture capital and trading, notably the Americas, came into prominence. The war and the previous centuries of commercial and colonial growth had provided Britain with an immense legacy: global reach. The opportunity was not to be lost on the commercial sector, but all the while, save for ensuring the protection of trade, statesmen fought hard against tendencies to enlarge the imperial estate. Theirs was a mission impossible, as will be seen, and with the acquisition of such a rich inheritance as was exhibited in 1815 came, oddly, seeds of decline.

All that lay in the future. The immediate task was to proclaim and keep the peace, and to guard against the resumption of war in the future.

The technique of management came forward in 1815 from centuries of trial and experimentation. Schemes of merchant mariners under protective charter, of colonization by companies and agencies, of self-government, of the creation of Crown colonies and of commercially dominated ones, too – all these ways of empire-making featured in the years 1815–1914. They had their basis in the long-nurtured preference of the British for incorporating these schemes under some substantially autonomous local authority, "standing intermediate between them and the imperial power", as D.A. Low explains, reverting to the tradition that dates from the reign of Henry II. The empire after 1815 inherited some older schemes of growth and management – the East India Company and the Hudson's Bay Company, for instance – and was obliged to deal with the legacies of others. The British Empire in India, the so-called jewel in the crown, survived the Great Mutiny of 1857 experienced by the East India Company. The Hudson's Bay Company likewise made a transition to a more modern world after a parliamentary inquiry in 1857, and it had a powerful presence in the Canadian west and north long thereafter. Corporate empire may have seemed out of fashion, but this did not prevent the Crown from creating, by chartered rule, other commercial enterprises that were advantageous to the state, notably the colony of Vancouver Island, the British North Borneo Company, the Imperial British East Africa Company and the British South Africa Company.[9] Proprietary grants and licensed concessions often ran their course, or came to be overtaken by events, but this technique of devolving power under centralized control was an old English mechanism; it had been variously in evidence for almost eight centuries.[10] Whitehall encouraged self-government after 1846, and lauded free trade at the same time. Even so, Downing Street was not averse to advancing Britain's interests in other ways and in other such schemes as the peculiar circumstances required. Various colonization schemes found support with limited obligation to the parent state. It backed explorations such as David Livingstone's and Robert Falcon Scott's. It encouraged scientific method and experimentation at home and abroad, and it made the globe a laboratory for British science. By mid-century even, a notion of national destiny had captured the attention of the informed public. Britain's obligation to the world was taking on new considerations of mission, as of yet largely undefined but clear to its adherents. In 1850, Lord John Russell told the House of Commons: "It appears to me that if we give up this high and holy work...we have no right to expect a continuance of those blessings, which, by God's favour, we have so long enjoyed."[11] As of mid-century there was no going back.

All of this happened under the umbrella of naval paramountcy. For, above all, Britain possessed a Navy that was second to none, capable of securing the home islands from invasion and, at the same time, of holding the Narrow Seas against Dutch, French or Spanish fleets. Concentrating naval force in wartime in the "Western Approaches" to the English Channel, it could fend off any rival. From the command of home waters, the command of the world derived.[12] The traumatic experiences of losing the American colonies and then countering the French during the revolutionary wars had a powerful effect. British leadership, particularly under Pitt and Dundas, was driven by defensive, financial and naval considerations rather than aggressively imperial or territorial ones. Crisis had induced an absolute determination "to establish beyond future hazard financial and naval supremacy over their rivals". By "prodigies of exertion" and "by destroying the colonial resources of our enemies and adding proportionately to our own", as Dundas put it unerringly, the peace dividends came – a political dominance in India against all rivals, dominance over all navies in Europe, and new colonies. "The twenty-six colonies of 1792 had grown to forty-three by 1816", and, more than this: "Britain was now in a position to impose an extra-European *Pax Britannica*."[13]

The Navy formed the shield of Achilles. "Britain's best bulwarks are her wooden walls," wrote the poet Henry Green.[14] "Britannia rules the waves!" became the axiom of the eighteenth century. The Navy owed its strength to British seamen and the power of the Admiralty.

> The great figure we make in the world, and the wide extent of our power and influence, is due to our naval strength, to which we stand indebted for our flourishing plantations, the spread of British fame and, what is of far greater consequence, British freedom, through every quarter of the universe.

That was the view of the historian John Campbell, writing in the epigraph to that early work of collective biography, *Lives of the British Admirals* (1742).[15] A British journalist or commentator could have written the same on naval affairs on the eve of the First World War. This was a time of golden British ascendancy on and over the seas, an epoch unique in the history of humankind. The impacts of British sea power were immense, not least the spread of liberties and democratic traditions in self-governing colonies and in states freed from old tyrannies of Spain, Portugal and France. Britain became guardian to many smaller states lying adjacent to the sealanes. The improving instinct of the age was undeniable, and the extension of missions and the freeing of slaves, the checking of piracy and the ending of the slave trade were gifts to the modern world that were brought with the display even of a single warship wearing the White Ensign and crewed by British officers and seamen. For behind that man-of-war lay the mightiest fleet of ships then known to humankind, steeled in tradition and enriched by honour and victory.

Napoleon's grand strategy to establish an empire in the eastern Mediterranean and India was checked by the British on the sea at Trafalgar and during the next decade, when there was a French naval resurgence, and while the war raged on the Continent it was the British mastery of the seas that contained France's ambitions under the emperor. "So I, had I remained in Egypt, should probably have founded an empire like Alexander," said Napoleon. He was received on board HMS *Bellerophon* and taken into custody, his eventual destination one of exile in St. Helena. He complained acidly to Captain Frederick Maitland of the British man-of-war: "Had it not been for you English, I should have been Emperor of the East; but whenever there is water to float a ship we are sure to find you in the way."[16] In the words of the distinguished American naval historian, Alfred Thayer Mahan, "those far-distant, storm-beaten ships upon which the Grand Army never looked, stood between it and the dominion of the world".[17] In his own times, Napoleon had declared that England could not become a continental power and, should the country attempt to do so, it would be ruined. He had the greatest insight into this matter and was entirely correct. In *King Richard the Second*, Shakespeare compared England to "a fortress built by Nature for herself against infection and the hand of war", and called it "This precious stone set in the silvers sea, which serves it in the office of a wall." It was far better as policy to pursue a colonial empire rather than being a continental power, as the great statesman Chatham had said. In that way, England could go from strength to strength.

British statesmen down the years until 1914 understood this. Canning gave three conditions of engaging in any war: it must be just, it must be one in which England could do justice to it, and it must be one in which England could "so interfere without detriment or prejudice to ourselves".[18] Disraeli had the same view:

> The abstention of England from any unnecessary interference in the affairs of Europe is the consequence, not of her decline of power but of her increased strength. England is no longer a mere European power; she is the metropolis of a great maritime Empire, extending to the boundaries of the farthest ocean. It is not because England has taken refuge in a state of apathy that she now almost systematically declines to interfere in the Continent of Europe, England is ready and as willing to interfere as in the old days when the necessity of her position requires it.[19]

1
Defining *Pax Britannica*

This is the history of an idea as much as it is an account of the practice of exerting power. Inasmuch as it bears partly on matters of intellectual history it is really, when you think of it, a form of biography "of the means whereby ideas are formed by men, are applied to their daily affairs, and are changed in that process of application".[1] During its most potent years, its adherents, proponents or critics did not call *Pax Britannica* that. It had no currency in its most formative years. It is a term with retrospective associations. Only late in that epoch did it come to be called that. At the outset of the period, 1815, the practitioners were far too preoccupied with reorganizing an efficient system of global influence and reach to presume that they had come to a state of *Pax Britannica.* They were, too, mindful of the possible resurgence of those two powers with which they had recently fought major wars: France and the United States. It may be kept in mind that towards the end of *Pax*, those two powers became complicit or actual allies of Great Britain and the British Empire. They, too, had gone through long changes and accommodations to British power. Throughout most of the years here under consideration, the British contended with the rivalry of these two foreign powers and did so with others of intractable character – Holland in the 1820s in Southeast Asia, Spain in regard to slavery and its nest in Cuba, and Belgium in equatorial Africa in humanitarian matters. Russia, with its interests in the Eurasian heartland, was never far from British strategic postulations.

Only when well into the game, so to speak, did the British become conscious of the unique state of affairs that they possessed in regards to world power and world influence. At that stage they were able on the basis of hard-won experience and success to laud and magnify their rule of law. They were in a position resoundingly to preach legal trade, to advance human and civil causes, to preach the end of slavery and piracy, and to advance a system of peace that they hoped would endure forever. They were mistaken in the latter: it was beyond them, and they were sadly overtaken by events. But in these late years of appreciating their power and of fearing that it might someday decline, they were conscious of a state of affairs that they believed existed during the Roman Empire – a *Pax Romana.*

It was a storied construction based deeply in the history of the British Isles and of seaborne ventures overseas. It was a record of wars successfully carried to conclusion, of heroes and of ships, of difficulties overcome, and of fights for freedom against enemies and states regarded as tyrants and demigods. It was written like a code of the nation, the credo of the policy-makers. It bore the mantle of divine direction.

> When Britain first, at Heaven's command,
> Arose from out the azure main,
> This was the charter, the charter of the land,
> And guardian angels sang this strain:
> 'Rule Britannia, Britain rule the waves;
> Britons never will be slaves!'
>
> James Thomson

Pax Britannica, according to the *Oxford English Dictionary,* means the peace imposed by British rule – that is, the practice of implementation of it. Put differently, *Pax* was a system of force from which, it was argued by its practitioners and propagandists, devolved the benefits of peace. Peace for the purpose of profit was one such benefit, and it hastened the free-trade movement. Humanitarian advancements, the attempted elimination of piracy and slavery, and the propagation of Christianity and education also derived from *Pax.* The British Empire of the nineteenth century was based as much on the official use of violence as it was on seaborne trade and industrial leadership. The high-minded aspirations of colonial secretaries, governors and consuls for sustaining *Pax,* or of increasing its influence, were only as good as the forces readily available and the willing cooperation of native rulers and allied states.

In the strictest terms of international law, peace constitutes the normal state of relations in international society. To the student of the history of the British Empire, this may well appear to be a curious definition. For as the historian Sir John Seeley explained in his *Expansion of England* (1883), the eighteenth-century additions to British dominions were acquisitions by conquest. The empire was won by the sword and kept by the sword. It was not acquired in a fit of absentmindedness, for when Seeley said that he was merely attempting to get our attention by a deceit or slight of hand. For a variety of reasons the empire had grown despite many intentions to the contrary. Acquisitions won by the sword were often returned to the defeated party at the peace, so as to encourage stability and prevent renewed rivalry in those parts of the world. Britain could well afford to return many conquests at the peace table, all the while retaining those places won by the sword the increased the strength and security of the empire and its trade. As of 1815 an altogether unimagined state of affairs had been entered into: the fruits of hard-earned victory now presented themselves. A look at the reason for rationales for keeping or discarding acquisitions of war helps to explain the motivations of *Pax Britannica*. Military advantage had to be coupled with diplomatic effort – two sides of the same foreign policy, as it were.

By 1815, Britain possessed a worldwide empire based on certain communications points, or nodes, some of them of obvious commercial advantage, all of them of strategic merit. Most of these "keys", according to the Secretary of State for Foreign Relations, Lord Castlereagh, gave their possessor military advantages. As such, these had been kept at the peace of 1815 in order to insure British pre-eminence in such outlying spots and beyond. And what were these strategic outposts, newly acquired? Helgoland was retained from Denmark to keep it from being used by a former enemy. Malta and the Ionian Islands, to accompany Gibraltar, strengthened the Mediterranean corridor and the links overland to India. Gambia was reoccupied. St. Helena, an East India Company way station, had received notoriety as the jail of Napoleon, guarded by the Royal Navy and a garrison. The British seemed alive to every contingency and, taking no chances, Tristan da Cunha and Ascension Island in the South Atlantic were occupied to prevent a repetition of Napoleon's flight to Elba. Mauritius, Rodriguez, the Seychelles and the Chagos Archipelago increased Britain's authority in the Indian Ocean. The British gave up minor claims to the fever-stricken French stations in Madagascar. Ceylon (Sri Lanka), with its magnificent Trincomalee Harbour but of scant trading value, was gained from the Dutch. The Cape of Good Hope, first captured then relinquished to the Dutch, was kept once and for all from falling into French hands and was a profitless possession. The Maldives to the southwest of Trincomalee, the Laccadives off the Malabar Coast, the Andaman Islands in the Bay of the Bengal, and Malacca and other trading stations in Sumatra – all were kept to augment British strategic leverage and trading power in eastern seas. In the West Indies, imperial advantage was strengthened in two ways: by the acquisition of St. Lucia, the great strategic prize of the eighteenth century, and by the reoccupation of Trinidad and Tobago, the latter boasting safe anchorages. On the American mainland, Britain acquired a section of Honduras and the colonies of Demerara, Essequibo and Berbice, together forming British Guiana. Newfoundland was a place of longstanding economic and strategic benefit but it required naval protection for the fisheries. Canada[2] and India were huge continental possessions, but even then in naval strategic thinking they formed enclaves of inference. "The British Empire is an Empire of islands," wrote Admiral Sir Herbert Richmond, historian and strategist, "islands either in the physical or economic sense". Practically all of the external trade of each member of the empire moved by sea. And on the safe and unimpeded passage of this seaborne trade rested the profit and power of the British Empire.[3]

Historical accounts of these accretions to the imperial estate, undertaken for strategic purposes – to give new leverage and to prevent possible enemies from using the same – seem almost lost in the chronicles of the nineteenth century, which focus, unavoidably, on the imperial scramble of the late century. But make no mistake: these early gains gave leverage to sea power and, more, mobility and capabilities of power projection, for one could, and often did, reinforce one another. When reviewing these acquisitions gained by 1815, Brian Tunstall, an historian of imperial defence, observed, with understatement:

> As she possessed also bases or stations at Gibraltar, Sierra Leone, St. Helena, Halifax, Bermuda, Antigua and Jamaica in the Atlantic, and Bombay, Madras and Penang in the Indian Ocean and East Indies, no power was in as good a position to attack British trade or territory as Britain was to defend them.[4]

True it was, as Viscount Castlereagh, the premier statesman of his country, informed the House of Commons in 1816. "Our policy", he said without exaggeration, "has been to secure the Empire against future attack. In order to do this we had acquired what in former days would have been thought romance – the keys of every great military position."[5]

If military advantage was a burning concern to the British, equally important was the rivalry posed by foreign states, individually or as allies. Britain had not kept everything at the peace of 1815: to France had been restored Martinique, Guadeloupe, Newfoundland fishing rights, Goree, Senegal, Reunion and French factories in India. Java had been restored to the Dutch, and large indemnifications made for the loss of Dutch possessions in the late war. With the exception of a few islands, France and Holland were left with the bulk of their possessions overseas. Those kept by the British were done so for strategic advantage. Not coveting the mastery of the world, explained Castlereagh, Britain had no intention of humiliating France and leaving it with a sense of grievance. At the same time he sought to strengthen the new Kingdom of the United Netherlands, consisting of Holland and Belgium combined, as a restraining force upon a potentially resurgent and aggressive France. In short, British motives entailed the restitution of rich colonies conquered in war. Strategic advantages were trumping old mercantilist connections. No conquered place was retained because of its natural wealth. As Castlereagh put it in commenting on the British, and their policy,

> They do not desire to retain any of these Colonies for their mere commercial value – too happy if by their restoration they can give other states an additional motive to cultivate the arts of peace. The only objectives to which they desire to adhere are those which affect essentially the engagement and security of their own dominion.

Castlereagh, explained the British diplomatic historian Sir Charles Webster, was more interested in building a stable Europe than in riveting the ascendancy of the British Empire over the rest of the world.[6]

British pre-eminence in the imperial and commercial fields existed, in part, because of the relative weakness of the contending nations and their empires.[7] Russia confined its ambitions to strengthening its dominions, securing its rivers and estuaries, and expanding eastwards overland. The French colonial empire had just about disappeared, and the French navy was in a recuperative mode. Although adventurers, traders and diplomats extended that nation's interests in the Levant, elsewhere the French were in a recuperative situation in the first decade after Waterloo. By and large, Spain had relinquished its colonial estate, while in many of its dominions the return of royal government sparked civil war or mutiny. Only Cuba, Puerto Rico and the Philippines remained, and much of their trade was conducted with the British. The Spanish did not reinvest in their empire, and the previous three centuries were regarded as the draining of Spanish strength rather than one of extractive gain. The old Spanish mercantilist order had broken down almost completely, and not until the mid-century did a Spanish navy present itself as a strong force. For their part, the Dutch recovered most of their colonial empire and set to the firm task of developing as a national estate the eastern archipelago rich in spices. They had to do so against British encroachment in Singapore, but without sufficient naval power they were obliged to allow the British to exploit the Malay Peninsula, use the Strait of Malacca without hindrance and develop trade to China. The Portuguese Empire, now much weakened, survived in an attenuated form, with places such as Timor, Macau and Goa, plus Angola and Mozambique, and above all Brazil, the most productive possession, which separated from Portugal in 1822. Portugal was to quickly come under British influence in the suppression of the slave trade but did not agree to the formal abolition of slavery until 1842. Brazil, to some degree a child of British policy backed by naval guarantee, posed no imperial threat to Britain's empire; indeed, trade there benefited British commerce.

Taken altogether, British hegemony operated in a vacuum provided by the weakness of its rivals. Only the United States, with its formidable oceanic commerce to all major seas and annexes, posed a threat to British commercial pre-eminence, though here and there the Stars and Stripes posed as rivals or co-associational trading partners to the Union Jack. The general state of affairs as here described – the dominion of the sea – continued until well into the second half of the nineteenth century, when all of these powers, plus the new ones of Germany and Japan, presented an altogether different scenario from those occupying prominent positions in the Colonial Office, the Foreign Office and the Admiralty.

Nelson's victory over the combined fleets of France and Spain at Trafalgar in 1805 provided a definitive lustre to the Navy that has never really lost its sheen. To add to the public adoration was a faith in the stewardship of the Admiralty, the sea kings of Britain. For a century-and-a-half after Nelson's death, the public persona of "the immortal memory" has never faded no matter how savagely the defence budgets may cut into naval requirements.

At the end of the Napoleonic Wars, Britain remained the only great naval power. "British sea-power, notwithstanding the first year of the war of 1812, had come out of the great European conflict unshaken and more pre-eminent than ever."[8] So wrote Admiral Sir Cyprian Bridge, former Director of Naval Intelligence and a noted commentator on British maritime prowess at the outset of the twentieth century. Britain had indeed riveted a maritime ascendancy on the world, and had grown strong by war. The fruits of victory were abundantly clear to all, not least to the French. It had not been the British Army that had prevented a French seaborne invasion of the British Isles. As a French encyclopedia writer expressed it, "The Empire of the seas is the most advantageous of all empires. The Phoenicians possessed it in other times, and it is to the English that this apparent glory now comes into sight among all the maritime powers."[9] Another French authority, observing the vaunted power of Britain's maritime influence, put it this way, in shocked awe: "The trident of Neptune is the sceptre of the world."[10]

Britain was now in a position to take full advantage of the Industrial Revolution, and to extend trade so as to enlarge the empire into a world-wise business concern. Britain had no desire to enlarge the colonial estate, but, as will be made clear, circumstances presented themselves requiring expansion. It was a fact of British life that the British fought against imperial expansion in the years of *Pax Britannica* – and yet the empire grew, and national obligations similarly.

In addition, when peace was declared in 1815, Britain's sea power "was supreme in all its elements".[11] In addition to the acquisition of bases, already mentioned, in ships of war, Britain was superior to the combined fleets of the world. There were over 200 ships of the line, nearly 300 frigates and corvettes, and some 400 smaller vessels. It was a prodigious marine establishment but only suitable for waging war. The new era meant that severe economies had to be made to the fleet. Many three- and two-deckers were cut down, or "razeed", so as to make a still powerful gun platform to be manned by reduced ships' companies. Old brigs were retained, and some converted to steam tugs. Corvettes and sloops-of-war proved to be useful implements of imperial purpose. Some new construction continued but, by and large, by 1830 a far different fleet existed than in 1815. A clerk of the Admiralty, recalling these days, stated flatly that the Navy consisted of

> nothing more than a few old but serviceable 120 and 80 gun ships, mainly 74's and 60's and too many 46 gun frigates, donkey-frigates of 26 guns, over-masted sloops (the 18 and 16 gun brig-sloops) and the coffin brigs (the 10's); of the last name, several foundered annually, and hence the name.[12]

The Navy ran the Packet Service, with its enlarging tentacles of a communications empire. The Coast Guard, or Preventing Service, guarded against piracy and smuggling in home waters, seeking means of raising revenue for the state. The merchant marine was the great carrier of the oceans, carrying the bulk of the world's trade. Britain possessed eleven-twelfths of the world's shipping.[13] The carrying trade of the globe was in its hands. The navigation acts continued in force and with them the provision that British seamen would man the vessels. A healthy, expanding shipbuilding industry stood behind the merchant world. Britain had all of the essential prerequisites to exercise influence on and over the seas, to the profit of the home islands and the security of the empire.

Thus, when Britain entered upon a remarkably long era of general European peace, statesmen and politicians became increasingly interested in the longevity of this state of affairs. They earnestly trusted in its continuance if not permanence. The long war against France and Napoleon had been a war of unexampled duration. "Throughout the whole of that eventful period," recalled Sir John Barrow, a secretary at the Admiralty, writing in 1831, "the attention of all Europe had been absorbed in the contemplation of 'enterprises of great pith and moment,' – of revolutions of empires – the bustle and business of warlike preparations – the movements of hostile armies – battles by sea and land, and of all 'the pomp and circumstance of glorious war'."[14] In regard to foreign rivals, Castlereagh contended that France and Russia posed the most likely threats in the future, and he dreaded the thought of a combination of the two as "the only one that can prove really formidable to the liberties of Europe".[15] Here lay the basis of the "Two-Power" naval standard. British diplomacy aimed to prevent such a combination, and it suited the country well when in the Crimean War it fought in concert with France and the Ottoman Empire against Russia. Maintaining the Ottoman Empire was a cardinal policy in the early years of *Pax* but it could not be sustained in its latest years – and therein lay the source of some of the future difficulties leading to 1914.

Now, in the plentitude of peace, British statesmen sought stability among the European powers. Castlereagh worked urgently to construct the Concert of Europe, but in the end it was British interests – and British freedom of action – that most concerned him.[16]

The various administrations that guided the affairs of state of Britain and the empire for the first half of the nineteenth century always acted with the greatest of caution, worried as they were that the revolutions that had convulsed Europe and the republican zeal that had developed in the United States and in the new Latin American republics would upset the British order. England had gone through its revolution in the seventeenth century, and with the restoration of the monarchy and then the establishment of constitutional monarchy by the supremacy of parliament equipoise had become the central feature of ministerial government. The war ending in 1815 had only reinforced in the mindset of British statesmen that strong central government, with a close watch to be kept against revolutionary principles at home and abroad in British territories, was to be continued unabated. These were the years of equipoise and convalescence. There were reforming impulses that changed the nature of British democratic institutions – the Reform Bill of 1832 being one and the emancipation of Roman Catholics another. But changes came slowly, and after much disputation and sometimes civil disorder. Britain was not immune to continental revolutionary tendencies. British statesmen guarded, as if a natural birthright of a Briton, that whatever changes should come to the home islands, the constitutional monarchy should continue, Parliament would reign supreme and Britain would remain secure from invasion. It was only under circumstances such as these that Britain would undertake reforms in its own way – setting aside the acts of trade and navigation, adopting free trade, continuing with the concept of the freedom of the seas under these new mercantile policies, ending slavery in the British Empire and fighting against the slave trade as its special national mission. Such measures as these were made possible by security at home and by statesmen who zealously guarded the primacy that had been acquired in 1815. They trusted in its continuance.

In this era, colonial growth under British auspices was a central tenet of policy-making, though it attracted many critics and self-interested persons. "England cannot afford to be little," proclaimed the President of the Board of Trade, William Huskisson, in 1828, adding, "She must be what she is or nothing... [She] is the parent of many flourishing colonies... [and] in every quarter of the globe we have planted the seeds of freedom, civilization and Christianity... [and] nations, kindred in blood, in habits, and in feelings, to ourselves." William Ewart Gladstone, sometime Colonial Secretary, stated a similar article of faith: "we feel proud when we trace upon the map how large a portion of the earth owns the benignant sway of the British crown, and we are pleased with the idea that the country which we love should so rapidly reproduce its own image... in different quarters of the globe".[17] No one of the age doubted that in the past the acts of trade and navigation had contributed to the power and prestige of Britain. The principle of protection, Lord Stanley proclaimed during the Corn Law debates of 1846, had given Britain its empire and its colonial system, and there was "not a sea on which the flag of England does not float, not a quarter of the world in which the language of England is not heard".[18]

As the nineteenth century advanced, greater recognition was given to *Pax* as a British favour or obligation to be bequeathed to the world and its "lesser breeds without the law", to employ Rudyard Kipling's well-worn phrase. This became a central tenet of *Pax*. Some have called it "the white man's burden". Others have spoken of it as a necessary atonement for past wrongs. But it was more than that; it was a basis of empire, naturally overshadowed by matters of commerce and security, but central nonetheless to British purposes and needs. Edmund Burke, political thinker, MP and historian, had written of trusteeship as essential in the extension of British authority overseas. The empire was a trusteeship to be administered with impartial justice. Moreover, the British name should not be tarnished by any suspicion of oppression in the governing of dependent subjects. After the loss of the Thirteen Colonies, the British policy of "exercising trust" became a distinctive characteristic of Britain as an imperial power. The seven-year trial of Warren Hastings had revealed wrongdoing and corruption. The trial and Burke's hysterical diatribes against Hastings awakened a sense of public duty to the peoples of India. As a concept, trusteeship soon expanded to include fighting against slavery in all forms and protecting indigenous peoples who inhabited the wider world and came within the British orbit of influence. Foolish it would have been to believe that these intentions could be carried to practical conclusion, but the flames burned bright and actuated the minds of many who understood that the state (and even the Church of England and dissenting churches) stood behind them and prodded them forwards. Fingers of suspicion had been pointed at imperial management. The Crown had fiduciary obligations. Colonial Office files bulge with reports about abuses of natives and attempts to correct the circumstances on turbulent frontiers.[19] The Aborigines' Protection Society was one of several entities, social and religious, that met at London's Exeter Hall and kept a sleepless watch (as best they could) on relations between settlers and indigenous peoples. As the nineteenth century progressed, the British mission towards the wider world – Christianity, commerce and civilization: David Livingstone's trinity – had a powerful hold on the British mentality. This formed an underpinning of *Pax Britannica*.

Law was an obligation borne by the British overseas. In the nineteenth century the British conscience became focused against abuses of empire and against persons not within the bounds of empire who were victims. So zealous was British public policy on this matter that the 1837 Select Committee of Parliament, which investigated the nature of aboriginal affairs, put the matter unequivocally. As Margery Perham, expert on British obligations and with expertise in colonial administration, puts it, "Had not Burke, commending his principles with willing eloquence, said of the American colonists, that the question was not whether the British Government had a right to render people miserable, but whether it had not an interest to make them happy?"[20] The British were moved to correct the abuses of the slave trade and then to legislate slavery out of existence, some 30 years before the abolition of serfdom in Russia. And the British had an obligation to protect aboriginal peoples in strife-torn British imperial settlements. As the same authority explains it, "God, it is said, would require at Britain's hands how it had used its power over 'untutored and defenseless savages,' and, again, 'our system has incurred a vast load of crime.' " The select committee's report cited how aboriginal territories had been usurped. It clinically listed the European vices and diseases introduced, and it railed against the poisons of drink and the destruction of guns imported.[21] These views were promulgated at exactly the same time as capitalism had freest rein. Peace for the purpose of profit was an imperial intention, and to have peace you needed law and order – and stable conditions on imperial frontiers where aboriginal rights were not usurped. Herein lay the conundrum of *Pax* in places where the Union Jack had been run up.

Beginning in the seventeenth century, colonial administrators had been sent to far-flung plantations and factories to regulate the business of trade and to provide a hand of authority. The Board of Trade in London set the rules for the empire and trade. Shipping policy was designed to develop the merchant marine, and a reservoir of masters and sailors, in times of emergency. "England's wealth by foreign trade" was the observable maxim. The old colonial system, with its powerful acts of trade and navigation, enriched the public coffers. The Navy and the Coast Guard policed the system. By the eighteenth century the Navy and its means of support constituted the largest segment of public spending and a central driving force in the British economy. The state grew rich on trade. It also grew rich on war and the fruits of war. At the outset of our period the old system remained intact. During the years when Huskison was at the Board of Trade, a rationalization of the acts of trade and navigation took place. This was preparatory to great changes that occurred in the 1830s and particularly in the mid-1840s. Thus by 1846, "free trade" had triumphed and British trade had been thrown open to competition. And, in 1849, the repeal of the navigation acts announced that the British were sufficiently assured concerning their merchant marine, shipping, and trading networks and practices – they were everywhere universally predominant and pre-eminent – that it seemed as if such glorious power and wealth on and over the seas had been the long-sought-after benefits of all of the years of war and tight regulatory commercial control.

The British approached the last half of the nineteenth century with undoubted confidence, with a clear lead in the various carrying trades of the world, dominance in merchant marine shipping, and full command of commodities traded in volumes and values. This dominance, powered by the Industrial revolution and aided at home by the Agricultural Revolution and food production, allowed for the sending overseas of millions of settlers and others. The Colonial Office and the British Government, having embraced the concept of responsible government in 1846, as a corollary of free trade, were enabling in those places of settlement under the Union Jack the evolution of liberties and freedoms that indicated that "little Englands over the water" were a natural offshoot of the home islands. Indeed, such colonial offshoots were seen as perhaps insurance for British interests in time of future difficulty.

In the colonies the governor was the guardian of the empire and the practitioner of its administration. As a class, colonial administrators form a unique cluster of Britons. Well educated at public schools, or former members of the armed services, or even prominent businessmen on the spot, they constituted in their human collectivity a personal extension of the expectations that the Colonial Office held implicitly and otherwise stated in commissions and instructions. What a young administrator described in 1913 upon entry into the colonial service spells out the general tenor of how the habit of authority that the British exercised seemed as if it was a God-given right. "The cult of the great god Jingo was as yet far from dead," wrote Arthur Grimble, who was destined for a cadetship in the Gilbert and Ellice Islands.

> Most English households of the day took it for granted that nobody could be always right, or ever quite right, except an Englishman. The Almighty was beyond doubt Anglo-Saxon, and the popular conception of Empire resultantly simple. Dominion over palm and prime (or whatever else happened to be noticeably far-flung) was the heaven-conferred privilege of the Bulldog Breed. Kipling, bard of Empire, had said so. The colonial possessions, as everyone so frankly called them, were properties to be administered, first and last, for the prestige of the little lazy isle where the trumpet-orchids blew. Kindly administered, naturally – nobody but the most frightful bounder could possibly question our sincerity about that – but firmly too, my boy, lest the school-children of Empire forgot who were the prefects and who were the fags.[22]

Power and wealth were preoccupations of Britons of the epoch. At the same time, they also had an obligation – one that grew with the decades and became more powerful still until it reached a climax at the turn of the new century. The *Pax* was an exercise in self-disciplining statecraft where higher principles operated side by side with the pursuit of profit and the protection of power. "They had a sense of mission," writes John S. Galbraith:

> Britain, they had no doubt, was particularly fitted to rule. British law, British morality, and British religion were priceless gifts to the peoples fortunate enough to come under imperial rule. Under the protection of the great queen the benighted of the earth would enjoy peace, order, and justice, and they would learn useful employments that would enable them to develop whatever capacities they possessed. This evangelical strain affected British policy through out the century.[23]

Of British arrogance and self-assurance there is no lack of evidence, and the British imperial century gave every opportunity for the display of British vanity and pride as well as modesty and self-effacement. As rulers or even born leaders, Britons could be a caricature, an oddity and even a subject for mirth. What made them and their kind unique was a sense of assurance and purpose. As a class, they represented a self-confident elite, not of meritocracy necessarily but of tradition, experience and station. Sometimes aristocratic and in other instances commercial, they were bred to wealth and the establishment. Public-school education had prepared them as the new Romans; their curriculum was their *vade mecum*. Admirers of public order, and victors over French republicanism and Napoleonic overstretch, they came to the wider world with a belief in their own capabilities. They were caretakers of nation and empire. They brought responsibility to their assignments, and they tended to act with restraint, reticence and a code of conduct that exemplified scrupulous behaviour. As the imperial century advanced, so did they come to reflect on their achievements, which they held with pride; but they also reviewed with pensive consideration the new world of peace, law, order and progress that they were bequeathing to the world. It was a considerable achievement, and this they knew with distinct clarity by the 1880s. And at this time, too, they began to think of their gift to the world – and their new role as the new Romans. Their elite status was linked to classical antiquity, for the era of increased imperial consciousness was that when the study of Greek and Latin was in full flower. In the circumstances, it was natural that allusions to Rome would find themselves expressed in British imperial thought.[24]

The term *Pax Britannica* appeared for the first time in print in 1878 in an article concerning the Indian Empire.[25] Its use gathered momentum with the years and we find it first uttered publicly on 12 July 1886 in a London venue. British statesmen, to repeat, had long been attracted to the history of the Greeks and the Romans of the classic age. Their curriculum at the public schools and in the universities was steeped in the classics. Most of the statesmen of the age had a command of Greek and Latin. They knew of the great battles at land and sea, of the lessons learned by the misuse of power, and of tactics and strategy as was worked out over the course of centuries. Lessons learned by generals of the classic age, the statesmen of 1815–1914, had been taken to heart. *Britain's Imperial Muse* by Christopher Hagerman[26] richly probes this field of inquiry and leaves us with no doubt that the British in their moment of full power were informed by the classical past even if they did not proclaim themselves as the new Romans. At the Royal United Service Institute in Whitehall, London, an address had been given by a retired officer in the Royal Marine Artillery, Captain John Colomb, who at that time was standing for election to Parliament in the Conservative interest (successfully as it turned out). Colomb was regarded as an authority on the naval protection of commerce, on imperial communications and on shore artillery establishments. A stout advocate of imperial federation, he thought not in terms of sentiment – the ties that bind – but in those of strategy. He advocated the protection of commerce, not the building of elaborate fortifications to defend major ports and arsenals. He saw the Navy as the "shield" and the army as the "spear" of imperial defence. Crucial to his way of thinking were coaling stations for an ever-expanding steam-powered Navy. His brother, Philip H. Colomb, a future admiral, had won popular acclaim for a book about his experience of dhow chasing in the Indian Ocean while on anti-slavery patrols. He was also a student of naval signals and a noted naval historian. He wrote long letters to *The Times* that earned him the epithet "column and a half", The Colomb brothers were part of that renaissance of military thinking that characterized the late nineteenth century in the run-up to the Anglo-Boer War. Already the rival dogs were nipping at the heels of British supremacy, and the big issue of the day was "blue-water" thinking versus matters of coastal defence, harbour security and naval base self-sufficiency (did the base serve the fleet or vice versa?).

Captain John Colomb had offered to the Institute a critique of imperial defence. He had chosen as his topic "Imperial Federation – Naval and Military".[27] Could a federation strengthen the defences of the empire? Could the blood ties that bind allow the British to share their burdens? The rhetoric was not "for war" but to enhance security. Colomb and many there at the time – 21 persons spoke about the issue – were concerned whether Britain could face the challenges raised by its rivals. The issue was how to protect the state and its responsibilities on and over the seas. And among those duties mentioned were securing sovereign territories, protecting seaborne trade and fulfilling the myriad obligations of the British people on and over the seas.

When Colomb addressed the issue, and others eagerly responded, Britain stood alone in what some have called "splendid isolation". Britain's world power depended on a number of axiomatic truths: the crimson tides of kinship among the self-governing colonies and dominions, a skillfully nurtured European balance of power, extensive diplomatic and consular services, and a largely agreeable *modus vivendi* with the United States, notably in the Caribbean and Latin America. Britain's power equally rested on alliances of an informal sort with certain new states and the paternalistic position that Britain had taken in regards to their origin and current security. Britain's influence in the early nineteenth century had secured Greek independence from the Ottoman Empire. The same influence had guaranteed Brazil's national status. More generally, throughout Latin America, that same influence had afforded security to the new nation states of Latin America from external intervention by the archaic power of Spain. Even then, British pre-eminence was never universal, for it did not prevent France or Austria from asserting a presence in the affairs of the Americas, specifically in Mexico in 1848. Nor did it control Russia in its Alaskan holdings.

Daily, the British had reminders of their limitations of authority and were conscious of their inability to intervene in every circumstance. They let pass most of the domestic difficulties of the wider world, choosing only to intervene or guide the process when British interests were involved. When the Suez Canal was brought into existence, then and then alone did the British take up a role of indirect interest, notably in the financial conduct of the canal. The canal did not bring political or strategical control, for that rested with the Egyptian Government.[28] Even so, it modified British strategic thinking in remarkable ways: it heightened geopolitical awareness in a public that was previously unconcerned with such matters; it led to further territorial obligations to guard that route; it allowed new commercial dealings in the Near East; and it resulted in increased British commitments on the Asian continent, the Indian Ocean and the China Seas. Technological change enabled these shifts, and steam power and particularly railways changed the ways of imperial reach. Railway construction – across Canada, the United States, Siberia, Eastern Europe and elsewhere – likewise altered the character and speed of troop deployment. Telegraph lines and submarine cables were similarly shrinking the world. This technological revolution was challenging, even subverting, the seaborne pre-eminence upon which British influence and defence had rested for so long. In short, the challenges to British authority and supremacy were prompting a re-evaluation. The old order was changing quickly, more so in the 1880s than in any previous decade since 1815. This was a subject for discussion in Whitehall.

Ably contributing to the discussion of Captain Colomb's paper was one of the greats of his age, the Rt. Hon. Sir George Ferguson Bowen, KCMG, DCL (Oxon). He embodied that link between the classical world and the late-Victorian age. He enjoyed a wide-ranging service in colonial administration – as governor in Queensland, New Zealand, the Colony of Victoria (Australia), Mauritius and Hong Kong. He was the author of numerous works, notably *Ithaca* (1850). Irish born, and educated at Trinity College Dublin, Brasenose College Oxford and

Lincoln's Inn, he had entered the colonial service in Corfu, one of the Ionian Islands. He had served as Corfu University's president. He had devoted spare time to classical studies. To him (and to many of his class and station) the British Empire and the Hellenic tradition had much in common. Like many a colonial governor, he was schooled in Greek and Latin with a deep knowledge of ancient history. Like many of his kind he was aware of the traditions of the Greeks and the Romans. A recent scholar has called this the "classical discourse".[29] He had been educated in a public school that was in its own way a cradle of empire. With 30 years of colonial service behind him – in the Mediterranean, China and Australasia – he was a well-informed commentator on the imperial estate and its issues and intentions.[30] In 1885 he had been invalided home in time to take part in the last phase of the Carnarvon Commission's expansive review (conducted in secrecy) of the defence of British possessions overseas.

Bowen ranked as a premier authority on the colonial issues of the day. He had recently published *The Federation of the British Empire* (1886), a popular work that led to a second edition, published in 1889. The belief held by his peers that Bowen had ended the protracted Maori Wars through his special breed of tact, discretion, strength and firmness was a matter for particular admiration. This colonial veteran would have been a force to reckon with in any discussion of imperial defence. On the occasion, Bowen voiced concerns about the empire's security. Locally raised naval forces were needed for local defence, he said, while imperial naval forces were required to guard the high seas. These were points of view particularly being advanced in the Australian colonies, though not always elsewhere. To his way of thinking, self-governing colonies ought to have a voice in the formation of the empire's foreign policy: the mother country and the daughter dominions would be linked by responsibility.

Then he said, in terms that brought to mind *Pax Romana*: "So should we see *Pax Britannica* far transcend what Pliny called the '*immense Romana Pacis Majestas*'." He hoped to view not only an imperial union but also a conjunction with the English-speaking American Republic. At the time there was much discussion of an Anglo-American reunion, or co-association, and to Bowen's way of thinking the larger association would afford "a guarantee of the peace and prosperity of the whole world."[31] Bowen was a visionary, and his many years in colonial administration that well might have jaded the viewpoints of fellow governors had done nothing to subvert his belief in the future of empire and the value of federation. Many others held to the idea of an imperial federation. His scheme was impractical owing to political realities, in both the home islands and the self-governing colonies.[32] But the concept had a long and slow death. It still showed signs of life in the colonial and imperial conferences that marked the years from the 1897 Jubilee of Queen Victoria to the more urgent discussions of the Edwardian age, notably that of

1911. It was precisely Bowen's perspectives on dominion contributions to the Navy that led zealously independent Canadian and Australian politicians to do just the opposite: to establish their own naval services in 1910 and 1912, respectively.

Bowen's was the first known public utterance of the term *Pax Britannica.* Joseph Chamberlain, MP, employed it in a speech in 1893 to illustrate the beneficent results of British rule in India. He used it again, when Secretary of State for the Colonies, in an address before the annual dinner of the Royal Colonial Institute in London in 1897. Belief in the sense of colonial possessions, dependencies and self-governing colonies had given way to "the sentiment of kinship". The imperial idea, he said, had also given way to "the sense of obligation." Happiness and prosperity had been brought to peoples by British rule: "our rule does, and has, brought security and peace and comparative prosperity to countries that never knew these blessings before". This work of civilization, said Chamberlain, was the fulfillment of the national mission; "we are finding scope for the exercise of those facilities and qualities which have made of us a great governing race". And thus:

> I do not say that our success has been perfect in every case, I do not say that all our methods have been beyond reproach; but I do say that in almost every instance in which the rule of the queen has been established and the great *Pax Britannica* has been enforced, there has come with it greater security to life and property, and a material improvement in the condition of the bulk of the population.

This had not been accomplished without bloodshed, he admitted, but the benefits to humanity "with the price which we are bound to pay for it" were worth it.[33]

Missionaries espoused the concept of *Pax* but often complained of its most violent and forceful aspects. It had its acolytes and its attendants in many aspects of life, and some have left their testimonials. Governors, admirals and generals wrote memoirs; and in these records of lives lived for the imperial purpose, statements about the British imperial moment are conscientiously stated and implicitly understood. Kipling, who knew empire and obligation first hand, kept the inspiration alive. Poet Laureate Alfred Austin penned verse under that rubric in 1896. His *Songs of England* (1900) talked of England's "long-armed sceptre". He spoke of the country's boast that "the fettered must be free". As Rome's power was built by the heroics of its sons carrying out the traditions of its peoples, with the divine decree determining, wrote Austin, so too with Britain. A universal peace and empire constituted the highest object of the new Romans.

Bowen and others at that famous meeting knew that with power went obligation. They were familiar with the powerful clusters of persons in Britain that had advanced, and continued to advance, the cause of imperial trusteeship. The concept grew in influence in the fight against slavery and the slave trade, and it became a central point of discussion as emigration from the home islands flowed in dramatically increasing numbers during the years of *Pax*. This unquenchable outward flow of human bodies brought Britons into contact and conflict with native peoples in all portions of the globe. Because the empire grew in global proportions with the years, the British at home who concerned themselves with the ethics and morality of such often-fatal impacts expressed strong views. They peppered the Government and the Colonial Office in particular with questions of conduct and charges of misdemeanours.

One sophisticated, highly organized group that took the duty upon itself was the Aborigines' Protection Society. It wanted to see a *Pax Britannica* but not at the expense of native interests. It saw itself as an agency for assisting those who were powerless to protect themselves. Its province was all native peoples in the British Empire, all persons who might unwillingly be caught up in slavery or indentured labour, and all non-Europeans not under the British flag who might be subject to abuse. By definition its roles were advocational and, more often than not, antagonistic to the policies of government. Its techniques involved diffusing correct information about the character and condition of aborigines, appealing to Government and Parliament when circumstances dictated action, and bringing popular opinion to exert an influence in advancing the cause of justice. By these means, and in these ways, the society hoped that much could be done towards what was said to be "the diminution of those gigantic evils the continuance of which reflects such deep dishonour on the British name".[34]

Always in the background, and not far from the minds of its practitioners, lay the fear that somehow the British Isles would be invaded, British trade overseas interrupted and the British Empire torn asunder and attacked by enemies, real or imagined. For all their internal strengths, the British worried about their future. Their island and overseas positions they saw as vulnerable unless they had adequate naval and military forces. "The British Empire, in short, is the possession of the sea," wrote Sir Charles Dilke and Spenser Wilkinson, the great authorities on imperial defence, in 1897, the year of Queen-Empress Victoria's Diamond Jubilee, and this was undoubtedly true.[35] How that predominant sea power was to be continued was one vital question. How long could it be sustained was another. The British might be able to answer the first. They dared not answer the second, though they tried mightily to sustain the fabric of commerce and armed authority, backed by diplomatic zeal and cunning, in the hope, if not the expectation, that *Pax* might continue indefinitely. The First

World War would ruin all of these hopes and interrupt the progress of the previous 100 years. It was not imperial decay that led to the downfall and collapse of *Pax Britannica*. Nor did British naval primacy, and command of the sea, disappear. But the shadows were gathering quickly around this imperial edifice built upon sea power, and new rivals were coming forward to grasp the trident of Neptune. The first of these was imperial Germany and the second the United States. As will be seen in subsequent chapters, it was the latter which became a suitable ally and then the supreme power at sea.

2
Empire of the Seas

In the era of *Pax Britannica* the Royal Navy won most of its battles while riding at anchor, in showing the flag on distant seas, and in undertaking a myriad of gunboat actions or of landing parties on faraway coasts. In the long history of British statecraft, it had been a tacitly accepted rule that the operation of British sea power was to be felt in the enemy's rather than in British waters. "The hostile coast was regarded strategically as the British frontier, and the sea was looked upon as territory which the enemy must be prevented from invading."[1] Acceptance of this led to blockades and to watching the enemy's movements. Having a navy stronger in number of ships or in general efficiency than that of the hostile nation was a British necessity. This was an accepted British policy. As a force for mobilization in time of need, the British Navy had no rival on the world stage.

The Navy of *Pax Britannica* was the progeny of at least three centuries of fighting at sea. British admirals and sailors inhabited a world of heroes of their own race. Tales of daring exploits and of cruel sacrifices necessarily rendered to king and country were the stuff of legend and even sacred memory. Cathedrals and churches housed the statues, tombs and plaques of the naval fighting race. Those men who as admirals and captains wielded the trident of Neptune in 1815 brought to their various tasks a systematic rigor and defined purpose that was invariably warlike. They formed a caste, unique in English and possibly world history. They differed from the independent-minded Elizabethan seadogs. Neither had they any similarity to the opportunistic generals at sea of the Cromwellian or Restoration navies. Theirs, by contrast, was a service steeled by fully a century of waging war against the Dutch, Spanish, French and Americans. And those who directed the affairs of the fleet ashore and afloat knew that they were guardians of the prime instrument of the state. They understood that the security of the home islands as well as the empire overseas was theirs alone to preserve and protect. The safeguarding of waterborne commerce likewise came under their knowing charge, and, as to banks and other financial institutions owned by British investors in foreign parts, they likewise regarded them as worthy of British protection, though within well-defined limits.

The Navy – or the Service – understood its responsibilities. Perhaps no armed instrument of government had been entrusted to that time with such obligations. The strength of the Navy consisted in naval discipline and in the complete loyalty and good comradeship between officers and men. To many an officer the Navy was not a collection of ships but a community of men with high purpose.[2]

In 1815, at the outset of *Pax*, the Navy ranked as the world's pre-eminent naval service. It possessed, theoretically at least, sufficient size and strength to protect Britain's interests on and over the seas. Already its duties were global. In the generation after Waterloo it faced some of its greatest difficulties "at home" owing to trenchant reforms at which the Treasury was the centre.[3] Despite severe fiscal restraints, the armed services of Britain were obliged to maintain and secure British possessions, to show the flag, to defend colonial outposts, to man garrisons and to secure the seas for "those who pass on their lawful occasions", besides undertaking a number of duties under the general heading of "humanitarian obligations". These were the requirements of *Pax*, and politicians and parliamentarians did not always recognize their costs.

At one time, British practitioners of sea power had thought in terms of fleets and cruising squadrons. Men-of-war ranged in line ahead had been their preferred tactical disposition in readiness for a fight at sea, while their frigates and sloops dispatched on scouting or particular duties were the eyes of the fleet. Now, in 1815, fleets would be assembled only for specific tasks. In the next year, for instance, Lord Exmouth commanded a fleet to free Christians who were held as slaves in North Africa. Yet again, in 1854, the Admiralty would deploy fleets to the Baltic and Black seas to control the Russians; they did so in concert with the French. Otherwise, and in other circumstances, the fleet had really ceased to exist as a tactical force of British sea power. By 1869 the British had "foreign stations" on every sea – South America, Pacific, Australian, China, Cape of Good Hope, North America and West Indies, Mediterranean and Indian Ocean.[4] The ships on station seldom acted as a unit on manoeuvres (except for the Mediterranean late in the nineteenth century). The sole concentration of force, an intended economy measure of the times, was the 1869 Flying Squadron, which circumnavigated the globe in the following year, showing the flag and encouraging outlying dependencies of the Crown to believe that they were not neglected in the course of imperial defence retrenchment. Only by the century's end, and in the run-up to the 1914 war, did the Admiralty again see the necessity of maintaining fleets proper. Even then a gigantic quarrel ensued when it was proposed, successfully, that the Mediterranean fleet be sacrificed in primacy to that of the Grand Fleet, a new concentration of force designed to be based in home waters as a counterweight against the rise of the imperial German navy. In other words, throughout most of the years of *Pax Britannica*, units of the Royal Navy were deployed around the world on what now appears to be hardly any warlike disposition.

Running this great instrument of state was a distinct officer class – what might be better described, as has been said, as a caste, or a self-selecting society.[5] Many officers were of aristocratic heritage or might soon find themselves with a baronetcy, even with a seat in the House of Lords. Others were members of the gentry. Some officers stood for election as MPs. Country houses were popular with these sets of men, with a residence kept in London for social and professional duties as required. Not all officers came from wealthy circumstances. Others, including indigent parson's sons or those who came from large and hard-pressed middle-class families, were sponsored entries to the Service and before the status of cadet was introduced. They were entered on the books as "Volunteers First Class" and under the captain's protection. There were a large number of "rectory admirals". Officers, generally speaking, were communicants of the Church of England. Being properly nominated was the route to acceptance. The formal examination consisted, as a future admiral of the fleet, Lord Fisher, recounted of his in 1854, as being able to write out the Lord's Prayer, drink a glass of sherry and compute by the rule of three (e.g. "If a yard of cloth costs 1s. 4d., how much will three yards cost?)." Many successful candidates rose from midshipman to lieutenant and then upwards, in some cases to admiral, or even to exalted admiral of the fleet. They were commissioned – that is, bore signed commissions from the monarch of the day. Very few were those officers who had come up through the ranks, or "through the hawse hole", as it was said (as if to describe the rats that somehow found their way aboard ship).

The Navy adhered to the philosophy of catching them young. An officer in 1870 would enter at the age of 12, then spend two years in a training ship and five as a midshipman. Taking a youngster from a private school was opposed on grounds, as the Admiralty stated, that "it is our opinion essential that he should receive practical training in seamanship while still a boy. To abandon this for the sake of a more perfect theoretical training would be, we are convinced, a fatal mistake."[6] Such a system, appropriate for securing England's "wooden walls", had decreasing utility to the needs of modern warfare. Cadets might have a good grounding in signals and rigging, and also in navigation and seamanship. However, their scientific attainments were inconsequential and their engineering competence doleful. The training ships "became merely a floating dormitory to satisfy the old traditions".[7]

With the establishment of *Britannia*, a college for naval cadets, towards mid-century, leaving behind the old pattern of being under the protection of the commanding officer and then taking your place as a midshipman (and messing in the gun room with others of your lot in life), the officers in training found themselves in classrooms for the first time. As technological changes advanced with exponential speed, engineering officers were needed, and eventually a separate engineering establishment, Keynam, was commissioned. A school for gunnery, *Excellent*, with an attendant shore base at Whale Island, Portsmouth, was established in 1830; another for torpedoes and mine-laying, *Vernon*, followed and by century's end the training of naval officers was radically different from that of 1815. The gunnery officer was an admired specialist. Even so, cutlass drill got much attention, and there was much drill in small arms and field pieces. Officers of the *Excellent* liked to proclaim: "Attitude is the art of gunnery – and whiskers make the man." The Navy sought to emulate the Army in the development of ordnance and in the training of gun crews. However, this was a preoccupation begun only at mid-century. At the outset of *Pax Britannica*, all training was done aboard ship – "learning the ropes" and much else. In 1860, for instance, a cadet, having passed the entrance examination, joined the *Britannia* training ship moored off Haslar Creek, Portsmouth. There was then no shore establishment or school, and that vessel, a first-rate three-decked line of battleship pierced for 120 guns and fully rigged, was still a seagoing one, and, when it was decided to station her at Plymouth, she was sailed round from Portsmouth.[8] Eventually she was moored in the River Dart.

If we could see her at century's end there would be the old *Britannia* in the river, moored fore and aft, with bows close under the stern of an old two-decker, *Hindustan*, the two ships connected by a covered gangway. Electrical cables ran to the shore, but it did not take long for prankster cadets to cut off the connection to shore, sending the ships into unwelcome darkness. Here was another reason to move the establishment ashore.

Recalling days when in floating *Britannia*, one of the many cadets who rose to become a distinguished admiral commented:

> Each cadet stowed all his clothing and uniform in a great sea-chest which he subsequently took to sea with him and retained all his time as a midshipman. The two junior terms slung their hammocks on board the *Hindustan* and the two senior terms on board the *Britannia*. We were well fed, with plenty of meat, vegetables, Devonshire cream, eggs, and so on, and well looked after. It was a grand time.

There was a bark-rigged steam yacht, *Wave*, a schooner, *Siren*, and cutter-rigged *Arrow* that served as tenders or training vessels, and in these the cadets learned the rudiments of sailing and taking soundings under way with the hand lead and the deep-sea lead. The cadets would go aloft on *Britannia*'s single jury foremast, with lower, topsail, topgallant and royal yards crossed, under which a safety net had been spread just in case a cadet should mistakenly fall from the futtock rigging under the lower top. Mathematics, trigonometry, physics,

French, nautical astronomy, navigation, pilotage and seamanship were the standard course requirements, as well as nautical surveying, chart-drawing and lectures in naval history.[9] Prizes were given in a number of fields, marks of distinction duly acquired that gave advantages to the recipient when faced with climbing the long ladder to the top.

In 1905 a new college was built ashore, also called *Britannia*. This magnificent Edwardian edifice gave an altogether imperial demeanour to the serious business of a worldwide navy. From makeshift billets afloat, all of a sudden the cadets and those responsible for them found themselves ashore in a school of learning that was rather novel when compared with past circumstances of making do. The gunroom was a hall of British naval prowess, with splendid oil paintings displaying the victories over all comers. Even King Alfred was venerated for naval exploits. Portraits of the great admirals decorated the corridors – the "sea kings of England". Tradition and honour ruled, and the road to the top was long and hard.

Advancement depended on seniority, as you rose, with luck, through all of the ranks to the much-coveted admiral of the fleet. Having passed out of *Britannia*, a cadet would be appointed to a ship. It was time to see the world. The vessel in question might happily be sent to the eastern Pacific, then on to the palm-fringed Society Islands and north to salubrious Hawaii, and possibly across to temperate Vancouver Island, with its charming colonial women, parties, and fish and game entertainments, then south to San Francisco, on to the lucrative export locale for Mexican silver at San Blas, Gulf of California, then south again to the Galapagos and to Valparaiso, Chile, before rounding the fabled Cape Horn once again, looking in at the desolate Falkland Islands, and then home at last – after perhaps four years, when the ship was "paid off". Then other opportunities were sought – a new ship, perhaps, and a new commander and a new foreign station, maybe the China station this time, with the delights of Hong Kong and Japan in view, or perhaps the Australasian station, with its wide reach out to Norfolk Island, New Guinea, the Cook Islands and Fiji. If in the Indian Ocean, it was steamy Zanzibar and perhaps Mauritius in the pleasant trade winds. Thus the Navy had eyes on every ocean and annex, and by the time the cadet had risen to captain he had very much seen the world. Of course, there had been great storms and ferocious winds and seas, and along the way, too, a shipmate might have tumbled from aloft and disappeared in the turbulent waters or crashed onto the main deck. Complete sets of sails may have been torn away and main and topmasts come crashing down, necessitating all wreckage to be cleared away, the captain declaiming to the lieutenant that he was no more use than a pump handle (he did not long remain on the ship), and the lower deck got to work under seasoned supervision to repair damage and proceed with the voyage. But soon Tahiti might be reached, and there was then frolic ashore in Polynesia, with fishing and bathing inside the coral reefs, the surf drumming out its plaintive music on the reefs outside. The sailors lived in a world of danger and a world of enchantment, curiously in contradistinction. Hearth and home might be very far away, not to be seen again for a year or probably more, but there would be tall tales to tell upon return, and happy shining faces to greet the wayfarer. Flying fish, penguins, iguanas and sealions all had describable characteristics of delight, and then there were the natural wonders, such as erupting volcanoes, tsunamis, a fire in the rigging during a storm known as St. Elmo's Fire and, perhaps of greatest entertainment, rounding Cape Horn in the highest seas and the worst weather. Hardship had its compensations, and experience gave the teller bragging rights. It's a world we have lost, the Victorian sailor's, and regretfully so few of their stories survive in print.[10]

There was a "swank" in the Navy that gave it special flavour and distinction. Admirals prided themselves on individuality. An understated bravado marked the Navy's every progression. Admiral Sir John Fisher liked to say that the Navy "travels first class". In their tailored clothes, bearing and detachment, the young midshipmen, or "snotties", were always on good behaviour, representative of "the Queen's Navie" and eminently proud of the Service. And why not? For they were in the elite of services, and in an enterprise of government that ruled the world. They might soon be sent to solve some particular problem – bail out a missionary or an archaeologist, free some British subject in a jam, or even just to show the flag or send up a warning rocket, or fire a bursting shell to keep native piracy in check. Britain ruled the waves and, when out of necessity, might waive the rules – though heaven help the commanding officer in question if he exceeded his rightful duties. On such an occasion a stout reprimand would be sent, and with it, possibly, an underlying message that he had "blotted his copybook" and that further assignments might be difficult or even impossible. There were lots of captains and lieutenants waiting to fill his shoes.

"Where shall we sail today, Admiral?" That is what the boyish flag captain is supposed, delightfully, to have asked his exalted superior. And did it really matter, the seven seas being essentially British? In fact, the admiral had specific duties and was probably under the constraints of his instructions. That having been said, it is true that certain officers spent most of their careers on a particular station – the North America and West Indies station being one such – and thereby became experts on the local planter class, the intricacies of dealing with the Americans on anti-slavery matters, and how to cooperate with the United States Navy in eradicating piracy. West Africa was not a desired location to be long on station, on account of disease and heat, and East Africa and the Indian Ocean weren't much better. Each station had its challenges and each their magic. The Royal Navy's remit was the Seven Seas. As befitted his station, a flag officer (e.g. a vice- or rear-admiral or commodore) commanding on one of the stations (because by mid-century the Navy had divided the world's waters into various such) would fly, or wear, his flag in what amounted to a capital ship. As late as 1859 a three-decker such as *Ganges* would be the admiral's flagship on the Pacific station. As late as that year, what an observer in 1809 said about the 120-gun *Caledonia* at Portsmouth would hold true to lookers-on in Esquimalt, British Columbia:

> What a sublime and terrible simplicity there is to our Navy! Nothing is admitted but what is absolutely useful. The cannon, the decks, the sailors, all wore the appearance of stern vigour, as if constituted only to resist the elements. No beautiful forms in the gun carriages, no taste or elegance in the cannon; the ports square and hard; the guns iron; the sailors muscular. Everything inspired one with awe.[11]

A midshipman had no clue as to where he might be sent, but often a captain would speak for him, and so he would be so appointed. Political patronage always helped. In the years after the Napoleonic wars, a man might wait for 40 years for promotion to lieutenant. In other cases, by age 22 a chance existed that lieutenant's rank could be reached, when a new set of prospects presented themselves and a new set of hurdles. Because a captain commissioning a ship could recommend the name of his executive officer, and because the latter could similarly advance the interests of those whom he knew, the officers of a certain ship were often bound up by systems that might be described as deferential – mutual obligations needing to be preserved. However, often there were outsiders appointed to vacancies. A young lieutenant always looked for an opportunity to prove himself worthy of command, and so, if competent and with "interest", his name would advance on the Navy List until such an opening occurred. Even then such an appointment had to be made or confirmed by the all-supreme lords of the Admiralty. "A war and a sickly season" could bring fast possibilities of advancement, but "Fear God and Dread Nought" (that old Cromwellian adage) was the central accepting purpose of every naval officer. He made sure that all under him knew this belief, and the King's Regulations and the Articles of War defended the whole structure. The whole was tied together by customs and conventions; it was similarly wrapped in a legal world that listed crimes and defined punishments – all designed so that each and every person in the Royal Navy knew the rules and conducted himself accordingly. The system had been built up over centuries and was as tough in the early years of *Pax* as it was, say, in the mid-eighteenth century during a siege of Gibraltar or Minorca.

Advancement on the Navy List invariably depended on seniority, and so the sooner on the list the better. If a lieutenant was fortunate enough to reach the rank of captain, he then took his place at the bottom of the advancement ladder, climbing slowly up as those above him died. Once made post-captain – that is, "posted" on the list – he stood in line for a sea command which would give him the necessary sea time, towards the end of our period, for flag rank – first rear admiral, then vice admiral, then admiral. He then progressed by the same process of "dead men's shoes". The ultimate rank was admiral of the fleet, which was a rarity. If in charge of a number of ships, even a squadron, a captain would be called commodore, an honorific title in those days. In the early years of *Pax* there were countless "Trafalgar Admirals" or "Admirals All" – that is, those who had served in one way or another at Trafalgar. Most were on half-pay, and they would wait and wait in the hope that their name would come to the top of the list. One such was Rear Admiral David Price, appointed commander-in-chief of the Pacific at the outset of the Crimean War. A former magistrate and with little recent sea command experience, he was demonstrably unsuitable to lead a British-French attack on the Russians at Petropavlovsk and shot himself mortally just before the event, sending the command structure into some doubt, for the French admiral would presumably have become head of operations. However, the ranking senior British officer, Captain Sir Frederick Nicolson, became commodore and pressed on with the attack. That it was a failure was owing to poor reconnaissance, underestimating the enemy, and geographical obstacles. Still, the whole event cast a dark shadow over these ancient admirals. Price had not taken advantage of a retirement scheme, and other officers similarly disregarded the dreary prospects.[12] The old arrangements for seniority and appointments were slow to change. When he became first lord of the Admiralty, Erskine Childers, fighting hard for economies, found himself embroiled in fights with officers on the Navy List who were unwilling to be superannuated. But political will carried the day: Childers dealt with a large list of unemployed officers. He offered a volunteer retirement scheme, with a higher pension and an advance in rank (rather than remaining on half pay). In a flash, however, the possibilities of reaching flag rank or rising in its various stages vanished quickly, resulting in many a saddened heart.[13] The new system of younger officers was important to national naval renewal in the 1890s. Those admirals who were too old to fight were still in a state of fealty to the Admiralty. One of them, Vice Admiral Cherry, apparently too weary to seek any sort of active employment in the Service, wrote to their lordships this last pathetic submission: "Request I may be received into Chatham Naval Hospital for the purpose of dying." To this the first sea lord, Admiral Sir Arthur Wilson, VC ("Old 'Ard 'Art", as he was known) minuted laconically: "Approved."[14]

As a caste, or breed, of men, admirals were "the joy of onlookers and sometimes even of their shipmates". So recalled an officer who had sailed with so many of them. *Pax*, he noted, was not based on the power of a gunboat (invariably puny) but "was due to the characters of those who represented the unseen and unchallenged power of Great Britain".[15] Eccentricity existed and was accepted, individuality applauded, oddities lauded. What counted most was the ability to command. John Rusworth Jellicoe was a slip of a man and short at four feet eight-and-a-half inches, the son of a captain in merchant service. He passed first out of *Britannia* in 1874 and then became a gunnery officer. He commanded *Victoria* when it was rammed by *Camperdown* off Tripoli during a tactical exercise but survived. He had been in the international naval brigade that advanced to Peking during the Boxer rising and was severely wounded. Fortune smiled on him, and he went on to successive commands at sea, winning the approval of many, and thus on 4 August 1914 he became commander in chief, Grand Fleet, flying his flag in *Iron Duke*, based on Scapa Flow in the Orkneys. He was a selfless character with deep religious convictions. Men who served with and under him were devoted to him; they implicitly trusted his leadership. Imperturbable in battle and a quick thinker, he was regarded by many as the coming Nelson, and Winston Churchill, when first lord of the Admiralty, thought similarly. He was a product of the Victorian age: "prudence" and "preparation" were bywords, as were "care" and "economy". Britain could lose command at sea by foolish action. Jellicoe did not intend to disappoint. That he had joined the Navy at a time when it was most reactionary gave him many challenges, and he witnessed the full sweep of changes that came over the Navy in the years running up to the outbreak of war and were exhibited at Jutland in 1916, when his fleet lost 14 warships, and 6,097 British sailors were killed, 510 wounded and 177 picked out of the water and taken prisoner. The Germans suffered nearly as much. Jellicoe's leadership came under question and the Navy and Admiralty suffered a severe blow. Problems of command and control failed Jellicoe in the end. As a character study he fascinates us still – the only man on either side, said Churchill, who could lose the war in an afternoon. All that lay ahead in the dreamy summertime atmosphere of the cruiser or gunboat sailing Chinese waters or undertaking manoeuvres, no matter how dangerous, in the war-free waters of the Mediterranean. Other naval officers were more ambitious and high profile. David Beatty, who commanded the Battle Cruiser Squadron at Jutland, for instance, or Sir Percy Scott, the gunnery enthusiast who developed director fire for guns, or volatile Lord Charles Beresford, Admiral Lord Fisher's nemesis, who caused all sorts of strife. Jellicoe was the epitome of the best that *Britannia* naval college could produce and the best that the Service could train and develop through the various levels of command. Talent-spotted early, he did not disappoint, and on his death in 1935 he was buried near Nelson in the Crypt at St. Paul's Cathedral.[16]

As for the "lower deck" as of 1815, the ratings, as they were called as a general category, were enlisted men. Some had been impressed during the recent war and had stayed on in the service.[17] The practice of impressment (never disavowed by the Navy) was not employed after 1815, when, with the coming of peace, there was a surplus of seamen and a downsizing of the naval establishment. The paying-off of ships during the first three years of peace meant a reduction in naval manpower from a peak of 145,000 to a mere 19,000, barely enough for the Service's peacetime requirements.[18] The number of sailors was voted by Parliament. The sailors – able seamen up to warrant officers – were invariably from a different social stratum than the officers and midshipmen. Most were from London, the Thames Valley and the southern counties. They had little or no schooling, and they ate and slept in different circumstances than did the officers. The lower deck was heavily graduated in rank and station, from warrant officers right down to ordinary seamen and those recently entered in the books as being "subject to the requirements of the service". There was a pecking order of severe classifications, every man to his duties and to his station. It was, too, a world of hard knocks, strict rules and severe punishments to offenders. If there were a chaplain on board, his spare time was used little beyond educating the young boys who were destined for the quarterdeck. Class ruled in all things naval ashore and afloat, and merit was the principal ingredient for a rise in rank and opportunity. And there were many opportunities for someone in the Queen's Navy to distinguish himself. Such opportunities were awaited with keen anticipation.

Boy seamen ratings had begun in the eighteenth century as "Officer's Servants". Many came from seafaring families while others were waifs or runaways, invariably from cities and towns. Some entered from naval orphanages. Others were brought forward from the Marine Society, a philanthropic institution founded in 1756 that provided not only a great patriotic service but also a humanitarian one in rescuing and nurturing derelict children. "Unlike later," writes the author of *Band of Brothers*, all about boy sailors,

> when men and boys on shipboard were strictly segregated, boys in the Georgian Navy lacking a more privileged berth were lumped in with the seamen, victualled in a broadside mess and slung their hammocks among them on the gun-deck. They were employed on such deck duties as their age and strength allowed. The smartest of the older boys worked aloft on the highest yards, the royals and topgallants, whose sails were the smallest and lightest. Some of these 'upper yardmen', who included potential officers, were killed in falls, an occupational hazard of all seamen, but those who survived the experience gained valuable skill and confidence in working aloft. The Admiralty enjoined that all boys should be exercised in bending and reefing sails daily, and should compete with other ships in performing drills smartly. In a ship with a captain who took an interest in the welfare and training of boys, of which there were regrettably few, the youngest of them enjoyed the benefit of a 'sea-daddy', an experienced seaman charged with the responsibility of looking after the boy; showing him how to prepare his food and mend his clothing as well as teaching him seamanship and the ways of the Navy, until he was old enough to stand on his own feet.

> Collingwood was such a captain: he, first among Nelson's 'band of brothers', was sympathetic to the plight of boys, having himself gone to sea at the age of eleven in 1762.[19]

This was not a sheltered life for boys of tender years, and they lived in the promiscuous conditions of a man-of-war's 'tween decks. Sodomy was the one capital offence in the old Navy for which, on conviction, the sentence was invariably carried out. Moral corruption emanated from a more likely source. After years at sea or months on blockade, a captain might allow boatloads of women on board. Grog was then freely issued. One ringing observation, dated 1821, presents the scene of

> the shocking, disgraceful actions of the lower deck... the dirt, filth and stench; the disgusting conversation; the indecent, beastly conduct and horrible scenes; the blasphemy and swearing; the riots, quarrels and fighting; where hundreds of men and women are huddled together in one room and must be the witness of each other's actions... a ship in this state is justly termed by the more decent seamen 'a hell afloat'.[20]

This appalling state of affairs changed with the passage of years. But chaplains were only assigned to larger ships and, in any case, they customarily attended to the education of future officers. An able seaman's lot was a rough-and-tumble one, not for the faint of heart. In peace as in war, injuries occurred at sea, as did death from accident or drowning.

As of the opening of our period, the Greenwich Hospital, which stands on the site of the ancient royal palace of Greenwich, was run by a foundation with enormous revenues (gathered from prize money, "gathering the flowers of the sea", Admiral Anson nicely called the system). At the time of its greatest prosperity, 3,000 inmates and 32,000 out-pensioners were maintained by the foundation. Queen Mary had found it difficult to provide shelter and maintenance for the thousands of brave men who had come back wounded after the battle of La Hogue. Eventually a plan was furnished by Christopher Wren, and the edifice built surpassed that built upriver for the Chelsea Pensioners. So the wounded and worn-out seamen were provided for, in magnificent surroundings that eventually – after the dissolution of 1869 – became the Royal Naval College and are now the University of Greenwich. As for the sailors in need, they were as of that year given pensions as compensation. The majority of the 1,000 who took the pension sadly died within a year of leaving the hospital. The whole was a questionable Victorian reform, and rather instructive to this day regarding the politics of how to deal with those injured in war.

As a rule, the situation of seagoing sailors has been portrayed as one of hardship and brutality. Winston Churchill is said to have claimed that the history of the Royal Navy was one only of "rum, sodomy and the lash". John Masefield's portrait of life at sea during Nelson's time shows the harsh nature of shipboard life. However, the sober perspective as given by Nicholas Rodger in his *Wooden World* shows a more benign existence and a healthier one, too. Life at sea, with food, drink and medical care, could be preferable to life ashore in, say, London, runs the argument. Given the fact that ship's companies could diminish over time (from death, disease, desertion or calamity), it was in the interest of the commanding officer to ensure the good health of the seamen. In short, tyranny had ended with the close of the wars, and as the century advanced the condition of sailors improved. Jack Tar presented an attractive figure in the popular view: a rough-and-tumble fellow with large, tattooed arms and biceps, swarthy of appearance because of hours under the sun and in the wind, capable of tying any knot, and noted for having sailed the seven seas in all sorts of conditions and dangers. He was a man of the world – a British sailor in the Royal Navy.

Completing a ship's complement by impressment had been an evil necessity during the Napoleonic War and the War of 1812. Afterwards the system was phased out, though in theory it seems to have enjoyed a lingering death.[21] For the new years of peace, the Navy depended on old-fashioned and time-honoured measures of providing an adequate supply of seamen – offering bounties for enlistment and paying off the ship's company at the end of the commission. At the outset of our period, no permanent measures were taken to provide for forming a regular body of seamen. Castlereagh's dictum that "the power of your establishments should be contrived so as to admit of a rapid expansion at the outset of a war" was disregarded in connection with the manning of the fleet. But the manpower requirements did not diminish for a navy policing the world's seas, and, rather than taking in foreign sailors and non-Caucasians, as a rule, it was better to keep those who came from the customary places – the Home Counties, the Thames Valley and the Southwest, plus Ireland. In 1835 the newly formed Manning Committee decreed that all boy seamen upon reaching the age of 18 were to be signed on for a ten-year period. Then years later this was extended to all ratings. Thus was begun what was meant by "continuous service". Seamen gunners was a class of sailor introduced in 1832, the intention being to have a core of duly instructed gunners, gunners' mates and yeomen of the powder room who would communicate to the whole crew of the ships to which they were appointed the knowledge that they had acquired at the depot, HMS *Excellent*. Thus, as the Victorian age dawned, the seamen gunners, the boy seamen and others on continuous service formed an altogether improved nucleus of the lower deck. In 1852, continuous service became universal throughout the fleet.[22]

These changes took years to effect, and in 1839 a senior naval lord resigned over what he described as "the rotten system of manning". In 1840 his point was proved when it took over four months to raise 4,000 men during a critical situation with France over Syria. There were prolonged delays during the Crimean War, too, particularly in the Baltic, the commander-in-chief complaining that given the fact that the ships were manned, with untrained and undisciplined crews, the fleet was not fit to go into action. As a lord of the Admiralty reviewing the matter said at the time, "If you will find 300 able seamen on board each ship, I shall be greatly surprised."[23]

HMS *Illustrious* was designated as the first training ship for boys in 1854, and before too long, line-of-battle ships, stripped of their sails and rigging, could be seen moored in Falmouth, Portland and Portsmouth as detested "hulks". These served as schools for the new sailors of the Victorian and Edwardian ages, who would also have sea time in seagoing training ships. HMS *Ganges*, a hulk moored at Falmouth and the principal training establishment, witnessed the heavy powers of the Ship's Police and petty officers who ruled this lower deck in its education and training. In 1892, Thomas Holman recounted that the old brutal days in the training hulks had passed, and the newer regulations required any instructor to be reduced from a petty officer to an able seaman and sent out of the Training Service if he struck a boy.

> This is placing dangerous power in the hands of the boys, who are sometimes not above using it in combining to ruin a Petty Officer; still it is, in my opinion, the lesser evil of the two, and the Instructors are certainly much more able to look after themselves now than we boys were then.[24]

Even so, the Admiralty continued to maintain a tough system of discipline that was beneficial to the efficiency of the Service. The system of corporal punishment continued, and sailors were dismissed for drunkenness. Watered rum, or grog, was issued to boys until 1851. Later, in 1881, the issue was restricted to men over 20 (it was finally abolished in 1970). In 1848, as an attempt to maintain discipline, sentences of courts martial were ordered to be circulated throughout the fleet and to be read to ships companies. They were read out immediately after the monthly reading of the Articles of War.[25] When the Admiralty had learned, to its regret, of secondary punishments having been introduced in lieu of corporal punishment, it sent, in reference to this unwelcome news, the following circular issued to commanders-in-chief on foreign stations: "They cannot but consider that such a practice, however plausible, or praiseworthy of motives, that have led to it, is contrary to the Rules established for the good of the Service, and the due protection of all engaged in it...". Further: "My Lords will always hold it to be the imperative duty of an Officer in command, to make himself acquainted with the most trifling Punishments inflicted on board his Ship, and to satisfy himself, as to their justice and necessity."[26] And to regulate the punishments, and have oversight over the same, captains were ordered to keep a defaulters' book, wherein was to be entered every offence and punishment. This was a further attempt to avoid excessive punishments then being handed out, or to prevent too lenient ones. Captains disliked this intervention, which they thought subverted their independent authority. Before long, bosuns were obliged to live under new rules in the exercise of punishment. Parliament was calling for accountability and demanding reforms.[27] Even so, drunkenness remained a nagging problem, particularly in locales where rum was available, and debilitating if not fatal diseases (malaria, yellow fever, dengue fever and others) could cut savagely into a ship's company. There were storms and accidents at sea, of course, and the Admiralty and Navy Board seldom gave out salaries and wages that put a smile on anyone's face. The mutiny of 1797 had laid bare grievances, and as of 1900 the seamen were once again demanding higher wages and better conditions ashore and afloat. As usual, their women and children ashore fared even worse. In the age of *Pax Britannica* the prize money that had been much more available during the wars with France and the United States no longer existed as a source of revenue, though capturing privateers and slavers had some joint benefit. The crew shared some of the proceeds from the freighting of bullion as undertaken by their vessel, but by and large the spoils of victory from a good and successful fight at sea had vanished during the years of peace.

The training of officers and men remained an undeniable of concern to the lords of the Admiralty, but rigid economies and old-fashioned attitudes invariably stood in the way of social improvement and the amelioration of working conditions. In 1904 the old *Ganges* was towed to Harwich, and Shotley Barracks, a shore establishment also known as *Ganges II*, was opened there in October 1905. It was the first and largest of the shore establishments for the training of boy seamen. It rather resembled a public school with its dormitories and laundry. Physical and mechanical training took the place of mast and sail drill. Marine instructors had charge of the drill. The old guard hated these changes, and Lord Brassey, not a naval officer but a well-known yachtsman, a civilian lord of the Admiralty and founder of the *Naval Annual*, wrote in that publication in 1905: "it seems regrettable that all masted ships should have disappeared from the training service for boys. Stationary ships are now mastless; the brigs are paid off... physical drill in the gymnasium is not a satisfactory substitute for training aloft." Senior officers, serving and retired, had joined the chorus, and they were not wholly prompted by nostalgia: the Navy was alone among the world's sea powers in abolishing sail training for its cadets and young seamen. As a compromise, the first sea lord, who was insistent on reform and bringing the Navy forward into the new century, ordered the erection of a 140-foot mast on the Shotley parade ground. It stands there today, a prominent Suffolk landmark, high above a police training college – symbol of an older order of the Royal Navy, one in which the wind was free and of a time when, as Drake said, "the wind commands".

Technological change was driving the Navy ashore for its training. In-class education was taking the place of shipboard experience. Coal had replaced sail almost completely, and wood had been supplanted by iron and steel. Manning the yards was out of fashion; looking at pressure gauges and reading firing range estimates was the new reality. Torpedoes and wireless had come into their own, and the industrial age was coming on at prodigious speed both ashore and afloat.

In these circumstances, Shotley Barracks may have seemed a lovely place by comparison with the old crowded, unsanitary and dark hulks, but like many another new establishment, often the old social mores and traditions continued. The corporate and corporal structures of the old Navy persisted. As the historian of boy sailors has observed,

> Most boys would have preferred working aloft on sails and rigging to coaling ship... but this particular bane of a Boy Seaman's existence was to be comparatively short-lived, with conversion to oil-fuel beginning in the second decade of the century. The ultra-traditionalist Royal Navy was no enemy of scientific progress where the matter of fighting efficiency was concerned; only in its treatment of ratings in general and its boys in particular. No progress there...[28]

Those ships wearing the White Ensign in the oceans and annexes of the world were backed up by many others that lay "in ordinary" – that is, in reserve and capable of being rigged, provisioned and manned as required in any emergency. The Navy's reputation was legendary, for it had fought the enemy, or a combination of enemy nations, over the course of two or more centuries. It had not won every fleet action or single-ship engagement. But overall it was the world's premier naval force in 1815, with a vaunted reputation, a tradition of victory that rested in superb seamanship and gunnery, and a proven officer corps. Its discipline was equally legendary, and its record in close combat – "Engage the enemy more closely," Nelson instructed – made the English sailor the terror of the seas. Always aiming for tactical advantage when in the line of battle, admirals and captains had learned the advantage of position – and how to put the enemy at a disadvantage in a sea fight. Innovative tactics, as employed at Trafalgar, had further kept the rivals off balance. Blockade was another successful means of controlling the enemy, preventing them from going to sea. While convoys in wartime had proved their merit, all the while British warships and letters of marque preyed on enemy merchant commerce. In every respect, in 1815, the British were the rulers of the waves. They stood at the doorstep of their great century, and they still held that status in 1914.

All the while that Britain's glory had been acquired by means of armed combat on and over the seas, Britain was progressing through the Industrial

Revolution, a process that made the country the workshop of the world and the remarkable industrial power of the early nineteenth century. That pre-eminence, in these fields, would diminish with the century, not because of British decline but because of the more rapid advance of rival industrial nations, notably Germany but also the United States, France and Japan. The "fear of falling" was actually the fear of being overtaken and left behind. In other words, British supremacy was actually shrinking in relation to its rivals, who were closing the gap, so to speak. This was the cause of the great concern in the years from 1890 to 1914. Rival industrial output, merchant shipping, oceanic passenger traffic and systems of communications naturally concerned the British, who long had enjoyed the fruits of victory and the influence that came with being the world's greatest banking and industrial power. Pronouncements concerning German ambitions on and over the seas caused the greatest worry.

The envy of the world, ships and sailors of the Royal Navy were the symbols of Britain's greatness. The White Ensign gave security to investment overseas. Banking houses, corporations, agents and consuls all leaned on the gunboat or even the fleet for security. Peace and profit went hand in hand. This was an axiom of the age. With unmistakable oceanic control and rivals who dare not contest this dominance, the Navy held the trident of Neptune – and had no intention of relinquishing it. As Britain's power was legendary, it is not surprising that rival commentators and statesmen held many a strong opinion about the Navy as policeman of the world, or as arbiter in the difficult circumstances where indigenous problems festered or third parties threatened to intervene. It was observed by Sir Arnold Wilson, a political agent of great experience in Persia, that whereas the British had paid a heavy price in expeditions, military and naval, and also in hydrographic surveys so that order could reign in the Persian Gulf, a tremendous price of the Admiralty had been paid. Slaves had been freed and pirates put down, but the British "got little out of it ourselves, for it is open to the commerce of all nations and we enjoy no sort of preferential rights".[29]

On the eve of the First World War the British Navy, like the empire, like the British merchant marine, like British capital and finance and like its communications networks overseas, was prodigious in size: plans effected for the manning of the fleet called for mobilizations that would bring in 136,000 on active service plus 11,000 recruits with an additional reserve of 24,000. The grand total of officers and men that the first lord of the Admiralty, Winston Churchill, estimated being available for March 1914 was 177,071.[30] The repeal of the navigation acts in 1849 had suspended the necessity of requiring British captains of merchant vessels maintaining British crews, and by the close of the century alarms were being raised that too many foreigners would be manning the fleet. The claim and fear might have been justifiable but naval recruiting averted the problem. Joining the Navy in time of need had huge popularity. "One life, one flag, one fleet, one throne" – the words by Tennyson – came like many a lad as a clarion call, and even an answer to counter desperate poverty, certain unemployment and urban depravity. The chance to see the world and serve in the greatest instrument of warfare afloat answered many a need, and it gave instant corporate identity – no small consideration.

3
Anchors of Empire

Naval power resides not only in ships and men, and on finance and national will; it rests on secure and adequate refuges and positions for repair, recuperation and resupply. In the age of *Pax*, when Britain took it upon itself to carry out policies of enforcement of the abolition of privateering, the suppression of the slave trade and the protection of seaborne commerce, strategically located naval bases were the direct result of the global nature of British interests. The state of Britain's foreign relations was always the commanding factor, and here again, power and profit went hand in hand. The selection of the sites of such bases and the construction of the same remain part of the imperial naval story relatively unappreciated as a subject of inquiry. Yet investigation of this shows how the prosperity of British trade and empire depended mightily on the projection overseas of human skills, architectural design and engineering know-how. Moreover, it discloses why statesmen, far from acting in a fit of absentmindedness, were willing to enlarge the imperial estate bit by bit so as to give strategic advantage to the whole.

By the early twentieth century, British bases girdled the globe. Numerous places, such as Weihaiwei, north China, and Aden, at the entrance to the Red Sea, had been grabbed for the purpose of maritime security and often so as to keep rivals out of these potential spheres of influence. With sovereignty or paramountcy over these places, the British came to possess a ring of bases from which to exercise power and coerce rivals. "Five keys lock up the world!" proclaimed the ruthless British naval administrator Admiral Sir John Fisher in 1904. These were Singapore, the Cape, Alexandria, Gibraltar and Dover. And he noted with pride that these five keys belonged to England and would be kept by the great fleets of England. Fisher's predecessors as of the year 1815 were equally anxious to have proper basing for the fleet, wherever it might be required. Even in the day when a single frigate or sloop-of-war might be called upon to "show the flag" and obtain results by a display of armed might, the leverage of sea power depended on basing or on the assistance of allied even client states.

By the 1830s the union of trade and sea power was established and secure. Free-trade lobbyists demanded protection of seaborne trade, just as had merchants and companies working under the old mercantile regime. But British trade overseas was growing. The ministers of state, and the opposition, who made policy at the heart of empire, implicitly understood the trade–sea power complex. Mobility of force and economy of movement demanded springboards of power and influence. The adroit guidance of Lord Melville, first lord of the Admiralty 1812–1830, and the caustic supervision of the Duke of Wellington, master general of ordnance and later commander-in-chief of the British Army 1827–1852, steered the long-range processes of base-development and security.[1] "No developments during the nineteenth century served to undermine the doctrine that national power and prosperity depended upon industry and overseas commerce, which involved in turn the upkeep of combined commercial and naval bases," wrote Gerald Graham. He also explained how the older acquisitions took on a new value in the mid- and later nineteenth century: "And with the development of steam in the thirties, colonial bases along the main trade routes doubled in strategic importance. Such bases served not only as depots for coaling, watering, victualling and repair, but as entrepôts and centres of influence expanding British commerce." Apart from India, where the expansion had been predicated on defensive needs, the British continued to exercise their influence "through the Open Door". And "not until the later nineteenth century did Britain begin to penetrate and sometimes assimilate neighbouring hinterlands in order to safeguard existing commercial establishments on the coast".[2] The technological imperative of the age – steam power – was enhanced by communications revolutions in the telegraph and submarine cable (and eventually wireless). With Britain as the driving force in these changes, developments in bases and their defences had to be kept up, and throughout the epoch the British did just that.

"If naval exploits have tended to capture the attention of historians and journalists, these exploits depended absolutely upon the ability of the royal dockyards and the ordnance and victualling yards to build, equip and sustain the fleet." So writes Jonathan Coad, who has brought the architectural edifice of the Navy at home and overseas to the reading public's attention. Dockyards lacked the glamour of the seagoing fleet, and shore establishments bore the brunt of many a charge of inefficiency and waste. But the British Government invested hugely in them. Royal dockyards, continues the same authority, "were the heart of the country's defence effort. Behind their walls they represented the government's greatest continuing capital investment in protection of the realm".[3]

Hand in hand with the expansion of the British Empire went the acquisition of naval bases. Some – Portsmouth, the Nore and Plymouth – were on home soil, while others were situated in foreign places of convenience where English was rarely spoken (e.g. Río de Janeiro and Valparaiso). During the wars that ended in 1815, the British built bases at Malta, Trincomalee and the Cape of Good Hope. Within a few years of the return of peace, they had laid the foundations of a new naval authority in Singapore, Aden, Valparaiso and elsewhere. They had erected Halifax, Nova Scotia, as a base in 1749, purely for strategic reasons, and thereby to keep an eye on the restless French, and they followed on, in the next century (principally the 1860s), with another "anchor of empire" at the westernmost reaches of the Canadian dominion at Esquimalt, Vancouver Island. This was Britain's window on the North Pacific, there to watch on the schemes of Russia, the United States, imperial Japan and other powers. In an era of overall entrenchment, government placed a growing reliance on bases of strategic merit so that the rapid rearrangement of forces, or the deployment of ships and men, could meet the needs of the day as they arose. Thus during the double difficulty of the British Columbia gold rush and the crisis with the United States over the San Juan Islands boundary, the Admiralty shifted naval units from the Far East to Vancouver Island as required.[4]

Now we turn to a specific case of base development: Bermuda. It was out of changing circumstances and an unannounced doctrine, which would in our times be called a "flexible response", that Bermuda, one of the earliest English colonies (1684 as a formal possession), arose from its volcanic bed and colonial slumber into a great imperial fortress – a British citadel in American seas. It became the new Gibraltar and the great bulwark of the empire. It is worth looking at its unappreciated history as a case study on how the British projected their power and how the base was built, against the odds.[5]

In the immediate years after Sir George Somers had been shipwrecked there and discovered its value for settlement and tobacco growing, a small colonial edifice had been established at St. George's, the capital – a Georgian town square replete with flagstaff, a parish church near to hand, some docks and jetties, and a strand of businesses, banks, import agencies, liquor vendors and clearing houses – altogether complete as an outcrop of the empire. Hard to defend from a seaward attack and useless as a harbour for a fleet, it would have been bypassed had it not been for the urgent need for a naval base in these mid-Atlantic latitudes, and the designing efforts of naval captains and Royal Engineers to conquer some of the geographical obstacles and create a bulwark of empire out of choral islets and a rocky mount known as Ireland Island, the westernmost of the Bermudas.

Like other naval bases, Bermuda owes everything to its location. The Bermudas, or Somers Islands, are not, as might be thought, situated in the West Indies; they lie in the shape of a sickle in the western Atlantic, 667 miles east of New York and 580 east of Cape Hatteras. They consist of a group of 300 small coral islands situated on the summit of a large cone rising from the submerged plateau of the Atlantic. The Virginia Company settled the islands in

1612 but found no fresh springs, only rain. Representative government was introduced in 1620 and, next to the House of Commons, the House of Assembly of Bermuda is the oldest legislative body of its kind in the British imperial experience. The islands passed from hand to hand among proprietors; pirates made them their base; and fearful mariners sighting the islands often called them "Isles of the Devils" because of the reefs surrounding them.[6]

Bermuda, if in enemy hands, would sorely test Britain's strength and confound its shipping. "The possession of Bermuda as the key of all our western Colonies", recounted a strategist after the War of 1812, "is of the first importance to England, for if a foe of any maritime strength had possession of it, our trade would be exposed to much annoyance if not total destruction."[7] Another contemporary authority put it this way: "The Bermudas are, in fact the Gibraltar of the West Indies, and Washington was very desirous of annexing them to the republic, to make them a nest of hornets to any English commerce."[8] As the century advanced, so did the high-minded discussion of Bermuda's value, which was lauded by many visionary strategists, including one who proclaimed Bermuda "central to the mouths of the Amazon, the Mississippi, the Oronoko, the St. Lawrence, and to the innumerable tributary rivers that send their waters through these mighty vomitaries of the ocean".[9] Halifax was a secure base, but in winter, refitting ships above decks was delayed by the weather. Besides, it lay 2,000 ocean-miles from the Caribbean, which was the centre of action against the French and other rivals. In the wars against pirates and slave-trading ships, Halifax gave way to Bermuda as being closer to the scene of crimes, so to speak.

No matter how high-sounding the strategic rhetoric, Bermuda's advantages as a base of military authority had already been demonstrated by recent events. The War of the American Revolution provided such proof. So did the war against France, begun in 1793, and, once again, the War of 1812. Until the revolutionary war, the islands were of little consequence to Britain, wrote an early historian of Bermuda in 1848. After that event, however, their importance became every day more apparent "and immense sums have since been expended to fortify them".[10] Cruisers based there helped to tighten the ring of maritime authority around the Thirteen Colonies and enforce the blockade. As a naval base, arsenal and garrison, Bermuda offered a tempting prize to American powder-seekers and privateers. During the war against France, British naval commanders worried about "that swarm of marauders out of Charleston",[11] and their attention was drawn south from Halifax and New England to the mid-Atlantic and southern states. Much the same set of circumstances existed during the War of 1812, at which time the United States had a clear eye on Bermuda, and intended to ruin it as a place from which British cruisers could prey on American commerce and interfere with American communications.[12] During that war, British warships sailed to blockade the American seaboard, with such success that by 1813 the throttling of enemy commerce had been achieved and American privateering reduced. The naval force sent for the pillaging of Washington assembled under the guns of Fort St. Catherine, near St. George's, Bermuda.

Bermuda gave more flexibility to naval power in more southerly waters into the Caribbean and the Spanish Main. Because Anglo-American tensions failed to ease through the 1820s, contrary to hopes and expectations, and were in fact made more volatile by the pronouncement of the Monroe Doctrine and the inability of statesmen on both sides of the Atlantic to reach accord on how to eradicate the slave trade, British military planners continued to build up the advantages of Bermuda. They therefore made plans for its adequate defence. New plans of 1827 dwarfed all previous schemes. Urgent completion was called for. During the 1830s, troubles on the Maine–New Brunswick border, sparked by a lumberjacks' fight, plus rebellions in Lower and Upper Canada, the invasion of Canadian territory by republican-inspired Hunters Lodges, and then, in the early 1840s, the crisis over Oregon (plus instability in Texas and California) all intensified the need to press on with the construction of facilities of replenishment and repair at Ireland Island. But construction proceeded at a tediously slow pace, and contracts either did not work or were altogether unsatisfactory.

To convert a cluster of soft stone or coral islands, 24 miles long, and guarded by storm-swept reefs and with some inshore anchorages only approached through narrow, dangerous channels, presented many challenges to hydrographic surveyors and pilots. Nonetheless, workable approaches and channels were found. The Admiralty purchased Ireland Island, and improvements and expansions were made to the establishment that dated as early as the American revolutionary war. Lieutenant Thomas Hurd undertook an urgent survey. He found "safe and secure anchorage among those islands for the whole Navy of England". In 1806, fearing that the United States or France might seize the islands as their own, the lords of the Admiralty, on the advice of Rear Admiral George Murray, began the process of making it a well-fortified location.[13] Murray was delighted at the prospect because ships could be sent swiftly and secretly from Bermuda to any part of his station. Hurd continued his surveying, erected landmarks, laid channel buoys, built surveying boats of native cedar, and trained Bermuda pilots (who earned their freedom from slavery) for the fleet.[14] The Navy Board, with charge of the dockyards, superintended the base's management and construction. Local materials were in short supply, with the indigenous cedar trees soon being chopped down for small shipbuilding requirements, notably for building many fast-sailing schooners and packet boats of such utility in waging wars against enemy privateers and slavers. When used for construction, cedar made good window frames and doors. Frames for storehouses and buildings were contracted for in Halifax. Local limestone could be used, and it was, extensively; but obtaining it was both expensive and time-consuming. Fire set back progress from time to time, as did hurricanes. Such disasters led to the realization that frame construction would have to give way to the more stable stone structures, and that, in turn, would require much more labour than was required for frame construction. Prefabricated buildings, from Halifax and England, using the latest techniques and materials, such as iron roof trusses, eased the problem of the paucity of local building materials. All the while, Halifax deteriorated and lost its old pre-eminence: by 1819 the establishment had been reduced to a careening wharf, a mast pond, a storehouse and a hospital.[15] Its essential value was not regained until late in the century, though it never disappeared totally from British imperial defence strategy.

Construction came under the gaze of Captain A.F. Evans, superintendent of works. He inhabited a great iron-ribbed, stone-walled, tile-roofed and strangely oriental-style house that looked out over the approaches and almost all of the buildings and yards of the establishment, the jail and its yard included. Master of all he surveyed, he was victim of the unremitting problems of supply, contracts and labour. He needed tradesmen. He wanted English artificers on account of their skills, and he could pay them well if he could get them. Owing to his urgent entreaty, the Admiralty sent him ten house carpenters on a three-year term. In other years, as in 1815, 36 artificers were sent and 39 labourers. Some prisoners from the recent wars were engaged, though at lower wages, and they were put to work fitting out prison and hospital ships, and constructing residences for dockyard officers.

Bermuda seemed then, as it is now in the telling, a big sump for labour. The yard could never get enough hands for the imperial construction project. While white labour was in special demand during the wars for serving the monarch ashore and afloat, in the subsequent time of peace, blacks provided the main source of labour for the Navy at Bermuda – principally ashore. Here again, the imperial presence is felt, for these were not usually freed slaves – they reflected the diaspora of blacks of the early nineteenth century. What strikes the historian are the several, well-defined categories of black labourers. All represented in their own distinct classification some peculiar aspect of *Pax Britannica*. Dockyard records indicate five distinct groups: Bermudian negroes, King's negroes (i.e. captured slaves), French negroes, American refugee negroes (former slaves) and Florida negroes (former Spanish slaves).

Brief descriptions of these show how diverse their backgrounds were and how constrained their futures would be. Bermuda negroes were held in highest trust and they operated the yard craft. They worked in storehouses and at wharf side, where their local knowledge found scope for action. They were hired by the government from the colonists who owned them, and their owners pocketed their dockyard wages. Lodged and victualled in the yard or on board the receiving ship, they had Sundays to themselves. As their masters received their monthly wages, they also had an interest in ensuring the slaves' safe return to the yard. On 1 August 1834, when slavery was abolished in Bermuda, these men were kept on as free labourers and were entitled to wages and rations. Second were the King's negroes, and they ranked behind the Bermudians in preference. Hired as freemen, some of them entered the Navy or the Army, under an act of parliament, upon the payment of £40 to the captors. As a class they came under martial law, in distinction to the Bermudians, who were under civil law. Some of the slaves were French and others Spanish, seized by Sir Alexander Cochrane at Martinique and Guadeloupe in 1808 and 1809. We can now see them as having passed from one empire to another and in the process found liberty and work with wages. The next category was refugees from American slavery. Black families had been taken from the Chesapeake in British warships and transports during the 1812 war. They arrived in states of destitution and misery, and were often helpless from dysenteric diseases. The British, already overtaxed in obligations, found it difficult to feed and clothe them from the warships. At length they became an embarrassment to their guardians. New warrants and colonial regulation curtailed their activities – these "free negroes" were prohibited from entering any parish with a view to settlement therein. They were employed as day labourers at Ireland Island, and could have their wages held for idleness or neglect of duty. Their women and children also came under regulations – they were employed picking oakum and were paid at the contract price, although deductions were made for food rations. The liberated American slave men acquired permanence under the Union Jack. They were given long-range contracts to keep their employment. They were housed ashore, eligible for victuals and medical care, and lived under Crown fiat. The contract that they signed makes clear that they were volunteers in British service, having been released from bondage by British favour, and those undesirous of signing and had who not receiving the King's Bounty were shipped to Halifax. As for those who stayed and went into imperial service, it may seem like an ironic twist of history to discover that, although some were employed in the dockyard and still others in the works and machine shops, the majority found themselves in uniform in the Royal Marines Colonial Battalion, a locally raised force on imperial/colonial police and garrison duties. Put differently, ex-slaves now served the master of their liberation, just as blacks freed from captured slave vessels and released in Sierra Leone found their way into the West India Regiment stationed on the West African coasts. Imperial history is full of these odd twists.

Next come the Florida negroes. Outcasts and misfits under the law, though valuable workers, they had been carried to Bermuda in warships from what were then Spanish possessions that were quite at peace with Britain. Neither captives from an enemy nor refugees from war, they had escaped in British warships believing British slavery to be more benign than that of Spain, which perhaps it was. When Britain occupied the Floridas in 1763–1781, some of them may have been colonists under the Union Jack. Their position remained invariably anomalous, for it is doubtful by which means they could be emancipated from slavery, except by remuneration of their late owners. At the outset the British failed in their attempts to return them to their country. They even obtained from the former masters a promise of freedom from mistreatment but the Floridians would entertain none of this: they accordingly remained a burden on the Navy. Eventually, in 1822, they were shipped to Trinidad, where the state of the law allowed for their newly acquired legal status and where, now emancipated, they were made British citizens. They, too, went from one empire to another, and from colony to colony, though no colony was an exact replica of another. American refugee negroes, free because they had served in the British forces during the 1812–1814 war and wished to settle on the land rather than be apprentices to any particular trade, also came in numbers – 50 in 1815 and more the next year – found themselves under the superintendence of a government agent appointed to look after their needs.[16] They had faced a remarkable social revolution under the emerging *Pax*, finding freedom for having served in British West Indian forces during the war against Napoleon or in British regiments fighting against the United States. Trinidad was ruled as a crown colony and Bermuda was a settlement colony. In the former the governor and executive had ways and means of authority that were unencumbered, so to speak, by a legislature. The will of the Colonial Office was far more influential in Trinidad, which, incidentally, had been captured from the Spanish and confirmed to Britain by the Treaty of Amiens in 1802. Here, as with Tobago, captured from the French, labour was in demand, though the Colonial Office and particularly James Stephen, the permanent undersecretary, swore against the expansion of planters' influence that would extend slavery, and make amelioration and abolition even more difficult. Downing Street prevailed.[17] The former dockyard workers of Bermuda were shipped there.

Lastly we come to the English white workers, with which we began. English citizens had no desire to remove to Bermuda, even at a time of massive unemployment at home. The earliest historian of the Bermuda dockyard attributed this unwillingness chiefly to the following reasons: life in a new colony separated artisans from their families, and obliged the former to live and do all things under authority. Not until 1824 did the Navy Board awaken to the need for housing for families on Ireland Island, and accordingly wives and children were permitted free passage outward bound in the flagship HMS *Jupiter*, and thereafter artificers enjoyed the privilege of free passage with their families to Bermuda. During this time the Royal Engineers constructed dockyard defences and dug ditches, but the scale of the proposed yard was so vast and the expense so great that contracted labour had to be provided, and provided quickly. Keeping artificers in good health was a difficult matter. Intemperance produced deplorable results; this was a hot climate and rum was very cheap. Dismissals from the service for drunkenness were common. Heavy drinking made men prone to epidemics, or so officials argued, and it induced carelessness of duty, want of punctuality and disrespect of officers.

The difficulties did not stop with drink. Disease was common and highly dangerous. Yellow fever, an acute infectious disease of subtropical and tropical areas, characterized by jaundice and vomiting from haemorrhages, was common. There were epidemics in 1812, 1818, 1819 and 1843, for instance, and another in 1864. In 1843 a quarter of the Royal 42nd Highlanders there on garrison duty succumbed to this dreadful scourge.[18] In 1864 the peril spread through the artificers and families of officers, as local cemetery inscriptions relate so sorrowfully. From the exalted commissioner to the lowly labourer, all were visited without differentiation as to rank or station. Even the paltry sums realized when a deceased artisan's effects were auctioned off (as was the pattern aboard ship) testified to the resigned state of the survivors. It is said that the only persons attending such a sale did so "under the gloomy impression that they may next become victims, and the market being glutted with dead men's effects is the cause of their not selling for their full value". "Yellow Jack" laid its deadly hand on Bermuda in yet another way: those artificers lucky enough to return to England at their contract's end personally advertised the unfavourable nature of Bermuda. This spread repugnance for the disease-infested coral islets among fellow dockyard workers at home. Insufficient numbers of men remained to effect the normal needs of the yard, and so the establishment deteriorated. The old chief of works, worn down by care and woe, shipped for England in a state of dejection. He did so at about the time that the commissioner, his superior, was about to complete his own term and go home, too. In these circumstances a revolution in administrative thinking was required. There were insufficient numbers of blacks and insufficient numbers of artificers. Royal Engineers could not undertake such a vast work, given their other obligations and their attention to matters of surveying, design and fortifications. Besides, this was a naval matter. Accordingly, the Admiralty at the British Government turned to another possibility of the times, and one made possible by social matters at home – convicts as labourers.

In 1824 the transport *Antelope* brought 300 convicts to Bermuda and with them came 100 Royal Marines, who took up garrison duties, with the special task of keeping a close eye on the workers. Turned into a convict hulk, the *Antelope* passed under the administration of the Navy. That same year another vessel, the *Glasgow*, had brought an emergency team of convict carpenters, smiths, joiners, masons and bricklayers to rebuild buildings that had been damaged by a recent hurricane. The discipline of the convicts remained one of concern to colonial governors. The Navy worried about the smuggling of spirits into the yard and thence onto the ships housing the convicts. The convicts found themselves under Home Office control. Their numbers swelled: 300 in 1824, 1,168 in 1844 and 1,662 in 1853 (their largest number just before yellow fever ravaged the stinking hulks in which they were housed). We can now calculate that between 1824 and 1860, the Bermuda naval establishment received a total of 9,094 convicts. We also know that the number sent home, including those last serving there, in 1863 amounted to 7,053. The number accounted for as "dead" totalled 2,041. For every nine sent, seven went home and two died. The convicts left a great legacy. One historian, looking at these accomplishments 100 years or so ago, and at the zenith of British imperial might concluded wisely: "The Convict establishment has been the great moving power by the manual efforts of which the Dockyard as we behold it, with its breakwater to protect it from the violence of storms, and the lofty fortifications for its defence in war, have been constructed."

No sooner had one great project been built on Bermuda to sustain the place than technology – particularly greater firepower (shells and rifled guns, in particular) – presented possibilities of vulnerability never imagined a decade earlier. Thus, in 1826, Lieutenant-Colonel Edward Fanshawe, RE, arrived with orders to make an extensive survey of the gun emplacements, arsenals, channels and barracks. He drew attention in his report to the main channel entrance below St. George's as being equivalent to that to the dockyard itself. Thus a new channel was cleared and the general plan became fixed in the mind of the War Office for the balance of the century.[19] New gun emplacements and forts were thrown up, and the Royal Engineers and Marine Artillery experts had ample scope for their professional capacities.

When steam arrived in Bermuda it gave the location enhanced benefit in the chains of communications and transit of men, material and supplies. The old West Indian bases, set up because of the dynamics of winds and currents, lost their importance. Bermuda changed with the times. Ships of war grew larger in tonnage, and by mid-century the need was felt for a dock capable of receiving such vessels at this strategically important port. The porous nature of the local rock precluded a permanent construction. British engineering responded to the challenge, and before long, in 1869, an ironclad 381-foot floating dock arrived undertow from the Medway.[20] This monumental project, carried to successful conclusion, increased British leverage in the waters flanking eastern North America and prevented vessels having to go home for repairs. Later, in 1902, a larger floating dock, the largest in the world, built at Wallsend-on-Tyne, arrived under powerful tugs from Britain and was placed off Ireland Island. It was capable of receiving a vessel of 17,500 tons, the largest of the pre-dreadnoughts.[21] This gave immense leverage to British sea power. A confidential wireless station was set up early in the twentieth century, and Bermuda took on yet another role that was important to the functioning of British sea power.

By mid-century this great Atlantic citadel had been quietly created at the crossroads of the American seas. American spies came to take note and report on the new fortifications.[22] During the next half-century, and up to the close of

Pax, it would be transformed in other ways. As long as the state of international affairs required an appropriate British response, government offices such as the Admiralty and the War Office were obliged to construct defences on coral islets on a volcanic mount so as to safeguard ships riding at anchor and the stores and supplies housed ashore. Equally important, they were required to make ready for the demands of the seagoing fleet.

In retrospect, Bermuda rose to prominence out of the wars of the late eighteenth and particularly the early nineteenth century. Sitting athwart the coastal sea routes of North America and the western Atlantic stretching down to the Caribbean and Panama, it was one of those locales – those hubs of British authority – which had ongoing value. During the War of 1812, Halifax had proved to be less than advantageous as a base from which to blockade the American seaboard, though it was more than adequate as a place from which British privateers could operate with great success.[23] During the early years of *Pax Britannica*, Britain sought to shore up its outer ramparts, and to secure to the country that which other nations and navies prized – advantageous geographical positions. The statesman Lord Castlerereagh said:

> The power of our establishments should be so contrived as to admit of a rapid extension at the outset of a war, so as to place us at once in security at home whilst we are enabled to reach the full fruits of our maritime superiority in striking an early blow against the colonies of the enemy.[24]

Today this would be called "forward basing".

The Napoleonic Wars and the war with the United States had left Britain with confirmed anchors of empire or new additions to those bases of influence and authority – new places of leverage, if you will. Many new acquisitions for the imperial estate were pressed on the arguments of the advocates of free trade, and additions were often a last resort or, indeed, to encourage legal trade. But it may be observed that the British, always conscious of their own potential weakness, and always fearing foreign advances, engaged in the pre-emptive impulse so as to maintain their advantage. Bermuda is a case in point of beefing up authority. The Falkland Islands, where sovereignty was asserted by naval influence in 1833 so as to enhance British protection of trade routes in the Southern Ocean and keep the Americans and Argentineans out, is another case, though of a slightly different order. Aden was acquired in 1839, and New Zealand likewise in the same year. Esquimalt was made station headquarters in 1862. Singapore grew as a naval establishment and towards the end of the century the British, using Hong Kong as their central place of rest and repair, extended their way north, to Weihaiwei, just as the Chinese Empire was facing collapse and imperial rivals, including Russia, were threatening in this portion of East Asia. The stone creations at Bermuda testify to Whitehall's resolve to construct a place of imperial concentration of power, a fist in the water wastes of the western Atlantic, a political projection of force that was a direct implementation of Britain's power, and of its authority in the Western Ocean.

For a century or more, Bermuda saw a succession of flagships of the commander-in-chief of the North America and West Indies station. From the days of the three-deckers, such as Admiral Sir John Warren's *San Domingo*, mounting 74 guns, through Vice Admiral Sir John Fisher's *Renown*, a fast and lightly gunned battleship, to the last large warship on this station, almost every version of capital ship was seen entering the Narrows and mooring in Grassy Bay. The admiral had a house there, Clarence House, purchased by the colony in 1816 and presented to the Crown for the use of the admiral. Not far distant was Mount Langton, the governor's residence, with its splendid grounds with superb bougainvilleas and other flowering shrubs and plants. For the admiral on station, Bermuda was a great relief from Halifax, with its colder climate and awkward politics, which always seemed to make a claim on the Navy. When Fisher went out to Halifax to take up the command in 1897, a previous commander-in-chief wished him well in that interesting assignment (far from the hectic activities at the Admiralty where Fisher had recently been) and added with a note of nostalgia: "I wish I could see Clarence Cove again & its beautiful phaeton birds sailing overhead and catching the reflected colours of the coral bottom."[25] In these palmy days, romance could find itself present in an admiral's recollections; memories of war were far distant. In a subtropical paradise like Bermuda, with its charming white or pastel cottages, its dingy regattas and its small though charming society of merchants, small landholders, churchmen, colonial officials, officers of the garrison and the naval establishment, the admiral remained supreme – all except for the governor, with whom he kept on the closest of terms.

The naval establishment had kept pace in size and importance with the enlargement of the economy and trade of the Americas in the nineteenth century. The American Civil War enhanced Bermuda's valued place as a watchtower, with blockade-runners coming and going, and the Royal Navy retaining strict neutrality. The War Office's inspector general of imperial fortifications sent their experts from time to time, Lieutenant Colonel William Jervois, RE, being one such, and on his recommendation of 1864 all sorts of new defences were thrown up.[26] The British exchequer groaned under these additional obligations. But gunnery was increasing in range and accuracy, and approaches to the anchorage had to be guarded against some fitful raid of an enemy cruiser squadron – a recommendation rather par for the course in other bases of empire: Esquimalt or Sydney, for example.

The British maintained a raft of naval bases in the Americas from St. John's, Newfoundland, to Port Stanley in the Falklands. Bermuda was the lynchpin of British strategy for the Americas, with Halifax as a necessary warden of the north, a place for shipbuilding and repair, and a location for stores and naval supplies, plus a hospital. Halifax boasted a new dock capable of accommodating battleships of the first class, such as the 11,800 tons displacement *Inflexible*, and was designed to give Britain renewed authority in the western Atlantic. Because of the rise of American commercial and naval power, British admirals "on station" were regularly instructed to give evaluations of the British anchors of empire in these seas.[27] Port Royal in Jamaica ranked first in importance in the British West Indies, with coal, naval stores and provisions, and a machinery shop for ship repairs. Ironically, Jamaica's strategic value grew with the likely possibility of an isthmian canal. In the late 1880s, Lord Brassey, later a lord of the Admiralty, complained that the place had been treated cavalierly by defence planners, despite the trilogy of its naval pre-eminence – that is to say, its excellent harbour, its naval facilities and its close proximity to the Isthmus of Panama, which was a mere two days away under steam. In need of modern guns to protect it from an enemy's ironclad fleet, it needed major renovations.[28] Meanwhile, at each of Antigua, Barbados and St. Lucia were kept a few hundred tons of coal in well-defended storehouses. These bases, whose importance had been demonstrated in yesteryear, were always capable of enlargement, and thus in influence, should new needs of the day arise. Elsewhere, as in Trinidad, St. Vincent and Demerara, the British maintained small garrisons. Altogether, Britain's Caribbean empire was sizeable. Small wonder that American defence planners looked on Britain's naval might with awe – a force to be reckoned with. In 1848 the United States added "an immense empire" to the republic by the treaty that ended the Mexican War. Visions of an empire reaching down into the Caribbean and then across the Pacific to China appeared, and eyes were on the possession of islands in the Caribbean to serve as naval bases. During the American Civil War the federal administration began consideration of having a base in this "American middle sea". Officers argued that the blockade of the Confederacy could be more effective with a Caribbean base of operations. At the close of hostilities they persisted in the argument that such a base would give the nation the means to "defy the navies of the world".[29]

In the early days of *Pax Britannica* the Admiralty and Post Office sailing packets, based on Falmouth, carried mail and small parcels to Bermuda, but inefficiencies and slowness led to many complaints from the West Indies and Britain. Steam reduced the problem, and in 1842 the Royal Mail steam packets to Bermuda and the Bahamas commenced service. The routes linked some 60 ports, and wove an imperial network of influence that was previously thought only to be of dreamlike proportions. The company sent out sailing vessels with cargoes and supplies for the sustenance and maintenance of the mail steamers. The Admiralty maintained residual control because the ships had to be wooden hulled, for their lordships were as yet unconvinced that iron hulls were superior. The ships were expected to be constructed so as to be armed for war if necessary, as indeed proved the case during the Crimean War. Troops and military supplies were transported at preferential rates. Admiralty agents sailed aboard the ships, and the Bermuda yard and others in the Caribbean under British control were available to the Royal Mail boats. New routes were devised, as required. Southampton, which was connected by train, supplanted Falmouth, which was only connected by road. Mexico got its own direct line, in keeping with its rising value regarding commerce and shipment of specie. The Cunard Line initially ran sailing, and then steam, vessels from Halifax to the Britain, and Bermuda was brought into that network, as was New York. British commerce was strengthening and expanding, with technology answering to commercial requirements. The British Post Office appointed agents in each port to supervise the mail, and the whole operation was an imperial and maritime spider's web of communications authority.[30] It was a triumph of industrial organization backing business requirements, underpinned by the nurturing imperial state. Units of British sea power were more in touch with Whitehall than ever before, while connections between Halifax and New York drew the transatlantic network even tighter. Colonial governors, consuls and agents found themselves drawn more closely together, the imperial pulse and purpose strengthened.

The transatlantic cable laid successfully in 1866 brought the admiral commanding in almost immediate touch with Whitehall, and advice from the governor general in Ottawa, the British ambassador in Washington or a consul in New York would flow in on a regular basis. When talk turned to a possible isthmian canal linking the Caribbean and the Pacific, the geopolitics of the Americas changed vitally. The Americans began to press for dissolution of the old 1850 Clayton–Bulwer Treaty that demanded that both Britain and the United States should be party to any future development in building, such as a canal. But by 1900 (see Chapter 13, where the subject is dealt with in greater detail), that requirement was dropped, and the British were all too soon to be happy to have the United States Navy police the waters of the West Indies, the Gulf Coast, and the shores of Central and South America. But the British never let go of Bermuda, and right through to 1914, and for almost a century after, it had distinctive merit in the strategy of worldwide influence. Here was an example, and there were many others besides, of a naval base developed by the British during *Pax* that would have a powerful influence in the safeguarding of the seas in the twentieth century and after.

In our own times, if you were to gaze from the anchorage of Grassy Bay at the massive, man-made shore establishment Ireland Island, with its component parts, you would immediately recognize it as British, not only from the Union Jack that flies from the pole but from the design of the buildings that project the British imperial ethos. However, you would have no knowledge of how these buildings were built by Bermuda's slave and then ex-slave populations, European artisans when available and eventually convict labourers.

All of these came to build this great key of authority athwart the Americas, hard by the waxing power of the United States and not far from the maritime provinces of Canada or the British West Indies or, for that matter, the ports of the Gulf of Mexico and the shores of Latin America. And it might come as a surprise to learn that later in the century, during the Anglo-Boer War, the base was the administrative centre for guarding 4,619 Boer prisoners housed mainly in tents on various islands in the sound, under the watch of the Army. In the two world wars and in the subsequent Cold War, Bermuda never lost its strategic importance. It finally closed as a British naval station in 1951, and the Ireland Island establishment became the Bermuda Maritime Museum. In our own time, Bermuda is home to a US naval air station, but throughout the age of *Pax Britannica* it was strictly a base of British sea power.

"The character of the British Empire will be found by tracing its distribution over the world," wrote two powerful commentators on British power in the late nineteenth century, Sir Charles Dilke and Spenser Wilkinson. "It follows everywhere the margin of the ocean." True this was, for British settlements and places of authority could be found along the coast of Africa, dotted all round the shores of the Indian Ocean, and on numerous islands, great and small. At all the critical points where the character of coastlines makes the land peculiarly accessible to influences of the sea, British seaborne energy seems to have established itself. The same authorities put it this way: "Witness the long possession of Gibraltar and the steady progress of British power in India and in South Africa. It is as though the sea had been saturated with British influence, and had deposited it along all the unprotected portion of its margin."[31] That influence rested on the primacy of the Navy. A French historian wrote, with admiration, that the Navy had won most of its battles at anchor, which was undoubtedly true. A French commentator of 1902 put it this way when describing the overall predominance that gave Britain global reach and global power:

> For England the sea is not to be looked upon as a means of transport... but as a territory, a British territory of course. The English fleet which owns the Empire of the Seas, places its frontiers at the enemy's coasts, and will dispose of all commerce behind that frontier, just as any army disposes of the resources of a conquered province.[32]

That comment was made in 1902. The same could have been said in 1837 at the commencement of the reign of Queen Victoria or, for that matter, in 1815 in that of George III. Of all the reasons for this pre-eminence, that of unquestioned importance was that Napoleon had been defeated in 1815 after a titanic war on land and sea. His ambitions towards India lay by way of Egypt. The Royal Navy stopped these ambitions. Plans to invade England were thwarted by British sea power and the control of the narrow seas. British naval units checked French overseas expeditions. British warships, individually or in squadrons, throttled French communications by sea, interrupted seaborne commerce and checked French ambitions. For their part, by forging a grand continental alliance to end the war in victory for themselves, the British used their sea mastery to bottle up the French and to interdict the trade of neutrals, such as the United States, whose activities were aiding and abetting what the British regarded as the enemy. In short, this empire of the seas had been acquired by war and grand strategy. Although the American revolutionary war had cost Britain almost all of its colonies except for the West Indies and Canada, the Napoleonic Wars produced the nucleus of a new empire: Ceylon, the Cape, Mauritius, Seychelles, the Ionian Islands, Heligoland, three provinces of Dutch Guiana and the three West Indian islands of St. Lucia, Tobago and Trinidad.[33]

4
Surveying the Seas, Expanding the Empire of Science

In the safe, languid and restorative years after Trafalgar, the Royal Navy became a worldwide instrument for conducting scientific research. The absence of war presented new opportunities in the line of human progress. The Navy was, in fact, a human mechanism for gathering global data about the seas and its margins, even its cavernous subsurface features. The fruits of its labours were prodigious. By the end of the nineteenth century the scientific achievements made possible by the Senior Service had made Britain into the leading scientific nation, and the focal point of scientific inquiry and knowledge. The empire of science brought a British order on a global scale, not only in terms of nomenclature and definitions but also in terms of quantification. The Navy was a force of measurement – depths of water, force of winds, patterns of climates, shifts in seasons, flows of tide, speeds of currents – all of these came within the Admiralty's purview. Lords of the Admiralty were conscious of their exalted position at the head of a global empire of the seas, and they were bound to be patrons of scientific inquiry no matter how grudgingly they might resist underwriting such schemes when the military requirements of the Service seemed to stretch their capabilities of response to the limit.

For an expanding maritime society, exploration, hydrography and surveying remained priorities, as they had during the preceding, pre-war era of Captains James Cook, George Vancouver and William Robert Broughton. These expeditions made during the reign of George III were the gloss on a larger purpose. Commercial reasons underpinned the whole rationale of discovery. The cynic might easily come to the conclusion that the work of the hydrographic service was entirely self-serving. This is not so, however, for its work was a gift to the world, its findings readily available to any who should seek the same. As part of the liberalizing modes of activity that characterized the years after 1815, the surveyors of the sea delivered up to the wider world all kinds of secrets – and they gave all sorts of advice to encourage safe navigation on and over the seas.

This great burden, borne by the British exchequer, had wide-ranging support within the British nation. After the Napoleonic Wars, an energized enthusiasm for scientific knowledge developed, especially among the broadening middle classes. They expanded beyond the scope of the older, esteemed private circles of the Royal Society, the Board of Longitude and the Office of the Astronomer Royal. Societies with specific scientific aims and with new niches to fill became popular. Just as travel-writing satisfies those who often cannot travel themselves, or dare not venture into dangerous corners of the world, they seemed to fill a psychological need resulting from the desperate days and years of the French and Napoleonic Wars. As one writer cheerily put it, "In so far as the new societies were concerned with the promotion of travel and exploration and with the accumulation of knowledge about foreign and unknown lands, they provided a most welcome avenue of actual or vicarious escape after thirty years of national isolation."[1]

Britain's global position as "Mistress of the Seas" allowed it with ease to send ships to the Pacific on exploration and scientific missions, to "show the flag" and to investigate as required. Scientific inquiry was a natural extension of naval primacy, and as essential to the lifeblood of the nation as clean air and water, food and fuel, and equipoise in world affairs. By this time the main features of the Pacific, as in almost every other part of the globe, held no great surprises. Thus the period can be characterized as one of elaboration – some meticulous hydrographic surveying of long coastlines and complicated archipelagoes, the gaining of description of the natural and social environments of these areas, and, towards the close of the era, a scientific analysis of the ocean basin.[2] The world's ocean wastes lay before the advancing Britain. A new world of discoveries opened up after 1815 with the arrival of peace. It is certain that old Tudor and Georgian ambitions reasserted themselves at this time, and with the coming of the new age, public subscriptions in aid of geographical discovery gave popular support to the customary zeal for exploration that had been a hallmark of the Admiralty. In other words, their lordships found themselves with allies in that line of work. In these new and welcome circumstances, exact and more specialized investigations took place during the early nineteenth century, as opposed to the broad studies of the late eighteenth, and the expedition of Commander Frederick William Beechey to the Pacific and Arctic in 1825–1828 exemplifies the then popular enthusiasm for the promotion of science through geographical discovery and exploration.

Moreover, the Geographical Society (later the Royal Geographical Society, with the sailor-king William IV as patron) was founded in London in 1830. Its existence rested on the belief that geographical knowledge was of

> the first importance to mankind in general, and paramount to the welfare of a maritime nation like Great Britain, with its numerous and extensive foreign

> possessions; that its decided utility in conferring just and distinct notions of the physical and political relations of our globe must be obvious to everyone, and is more enhanced by this species of knowledge being obtained without much difficulty, while at the same time it affords a copious source of rational amusement...[3]

Prominent in its interests was Africa, exploration of that continent and the abolition of slavery; and in due time the Royal Geographical Society absorbed the African Association.

At the Admiralty the congruence of the aims of science and empire was personified by Sir John Barrow, a permanent secretary of the Admiralty for most of the period 1804–1845. The author of 12 books and 3,000 articles in some of the great journals of the day, he was a heavyweight in founding the Geographical Society. Barrow, a north countryman from Lancashire, was a droll fellow, and one of his greatest strengths was that he had the capacity to keep to an agenda. His influence and persistence had the uncanny ability to prevail against indifference and ignorance in high places. Fortunately he had the ear of Viscount Melville, first lord of the Admiralty and Sir Joseph Banks, the presiding genius of British science and President of the Royal Society. Sir John Wilson Croker, principal secretary of the Admiralty, likewise gave Barrow all the freedom he needed.

In these circumstances, Barrow became the ardent promoter of exploration in the torrid and frigid zones alike, and became the father of modern polar exploration. His principal motive in promoting it lay in the adage, which evolved in Tudor times, "knowledge is power". Barrow considered science to be subservient to British naval and commercial interests; to him it constituted a means of acquiring power.[4] He had many critics, some of whom despised his self-appointed role as "*Oracle* on all matters of inquiry".[5] Others disliked his devious and mischievous ways. Admiral Sir Thomas Byam Martin grumbled that Barrow, who had set his face against the use of lightning conductors on British warships, was "the most obstinate man living".[6] Barrow had "presumed to set his face against it. This comes of permitting subordinates in office to acquire a sway and habit of dictation which belongs not to their station."[7] Barrow stood in opposition to some of the worthiest scientists of the realm, including Sir Humphrey Davy and Michael Faraday and the Royal Society, who backed the proposal brought forward to the lords of the Admiralty by John Snow Harris of Plymouth. Lightning rods were eventually adopted in 1840 and fitted to Her Majesty's ships.

Barrow got off to a bad start, for in 1814 he arranged for an expedition to explore the lower Congo River. Commander James Tuckey, who had commanded the schooner *Congo*, led a party upriver 150 miles in steam boats, but he and five of his officers and many other men died of fever, and the master brought the schooner home with the survivors.[8] The deadly climate checked African exploration for a time and the Admiralty turned to exploration adventures in cooler climates.

Times favoured Barrow, even if he fudged the commercial advantages of these arduous enterprises in polar seas. The coming of peace in 1815 made possible the renewal of polar exploration. Small warships, otherwise redundant, could be employed in voyages for the advancement of navigation, geography and, it was hoped, commerce. What did the cost of outfitting and provisioning a couple of barks amount to, he asked, when the benefits to England were so great? He liked to point out that the chances of dying at home were the same as they were on a distant voyage among ice flows and polar bears. He was always on the side of the Navy: "The *Physical* power of the navy of England", he proclaimed in his 1848 testimonial to Arctic science and the achievement of officers and men of the Navy,

> has long been duly appreciated at home, also by most foreign nations, and is a matter of public record; its *Moral* influence, though less the object of publicity, requires only to be more extensively known... and nothing can be more conducive to this end, than the results to be derived from voyages of discovery... whose great aim has been the acquisition of knowledge, not for England alone, but for the general benefit of mankind.[9]

And who could gainsay the fortitude of English sailors on ice as in water? "Arctic service", claimed the historian of the Navy at the end of the century, "is arduous and difficult, but it offers admirable opportunities for gaining habits of forming quick and right decisions and for cultivating presence of mind, and all the qualities that are needed for success in war. This is its most useful and important side."[10]

Captain Sir John Franklin exhibited high-minded purposes concerning the results of discoveries to the nation, the empire and mankind in general. This is what the brave, veteran seaman wrote in closing the narrative of his second polar voyage:

> Arctic discovery has been fostered principally by Great Britain; and it is a subject of just pride that it has been prosecuted by her from motives as disinterested as they are enlightened; not from any prospect of immediate benefit to herself, but from a steady view to the acquirement of useful knowledge, and the extension of the bounds of science. Each succeeding attempt has added a step towards the completion of northern geography; and the contributions to natural history and science have excited a general interest throughout the civilized world... And it is sincerely to be hoped that Great Britain will not relax her efforts until the question of a north-west

> passage has been satisfactorily set at rest, or at least until those portions of the northern shores of America, which are yet unknown, be laid down on our maps; and which... are the only intervals wanting to complete the outline of Europe, Asia, and America.[11]

In a letter to the Admiralty, Franklin argued the case to continue the quest in the far north: "Each succeeding attempt has added a step towards the completion... and it is sincerely to be hoped that Great Britain will not relax her efforts until the question of a north west passage has been satisfactorily set at rest."[12]

Geographical and scientific inquiry, trade, imperial expansion, foreign completion, national honour, prestige, security, preparedness and defence, not to exclude professional advancement and political advantage on the part of those promoting it, were the interrelated themes which lay at the bottom of a most expensive enterprise that occupied the attention of the Navy and attracted the interest of the British Parliament, press and public of the age, especially during the search for the ill-fated Franklin expedition commenced in 1845.[13] Some 32 separate expeditions were mounted. Lady Jane Franklin began a drive to make sure that Franklin's place, as the discoverer of the passage, was not forgotten. Franklin's epitaph, penned by his nephew Alfred, Lord Tennyson, is in Westminster Abbey: "Not here: the white North has thy Bones; and thou, Heroic Sailor-Soul, Art passing on thine happier voyage now Toward no earthly pole." Reports circulating about the fate of Franklin's last expedition attracted the attention of the Victorian age, for in the words of one historian, Franklin's narrative presented "a new Arctic; starvation, murder and cannibalism, the extremities of human suffering".[14] In due course novelist Charles Dickens would enter the lists on the matter of cannibalism as practised during such expeditions as this, and the matter cut to the quick of the British conscience of the age.

Scientific results of this century-long examination of Arctic waters were prodigious.[15] This collective enterprise vaulted Britain into the top position in polar studies, and this long before the voyages of Robert Falcon Scott and Ernest Shackleton riveted the public's imagination on icy and snowbound wastes at the ends of the earth. But there were other progressions as well. In 1908, Captain Scott, who died a similarly miserable death in the icy wilds, had this to say about Franklin and his book *Journey to the Polar Sea* (all about the expedition of 1819–1822): that it was astonishing that the years since Franklin's journey and down to Scott's own time had seen such rapid change. "Such a period has never held a fuller measure of change or more speedily passed current events into the limbo of the past," mused Scott, who added that in less than a century those vast tracts of the Canadian northwest through which Franklin and his men had ventured had been succeeded by season without change "where few have passed since his day and Nature alone holds sway".[16] Elsewhere in more southern latitudes, that locale "would one day provide largely the bread of his countrymen". He was referring to the grain-growing areas of the Canadian west.

But this remarkable century of scientific exploration with the Navy at its centre had begun somewhat differently under other demands, mainly commercial. The business of the Hydrographic Department came to be put on a firm footing only by degrees. Alexander Dalrymple, examiner of charts for the East India Company, received the Admiralty's appointment as hydrographer to the Admiralty in 1795, the first, and in that office brought regularity to the chart-production business, but his achievements were little known even in the nineteenth century. His successor, Thomas Hurd, had taken up a more regularized appointment in 1808. However, his success depended on support from his superiors, which were not often forthcoming.[17] After this came W.E. Parry and Francis Beaufort, then later in the century John Washington, George Henry Richards and J.F. Parry. They were all lions and good at their work as sailors, scientists and, not least, administrators and diplomats.

In May 1814, Captain Hurd, the determined and progressive hydrographer of the Admiralty, penned a lengthy memorandum for the Admiralty on the theme of the relations of science and empire – and the need for Arctic exploration. We have already met Hurd in connection with his survey of Bermuda, a notable achievement that made possible that great bulwark of the empire. "The return of Peace to this Country", he wrote compellingly in 1814,

> makes me consider it as an official duty to represent to the Lords Commissioners of the Admiralty the great deficiency of our nautical knowledge in almost every part of the World, but more particularly on the coastline of our own Dominions and also with the hopes that the present favourable moment for remedying these evils will be made use of, by calling into employment those of our Naval Officers, whose scientific merits point them out as qualified for undertakings of this nature – of which description of Officers there are I am happy to say many who stand eminently conspicuous.

He then listed the needs of his department: surveys of China and the Eastern Seas, Kamchatka, Tasmania, East Africa, the Mediterranean and even the British Isles. He noted that surveyors had been sent out to the "Newfoundland and American Stations". The eastern side of South America was erroneously laid down in charts and maps, he said, and wanted rectifying. In addition, various situations and harbours were just growing into use and notice. Knowing the commercial prospects of South America, he concluded:

> In acquiring the nautical knowledge here recommended, much good might also result there from in other points of view as an excellent opportunity

> would thereby be afforded for the exertions of abilities both scientific and commercial, by uniting as Companions of their researches, persons of the description who of course would become accountable to the Nation for all the knowledge they might thereby acquire.

He was thinking of the prospects of bringing men of science into the business of discovery by HM ships. He went on to repeat the make-work benefits for meritorious officers whose abilities would otherwise lie dormant. This would be a means of amassing information that would doubtless prove highly advantageous to the British in a future war, and "would otherwise redound to the Credit and Glory of this great Maritime Empire, whose flag flies triumphant in every part of the World".[18]

British governments always seemed financially hard pressed in this epoch, but, despite this, successive British governments took the matter of scientific discovery with utmost seriousness. This was an age of exalted science, and of energetic discoveries of distant lands and peoples. In the 60-year period after 1800, no fewer than 190 Admiralty ships were employed on missions of discovery.[19] In the 1820s alone, 26 ships were sent. This number may not seem great when the size of the British fleet is recalled, but the forced economics of that period did not allow for the active service of any warships, on scientific duties or not, unless they were needed for the maintenance or promotion of national security and prosperity.

As Barrow, Hurd and others knew, hydrographic surveying was of essential importance to a maritime state. Accurate charts would facilitate trade overseas and economic expansion at home. Charts were spoken of as the harbinger of commerce, and from commerce flowed many other benefits. In 1828 the decision was made to sell charts to the public. As the principal industrial nation, Britain sought not only to protect but also to strengthen its commercial interests, colonial and foreign. The extensive charting of the seas undertaken by the hydrographic branch of the Royal Navy in the nineteenth century reflects British pre-eminence during this period, and on almost all oceans, seas and annexes British warships on survey were symbols of national and maritime power in distant quarters of the globe. On two occasions, swift surveying aided strategic objectives: on inshore waters during the capture of Canton, and in the Baltic and Black seas during the Crimean War.

The Navy served as a conduit of scientific observation and collection. The process demonstrated systematic thinking. By the time of Queen Victoria's Jubilee, 1887, the fifth edition of the widely distributed *A Manual of Scientific Inquiry... for Officers in Her Majesty's Navy; and Adapted for Travellers in General* (London: Eyre and Spottiswoode, 1886) provided just such guidance. Nothing seems to have been taken for granted. It was noted in this work, for instance, that quality of writing as a preparation for advancement in the Service was essential. The work lauded the importance of powers of observation and scientific understanding. The brains behind this work belonged to the astronomer and mathematician Sir John Herschel, by this stage of the imperial progression a giant of imperial science. Its telling introductory memorandum reads:

> It is the opinion of the Lords Commissioners of the Admiralty that it would be to the honour and advantage of the Navy, and conduce to the general interests of Science, if new facilities were and encouragement were given to the collection of information upon scientific subjects by the officers, and more particularly by the medical officers when upon foreign service... They are sending a survey vessel to New Zealand, and have others in the Torres Straits and in other parts of the world. A new establishment is contemplated in Borneo. Expeditions are proposed in search of Sir John Franklin. They have cruisers in every sea; and where the ships of the navy are not present, it sometimes happens that the vessels of the merchant are conducted with much intelligence and enterprise, and for all these the work proposed would be valuable.[20]

As in almost every line of national activity, an underlying factor in the long history of British expansion was Britain's keen awareness of the threat posed by other nations. In this connection, international rivalry provided a spur to British Arctic exploration. Along the northern and icy fringes of British North America, foreign (notably Russian) activity produced apprehension on the part of the Colonial and Foreign offices. To the south of Upper and Lower Canada, the United States lay somewhat dejected after an unsuccessful, frustrating war against the British Empire in North America. American expansion into Canada had been checked and, in 1818, the two rivals had, by convention, divided the continent along the 49th parallel from the Lake of the Woods to the Rocky Mountains. The Pacific slope remained open to both nations, without prejudice to either's claims or, in fact, those of other nations. By the Monroe Doctrine of 1823, a unilateral presidential enunciation of foreign policy, the United States announced that future European colonization in North America would be challenged. This dictum was no stronger than the power and influence of the parent state. The Oregon question remained unsettled until 1846, when partition of the area from 42° to 54° 40′ N latitude between the Continental Divide and the Pacific occurred, leaving Vancouver Island in British hands and the San Juan archipelago in eventual dispute.[21]

The Russian American Company, chartered in 1799 by imperial ukase to extend the commerce and territory of Russia and spread the Russian Orthodox faith, had bold schemes afoot. From a new headquarters at Sitka in southeastern Alaska, it sent a naval expedition under Commander Ivan Krusenstern to treat with the Hawaiian monarch, Kamehameha, and then sent ships to the islands for food supplies. In 1815 an ill-trained agent built a fort, raised the Russian flag and acted as sovereign lord. Hawaiian, British and American persons turned against his attempts to monopolize trade, and he fled to China and then to Russia. The Russian government became well aware of the resistance that Britain or the United States would have shown to Russian annexation of the Hawaiian Islands.[22] The Russians had aspirations for dominion in western North America as far south as San Francisco Bay.[23] They made an attempt in March 1806 to enter the Columbia River, there to establish shipbuilding, but foul weather and heavy surf prevented this, and consequently they looked to California as a place to solve their logistical problems. They missed Lewis and Clark by a short interval. The British had an inveterate suspicion of Russian designs, and it is to this theme that we turn, if briefly.

By controlling Alaska, Russia possessed the westernmost approach to the Northwest Passage. Otto von Kotzebue in 1815–1818 sought a passage that way to the Atlantic. At the Admiralty, Barrow, acting on intelligence about Russian movements, warned that the Russians were "strongly impressed with the idea of an open passage round America". Then, in morbid but telling tones, he advised: "It would be somewhat mortifying if a naval power but of yesterday should complete a discovery in the nineteenth century, which was so happily commenced by Englishmen in the sixteenth."[24] Under this warning, Parliament offered a substantial reward in 1818, similar to an earlier one of 1775, for finding a Northwest Passage or for attaining the farthest north should a westward route to the Bering Strait be impossible. It is one of the ironies of history that Britain turned down, twice, the opportunity of a close association with the Hawaiian monarchy – first, when Captain Vancouver became the special associate of Kamehameha and was offered the islands, and second, when Captain Lord George Paulet of HMS *Carysfort*, in 1843, proclaimed British dominion over the Hawaiian Islands so as to keep the French from grabbing them. The measure was disavowed by his superior, Rear Admiral Richard Thomas. It was also overturned by London, principally the Foreign Office, on the grounds that as long as British interests were protected, Britain did not want to find itself in a wasp's nest. The government did not want paramount influence in the Hawaiian Islands, only fair recognition of commercial and political interests on a similar footing to the two rivals, the United States and France. The same policy held true for a claim to California. To the Hudson's Bay Company's urgings for a port on the Northwest Coast under British protection, the ministry was clearly against "the formation of new and distant Colonies", and as of the year 1841 even a secret evaluation of the commerce and navigation of the North Pacific as proposed by the imperially minded Sir George Simpson, the governor of Hudson's Bay Company territories, was rejected. Lord John Russell, at the Colonial Office, beset by complaints of colonial overstretch, replied somewhat diffidently that the British Government had no desire to colonize the Hawaiian

Islands, which would become American in any event. At the Admiralty, Barrow held a similar view and pointed out that as long as British cruisers had free access to ports, that was all that was needed. Only a port near the Columbia River would be useful, said Barrow, and here are the origins of the idea that a harbour on Vancouver Island might solve the need for a British base there, something that developed at Esquimalt after the Oregon boundary resolution. The British policy was a blanket one: Britain did not contemplate "any new acquisitions at present... either on the Shores, or among the Islands of the Pacific."[25]

Whaling captain William Scoresby announced that the seas near Greenland were open to navigation, and before long a voyage of exploration was authorized – to go as close to the North Pole as possible and thence to the Bering Strait. It was on this expedition that Lieutenant John Franklin, a veteran of Trafalgar, first made his appearance as a polar voyager and traveller.[26]

Franklin, like Barrow, fully grasped the need to check Russian power in order to prevent it from pressing into the rich fur-bearing region of the Mackenzie River basin, first explored by Sir Alexander Mackenzie and since developed by British fur-trading firms, the North West Company and the Hudson's Bay Company. These companies were allies of the Navy in northern exploration. In 1823, Tsar Alexander I sent a frigate on discoveries, with astronomical apparatus, and although this ship never entered the Bering Sea, news of it was sufficient for Barrow to set in place another expedition, of which more presently. It was also of sufficient alarm for the Foreign Office to check Russian "pretensions" in this area. Worry existed that the Russians would end free coastal navigation. Meanwhile, the Hudson's Bay Company sent a land expedition under trader Samuel Black to "keep the Russians at a distance" by drawing the trade in the Stikine River, west of the Rocky Mountains, into the interior, away from the Russians on the coast. The Americans, meanwhile, had become alarmed at the growth of Russian operations.

At the Foreign Office, George Canning, anxious to check Russian expansion southwards, opposed any attempt by the Russians to control coastal navigation by a haughtily proclaimed ukase that had no credibility in international law as the British saw it. By a convention of 1825, Britain and Russia agreed to establish the southern boundary of Russian America at 54° 40′ N latitude and its eastern limits along Portland Canal, and thence by a line to the Arctic Ocean. The northern line gave Canada its most westerly limits in this latitude. The coastal boundary was vague, however, and a subject of later Anglo-American dispute involving Canada. This convention, like the one signed the previous year between the United States and Russia, stayed Russian progress eastward and southward. At the same time it restored British and American maritime rights. By trade and diplomacy, therefore, the British had entrenched their own position in northwestern North America, including the Northwest Coast, and got freedom of navigation, their greater goal. Although British Columbia is usually seen as a bulwark to American expansion, in fact, as this progression shows, the Russian threat had been countered. It did not mean that Russian cruisers might pose no further challenge, as they did later in the century, but for the moment the territorial equilibrium had been established. As a side benefit, the interests of the Hudson's Bay Company, an empire within an empire, were reaffirmed.[27]

Meanwhile, on Foreign Office advice, the Admiralty set in place the plan to find the Northwest Passage. In September 1823 the Admiralty sent instructions to the commander-in-chief of the South America station, to dispatch a vessel to the Bering Strait. At first sight it appears that the aim was to match Russian naval strength there, in high latitudes, with hopes that news of this would find its way back to St. Petersburg. The intention was to meet up with Parry's attempt to transit the Northwest Passage from the east, via Prince Regent Inlet. In addition, a rendezvous might be made with Franklin, then going by canoe and overland, down the Mackenzie River to the Arctic shore, then west. The frigate sent via Cape Horn to the Bering Strait was the third part of the plan. In the event, the frigate was replaced by the sloop of war, HMS *Blossom*, under Commander Frederick William Beechey, son of well-known portrait painter Sir William Beechey. Young Beechey was himself a distinguished artist and a person of scientific as well as artistic accomplishment.[28] As his portrait shows, he seemed cast in the Byronic mould, and his almost rosy-cheeked bearing and lovely eyes show no evidence of the hard world of knocks that had led him to the top of his profession as a scientific naval officer. He had entered the Navy under the patronage of Earl St. Vincent and was only 29 when he sailed for the Pacific. However, he was fit, able and experienced – and battle hardened from extensive service during the later stages of the Napoleonic Wars.

Blossom entered the Pacific via Cape Horn and reached the Bering Strait almost on schedule. There was no sign of Franklin. Reconnaissance in the immediate vicinity showed the country to be impenetrable, uninhabitable and oddly infested with mosquitoes. At various places, Beechey left caches of supplies for Franklin. In a last great search attempt the ship's barge, under the master's mate, Thomas Elson, pressed along the coast, eastwards beyond Icy Cape (which had been James Cook's limit of discovery), and against crushing ice (and the fear of entrapment) and the opposition of hostile natives, the Inuit. In the meantime, Franklin, working west, had decided to go no farther than what he called Return Reef. This he reached five days before Elson made his utmost Point Barrow, a mere 146 miles to the west. It would have been an historic meeting at that end of the earth had it happened. They were ignorant of each other's positions, of course. Still, there is no doubt that Elson and Franklin acted wisely in not pressing on in the approaching early winter conditions. Franklin retraced his steps. Beechey stayed in Kotzebue Sound so as to give Franklin a last chance of a rendezvous, and returned again the following year, by which time Franklin was back in England and scheming for his next opportunity, one for which he would have to wait.

This combined expedition was important for the advancement of navigation and trade. The mapping of the coast of Russian America east to Point Barrow was one result, and the delineation of the north and northwest coasts of Alaska was Beechey's achievement. Later he sailed into San Francisco Bay, then sailed south yet again and came to Pitcairn Island, a great rock which seemed to rise out of the sea, where he and the ship's company met John Adams, the sole surviving mutineer of Bligh's *Bounty*. Oral testimony was eagerly taken, and the whole sordid story of the last, violent years, months and days of the mutineers was scribbled down and later released to the inquisitive public. Accurate news was finally proclaimed about the ringleader: Fletcher Christian died at the hands of the last surviving Tahitian, who shot him in the back.[29] What happened to the Pitcairn Islanders, and how they were taken under the wing of the Royal Navy and missionary societies, is a chapter in imperial benevolence, and as that story lies outside the theme of this chapter it is dealt with later (Chapter 8).

The scientific accomplishments of Beechey's voyage were prodigious. George Tradescant Lay, who shipped aboard as a naturalist, supervised the systematic collection of specimens for the government, and the amateur scientists among the ship's officers and midshipmen. It was a coordinated effort, and doubtless the first of the age. It set new standards in cooperation with the scientific community ashore. The first lieutenant, George Peard, was an amateur geologist. Another lieutenant, John Wainright, was an astronomer and gathered data for use in London circles. Edward Belcher, later a famous surveyor, made a geological collection. The surgeon and his assistant made collections, while William Smyth, mate, made drawings of the specimens collected. *A Zoology of Captain Beechey's Voyage* saw print in 1839, brought to publication by Dr John Richardson, a naval surgeon. In the volume there was much for persons of scientific inclination – a chapter on ornithology, another on fish, yet another on crustaceans and a final one on batrachians, reptiles, and molluscs and their shells. A chapter on geology and mineralogy penned by the distinguished Oxford don the Reverend Dr W. Buckland completed this work, with 50 illustrations drawn by G.B. Sowerby. A second work, or catalogue, appeared, *The Botany of Captain Beechey's Voyage*, in which the steering hand was none other than Joseph Hooker, regius professor of botany at the University of Glasgow. The expedition produced many fine charts, notably of San Franciso Bay and another of Kotzebue Sound in Russian America.

In 1829, just after Beechey brought *Blossom* home with scientific treasures, there arrived at the Admiralty a largely self-educated officer, a battle-scarred veteran of campaigns against the Spanish and someone who had come close to death from a fanatic's bullet while surveying the Turkish coast. He was Francis Beaufort, an Irishman and son of a medical doctor, who in his time not only forged great alliances with the great and the good of the British scientific community but also made the Hydrographic Office into the finest chart-making and maritime science centre of its age.

Beaufort bemoaned any enforced state of indolence that their lordships threw upon him. "To a storeship! Good heavens!" he declaimed when appointed to the old *Woolwich*, a fifth rate moored at Deptford,

> It is for the command of a storeship that I have spilled my blood, sacrificed the prime of my life, dragged out a tedious economy in foreign climates, wasted by best hours in professional studies... For a storeship, for the honour of carrying new anchors abroad and old anchors home! For a ship more lumbered than a Dover packet, more weakly manned than a Yankee carrier – three fourths of her arms and ammunition on shore, three feet deeper than her trim, and with jury masts and sails! – so that she can neither fight nor run; in short, for a ship where neither ambition, promotion or riches... can be obtained.[30]

It was for a young officer a humiliating appointment, but at least it was on active duty and on full pay.

Beaufort made his name as a surveyor in the Mediterranean, producing *Karamania* (1817), which invoked the classical monument to the British cause. When he arrived at the Admiralty as hydrographer, the place is said to have been

> a kind of hybrid institution, the one branch of it inviting as it were the opposition of the civil element at Whitehall, the other calculated to encounter the ill-will of authorities afloat, from the circumstance that it was necessary the officers composing it should be in a measure independent of their authority.[31]

Beaufort was the right man, a progressive and energetic force, at a time when there was a rapid expansion of the merchant fleet, with steam supplanting sail in some trades, coaling stations required in distant spots of the globe, distant trades in the supplying of foodstuffs to the home islands being developed, and rapid expansion overseas of the formal and informal empires.

For a quarter of a century, Beaufort directed the explorations and experiments of the period, fighting indifference ashore while bemoaning the system of "influence" that dogged naval appointments. He sought and won a separate status for the hydrographic division of the Admiralty, and he presided over the greatest production of charts of any hydrographer, besides giving the

Beaufort scale of wind speeds, still used by yachtsmen. Like Hurd before him, Beaufort placed naturalists on board Navy vessels bound on explorations of distant coasts. The Navy expected all of its ships to bring back information about a range of subjects. In terms of natural history, those expectations were not spelled out, though with regard to Captain King's expedition to northern Australia in 1817–1822, an Admiralty memorandum, which survives, sets forth the hoped-for gains: in climate, terrain, flora and fauna, minerals, tribes (their arts, crafts and languages) and "a circumstantial account of such articles growing on the seacoast, if any, as might be advantageously imported into Great Britain, and those that would be required by the natives in exchange for them".[32]

Beaufort remained emphatic about nomenclature, insisting that the giving of unmeaning names only confused geographical knowledge. "The name stamped on a place by the first discover should be held sacred by the common consent of all nations," he advised, while "in really new discoveries the name applied should convey an idea of the sense of place, some illusion to inhabitants, or even better to adopt the native appellation". He was a modernist, and he distanced himself from those of an earlier era who had "exhaust[ed] the catalogue of public characters and private friends".[33] He kept up relations with his French, German and Russian counterparts, broadening the connections of the Hydrographic Department in important diplomatic work as world leader. The Admiralty adopted the Beaufort wind scale in 1838 and ordered it to be put to use throughout the fleet. He gave aid to numerous scientific voyages of the age, such as that of James Clark Ross to the Antarctic to observe terrestrial magnetism in southern latitudes. He prepared a *Manual of Scientific Inquiry*, already mentioned, its purpose being to guide naval officers in making scientific observations and bringing home the results. He supervised the acquisition of instruments for the Royal Observatory at Greenwich. He kept in close touch with the astronomer royal. In all, he was the middleman in the exchange of scientific views and often the fixer of various schemes and plans.

Above all, Beaufort, a genius at administration, supervised the surveys of the age. His biographer puts the importance of the work this way:

> In the 1830s Britannia ruled not only the waves but also – such was her Empire – many of the shores on which they broke. In addition, there were vast stretches of coastline where suzerainty was more nominal than real and accordingly where no great political or military problems stood in the way of operation by British ships.[34]

Thus, permission to survey had to be requested of the rulers on occasion, such as in the eastern Mediterranean or in Spanish West Indian possessions. In other places, such as the China Seas, surveying was specified as a negotiated concession. Sometimes there were difficulties, as in Morocco, where the emperor objected. Sometimes, as in the case of the Columbia River, cautionary instructions were provided to guide the British surveyor. The worry here was that the Americans might object, and if that were the case the survey needed to be broken off. The Admiralty wanted no more difficulties and no more entanglements with foreign powers. Thus the surveying tasks continued when and where they could. It was the progress of the tortoise, and it was effective. Surveys were completed of East Africa, New Zealand, Ireland, the River Plate, the Strait of Juan de Fuca and other areas. As of 1842 the number of ships on hydrographic duties numbered 20 – a high point. Gradually steam replaced sail, and surveys became more rapid and more extensive. The work expanded with steam, and the work pressed into hitherto inaccessible waters – notably the coasts of British Columbia and Southeast Alaska.

Among the signal successes of his career as a hydrographer, that of opening up the ports of South America to safe navigation remains a hallmark. On the west coast of the Americas, that long flank of the eastern Pacific, the Admiralty chart was incomplete, and unsuitably so given the growing trade and political complexity of the component states and empires. "As always," writes a former hydrographer of the Navy and historian Vice-Admiral George Richie, "trade needs ships and ships need charts, and the Spanish had only recently begun releasing charts of their American colonies for use by others."[35] Thus, in 1826, to support the growing trade of Britain with the South American republics, and to encourage it even further, a hydrographic expedition left England to survey the coasts of South America from the River Plate southwards, through the Strait of Magellan, then northward to the island of Chiloe. It was a formidable task with prodigious consequences: it rendered the South American west coast easily accessible to merchant shipping from Europe. This was the expedition of Captain Phillip Parker King. The vessels were *Adventure* and *Beagle*. In 1831, Beaufort, reviewing the Beechey successes referred to above and the progress of King's survey, approved plans for further surveys – those of *Beagle*, *Sulphur* and *Starling*.

That doughty little sloop, rigged as brig and built in 1820, the 235-ton *Beagle* had been sent by the Admiralty to re-examine and extend the work of Captain King. The latter, in 1826, had commanded *Adventure* and *Beagle* in an examination of Tierra del Fuego and the waters from Montevideo on the Atlantic to Chiloe in the Pacific. The commanding officer of *Beagle*, Pringle Stokes, worried that his standards of surveying were not up to the mark (as indeed was the case, later attested to by Parker King), had committed suicide in the desolate location of Port Famine, Tierra del Fuego.

From 1831 to 1836, *Beagle*, now commanded by Captain Robert FitzRoy, surveyed parts of South America's coast as far north as the Galapagos. This made the British no longer dependent on Spanish charts of the area and it gave much more scientific precision to earlier British charts made by James Colnett, in 1793–1794, when he was examining, under nomination from the Admiralty, ports that would afford to British whalers the necessary advantages of refreshment and security of refit. He surveyed Revilla Gigedo Islands south of Cape San Lucas, the Cocos Island off the coast of Central America, the Galapagos west of Ecuador, and St. Ambrose and St. Felix Isles off the coast of Chile.[36] Still, there was much left for *Beagle* to do in the surveying line. The motives of this voyage deserve no repetition here, save to note that *Beagle*'s survey, like those before it, was undertaken to promote British commercial and political ends.[37]

The world would scarcely know of this voyage had not Charles Darwin, a 22-year-old gentleman, sailed in *Beagle*. FitzRoy, 26, perhaps mindful of the fact that the previous commander had committed suicide, wanted companionship in the form of a naturalist, and until that point in time, many a naturalist had gone on Navy voyages of discovery and exploration – Archibald Menzies with Captain Vancouver, for instance. He asked Beaufort if he knew anyone suitable. Word passed through a mathematician and astronomer in Cambridge, and then to a botanist and mineralogist. "I believe my friend Mr. [George] Peacock of Trinity College, Cambridge, has succeeded in getting a 'Savant' for you – a Mr. Darwin, grandson of the well known philosopher and poet, full of zeal and enterprise and having contemplated a voyage on his own account to S. America." And so it was arranged, and Beaufort had been the fixer. His biographer writes, in speculation: "Within days Darwin made his agreement with FitzRoy and the two young men discussed the voyage with Beaufort... Without Beaufort, Darwin would never have set foot on the *Beagle*; another man might not have drawn the conclusions that Darwin did from what he saw."[38] FitzRoy and Darwin spent five years together. They circled the globe together, but in the end they reached startlingly different conclusions about the origins of the natural world. In the end, FitzRoy came to regret taking Darwin with him. The scientific revolution was beyond FitzRoy's comprehension or appreciation, and it is contended that his knowledge that he had provided Darwin with the vehicle for his sacrilegious ideas propelled him down an irrevocable path to suicide.[39]

Then, in 1836, *Sulphur* and *Starling* were sent to complete *Beagle*'s work on the Chilean coast, examine the coast of Central America and investigate the coast of California north of Punta de Los Reyes, including the Farallone Islands, the Bar of San Francisco and the waters flowing into San Francisco Bay near Carquinez Sound. The British commander was under instructions to keep an eye on what the Russians were doing at Fort Ross. He found only a small and faltering agricultural community (which was soon to be sold to private interests).[40] This expedition was of considerable value in fact-gathering for the parent government.[41] All the same, London was in no mood to extend formal imperial obligations. Time and again, Britain could have had Hawaii and California, but rather than doing so by neglect it did it by conscious decision not to add these spots to Her Majesty's dominions. Trade not dominion ruled the official thinking of the day. And to improve trade and navigation the work of the hydrographers proceeded apace.

Indifference to the work of the hydrographer and the surveyors was widespread, as can be imagined. Beaufort is credited with the aphorism "The natural tendency of men is to undervalue what they cannot understand." And when facing massive cuts to his budget in 1851, he wrote sharply to the secretary of the Admiralty:

> I will not trifle with your time by repeating here the hackneyed truisms about the comparative expense to the country in the cost of surveys or in the loss of ships and cargoes, but I will just entreat you to weigh the small sum you propose to save against the large amount of mischief which may be the result.[42]

Not least, he brought to his task directness and good directions to his subordinates. When Sir Edward Belcher, a hot-headed and difficult fellow (though technically a wonderful surveyor), made some point that reflected his own exalted position and bias, Beaufort shot back:

> Your last letter is really all Hebrew to me: ransoms and dollars; queens; treaties and negotiations? What have I to do with these awful things; they far transcend my limited chart-making facilities, however well suited they may be to Admiralty Lords, to Commanders-in-Chief, to Governors of Colonies and to you; and with them my very good friend you must arrange your diplomatic enterprises, and to them you must look for applause. Fortunately the Board have not sent your dispatches upstairs, nor asked for my opinions which I beg leave to reserve for affairs of soundings, angles, and other humble things like that kind. That you may have been doing good service to the country I will not deny, but the harvest I look for at your hands does not stretch beyond the reach of a deep sea-line and all the credit I crave for you, and through you for myself, must be won in the Kingdoms of science and reaped in hydrographic fields.[43]

Barrow, good at self-advancement, mastered the technique of publishing scientific discoveries and voyage accounts. Using the *Quarterly Review* published by John Murray as a means of propounding his views, of advancing the cause of discovery and of answering his critics, he was tireless in directing the many expeditions sent forth, at least until his retirement in 1845. He used his connections with the Royal Geographical Society to advantage. Scanning the in-letters from captains afloat in distant, intriguing and hitherto unknown parts, he would copy segments in the office and send them to the society for printing in the *Proceedings of the Royal Geographical Society* or the *Journal of the Royal Geographical Society*. He did the same thing for the monthly *Nautical Magazine*, founded in 1832 to advance the cause of safe navigation through the publication of geographical information about the sea. Thus was information disseminated and the attractions of discoveries promoted. The Geological Society and the Zoological Society were other means of advertising the findings about the wider world, and the Ethnographical Society of London followed on, as did the various missionary societies, notably the Church Missionary Society. The Hakluyt Society, founded in 1846 to print in English the records of travel and exploration, was one of the giant creations of the age. Presided over by naval officers in the main, but engaging a wide segment of the learned classes, it concentrated initially on early Spanish, Portuguese and English voyages, many of the age of Drake and Hawkins. Like other "records societies" it made available, in inexpensive format, and by subscription, accounts of past travels largely unavailable in definitive edition or English translation. Meanwhile, such other organizations as the Colonial Institute, later the Royal Empire Society (and finally, as if by natural progression, the Royal Commonwealth Society), the Asiatic Society and various clubs (e.g. the Athenaeum, founded by John Wilson Croker, secretary of the Admiralty) came into existence. London was the natural centre for all of this, the fulcrum of power and the point on which all peripheral activities in all manner of types of learned discovery focused.

The price of the Admiralty rose in these distant expeditions of information-gathering. Arctic and Antarctic discoveries wreaked mental as well as physical havoc on officers and men, and many of them never returned from their ordeals. The story of Robert Falcon Scott continues to live in haunting memory but is far from a solitary case. That of Franklin is another, and to his story we again return. He went out to Tasmania (Van Diemen's Land) as governor, and then, in 1845, undertook his third Northwest Passage search, in HMS *Erebus* and HMS *Terror*. He disappeared into a deadly silence, and his firebrand wife, the wealthy Lady Jane Franklin, exerted such pressure on the Admiralty that their lordships were obliged to continue the search for Franklin and any possible survivors long after hope had faded that any living persons would be found in the icebound wastes of the Canadian Arctic. The story haunted the Victorian imagination, replete as it was with rumours of cannibalism (conveyed by Dr John Rae in the employ of the Hudson's Bay Company on flimsy evidence of some lacerated human bones recovered from Inuit).[44] Franklin has oddly been criticized as too old for the assignment, but we do not know the cause of his death. Armchair geographers and sit-at-home literary explorers have had a field day at his expense. Were they to spend 24 hours in the captain's cabin of the *Erebus* locked in the ice, and with no relief in sight, imprisoned by changing environmental circumstance over which no one had control, they would think differently and give more sober judgments than are currently in fashion. The quest for the Northwest Passage was indeed a tragic one, full of heroism and pathos, of dreams fulfilled and unfulfilled. Franklin was anxious to further the field of magnetic science,[45] a fact forgotten. History has not been kind to him: like many another heroic figure of the Victorian age, his life is surrounded by intrigue and many missing pieces.[46]

The Navy's contributions to polar discoveries and imperial science speak for themselves, Franklin or no. Admiral Sir Leopold McClintock's research confirmed that the Franklin expedition had discovered the Northwest Passage. Captain Sir Robert McClure was the first to pass through a passage while, later, Roald Amundsen was the first to do so entirely by ship. Arrowsmith, the noted cartographer, championed Rae's prior claims, and Rae and McClintock engaged in a lively correspondence in 1860. As McClintock said, "positive proof was wanting" and thus many another expedition had to be sent.

> My object in the *Fox* [Lady Jane Franklin's ship] was to examine the whole of the unexplored area . . . and I did so. Had your information as to locality been conclusive this great labour would have been unnecessary. Now in spite of these additional and important facts, Arrowsmith does me the injustice of giving you credit for the *Whole*, and simply mentioned me as having "fully confirmed" you, and talks of "the first intelligence of the Fate" as if anything could be *Discovered Twice*.[47]

We might note for the record that the good Dr Rae, a prolix and self-aggrandizing fellow, died in his warm bed in Kensington, having claimed that he and not Franklin and his fellow officers had found the last stretch of the water passage west to Cathay.[48] All the same, he got an award from the Admiralty – not for the discovery of the Northwest Passage, mind you, but for gathering materials, eventually accepted, concerning the fate of Franklin.[49] As to *Erebus* and *Terror*, the search for the remains continues, but the tantalizing tale of the sighting by a merchant ship, *Renovation*, of an iceberg with two ships fast on it, in April 1851, may indicate a grave somewhere on the eastern shores of Newfoundland.[50]

As to other pioneers of exploration, now safely home, many turned to good works ashore. For instance, Beechey, who never returned to the Arctic, continued a service to scientific inquiry until his death in 1856. The seaborne doyen of his age, he was elected president of the Royal Geographical Society. In his last annual address, he summed up the scientific aims of the age. After 40 years, he told his audience, "The major problem", that of the Northwest Passage, had been solved at last "and Science at least has reaped her harvest". And what was this harvest? All sorts of findings in geography, magnetism, botany and climatology. Arctic discovery had shown what men could endure with little loss of life, Franklin and his men notwithstanding. "They have, in short," he concluded in ringing tones, "expunged the blot of obscurity which would otherwise have hung over and disfigured the history of this enlightened age."[51] The cynics would have their own replies to this sort of statement, as might well be expected. Perhaps in saying this, Beechey had in mind Dr Rae's recent acerbic critique on Arctic discovery: that the way to get credit was to plan some scheme, "and having signally failed, return with a lot of reasons – sufficiently good to gull John Bull – for your failure".[52]

It is true that the surveyors responded to the needs of the day, as shipping increased and global trade by sea necessitated reliable charts and sailing directions. The freedom of the seas necessitated safe navigation. Hurd, Beechey, Beaufort and others did yeoman work, but an interesting and disinterested comment by a subsequent hydrographer, Rear Admiral A.G.N. Wyatt, makes this point: that it was not the great men but the times that led to the achievements of the nineteenth century in hydrographic matters. "The inexorable pressure of economic expansion would have forced some such results from any authorities . . . The Surveyor and the Merchant went hand in hand while British commercial prosperity was leaping to its peak . . . "[53]

At the time when the data were being gathered, the costs of surveys were not fully appreciated in the press and in Parliament. Once the politicians began to toy with the financial side (which was always small in relation to the seagoing, fighting navy), their prejudices often showed. In the case of the budget-paring Lord Goschen, in 1872 we find this:

> I am as much impressed as anyone else with the great importance of the surveying work which is being carried on and the ability with which the service is conducted makes one naturally wish to give every facility and development to it. But I constantly stand aghast at the enormous proportion of the Expenditure in men and time absorbed by the non-fighting part of the Navy (though surveying vessels are only a small sub-division of the non-fighting class).[54]

To this sort of position the hydrographer and indeed members of the Admiralty Board could give professional replies. George Henry Richards, the then hydrographer, pointed out that surveys must continue because, as he warned, his anxiety was caused "by a knowledge of how much the safety of these great iron ships of the present day depend on the labours of the surveying vessels". The cost of these vessels was rising steeply; their chances of sinking quickly was high in comparison with wooden hulls. Richards added: "I would venture to point out also that in all conflicts which have occurred during the last 25 years the surveying vessels have been the Pioneers of the

Fighting Fleet – hence the necessity of training officers and men for future contingencies." To this Admiral Sir Sydney Dacres of the board minuted: "The Hydrographer's remarks as to the distinguished part taken by the surveying officers in all our late wars, I gladly endorse and every officer engaged in China, Baltic and Black seas will gladly do likewise."[55] In 1865, two gun vessels were commissioned – *Serpent* for China and *Gannet* for the West Indies – which were intended to combine the duties of a surveying ship with those of a man-of-war. However, the experiment did not succeed, perhaps because the remuneration usually allowed to commanders and certain officers was reduced by about half and, more likely, because of competing obligations.[56]

Hydrographers of the Navy often found themselves in bureaucratic snares. They had to counter technical and bureaucratic shifts in the making and selling of charts, to deal with massive backlogs of charts in preparation (Beaufort insisted on approving all of them himself) and to oversee the timely preparation of sailing directions to accompany charts. It was a vast industry predicated on the laudable argument that information should be made freely available to the merchant services as well as to the Navy and, further, that foreigners were entitled to obtain these charts and sailing directions. Hurd and Beaufort exchanged charts with Russian rivals and had no fear of doing so. The British gathered information from their American counterparts, notably about lighthouses. Ocean conditions and sailing routes were developed on the basis of studying the myriad ships logs, and the American Mathew Fontaine Maury and the Briton A.G. Findlay by 1860 provided excellent compendia of advice for mariners setting out on voyages, near and far.

As Richards knew, the work of the Hydrographic Department remained neglectfully unknown outside its own field. The duties and obligations were immense and of incalculable benefit to the future. Thus in his *Memoir* of 1868 he had written of the department's usefulness and that previously nagging shortcomings had been dealt with. "The enlightened liberality of successive Governments meant that the time had arrived, and he thus offered a sketch of the department to its rulers with the aim of making clear to them what, even to himself, had for long appeared obscure." He stated what became an oft-quoted phrase: "A state of war had always proved to be the opportunity of the Hydrographic Department." The work of the department continued and expanded: the siting of lighthouses abroad; the research into forecasting the approach of storms; the training and examination of young officers in navigation and pilotage; the nomination of officers for promotion; the investigations into the loss of surveying vessels, such as *Osprey* in 1867, and much else. Richards had done much in his time, not least managing a surveying team that did vital work in the Strait of Juan de Fuca and the Strait of Georgia, while laying down the 49th Parallel between the United States and British Columbia. He must have been like the expert in intricate navigation of Conrad's *Shadow Line*: "His brain must have been a perfect warehouse of reefs, positions, bearings, images of headlands, shapes of obscure coasts, aspects of innumerable islands, desert and otherwise." High-minded, expansive in his views and a world traveller, he had provided great service to humanity, and upon his retirement from the Navy in 1874, age 54, Rear-Admiral George Henry Richards, Commander of the Bath (later K. C. B.), a fellow of the Royal Society and of the Royal Geographical Society, had become a pillar of the scientific world. It was time to leave the Navy that he had been in since he was 13. Like many a great hydrographer, he later went into the private world of commerce, helping to lay down thousands of miles of submarine cables across deep oceanic spaces, in this case the North Atlantic. But in his time, too, he had sailed the seven seas, circumnavigated the globe twice, and knew all about triangulation, chronometers and how to regulate them, the drawing of draft plans, the engraving of charts, and how knowledge was best disseminated in the Victorian world. He had the capacity, too, to keep his political superiors on their toes, and to be careful what he said about the workaday world of plumbing the depths of the oceans and shoals, and of finding reefs and rocks that posed a hazard to shipping.

And what a world Richards had seen in his short life at sea. He was an aquatic globetrotter. He had been out to the Pacific in *Sulphur* with Beechey. He had taken an active share in the Chinese war of 1838–1840, which had boosted his reputation as a seagoing fighter. He surveyed the southeast coast of South America, and he was promoted to commander for gallantry in storming the forts in the River Parana. He surveyed in New Zealand during the Maori Wars, and then went to the high Arctic to search for Franklin. He was a man of tremendous physical strength, and although he apparently was injured in the right hand, perhaps in the Parana scrap, he is said to have taken one of the most extraordinary sledging journeys on record, when he was searching for Franklin. But his monument lies in the waters of British Columbia, where he directed the massive survey under tremendous pressure, with the aggressive Americans searching out the gold fields of the Fraser and Cariboo, and the United States Army landing intemperately on the disputed San Juan Islands.[57]

In the South Pacific, surveys advanced in relation to political requirements because commerce in the islands was insignificant in comparison with British influence elsewhere. But there were missionary claims on British attention: kidnappers, beachcombers and blackbirders to be watched or stamped out. Since Beechey's time, the Admiralty chart had seen many new additions. Under a cloud of secrecy, Henry Kellett took *Herald* to the Galapagos, and he signified to London Britain's commanding position in wartime but reported that it could not be self-sufficient; designs for formal empire there died.[58] Henry Denham spent seven years mapping Fijian islands and Australian coasts. Owen Stanley surveyed the northeast coast of Australia, the Arafura Sea, the Torres Strait and southeast New Guinea. On board Stanley's command, *Rattlesnake*, was a young surgeon, Thomas Huxley, who was to make such a name for himself in biological research. In the paddlewheel warship *Acheron*, John Lort Stokes conducted the first major survey of New Zealand, 4,300 miles of coast – another heroic examination for empire, and influential in the closing of the maritime frontier of this future dominion, where a protracted war between Maori and Pakehas was in progress, and did not really end until 1872.[59] The value of steam power for surveying purposes was revealed by *Acheron*.

Stokes, typical of many of his time, saw steam as a means of imperial power and colonial advancement:

> As we steamed up this picturesque arm of the sea [Queen Charlotte's Sound], several Maori whaleboats, which have nearly superseded the use of canoes, passed, hastening out of the quiet nooks studding its shores, to gaze in intent awe on a vessel moved by the unseen agency of steam. As we drew near the head of the Sound, two densely crowded boats pulled into mid-Channel to meet us. On passing them, the *Acheron* suddenly stopped. The effect on our Maori spectators was very startling. Terror or admiration appeared to take full possession of them, in a moment afterwards their wild shrieks echoed from shore to shore. The violent manner in which they then threw their arms about and the contortions of their features showed intense excitement... The impression created by the visit of HM Steamer will not soon be effaced and may be useful in confirming the belief already generally entertained elsewhere that the English can promptly furnish any turbulence, or outrage on their countrymen, however remote from the rest of government their settlement might be.[60]

Stokes was keen for the advancement of steam navigation, and he recommended that steamers would allow the reduction of the number of sailing vessels on station and perhaps reduce the number of regiments required ashore. The telegraph and submarine cable were also inventions that he trumpeted for naval mobility, and he thought that they would yield many blessings of peace, civilization and Christianity over the darkened spots of the world. He waxed eloquent on this subject to Gladstone:

> Once a knot of enterprising people can be got to take root where there is prospect of commerce, a trade will soon spring up and a fresh tract be opened for British manufactures. England cannot... have too many well selected and well established colonies; they are to her like the rigging of a ship.

Gladstone, a former colonial secretary, was not so sure:

> I feel less sanguine than yourself, and I am disposed to shrink from the extent of duty, of highly arduous and honourable duty, which you would England

> to assume . . . I hesitate to admit the propriety of any indefinite or wide extension of our protectorate, by acts or by a policy of ours, to tribes not within our dominions by fresh assumptions with misgiving and even with dread. There is no country on earth so charged with responsibilities as we are: and I am by no means aware that we are not more ready to undertake them than ready to meet them.[61]

As a branch of science, oceanography was coming into its own, and out of this the *Challenger* expedition of 1872–1876 was born. The vessel was a wooden steam corvette, rigged with sails and fitted with a screw propeller that could be disengaged when not required. The captain was George Nares. The mandate was to find anything and everything possible about what goes on under the surface of what *Genesis* calls "the waters under the heavens". The scheme had its origins in the work of scientific societies, at the apex of which stood the Royal Society in collaboration with the University of Edinburgh. The expedition sailed from Portsmouth in 1872 and involved 240 scientists and crew. For the necessary laboratories and accommodations, considerable modifications had been made to inboard arrangements. The scientific passengers made zoological, botanical and geological collections. They saw the bleak penguin rookeries in the Antarctic, East Indian coral and spice islands; they met hostile peoples in New Guinea and the mikado in Japan. Details of the ocean's temperatures and chemical content were gathered. Deep-sea soundings and samples of the bottom of the ocean, plus meteorological and magnetic observations, were made. All together, after three-and-a-half years and 68,000 sea miles, and having sailed most of the world's oceans, the expedition gathered a body of data that has been matched by few voyages of discovery, and brought prodigious results, not least 4,000 previously unknown species.[62] As publisher John Murray said of the 50-volume *Report of the Challenger Expedition*, it was "the greatest advance in the knowledge of our planet since the celebrated discoveries of the fifteenth and sixteenth centuries". The *Report*, says one historian, is "a solid monument to the patience of the navy and the Victorian passion for accumulating knowledge".[63] And well into the late years of *Pax*, the Navy's hydrographers and surveyors continued to gather the empirical data that was so important for safe navigation.

By century's close the global reach of the Hydrographic Department had been largely achieved. In Canadian, Australian and other waters of self-governing dominions and colonies, surveying ships under the control of the Navy continued the exacting work, and it is a fascinating fact that some of the last remaining Royal Navy vessels at distant stations at their closure early in the next century were those dedicated to surveying duties. Most of them had sails, which were useful when coal was not available for steaming purposes. Submarines had made their debut, another consideration for the surveyors.

Moreover, mines and minesweeping had additional requirements, and the Russo-Japanese War of 1904–1905 had shown how powerfully this type of war could be waged on inshore waters. The work of the department had to consider these matters and, more generally, had to continue its larger mandate as trade and globalization continued. Yet at the same time there were revolutions afoot in naval affairs that were to have far-reaching consequences. Not the least of these was the scheme to close down the overseas stations and institute cruising squadrons, one based at Devonport and another in China. The location of cable stations needed attention and wireless ones, too. Approaches to the intended Panama Canal needed examination and verification. Of even greater significance, however, was that the scene was becoming increasingly clouded over by the challenge of Germany, a theme that we first meet here but which comes forward with enhanced dimensions towards the close of our period. Growing trade rivalry between Britain and Germany formed the initial framework of cooling relations between the two countries. With the German economy fast outstripping that of the British, Germany now represented a potential threat of a military sort. Domination of Europe would pose the greatest threat to the British Empire and would likely end *Pax Britannica*.[64] This was the state of affairs that even the hydrographers had to contend with.

As early as 1901 the first lord of the Admiralty, the Earl of Selborne, expressed great concern about the rise of Germany's global aspirations and activities on and over the seas, all buttressed by naval capabilities. "The naval policy of Germany", he warned a colleague, "is definite and persistent. The Emperor seems determined that the power of Germany shall be used the entire world over to push German commerce, possessions, and interests. Of necessity it follows that the German naval strength must be raised so as to compare more advantageously than at present with ours." All of a sudden, France and Russia assumed new importance in British naval calculations. As Selborne put it,

> The result of this policy will be to place Germany in a commanding position if ever we find ourselves at war with France and Russia, and at the same time to put the Triple Alliance in a different relative position to France and Russia in respect of naval strength to that which it has hitherto occupied.

He closed with this sombre observation: "Naval officers who have seen much of the German navy lately are all agreed that it is as good as can be..."[65]

Confirmatory information reached Whitehall, setting off more alarm bells. In 1902 the Admiralty learned from its British naval *Attaché* in Berlin of enhanced German naval aspirations. To this was added Foreign Office opinion and advice that the Kaiser's navy, built up under the energizing leadership of Admiral von Tirpitz, meant business on and over the seas. A "place in the sun" was desired, a seagoing fleet capable of meeting the needs of Germany for greater trade and colonies, and, naturally, bases of rest, repair and control. Doubtless the Germans were able to use British Admiralty charts to fulfill ambitions overseas. Even at the turn of the new century, Germany could not intervene in South Africa because the Royal Navy guarded the seas. From that bitter experience von Tirpitz came to his own conclusion: Germany must build, he told the Kaiser, a great fleet "unless she is prepared hereafter to go the way of renunciation" and to leave the colonial field "to the Anglo-Saxons and to the sons of Jehovah".[66] There was the challenge to the hitherto unchallenged supremacy of the Navy.

British data-gathering and the preparation of charts and sailing directions turned once more to European waters, notably the Baltic, the North Sea, the English Channel, approaches to the British Islands, the Straits of Gibraltar and the Mediterranean. The department turned its attention to defence measures. In January 1906 the hydrographer could inform the Admiralty that the war organization of chart establishments was complete. Destroyers and torpedo-gunboats could now be issued chart sets. A greatly enlarged chart of European waters had been prepared for admirals afloat. In answer to an appeal from the director of Naval Intelligence, a chart of the world was hastily completed in 1908. German charts were acquired and copied. In a paper discussing a possible German invasion of Britain, the hydrographer showed the ports from which an armada might issue. Harbours needed to be resurveyed and, in the Orkneys, Scapa Flow required particular attention as the intended haven for the grand fleet in wartime. The department provided advice about gun ranges and battle-practice areas.[67] The positioning of light-ships merited reconsideration, in conjunction with Trinity House, the ancient brotherhood that supervised navigation and aids to navigation around the British Isles.

In all ways the premier maritime nation readied itself for war. Yet it is always fascinating to read how in these darkening days the department was still fighting for recognition and a modicum of independence, and was often at odds with the sharp-end naval authorities, which were not quite so sure that the work of the surveyor was as important as its champions made it out to be. "It surely cannot be Their Lordships' belief that hydrography has ceased to be important to the Fleet," moaned Admiral Sir Herbert Purey-Cust, the hydrographer who had that important assignment in the years leading up to the First World War. His letters are wearying testimony about the Treasury's insistence that the establishment should be cut down because receipts from the sale of charts and sailing directions had fallen. His argument was that the department served the fleet and should be judged according to its efficiency in meeting requirements. "Some day," he warned, and with this we conclude our chronicle on this subject of *Pax Britannica*, "a mistake may lose a battleship or worse and will it then be sufficient excuse that the Hydrographer has been occupied with other duties?"[68]

In the end, the peculiar gift to the world of publishing charts and sailing directions for making possible safer navigation may be considered the British Empire's greatest legacy. The incremental building up of empirical data, and its codification in the hands of the Admiralty's Hydrographic Office, constitutes a monument of intellectual achievement. To this day, yachtsmen navigating the intricate waters of Georgian Bay know that they are the beneficiaries of the work of Owen, Bayfield and Bolton, and of their ships' companies working in boats who did the heavy lifting of hydrographic surveying. This is only one instance, for in all waters of the world where tankers and freighters, cruise ships and pleasurecraft ply the seas, they sail where British officers and men under guidance from the Admiralty demanded that perils to shipping be noted in "Remark Books", and that reliable information be provided for those who would, to employ the ancient Naval Prayer, "pass on the seas upon their lawful occasions". *Pax Britannica* has given the world many legacies, but none so important or so durable as its charts and sailing directions. The intention was purely scientific to the benefits of commerce, but it had altruistic and humanitarian benefits of incalculable proportions.

5
Informal and Formal Empires in the Americas

It was in the Americas that a repositioning of power took place during the first few decades of *Pax Britannica*. The British consolidated their authority in British North America, aided, as we have seen, by the development of Bermuda as a naval base, which supplemented their old anchors of empire at such places as Antigua and Barbados. There existed some nagging possibility that France would make an ill-judged attempt to reassert influence in the Americas. However, it was the ascendant United States that posed the certain rival to the British. Successive presidents and secretaries of state were anxious to assert their dominance in the Americas, even announcing, as President James Monroe did in 1823, the Monroe Doctrine. This was designed as a warning to European powers against asserting territorial claims. British naval power allowed such a declaration. The British, however, were not prepared to concede that a mere paper declaration sufficed, and in their formal as in their informal empires they continued to strengthen their positions, particularly in the Americas. As late as 1850 they still held to the ancient policy that they reserved the rights over any future isthmian canal, and entered into a treaty with the United States on that score.[1] It was not until after the Spanish-American War that Britain was able to accede to Washington's view that the Caribbean had ceased to be a British lake and had become a central point of American strategic thinking.

Reforms had been made to British imperial management after the loss of the Thirteen Colonies. Reviewing this new state of affairs in 1861, a former permanent undersecretary of state for colonial affairs, Herman Merivale, recalled that the British colonial empire was administered "after no very regular pattern, but in accordance with certain received usages". Most of the colonies had legislatures but the mother country jealously controlled their affairs through executive government. The acts of trade and navigation were additional means of this control until being cast aside in 1846, and slavery continued in many of the West Indian colonies until its abolition in 1833. In the British North American provinces, Britain possessed its finest strategic asset. Newfoundland, "fief of

Admiralty", under the rule of admirals until 1832, gave its possessors great security value adjacent to the sea routes leading to the New World.[2] For 130 years the Navy was the engine of law here and on the adjacent Labrador shore. Nova Scotia, with Halifax harbour, was an anchor of empire of undoubted value, not least as a preventative against any rebellion against the Crown there or elsewhere in those seas. In Quebec a great fortress protected the colonization process as well as the fur, grain and timber trades. Upriver, and on Lake Ontario, lay Fort Kingston, naval depot and yard, while upstream by portages and lakes the British imperial fact pressed right into the continental heartland at the head of Lake Superior. The government's policy of "shoveling out paupers", that is, assisted emigration, found fertile ground in Upper Canada (later Ontario), reinforcing the colony established by refugees from the American Revolution, the Loyalists, with Britons directly sent from home. In 1849 the British Government established under Hudson's Bay Company auspices the colony of Vancouver Island as a bulwark against American settlement. Its strategic benefits in the Pacific outdistanced its economic abilities, but by mid-century it gave an indication of the possibilities of a transcontinental Canada.

Indeed, by the 1840s the political climate at home had changed so rapidly owing to the rapid growth of the British population that the formal empire took on new meaning as a place of opportunity. Political thinkers looked to the Crown's vast overseas possessions as a prospect for relief. While on the one hand many sceptics called for the abandoning of a colonial system that only invited trouble (they gleefully cited the troublesome Canadian rebellions of 1837 and 1838, the costly colonial defences, the problems of maladministration and the incessant wars on the empire's frontiers), a new school contemplated a reconstructed and energized British Empire wherein universal free trade and on-the-spot colonial land control would attract emigrants from home, and free communities would thus be founded possessing characteristics of regulated settlement. To a large degree this school of thinkers was directing "the thoughts of the more speculative towards the renewal of the older and freer polity of our first American settlements", reflected Merivale.[3]

However, these innovators failed to see that each new colonial society would wish to free itself from the fetters of the land system of the founders, and to put in place a system of its own. They also failed to foresee that the colonial regulation that they wanted to implement would have to yield to colonial self-government, a scheme that the mother country was obliged to foster. In several locations, especially in South Australia and Christchurch, New Zealand, these "closet speculators" shaped the character of colony-building of that era. That they were so influential was not just because of their persistence. The government, under pressure, looked for ways of founding settlements in British lands overseas and to do this at little or no cost to itself besides the customary costs of naval protection. Hounded by zealous colony promoters, Colonial Office secretaries and bureaucrats fought gallantly to counter schemes for granting land at a "just or sufficient price". But the Colonial Office, notably under Sir James Stephen, the undersecretary, battled against what he regarded as the trickery of the proponents of Edward Gibbon Wakefield's scheme of systematic colonization, preferring to see potential additions to the imperial estate in strategic and financial terms. So "sufficient price" for land sometimes gave way to "reasonable price". One pound sterling per acre of land acquired by a settler after occupation for a set number of years became the usual real-estate price, and was the initial (and "reasonable", according to the Colonial Office) price of land available to prospective colonists on Vancouver Island. The absurdity of this price-fixing deterred settlement in places where it was applied and probably encouraged more and more emigrants to go to the United States to settle on much cheaper land, perhaps available by pre-emption. In South Australia, the system proved to be a failure and a Crown colony was instituted. In New Zealand, a colonizing company, founded on Wakefieldian lines, wrested control from colonists and Maori alike, and proved to be the bane of existence for Stephen, who had the matter corrected and brought about the Treaty of Waitangi, negotiated by the naval officer Captain William Hobson. A colonial war did not develop in South Australia but in New Zealand the contest for control consumed two decades, cost many a life among imperial and colonial soldiers, engaged many British men-of-war and set back British race relations with the Maori, which had deep-seated legacies.[4]

Despite all conscious attempts to the contrary, the British imperial estate continued to expand after 1815. In the first 50 years after that date, the empire's area expanded by about 100,000 square miles per year, very little less than the average annual expansion between 1865 and 1914.[5] The nature of this growth, long the preoccupation of historians, was more various in character and form than can easily be categorized in a word or a phrase. The philosophical radicals took up the task of analysing empire. Jeremy Bentham cried for an emancipation of the colonies as economically worthless, as seeds of war, and expensive to maintain and defend. John R. McCulloch might claim the colonies to be bereft of any benefit to the mother country. John Stuart Mill charged that the colonies were kept because of the interests of the "few" – the ruling class who were seeking governorships, judgeships and other appointments, for themselves or their friends.

This "countercurrent" to imperial control and expansion made little headway with statesmen. There were no decisions to drop imperial acquisitions or freeze the colonial state. However, it meant that the critics of imperial expansion had powerful positions, in and out of parliament. Historians have declared the mid-Victorian policy of anti-colonialism to be a myth because no responsible statesman held to the view of dispensing with empire. Robinson and Gallagher concluded that British expansion was "vigorous and uninterrupted" and combined "commercial penetration and political influence" in informal and formal areas, the last type being acquisitions only of necessity.[6] In essence, the pulse of imperial growth came from commerce. Industrial growth and advantage lay behind much of it, but the need for areas for the settlement of the burgeoning population in the home islands was another impellent. Missionary and humanitarian requirements – made concrete by the actions of the Aborigines' Protection Society – were potent additives to the mix, plus those of security, including preventing a rival from gaining an advantage in some newer area of concern. The demands of waging a war against the slave trade also brought accretions to the imperial estate, as did the need of finding places of resettlement for freed slaves. In all, the complications of running and holding world primacy may help to explain that for all attempts to reduce colonial expansion to a simple explanation, the complexities of trying to embrace all of the motives are truly an occupational hazard for the working historian. But one of the themes running through this book is that *Pax Britannica* rested on the materials of sea power – that is, the ships and bases (and garrisons of the same), and the political will exercised at home in Whitehall and in Parliament to maintain such primacy in the face of many other rivals.

The inseparable idea of free trade and naval power was finely manifested in the issues pursued by Palmerston, the dominant foreign policy-maker of the age. The pursuit of free trade, as Palmerston envisioned it, benefited not only Britain but also other commercial and industrial nations, and the fact that this mission had to be undertaken by the Navy he saw reciprocally as beneficial to the training of seamen and the naval establishment generally. It was a new twist to the old mercantilist theory of self-sufficiency, the dominance of trade in British "bottoms" (or ships), and the training of British officers and men as a reservoir of seamen for future naval and diplomatic assignments. Palmerston thought in wide-ranging terms about this, and nowhere was the benefit to be better to British commercial and industrial advantage than in the Americas, notably the United States but also in the nascent states of Latin America. Albert H. Imlah, in his *Economic Elements in the "Pax Britannica"*, puts it this way: "The matter of open sea lanes was, perhaps, the special task of diplomacy and, in crises, of the navy; but both diplomacy and, if it came to that, naval action were, if anything, rendered easier by free-trade policy which promoted mutuality of commercial interests."[7] In the circumstances, the British rarely used their strength in ways that might have given them real advantage. Rather, they reacted to circumstances as they arose. Given the greatness and superiority of England's possession of superior force, reflecting its industrial and commercial strengths, the Navy was the keen edge of the parent state.

As the first industrial nation, Britain had many advantages over its competitors. British coal, the fuel of the Industrial Revolution at home, was also a vitally important export, and a means of increasing the trade advantage. Used as ballast, it powered machinery overseas besides allowing an enhanced mobility for British armed steamers or merchant steamers. Iron and steel production rose at home, and was exported in raw form or manufactured items. Yorkshire worsteds and Lancashire cottons found ready markets overseas. Iron ships, military and merchant, were built for overseas sale; so were guns, rifles, pistols and machine guns. Although by the 1860s the United States was overhauling Britain in patents and inventions, Britain still retained its primacy in industrial exports. An indication of this primacy is given in this statement by Paul Kennedy:

> Economically, the Britain of 1860 was remarkably different, not merely from the German states, but from all other European countries apart from Belgium. If she was not the "workshop of the world", she was at least producing about two-thirds of its coal, about half its iron, five-sevenths of its steel, two-fifths of its hardware and about half of its commercial cotton cloth; 40 percent of the world's trade in manufactures came from her factories, and about one third of the total exports of all other countries went to the British market. In addition to being responsible for a large part of international, or better, transoceanic, commence, she was also the centre for banking, insurance, investment and commodity dealing and possessed more registered steamship tonnage than all other countries combined. Already by this stage, the greater part of the British workforce was engaged in manufacturing and the majority of the population lived in urban areas.[8]

Given the nature of the Industrial Revolution and the fact that Britain was "the workshop of the world", reliant on seaborne trade, it is natural to see questions of whether or not to expand the bounds of empire in commercial terms. The abiding expectation of the times was "trade not rule", but this was only half the truth of it. It was security that haunted the British official mind and not commercial prospects specifically. The reason for this is that British statesmen and strategists knew that it was security and security alone that would protect their commerce upon which British profit and power were dependent. British industry floated on the merchant marine. The Industrial Revolution crossed the oceans under sail (and later tramp steamers). The distant seas approached by either of the great southern capes were being drawn into the commercial network by better shipping and a fuller knowledge of wind conditions, thus expediting faster, more profitable voyages. Trade, therefore, was the beneficiary of sea power – that is, the instruments of a maritime statecraft, including ships, manpower and bases of influence and operation.

No one of the age quarrelled with the assumption that it was on the Navy and the merchant marine that the power and profit of Britain and the British Empire rested. No one saw this more clearly than Palmerston, who not only looked to British benefits but to those of other nations as well. In a sense, *Pax* was a gift to the world. Say what you might about imperial expansion, but invariably you will find that British statesmen when pondering the obligations of another accretion of empire always considered how such a place would benefit British security. Naturally, and unavoidably, defensive imperialism reared its head: what we might call the pre-emptive impulse so often directed the course of imperial affairs throughout this long century. And that was based on the assumption that it was better to take possession of that distant spot before a rival could do so. This was the *modus operandi* when the British took the Cape of Good Hope, for as Commodore John Blankett had advised some years previously, "Considered as an entrepôt between Europe and Asia, it has every advantage that can be wished, either in point of situation, climate, soil and productions. What was a feather in the hands of Holland will become a sword in the hands of France."[9] Dutch colonists had arrived in 1652 and the true mercantile value of the Cape seems to have been as "the tavern of the two oceans". For reasons far beyond British comprehension, the possession of the Cape had the same value for Britain as it had had for the House of Orange; on the other hand, it turned into a quagmire of responsibilities. No place in British expansion exhibited such an example of reluctant empire, where the turbulence of the frontier, the expansion of Boer and British settlement, and the spread of the missionary factor spelled altogether a most potent and unhappy mix. The British had gone there for reasons of security. That was the essence of it at the outset of the age of *Pax Britannica*.

Many such numerous examples come forward in the imperial experience, and we meet them several times during this narrative. The British, above all, were conscious of their security and mindful of the strength posed by their rivals, real and imagined. There is no denying the influence that commerce played in the expansion of British realms during this period, and it is true that "trade with informal control if possible; trade with rule where necessary" would be the preferred option, as Robinson and Gallagher argue. Overseas trade, investment, migration and culture, especially the first two, drove the imperial dynamic.[10] British statesmen, investors, industrialists and exporters looked to the wider seas for new opportunities.

After 1815, British seaborne commerce increased dramatically to eastern seas. India, Southeast Asia and China bulked large as places of British merchant activity, where competition from the French, Dutch and Americans remained keen. The convict colony of Botany Bay, New South Wales; the sea otter hunting base of Nootka Sound, Vancouver Island; the great transpacific trading crossroads of the Hawaiian Islands; and the Bonin Islands off the Siberian coast and the Marquesas in the South Pacific, both resorts for whalers, attracted attention. Commercial interests pursued new trades – in pelts and skins, in whale products, in timber and tea, in hides and tallow – relentlessly from Europe and eastern North America. And outwards from the Home Islands came machinery and implements, cottons and worsteds, prefabricated buildings, and coal in phenomenal quantities as ballast or fuel.

After 1815, too, oceanic commerce increasingly used the roaring forties. Cape Horn merchantmen shipped wool and oil from the Australian colonies, timber and flax from New Zealand, fertilizer-rich guano from the Chincha Islands, and nitrates and ores from the ports of Chile and Peru. Beginning in 1822, British men-of-war were conveying at least an annual freight of silver specie from shipment points as far north as Mexican ports in the Gulf of California. We will return to this presently. The discovery of gold in the Sacramento River drew shipping and capital to San Francisco Bay, a pattern replicated later at the Fraser River in 1858 and the Stikine River in 1862. In all of these ways, the quickening pace of seaborne commerce was fulfilling promoters' promises of rich returns in the distant ocean. Such cargoes were invariably destined for North Atlantic ports; others, of a more exotic nature (including sandalwood, the sea slug *bêche-de-mere* and edible birds nests), were shipped by European vessels in the Pacific to those celebrated ports of Canton and Macao, gateways of business and diplomacy for the Chinese Empire. All of these requirements necessitated an increasing naval armament for the Pacific. Lawlessness, real or imagined, remained the undying worry for the commercial sector, and for governors and consuls. Calling up gunboats to provide security and put down civil strife became the order of the day.

The greatest rivals to the British in these trades were the Americans, and rapacious competition was to have tragic consequences in the history of the Falkland Islands, discussed below. From Nantucket and Stonington, Connecticut, sealers were sent south to range the islands and beaches of the southern ocean. They needed places of rest and repair. Port Louis, Berkeley Sound, in the Falklands, was one place used by Fanning and other traders to take in sealskins or to engage in whaling activities beyond the Horn in Chile. From a temporary base in the Marquesas, American privateers and naval vessels had preyed on the large British whaling fleet owned chiefly by the London whaling lobby, Etches and Campion, and when the USS *Essex*, under Captain David Porter, had made such a tremendous haul of British whalers, cruisers of the Royal Navy hunted down the enemy in Valparaiso. The Royal Navy had sent warships round Cape Horn during the War of 1812, but none more successfully when *Phoebe* and *Cherub* captured *Essex* and put a stop to one of the most remarkable instances of *guerre de course* in history, rivalled only by the experiences of John Paul Jones and Maximillian von Spee. The Americans were latecomers to the Pacific, but in the years after the 1812 war their interests surged in these seas. "Everything conspires to render the Pacific of great interest to the people of the United States at the present time," commented

Commodore John Downes in 1833, adding: "Our future sea fights are as likely to take place here as on the Atlantic Ocean, for here we are acquiring a preponderating commercial interest, and here must be our navy also." *Columbia* and *Lady Washington* had been the first American ships to double Cape Horn, in 1788, bound for the Northwest Coast. Whalers and sea otter seekers had followed in number. In 1818 the Navy Board sent USS *Macedonian* to the Pacific to show the flag, and this quest for global influence led to a distant-station policy that was applied in the Mediterranean (founded 1815), the Caribbean (1822) and the Pacific (1821).

Since the days of Sir Francis Drake and Captain George Vancouver, the British held a special attraction to northern California, which had been named Nova Albion by Drake in 1579. He had careened *Golden Hind* at Drakes Bay, north of San Francisco Bay (which he did not see), and had proclaimed English dominion there. But, as secretaries of the Admiralty noted, the French cartographer Delisle changed the names and even deleted the placename Nova Albion from the maps. He also changed Puerto de Francisco Draco to Porto San Francisco. Some mischief-making was going on in the cartographic world. The Admiralty and the Foreign Office rightly sensed some fudging of the maps and reports by the French.[11] Maps now entered the equation as pawns on the chessboard of international rivalry.

Within a few years the rivalry heated up considerably. Alta California still lay under faltering Mexican dominance; its future was in doubt, though the Americans and the United States Navy had eyes on the great port and the crumbling authority of the governor headquartered at Monterey, a lovely bay but an open and exposed roadstead. In the 1840s, sleepy California, known to the world through the illegal hide and tallow trade, and also through its place for illegal immigrants to settle, was the focal point of naval rivalries and much jockeying for position. Rival European powers were watching each other's moves closely. Consuls appointed by their home governments each worked against the other, striving for advantage in trade, real estate and even religious advantage. The United States, France and Britain vociferously denied having any designs on California. The Americans came with various designs and various schemes, and Manifest Destiny seemed to embrace their project, backed by a virulent press. But all three governments had agents at work and warships protecting their nationals and commerce. Each watched closely the manoeuvres and movements of the warships of the others; and each had Pacific squadrons with spirited admirals, who had to be restrained by home governments. The prize, after a false start by an intemperate US naval captain, eventually went to the United States and its Navy in 1846. During this episode ships of the Royal Navy's Pacific squadron under Rear Admiral Sir George Francis Seymour were mere bystanders, hobbled by the stricture of a non-intervention policy ordered by the British Government.[12]

In the circumstances, the hands of the British admiral, Seymour, were tied. As the American commodore there at the time, Sloat, put it about his British opposite,

> The visit of the Admiral was very serviceable to our cause in California, as the inhabitants [Californios] fully believed he would take part with them and that we would be obliged to abandon our conquest, but when they saw the friendly intercourse subsisting between us, and found that he could not interfere on their behalf, they abandoned all hope of ever seeing the Mexican flag fly in California again.[13]

Had British foreign policy been different, the British could have taken Monterey, California, but that was not the will of the government, which, we are reminded, preferred trade to territory.

The War of 1812 had ended in strained relations with the United States. Suspicions ran deep in the American capital. Thomas Jefferson, a former president and secretary of state, let fly venom in a private letter:

> I consider the government of England as totally without morality, insolent beyond bearing, inflated with vanity and ambition, aiming at the exclusive dominion of the sea, lost in corruption, of deep-rooted hatred towards us, hostile to liberty wherever it endeavors to show its head, and the eternal disturber of the peace of the world.[14]

Others at the top of the administration shared his views, and John Quincy Adams, when secretary of state, once told his British counterpart that he expected sooner or later to hear that the British were claiming the moon as their own.

Meanwhile, urgent issues existed to bring peace and accord. Indian tribes south of the border in self-interested alliance with the British Crown in war as in peace found themselves expediently cast aside by British diplomats who were anxious for peace. In 1815, Congress passed a law prohibiting all traffic of British traders within the territories of the United States. The Treaty of Ghent of 1814 called for a return to the territorial status *ante bellum*. However, in a bold attempt to solve matters of trade and security west of the Great Lakes, a joint commission was immediately put in place to extend the agreed border between the United States and British North America west to the Continental Divide. Subsequent surveys of the Great Lakes boundary had to be undertaken and accepted by both parties. Another measure, the Rush–Bagot agreement of 1817, specified a reduction in British and American naval armaments on the Great Lakes, a first of its kind in international relations. But the British were wary of US naval and diplomatic intentions, as rightly they should have been.

In 1818, USS *Ontario* under Captain James Biddle carried out orders to take possession of the Columbia River in the name of the United States. He laid down markers on the riverbanks. Washington backed off under pressure from London, and a British sloop-of-war was sent as a countermeasure in this game of cat and mouse.[15] On the Great Lakes it was not until 1822 that rigid economies could be brought to the naval establishment at Kingston, Lake Ontario, and to the Great Lakes command.[16] For their part, the Americans watched the British closely, and such huge defence as the British ordnance department built up in Quebec, and the construction of the canal between the Ottawa River and Kingston under guidance of the Royal Engineers, was bound to be looked on as an indication of future British hostile intentions.[17] Not until 1871 could the British withdraw their last regiment guarding the Canadian frontier.

American continentalist ambitions and moves towards Texas, California and Oregon bulked up the republic in size, expanded its borders and fuelled its political bravado. The crisis of the federal union over states rights posed the next issue. The *Trent* crisis and complications of the American Civil War constituted a tense epoch. During the crisis the British had in the commander-in-chief of North America and the West Indies, Vice Admiral Sir Alexander Milne, and the British minister in Washington, Lord Lyons, the perfect combination of tact and strength, proportionally employed. There was no need of glory for a naval action, only the necessity of observing strict neutrality as proclaimed on 13 May 1861. When two Confederate officials were forcibly removed from a British mail steamer, *Trent*, by a Union warship, the great potential rift between Britain and the United States presented itself. British commercial interests were closely tied to those of the Confederacy in shipping, finance and cotton trade. Milne, based in Halifax and on Bermuda, depending on the seasons, acted on instructions from the Admiralty which in turn got its orders from the Foreign Office. He also took his cue from the British minister in Washington, Lyons, a smooth and careful diplomat who steered the British ship of state through unchartered waters. London showed to Washington that it meant business: regimental numbers in British North America were dramatically increased and the strength in ships on station rose to the highest ever – 40. But the work was truly of a diplomatic sort carried through to peaceful solution.

In the great cabin of the flagship, *Nile*, Milne and his secretaries scanned the incoming correspondence, tracked the proceedings of all of the ships under his command, read the New York and London newspapers, and fired off responses and directives as required. In the capital of Nova Scotia, the *Halifax Evening Express* of 13 May 1862, watching the goings-on at close hand, commented:

> we believe the amount of correspondence which the commander-in-chief of the Navy has to maintain not only with the flag officers under his command, but with the Ministers, Governors, and Consuls on the station – with all

> the public departments at home, to say nothing of the Admiralty itself – is something fabulous and would make a stranger believe that our admirals were merely sent out as diplomatists, instead of to fight battles.

The Foreign Office view was that the priority was to reserve the peace in international affairs, and this was duly observed. All such material matters, and there were many, including the claims for damages in consequence of the Confederate warship *Alabama* being equipped by British firms, would be resolved under the arrangements of the Treaty of Washington of 1871. (The San Juan Islands dispute was thus settled similarly.) However, the silent victory was truly Milne's, and that of the officers and men who served under him. He received the most complimentary sentiments of approval from their lordships, who had recognized the difficulties of his position. His tact and discretion won their unqualified approval. No victory medal was struck, because that could only be done for a battle. Milne's work on this station was of the highest order for peaceful work of the Navy during *Pax Britannica*, and he remains in the historical record that usually prefers to trumpet the successes of those in battle one of the great figures of naval diplomacy.[18]

Throughout the nineteenth century, even to the eve of the 1914 war, the naval armaments question regarding the Great Lakes was an incendiary in the diplomatic files. Gradually, British defence planners and British admirals, notably Sir John Fisher, came to the conclusion that Canada had to be left to its own devices: the dominion was a hostage to fortune; its security depended on good Anglo-American relations. Meanwhile, in 1880, Britain transferred to the dominion of Canada its sovereign claims to the lands and waters of the Northwest Passage. Canadian governments subsequently undertook various expeditions of discovery and flag-planting, all designed to strengthen the Dominion's claim against possible threats from rival American, Danish and Norwegian intruders. Early in the new century, Royal Canadian Mounted Police posts had been thrown up on the Arctic wastes, while dog-sled teams went on tours to "maintain the right". The pattern was familiar. Canadians were enforcing their own *Pax*.

No greater challenge to British requirements and aspirations of the age existed than in Central and South America, particularly the latter. Herein lay tortuous webs of influence and local rivalries. The Portuguese and Spanish empires in Latin America had been built on a grand scale, but they were prone to administrative difficulties, illicit trade and contraband, corruption and graft, and, not least, the perils of international relations. Napoleon's invasion of the Iberian Peninsula precipitated the revolutions in Latin America, from Mexico south to Argentina. "The nationalist monarchist movement in Spain", wrote the English historian R.A. Humphreys, "was paralleled by a semi-nationalist, semi-monarchist movement in America. It began ostensibly as an assertion of freedom from French control. It ended as a war of independence against Spain." At the local level, colonial conditions and aspirations led to various overlapping and sometimes competing political and administrative responses that British naval officers could only be amazed at, or more likely befuddled by. Naval officers were observers of the radical political changes that were transforming the map of the Western Hemisphere. Commenting on why the war became a revolutionary one against Spain, Humphreys explained that this was "due partly to the action of the Spanish, partly to threat of the colonial authorities, and partly to deeper colonial conditions and aspirations. Like the earlier revolution in North America that in Latin America was not merely a struggle for home rule, it was also a contest as to who should rule at home. The fulfilment by the Spanish Americans themselves, not least the inspired activities of their great leaders Bolívar and San Martín, remains "a legitimate source of pride to a people whose past has been too little understood and whose successes have been too little appreciated".[19]

British commerce made steady gains during the early nineteenth century in South America. The Manchester Chamber of Commerce pressed on Canning at the Foreign Office to recognize the New Republics. They wanted free trade agreements signed with them.[20] It was in this way that most favoured nation status came to Britain, which built up a powerful infrastructure in the ports and capitals of Latin America. Such activity required official protection from bureaucratic interference and local piracy. A British sloop-of-war lying in the roadstead of a trading port was always a salutary sight to British merchants, bankers and commission agents, as well as to those of other nations: similarly, it was a cautionary message to any insurgents or pirates who might consider tampering with an innocent British or foreign cargo vessel or warehouse ashore. Moreover, during that protracted period of insurgency, revolution, civil war and feared repression from the imperial powers that dominated the affairs of South America before the independence movements of the 1820s, the Navy's vessels "on station" provided a welcome reminder of British intentions. These policies were to foster the cause of peace for the purpose of profit, and to promote the health and trade of Latin American states. To a certain degree the pursuit of those objectives meant preventing the former imperial powers – Spain and Portugal – from reasserting their old dominance. Equally, the Navy watched the threatening rivalry of the two other nations that had extensive, indeed growing, commercial and diplomatic interests in South America, France and the United States. (Germany only entered the lists here in the early twentieth century.) In the words of liberator Simon Bolivar, "Only England, mistress of the seas, can protect us against the united force of European reaction."[21] As diplomatic historian Sir Charles Webster put it unerringly, "by two main agencies – her trade and her fleet", Britain was able to establish a very strong role in Latin American affairs.[22] This was a view fully appreciated by nationalists and revolutionaries seeking to establish states free from the dominance and potential interference of the Old World. There had been many discussions in the British Cabinet over the recognition of the independence of Spanish and Portuguese colonies in Central and South America, and the prevailing wisdom assured that the approach to be taken would be gradualist rather than assertive. In other words, the British would act from a distance, and informally, rather than take a direct line of approach. "I have long thought that the insurgent States must be sooner or later recognized, but in doing it we must be governed by circumstances."[23] So said Canning, and that was the policy adopted. "In promoting such revolutions," John Barrow, the Admiralty secretary, cautioned, "I trust England will never be concerned, being fully convinced that however much South America might gain by a quiet change of masters, she would very soon be thrown back into a state of barbarism by revolutions."[24] Given these occasional volcanic eruptions, the requirement was to undertake commercial treaties that assumed eventual independence: in 1825 they were concluded with Mexico, Buenos Aires and Colombia. By these gentle methods of statecraft, Britain acquired special status, as most favoured nation.

From the eighteenth century, British ships had been using Río de Janeiro as a port of call. The imposing entrance to the great haven, dominated by the Sugar Loaf, Pão de Açúar, always afforded a welcoming sight for mariners approaching after a usually long voyage. As they drew nearer, they spied two three-decker stone forts, one guarding each side of the entrance. Shore and island batteries lay within the entrance. A large citadel and a monastery dominated the town's skyline. This magnificent port, perhaps the best in South America, offered a safe refuge, a good place for refit and repair if necessary, and a beautiful, healthy locale for obtaining drinking water, provisions – especially fresh fruit and meat – and wood. From thence, ships of war would proceed outwardbound for either the Cape of Good Hope or Cape Horn on voyages of discovery, of consular duty or of war, as in the case of the War of 1812. And from Río they would proceed on more specific missions, such as hydrographic surveying or inquiring voyages to Antarctica. By 1771 that port had become the unofficial headquarters for British warships operating in South Atlantic or even Pacific waters.[25] During the old imperial order, British ships of war, even those on voyages of discovery commanded by James Cook or William Robert Broughton, faced pesky bureaucrats ashore and petty rules. The British and the Brazilians were on terms of friendship because the Navy's business there benefited the local economy. Even so, local government officials remained on the defensive – zealous guardians of rights and revenues.

Already, and in 1808, the state of British interests in South America had become sufficiently demanding that the Admiralty had established the "Brazils" or South America station. In consequence of the impending removal of the Portuguese crown from Portugal to some secure spot in Brazil, the requirements to have an adequate British naval presence on the Brazil coast were sufficiently strong that the new arrangements were mandatory. On 25 January 1808, Rear Admiral Sir William Sidney Smith, appointed first commander-in-chief of the squadron to be stationed on the Brazilian coast, received instructions to give "permanent protection" to "the coasts of the Portuguese dominions". The object was to afford security to the Prince Regent's government, and the whole scheme, including preparing a large enough naval armament of eight ships-of-the-line, was done in consequence of the decision and direction of the Cabinet and particularly of George Canning, secretary of state at the Foreign Office. That fleet, which arrived at Río on 17 May 1808, became the basis of the squadron that served permanently on the coasts of South America (and with growing obligations in the South Atlantic and the eastern Pacific).[26]

The establishment of the "Brazils" station was commensurate with diplomatic initiatives. That same year, 1808, Lord Strangford was sent as envoy-extraordinary to the Portuguese Court in Río. There, with its key trade and communications for the South Atlantic, eastern South America, and even trade and communications beyond Cape Horn, gave Strangford an advantageous location from which to communicate with the key cities and provinces of Spanish-held South America. He pursued several sensitive matters with the Brazil government. These included the attempted suppression of the Portuguese-Brazilian slave trade, and the attempted checking of Portuguese aggrandizement on the southwestern frontiers of Brazil, especially in the Banda Oriental, to which a force of military occupation had been sent in 1811. Strangford did not succeed in either mission, and the Republic of Uruguay came into existence in 1828. Throughout, his relations with Brazil's government remained on friendly terms.

The Royal Navy constantly sustained the continuing association of British diplomacy and Portuguese needs on both sides of the Atlantic. British naval help could be formal as well as informal, the latter unauthorized. For example, in the former category, when the Portuguese royal family sailed from the Tagus to Brazil in 1807 so as to escape Napoleon's dominance at home, it was a small British squadron that afforded security to the Portuguese fleet. The royal party duly arrived in March 1808, and Río became the new capital of the Portuguese Empire. Between 1816 and 1822, "Portuguese" forces and "Brazilian" forces fought campaigns in various parts of Brazil for control. The origins and success of the Brazilian fleet got no official support from Britain, but informal help was to hand. By good fortune and inspired improvisation, the Brazilian government created a new national navy. It solved its manpower problems by recruiting officers and men in London and Liverpool, and by bringing in that quirky genius Lord Cochrane it was able to sweep the Portuguese from the seas, force the enemy out of its garrisons, and suppress a difficult revolt. In all, this infant navy was significant in the evolution and continuance of

Brazil's independence.[27] The declaration and establishment of an independent empire of Brazil under Dom Pedro I came on 2 September 1822. For the British it was business as usual afloat and ashore, now securing the independent empire against insurgents who might upset the new order.

Successive British diplomats, including Lord John Ponsonby, advanced cordial relations with the local government. In Río, as in Montevideo, Valparaiso and elsewhere, British policy was peace for the purpose of profit. Thus diplomats such as Strangford, Ponsonby and Woodbine Parish in Buenos Aires, and captains of British warships visiting these ports, sought to maintain strict neutrality. As one captain's instructions ran in 1831, "to give countenance and protection to this extensive commerce and to support the influence of British interests in these countries is the first and indispensable duty of the squadron placed under your command". He was also reminded that the British had £10 million invested in the South American states, and that the civil condition of none of these states was tranquil.[28] Moreover, France, the United States and Portugal also competed strongly for commercial ascendancy in certain South American ports, more especially in the Río de la Plata. The Portuguese had a settlement at Colonia. Montevideo and Buenos Aires vied for primacy in the hide and beef export trades, and they also kept ambitiously watchful eyes on the interior provinces to the north drained by the Paraná-Plata system.

In these tight circumstances, officers commanding British warships had to be careful so as not to be seen as agents of British commercial bullyism. Moreover, they certainly could not take the side of the insurgents and the revolutionaries against the local legitimate government. This was the case even though the Foreign Office might have come to the conclusion that the independence of South American states constituted the preferable course of action if British commercial and political interests were to be sustained and enhanced. To send an armed party from a warship to secure a limited objective ashore afforded a tempting response for any frustrated commanding officer who saw British property and lives at risk. In 1831, for instance, British and French naval commanders combined forces, and landed seamen and marines to protect nationals at Río. The Admiralty denounced the practice as "inexpedient and unsafe", and stated in the clearest language: "Remonstrance with the civil authorities on shore is the duty of the British resident."[29] "It took adroit diplomacy", remarked an admiring Rear Admiral Sir Manley Dixon in praise of Commodore William Bowles on completion of his tour of duty in the Río de la Plata, "for the maintenance of friendly relations with the heads of the contending parties on each bank of the river; a relationship not very easy to maintain without having had a due observance to that system of neutrality, which has been so strongly recommended and so successfully adhered to." Bowes was well aware of the snares. Some years after leaving the station, he wrote to the first lord of the Admiralty complaining that other persons of his rank had been appointed companions of the order of the Bath but he had been overlooked on what was then the Honours List. Believing it to be his duty to bring the lords of the Admiralty details of his 42 years of service, he included these particulars about his subsequent work on the South America station in 1816–1820:

> having been entrusted with the command of a squadron...for the protection of British interests and commerce under circumstances of peculiar difficulty and delicacy, at a period when hostilities were actively carried on between Spain and her Colonies in that country, and when every duty, diplomatic and consular, as well as Naval, devolved upon me, not a single British subject sustained injury, or even serious molestation, within the limits of my command.

He went on to point out that during that time the British Government was never once involved with any dispute or unpleasant discussion with either of the contending parties. Surely, Bowles concluded, these are meritorious contributions deserving of recognition at the national level. He got the attention of the "higher ups", was made a CB and subsequently KCB, and ultimately (because he lived so long) became Admiral of the Fleet.[30] Bowles, a contemporary of the immortal Nelson, was one of the giants of *Pax*, and his intriguing story awaits the attention of a dutiful historian.

Apart from the unauthorized, aborted 1806–1807 expedition of Commodore Sir Home Riggs Popham from the Cape of Good Hope to occupy the Río de la Plata, Britain harboured no territorial designs on South America. Only on the most desperate of occasions would a British naval commander send a landing party ashore to secure a bank's assets, or to dissuade patriots from making a forced levy on British merchants, or protect a customs house against interference. In those rare instances when extreme measures of gunboat diplomacy were employed, the Foreign Office appreciated even more fully the foolishness of intervention. Every time the British attempted armed coercion, they got their hands burnt. Lord Aberdeen learned this to his regret in the Paraná-Plata system of 1845, when seeking to assist Montevideo's independence and to safeguard British trade in the face of "senseless and barbarous" interference from the Argentine leader, General Juan Manuel de Rosas.[31] On this occasion the Anglo-French blockade of the Río de la Plata showed the Navy, like it or not, as the agent of imperial diplomacy. Customarily the Navy's duties were confined to doing what it could effectively do: "to check piracy, protect trade, prevent the abuse of the right of blockade and keep any acquisitive European power from interfering".[32] Naval commanders by mid-century bore instructions to give assistance to consuls ashore, while protection of trade and safeguarding citizens were to be treated as obligations; at the same time, commanders were to avoid entanglement in civil wars, and were on no account to put naval parties too far from the shore.[33] Altogether the Service's task was a demanding one. Yet as long as Britain had command of the sea, real or imagined, during the wars of liberation of Spanish-held South America, Spain had no good chance of reasserting its former authority. Meanwhile, provided that local governments were in agreement, the whole continent lay open to commercial penetration by British and other European traders, and Americans besides.

Southwards and outwards from the home islands lay the course of empire. Safeguarding seaborne trade and promoting the maritime ascendancy of Britain were root causes of British policy to reoccupy the Falkland Islands or Malvinas in 1832 and 1833. These isles of misfortune, barren and lonely in the southern wastes of ocean, had long been claimed by England, and at one time France and Spain had settlers and agents there.[34] In 1820 the United Provinces of South America, otherwise Argentina, established a settlement on a spot that had long since been abandoned by the other powers. This state of affairs continued until 1831, when, in order to protect American sealing vessels from being interfered with, the American corvette, *Lexington*, with Silas Duncan commanding, laid waste to the Argentine residents and entrepreneurs who were engaged in cattle-raising, sealing, and supplying whalers and sealing ships that came for refreshment and repair.

In Buenos Aires the British minister in Argentina, Henry Stephen Fox, watched these developments with growing alarm. Of urbane charm and wit, he possessed tact and courteous manners that were to ease Britain's relations with Argentina at precisely the time when the United States was acerbating an already difficult position. Fox's dispatches to Palmerston reported a constant turmoil in Argentine domestic affairs. Factions quarrelled in Buenos Aires, while in the republic's distant provinces, "senseless, interminable, unintelligible discord" seemed to be the order of the day. There had been a furore in the local press about the *Lexington* business in the Malvinas, and the government had taken every advantage, Fox told Palmerston, to use the incident as a means of distraction from the internal discord which rocked the country. As to the incident, Fox reported to London that irritation and ill humour had been manifested on both the American and Argentine sides. It is one the great ironies of history that the British acted in reassertion in the Falklands to protect their interest against the Americans, not the Argentines. The British subsequently intervened on the grounds that they never had abandoned or lost their claims to sovereignty and that the Argentines were interlopers.[35]

To reassert British influence, the sloop-of-war *Clio*, mounting ten guns and commanded by John James Onslow, was sent from Río "for purposes of exercising the rights of sovereignty there, and of acting at the said Islands as in a possession belonging to the Crown of Great Britain".[36] In December 1832 and January 1833 – summertime in those latitudes – Onslow carried out his responsibilities with cold directness. The captain of the Argentine armed schooner

Sarandí, José Pinedo, was obliged to retire in the face of overwhelming British force, including seamen and marines landed from the British sloop. The Union Jack was run up. Periodically, British warships were sent to inspect and to report. For years thereafter, before a British colony proper was established, Britain's lonely imperial outpost in the South Atlantic was maintained as a "stone frigate" – that is, on the books of the commander-in-chief of South America. Argentina's heated and aggrieved response to British intervention fell on deaf ears: Palmerston at the Foreign Office told the exceedingly unhappy and distressed Argentine minister in London, Manuel Moreno, that not only was Captain Onslow's repossession authorized but that British rights were incontestable.

Palmerston's position, based on legal advice, was that Britain's claims had never been surrendered. The Argentine position was that Spain's claims had never been abandoned and that the occupation of the Malvinas was proof positive of the rightful direction of Argentine policy. Here was born the origin of a subsequent war, in 1982, which would claim the lives of 253 British and 655 Argentines, to say nothing of other casualties and disorders. I cannot resist recounting a personal anecdote of the year 1982. At the time I was working on a history of these isles of misfortune as a natural extension of my research and writing about British activities on wider seas, notably the Pacific, and I sent Mrs Thatcher a copy of my unpublished manuscript: "Britain and the Struggle for the Falkland Islands, 1832–1842". A polite letter in reply arrived from a secretary at Number 10:

> The Prime Minister has asked me to thank you for your letter... The Prime Minister has not yet appointed the Commission of Inquiry to which you refer, though an announcement about this may be made soon. I think it unlikely that the Commission will need to inquire into the early history of the British relationship with the Falkland Islands, but your manuscript will be read with interest here. Thank you very much for letting us see a copy.[37]

In the nineteenth century, too, historical understanding of the Argentine position was equally discounted, though the Foreign Office often pointed out that the British position on sovereignty was not as inviolate as was imagined. On reflection, any thoughts of establishing a naval station in the Falklands did not linger in the minds of British policy-makers, but they wanted to keep others out, and they wanted to safeguard the traffic of merchant ships going to and from wider seas. A company was established to develop British agriculture and fishing there, and, by late in the century, Port Stanley had become important as a coaling station. The introduction of wireless there early in the twentieth century added to its strategic value, and its importance in this regard helped to bring Von Spee's East Asiatic Squadron, then heading home for Germany, to account in December 1914, but not until after the tragedy of Coronel. These remarkable events do not have a place in this narrative except to point out that the geographical location of these windswept and desolate islands proved to be invaluable to the tactical ability of the British to deal with a wide-ranging threat from the enemy. This was an unintended dividend of *Clio*'s actions of 1832–1833 and demonstrated yet again how technological innovation, notably in steam navigation and wireless communication, were changing the flexibility of British naval power. British battle cruisers proved their effectiveness here, in circumstances that were suitable to their design specifications, including speed and armament.

By this time, throughout the nineteenth century and after, on either side of the South American continent, the British had unrestricted access to two great shipping and trading ports – Río and Valparaiso. Although each had disadvantages (exorbitant port duties in the case of the former; perpetual civil war in the latter, besides terrible winds known as "Northers" in November) – these could be endured. Both became station headquarters, the latter in 1837 when the Pacific station was established. Just as Río was the anchor of British naval influence on the eastern flank of South America, so did Valparaiso become that on the western side – but with remarkably wide influence in the eastern Pacific, the islands of the South and Central Pacific and high latitudes of the North Pacific, until such time as Esquimalt became Pacific station headquarters in 1862. Valparaiso never lost its utility to the Navy. For years an old warship, *Nereus*, lay at anchor in Valparaiso harbour, though Chilean governments protested at the existence of this "foreign" floating base and did their best to get rid of it. At Callao, the British kept another veteran vessel, *Naiad*, as a coal hulk. These vessels were well stocked with naval stores, food and drink, medical supplies, coal, spars – indeed, all of the necessities of naval global reach. There were surgeons aboard, and places for the sick and the hurt. In the absence of a shore establishment, these stone frigates served nicely. However, all dockyard work had to be done ashore in foreign yards where British naval rules, regulations and standards did not apply. The British learned from experience not to have storehouses ashore because they were subject to pilfering.

Valparaiso and Callao were the ports where British merchants were most in need of protection. The shipping and banking firms, and the merchants and mining interests, called out for naval protection. Earthquakes, storm damage and fires necessitated humanitarian responses, too. One British warship was always lying in each of the ports as an indication of a necessary response if a shore party were needed to safeguard a trading house or financial interest. In time of insurrection or civil strife, the warship from the other port would come to double the strength, leaving an unfortunate gap in security in the place that had seemingly been abandoned. At Panama and Costa Rica, a British consul would complain of being neglected by the state of affairs in Valparaiso or Callao, and would similarly complain when British warships seemed to pay more attention to freighting silver from Mazatlan and San Blas to the neglect of Central America. From Valparaiso, British warships were sent one at a time to the Pacific Islands, and their tours there were ranked of secondary importance to those of securing British interests in Latin America, where the big gains in trade were being made. International activity could not allow the Pacific Islands to be a backwater for long for British interests. However, during the 1820s, 1830s and early 1840s, Latin American affairs commanded Whitehall's attention.

From the commencement of the Navy's remarkable rise to prominence in the Pacific, unemployed British naval officers, becoming adventurers in distant seas, such as Lord Cochrane, aided the insurgents in throwing off the yoke of Spanish domination. They used Valparaiso as their base. Unlike Bowles, of which little is written, Cochrane and his kind have invited many biographies, some of extraordinarily high calibre (as befits their subject).[38] Cochrane, for instance, arrived at Valparaiso in the British merchant ship *Rose*. His object was to take control of Callao, the Spanish naval base and arsenal. At Valparaiso he took command of the Chilean squadron of seven vessels that he described as "a force, which, though deficient in organization and equipment, was very creditable to the energy of a newly emancipated people". British and American officers and seamen had been recruited, and the squadron sailed for Callao. The Spanish proved difficult to dislodge, and Cochrane turned to easier targets, including Valdivia. Cochrane worked in irregular contact with General San Martín, and eventually the Spanish navy suffered a death blow, according to Captain Basil Hall of HMS *Conway*, who observed the developments. He praised Cochrane's "matchless intrepidity and inexhaustible resources in war" and he noted that after Cochrane's decisive capture of the Spanish frigate *Esmeralda*, "The loss was a death-blow to the Spanish naval force in that quarter of the world; for although there were still two Spanish and some smaller vessels in the Pacific, they never afterwards showed themselves, but left Lord Cochrane undisputed master of the coast."[39] Getting compensation for services rendered was insurmountable to Cochrane, and he turned to other prospects, including those of Brazil. Reinstated into the Navy in 1832, he closed his remarkable life as commander-in-chief on the North America and West Indies station, and was a strong advocate for steam navigation and oil development in Trinidad. The Navy's role in the history of Peru in the early nineteenth century was equally significant, and in 1811 HMS *Standard* reached Callao, becoming the first British man-of-war arriving there without being considered an enemy by local authorities. Ships that subsequently visited the Peruvian coast played a role out of all proportion to their numbers.[40]

From Río and later Valparaiso, Navy vessels visiting the Pacific kept up a precious function for international financial security as freighters of bullion, specie, bank notes and bills of exchange. Gold from Peru and silver from Mexico were the most valuable consignments. The carriage of specie – that is, bullion or coins – by British warships had been authorized for centuries, but by the early nineteenth century it was virtually confined to the west coast of the Americas, especially to Mexico, which boasted half of the world's silver. This little-known function of the Navy is the subject of another contribution to the understanding of the peaceful benefits of *Pax*. Suffice it to say, conveyance of specie, or "freight" as it was customarily called, was authorized by the British Government and controlled by regulation. However, it was theoretically illegal in Mexico after independence in 1821 but carried on nonetheless. The Mexican government (or rather governments, for they were in constant turmoil and change) saw bullion as an export commodity and clamped a 10 per cent export duty on all such shipments. The British Foreign Office advised against this as an impediment to trade and commercial growth, but to no avail. Mexico needed revenue. The duty actually encouraged smuggling on the part of some in the Navy, and horror stories that reached the Admiralty led to strict regulations and promised punishments. Specie shipments favoured the Navy. Admiralty regulations controlled what admirals and ships' captains could receive for the conveyance of freight, specified in percentages. Everyone from the commander-in-chief to the captain and fellow officers, warrant officers and "the ship's paint fund" (which favoured the lower deck), even the Greenwich Hospital for Seamen, received some portion of the gratuity.[41] Admirals benefited the most, and news of Rear Admiral Sir Thomas Hardy's good fortune was the talk of the Navy in 1822. As Sir Thomas Byam Martin at the Navy Board wrote to Commodore Robert Barrie on the Great Lakes, "Hardy is picking up a good deal of freight money in the South Seas, and will no doubt return £20,000 the better for his command, which in time of peace is no bad thing...when you get your flag you must get a good slice of the good loaf."[42]

In an era of intermittent anarchy in Latin American affairs, HM Majesty's ships were a symbol of security to nervous merchants and anxious creditors. The Navy was the Securicor or Wells Fargo of that age. It suffered no "hold-ups" or heists. One British treasure-carrying ship, *Thetis*, was lost off the coast of Brazil. Salvage efforts were wonderfully accomplished and most of the bullion was recovered. On occasion, fraudulent practices occurred (one shipper fooled a naval captain by shipping lead instead of silver); and naval officers were not immune to corruption. By and large, however, the Service carried on the business according to the rules and to its credit. Ships took on "freights" from west coast ports as far north as Guaymas and San Blas, Mexico, and from Panama, Guayaquil, Callao, Valparaiso, Buenos Aires, Montevideo and, of course, Río. The last mentioned was the collection point for periodic shipments to Portsmouth and thence to the Bank of England's vaults. Almost every man-of-war returning from Río upon completion of a three- or four-year commission on the South American station took home a handsome "freight". Of immense mutual economic benefit to Peru and the City of London, to give but one national example of the times, is that from 1814 to 1855 at least 54 British men-of-war were involved in transporting bullion along the west coast of South America, calling at Peruvian ports or rounding Cape Horn bound for Río or directly for Portsmouth.[43] Of these ports, Guaymas, Mazatlan and San Blas were of critical importance, and by the late 1830s, naval captains calling there for the "annual freight" were noting the necessity of having a ship constantly on the coast so as to receive the deposits, and to give confidence and security to commerce. "England being the receptacle of almost all of this treasure," Captain Henry William Bruce advised, "the mode of its conveyance cannot but be of importance to her, and the inference is obvious, that this Mexican coast with its progressively improving state of commerce, demands the serious attention of our Government."[44]

Because the payment of the gratuity to a captain of a British warship on the Pacific station was one of the most sought-after benefits of naval service, obtaining such a command depended on "interest" and influence in high places. The Mediterranean offered much sun but the Pacific offered the chance of money, an Admiralty clerk recorded, and thus appointments to ships destined for waters beyond Cape Horn were much prized. The frigates in particular, he noted, "were commanded almost exclusively by captains who were noblemen or members of noble families: the former station being one of pleasure; the latter more lucrative, as their ships invariably brought home heavy freights".[45]

In the circumstances, the possibilities of gain could take priority over other demands on the station, as the case of Captain the Hon. John Gordon of the frigate *America* discloses. In 1843 the Admiralty directed the commander-in-chief of the Pacific to send a warship to the Northwest Coast in support of British interests in Oregon, where the Hudson's Bay Company was the nominal authority but where American settlers were beginning to make incursions that might threaten British claims to sovereignty that were then undetermined. In 1844 the sloop *Modeste* had shown the flag in the Columbia River, and the next year *America* entered the Strait of Juan de Fuca and Puget Sound for the same purpose. The hunting and fishing expeditions on southern Vancouver Island appealed greatly to the officers once ashore after their long voyage. But Gordon, a proud Scot, said he would not give "an acre of the barren hills of Scotland for all that he saw around him". That the local salmon were caught by bait or by nets and not by the fly as in Scotland apparently scandalized him, as Chief Factor Roderick Finlayson recalled, perhaps in exaggeration. From this the myth arose the tale that the Columbia country was lost to the British Empire "because the salmon would not take the fly". It makes a good story but it is not true. Chief Factor James Douglas (later governor of the colonies of Vancouver

Island and British Columbia) found Gordon apathetic about British interests in this quarter.[46]

Captain Gordon owed his appointment to the fact that his eldest brother was the foreign secretary, Lord Aberdeen, and another was a lord of the Admiralty. Disregarding his instructions to remain on station in support of British interests in Oregon, California and Hawaii, Gordon proceeded to Mazatlan and there took on one of the largest freights ever shipped there. The commander-in-chief, Rear Admiral Seymour, fumed upon learning that one of his two crack frigates had been taken home: "Gordon's ill-judged decision might have turned the fate of war with the U.S. against us." Captain Sir Henry Byam Martin, commanding the frigate *Grampus*, was scandalized that a man of family should disgrace himself for money by this act of sailing for England, without orders. Gordon was court-martialled and the charge was proved. Gordon retired from the Service, taking advantage of the newly instituted retirement scheme. The case attracted widespread interest in Britain and served as a lesson to other British commanders destined for an assignment on the Pacific station.[47] A lieutenant of *America*, commenting on the court martial, wrote in his private journal:

> after due deliberation to the pros and cons, our worthy old Chief was doomed to be reprimanded, as indeed, if a war with the United States had been brought on, he would have deserved to have been shot. Fortunately for him [President] Polk and [Foreign Secretary] Aberdeen made it up somehow.[48]

To correct against such abuses, the rules and regulations were tightened up, and administration "on station" improved. The Navy shifted its attention north when the California gold rush occurred. Regulations against smuggling specie on board Her Majesty's ships remained a problem and invited much investigation and further warnings against the practice. By 1881 the practice of shipping specie on British warships had just about dried up, and the freighting business was carried on in commercial shipping such as the pioneering British firm Pacific Mail Company, which ran steamers to Panama then transshipment by rail to the Caribbean and then to Britain and Europe. Aboard these steamers a Royal Navy officer was posted to guard the shipment, guide against smuggling and provide assurance against piracy, which was always a threat. The United States Navy also got involved in the specie conveyance business. The shipping of freight became big business in the nineteenth century, and not surprisingly the Royal Navy was the largest to undertake the task and to receive the benefits.

South American waters remained vital to British trade and security because on the east coast of the continent lay waters which formed part of the strategically significant South Atlantic corridor, through which substantial volumes of high-value goods passed inwards to the home islands and European ports. The geographical position of Río in relationship to the wider waters of the world had never really diminished. "There is no station that occupies so central and commanding a position as Río," lamented a senior Admiralty clerk in 1892, who hoped that the stations so important in yesteryear might be reinstated. He explained: "cruisers could be dispatched from thence, at a moment's notice, to the Pacific, China and Australia, as well as to the Cape, the east coast of Africa, India, and the Strait Settlements by cable room Whitehall with as much security as dispatch".[49] But economies were driving the redirection of naval deployments on distant stations, and although this same authority might have yearned for a return to yesteryear, when the great port of Brazil was the informal anchor of an informal empire in South America (and on both sides of Cape Horn for a time), the old order of keeping ships "on station" was giving way to the reorganization of naval units. In 1905 the South Atlantic station was closed.[50] The New World had been called into existence by the Old, as has been commonly said, and the role of the Navy in support of, and often in spite of, British diplomacy had been of supreme importance. Readers will be bemused to learn that the Admiralty abolished the South American station at just about the time as the German *Kriegsmarine* established its South Atlantic station.[51]

Throughout this long period that ended in 1914, the quarterdeck diplomacy that enabled *Pax Britannica* to function was greatly to the benefit of the City of London, the shipping sector, insurance firms and manufacturing interests. Hardly a sector of the British economy at home and abroad did not benefit from the hegemony supplied by British warships, officers and men. The merchant marine carried the trades of the ocean, and linked all great ports on all great seas and annexes. The Navy, its protector, was the enabler of British imperialism in formal and informal guises. Places of formal empire, British North America in particular, benefited from British naval pre-eminence. In locations of informal empire, notably Latin America, the benefits were no less influential. In Parliament, debates might arise about the relative merits of formal versus informal empire: why possess colonies in the first place when profits could be made in locations where the costs were minimal? But formal empire could not be given away. The proponents of "little England" were never successful, no matter how strongly they might argue their case.

In 1901 the first lord of the Admiralty, Lord Selborne, minuted that it was on its credit and its navy that the strength of Britain rested, and he noted that these were twin pillars of power. Nothing had really changed from Sir Josiah Child's maxim of three centuries before that in all things, profit and power ought jointly to be considered. In this connection the advancement of the theory of "gentlemanly capitalism" brings us closer to understanding the totality of the imperial achievement and British economic success in the nineteenth and twentieth centuries. It shows how new worlds have replaced old, how the movement of British wealth left the formal empire behind, and how former colonial structures and informal political links were often mere conveniences, designed to serve greater financial ends.[52]

Profit and power went hand in hand. The security of British investments overseas required gunboats and regiments. The technique of influence – the "how to" – rested very much with the lords of the Admiralty, with the commanders-in-chief on foreign stations, and with the commanders of British men-of-war, plus the ships' complements, naval discipline and much else. But the naval obligations, as shown, were often in excess of capabilities, as the Admiralty stressed in its relations to the Cabinet and to Parliament. The Admiralty, or so it thought in the absolute, zealously retained its independence from other government departments, refusing to be an instrument of the Foreign or Colonial offices. It would be a mistake to see the Navy as the tool of the metropolis; that is too narrow a view. Rather, the Navy was at the centre of a web of influence that came from London and the nation more generally. The financial gains from Latin America were large. The investments there were well worthwhile, though the risks were correspondingly high. This, then, is where the Navy features in *Pax Britannica*: it was a means of diminishing risk, affording security to investors and traders, and keeping the peace in the most challenging of circumstances. No legal corporation or enterprise had a better insurer.

6
Challenges of Europe, the Mediterranean and the Black Sea

Throughout the first half-century of that epoch which constitutes *Pax Britannica*, British statesmen always concerned themselves with the rights of independence in the Law of Nations and the international system. They might have moulded that situation to suit their purposes; they might have talked in high fashion of a community of law-abiding nations of Europe; they might, when necessary, have proposed multilateral discussions; and they might even have accepted invitations to the same. But, when placed in a corner, without equivocation, they kept to an independence of action. Truth to tell, they hated having their hands tied. The uniqueness of this had been demonstrated long before by their role in crafting the Peace of Vienna, where they cooperated mightily with the other powers in creating a post-war Europe (including Holland and Belgium and new borders). Castlereagh, however, refused to be a slave to the Congress system. A recent historian stated:

> he made it clear that he had become increasingly alarmed by the "abstractions and sweeping generalities" emanating from the Holy Alliance. In practical terms, the fear of Russian expansionism – rather than France resurgence – was the underlying, if softly spoken, threat to the successful operation of British foreign policy at this stage.[1]

Castlereagh, Canning and especially Palmerston were the architects of *Pax Britannica*, and of this trio, Palmerston was the essence of it. He had in 1807 been a lord of the Admiralty and secretary at war in succession to Castlereagh. His star was in the ascendant when, in 1829, he spoke powerfully about the foreign relations of Britain. In 1832 he became secretary of state for foreign affairs, and he soon took on an aura of authority which some likened agreeably to the spirit of the great Earl of Chatham, who steered the ship of state so successfully during the Seven Years War. He understood the power of public opinion. His views found favour with the often fractious commercial interests. He opposed large standing armies in peacetime because they were bad economy for the state and unnecessary for military matters. At the same time he knew how to use sea power. One historian puts it this way: "Having been at the War Office a score of years, he knew the British army was small, but that it could be used as a sword in the hand of the fleet at certain points such as Constantinople."[2] He had come to the conclusion that Turkey needed to be kept as a European power so as to offset Russian intentions, and he supported Greece against Turkey. To play the role of English mediator between Turkey and Russia was an esteemed contribution of Palmerston. He followed the interests of Portugal and Brazil, and the Spanish position with regard to possible reassertion of power in Mexico (which alarmed him). He urged forbearance towards weak powers, such as Brazil, as the best policy, and to use gentle coercive measures to make the British point. He knew how to make diplomatic friends. There were two kinds of interference, he concluded: "by friendly counsel and advice, or by force of arms", and the former was the British way. If Russia ever got hold of the Ottoman Empire it would be dismembered and partitioned. Thus the integrity of the Ottoman Empire was necessary to the maintenance of the tranquility, the liberty and the balance of power in the rest of Europe, he said in 1833. "England wishes for peace, but is not afraid of war... if we were called upon to take up arms in vindication of our honour, no country in Europe is likely to suffer less from a war than this country." No country was so advantaged as England, he reasoned, owing to the constitution that it enjoyed, the wealth rapidly accumulating and the enterprise of the British people.[3]

Palmerston was fond of saying that England had no natural enemies and no perpetual friends, only "eternal interests". These were three in number, and interlocking: first, maintaining a stronger navy than the likely combination of other powers; second, pursuing the independence of the Low Countries so that no hostile power could control the European shores of the English Channel; and, third, keeping a balance of power in Europe so that no single power could dominate that continent.

No one of the era questioned that the foundation of *Pax Britannica* lay in the ability of British sea power to command the Narrow Seas of western Europe. Thus a resurgent France was never far from the worried British gaze, and the watch was kept on the English Channel, the western flank of France, notably Brest, and the Mediterranean coast, notably Toulon. Fundamentally important Gibraltar and Malta (an acquisition from the recent war and designed to keep the Russians out) gave a commanding position in the central Mediterranean. As the fleet changed to armoured metal steam-driven warships equipped with even more sophisticated weapons, the Admiralty's Works Department had much to do, requiring specialized talents.[4] The hospital and drydock were notable additions of the 1840s, giving the fleet staying power in the central and eastern Mediterranean.

By 1815, Corfu and the Ionian Islands had come under British sway, and for a time the British were drawn into quagmires ashore that ran counter to the customary imperial logic which was to maintain way stations, or hostelries, and to avoid at all costs continental obligations. The eastern Mediterranean was a place of shifting and devious alliances, and into this oriental world the British moved to exert their pressures by floating armed force. Here they watched French ambitions closely. Britain needed ships on distant stations – 10–12 ships of the line for the Mediterranean, the secretary of state for foreign affairs, Palmerston, said in Parliament on 11 March 1839 – for "we have great interests in that part of the world, which require the presence and protection of a powerful naval force". In this case, Britain's line of argument was initially pacific. As Palmerston said, the commerce of Britain was best maintained by peace "because without that, it is vain to hope for a prosperous commerce; and not only must that peace be maintained for England, but also for other countries".[5] And peace, beneficial for trade and commerce, opened up new channels and markets. The material means of security was the Navy. There was no sense in having ships of the line in home ports, said Palmerston, they had to be "on station" so as also to give Russia an indication of British strength and resolve.

Britain aided Greek independence and elsewhere was largely successful in propping up island regimes suitable to its maritime requirements.[6] The whole imperial project in the Mediterranean was based on British diplomacy backed by the British fleet. That having been said, the British were able to obtain allies to provide stability and agreeable conditions to further their foreign policies. The Treaty of London of 1827, realized under Foreign Secretary George Canning's inspiration, created a great power concert for peace. This was a landmark agreement because it called for a force-in-being. Britain, France and Russia became allied with the optimistic aim of gaining Greece autonomy and tributary status under the Ottoman state. The combined peacekeeping force was to guarantee Greek waters, prevent military or naval reinforcements either from Turkey or Egypt, and suppress piracy. That same year the problems escalated. Lord Cochrane, tired of naval service in South American waters, was brought into an adventure to operate a fleet of six steam vessels, for a surgical strike on Turkish shipping at Constantinople. That never happened. Another scheme was soon mounted. The main duties fell upon the British Mediterranean fleet and Admiral Sir Edward Codrington, who would, if he had had his way, have exhibited the power of the West. He put it this way: "One strong act of coercion would place the Porte at our mercy and we would then settle the whole matter as we chose." That was the view from the admiral's cabin. In the event, a combined Egyptian-Turkish fleet sailed from Alexandria and took refuge in Navarino. Codrington then blockaded it. Then he sent in a naval force, which with superior gunnery fought a sharp action, ruinous to the enemy. War had never been declared. The cabinet covered itself by removing Codrington from his post for having allowed the Muslim force to enter Navarino in the first place.[7] It had been a mixed affair, with uncertain consequences save to offer the Greeks a promising form of freedom. That was a signal victory for democratic causes and reflected one aspect of *Pax Britannica*.

Eventually, diplomacy backed by force was employed. Admiral Sir Robert Stopford was sent with a fleet to demand the restoration of Turkish ships, and this ultimatum was delivered to Mehemet Ali. "Everything depends on the energy of our admiral at particular moments," Palmerston told Lord Minto, the first lord of the Admiralty. Minto may have had his doubts. Palmerston, like the French in alliance, was in for a surprise because Stopford was dilatory. Palmerston called the English admiral a "superannuated twaddler". On instructions, Stopford was summarily removed. Sir Charles Napier, previously second in command, became just the man that the foreign secretary needed. This operation, once renewed, was conducted with celerity and vigour, and it led to the occupation of Sidon and Beirut, and to the bombardment of Acre. In consequence, Mehemet Ali was obliged to evacuate Syria, and when he did so a relieved France abandoned its threatening attitude, thus easing tensions among the powers. In this case, as Palmerston argued, paramount sea power effectively displayed had brought untold commercial advantages and kept a European rival at bay. "No British ships at any time ever showed themselves more effective than those which captured Acre," said a delighted Palmerston.[8] Thus closed the crisis of 1840, one in which France had taken an independent policy and one in which British sea power had played a unique role.

With regard to naval expenditures, Palmerston was quick to back them. In 1836, for instance, he had stated that for a country like Britain, the defence of the country and the protection of trade ought not to fall below the strength of naval forces of neighbouring nations. Then world circumstances called for an increase in the present naval force. It was not a hostile measure, Palmerston insisted, but rather a necessary maintenance of peace, upholding the honour of the country, and the protection and extension of its foreign commerce. This enlightened, far-sighted view was not always held by foreign secretaries, but for Palmerston no telescope or binoculars were needed. He kept a narrow eye on the Russian navy, which at that time was increasing its naval armament at Cronstadt. No power could proscribe to another what naval power they could have, of course, but its government could ask questions in diplomatic fashion for what purposes such a force was intended. England had a theoretical right to be alarmed by Russia's build-up. Two years before the Royal Navy had been increased, when the secretary of the Admiralty dwelled on the Russian naval build-up. Britain needed a navy, said Palmerston, of sufficient size and readiness (within a very short period) to defend the nation, "not merely from aggression but even from insult".

Profit and power were the interlocking fixations of the proponents of *Pax*. The channels of British trade had become global by the 1830s. By and large the commerce was with foreign in greater proportion than colonial trade. Thus it was that statesmen concerned themselves with every situation in which a British subject, trading or not, might find themselves in difficulty. Thus a cardinal duty of guardians and practitioners of *Pax* was to protect British and, in certain cases, other European citizens around the world. At first the arguments were narrower, and more simply backed the concept of the British subject. In those days passports were not carried, though a letter of permission or a permit would ease passage through foreign lands. An Islamic leader might issue a *Firman* – a letter of permission to travel or to trade. The extraterritorial rights of a nation hardly existed in a codified way, and there were no general rules laid down about how to extract a hostage who had been taken by another power, or by a bunch of thugs looking for a ransom.

It was easy to define a Briton by their birth and lineage. The extent of the colonial empire spawned the English nationality overseas. A subject born in a garrison or fort in some distant locale obviously qualified for British protection. The dominions, conscious of citizenship status, had no doubt but that their nationals were British and lived happily under the Union Jack, their allegiance to king and country at home never in question. But years of separation and circumstances of war, and the sacrifices made, would blur that credo. Did an Australian fight for empire at Gallipoli or for his own homeland? Did a Canadian really find his country by fighting the German enemy at Vimy, or had that been won long ago against the invading Americans in the War of 1812? Until the Commonwealth Relations Act of 1972 put an end to the principle that a British subject overseas had a right to enter Britain as a member of the Commonwealth of Nations, the essential right was that a British subject overseas was the same as one at home. They were not Europeans then in the sense of citizenship; the East began at Calais. The world at Britain's portals led to other British colonies, or to outposts of empires – those little enclaves of compressed power that were watchtowers on the narrow passages or at the great trading ports of the world. The Royal Navy was the guardian of all this, and if one ship and the ship's company was in peril, so were they all.

Other persons not specifically British wished indeed that they were. And herein lies the conundrum of the celebrated story of being British in the nineteenth century. The Navy was "on call" especially, in Professor C.J. Bartlett's words, in "those parts of the world where respect for a British citizen and his property were not automatic, where conceptions of justice differed from those of western Europe, or were not reinforced with sufficient regularity or thoroughness". The early years of *Pax*, the same authority says, "witnessed a great expansion in duties of the navy, sometimes to the embarrassment of the naval and more purely political objectives of the fleet".[9]

But where did a naval officer stop in the business of rescuing persons ashore who had found themselves inadvertently in difficulty, their personal liberty suspended by what outsiders might regard as a religious fanatic, persons without or beyond the law, or non-state actors? British ambassadors and consuls knew who to talk to and who to bargain with. But when persons "on the outside" of nationality were calling for protection, what were the rules? Did a European in such circumstances trump, say, a Black or a Creole? Did the person worthy of protection have to be a Christian? Was that the defining point? These were some of the puzzles of those practising quarterdeck diplomacy. But Britons and Europeans met the qualification for rescue.

From the earliest years of *Pax*, the British undertook to free European captives, English or other, who for one reason or other found themselves hostages or slaves to non-European, ally or client powers. An early example of this dates from 1816, when the Dey of Algiers refused to abolish slavery. In doing so he insulted Admiral Edward Pellew, Viscount Exmouth, the commander-in-chief on the Mediterranean station. Lord Exmouth possessed unquestionable orders from Whitehall to obtain a satisfactory outcome, by intimation or by actual violence as the circumstances required. The object was to obtain reparation for the massacre of fishermen at Bona, to exact for the future an unconditional abolition of Christian slavery, and to treat Christian captives as prisoners of war. It fell to the admiral to determine the proportionate response. The foe was advantaged by shore position, ably defended, but the bombardment brought results eventually.

After the battle was fully joined and the outcome clearly realized, the British admiral offered terms of peace that were subsequently submitted to the Dey. The Exmouth in Egypt episode provides a microcosm of British policy. Here was the issue: freeing Christian slaves or hostages. This became the *modus operandi* of *Pax Britannica*: if British interests, economic, humanitarian or otherwise, were truly and unequivocally endangered, forces (used either as a threatening instrument or as a last resort) were to be employed to bring the circumstance to a conclusion that was satisfactory to the British. The latter knew the end state required; they set the rules, and they backed their force with their laws and their moral suasion. Their interest in individualism and equality under the law is strangely linked to a moral force and a militant capability which, when once released, is unquenchable. The outcome of the Algerian affair was regarded in Spain, the Netherlands and the Vatican as a Christian rather than an English victory. All the same, Exmouth did not eradicate piracy. Thus, in 1824, once again England had to send a fleet to Algiers to deal with the incorrigible nest of pirates. France solved the problem by annexing Algiers in 1830.[10] This conquest made France a Mediterranean power, and put the country "astride the Mediterranean route to India". The latent concept of that sea as a "French Lake" was revived. By this diplomatic turn, all of a sudden France had re-emerged as Britain's most formidable rival. French adventures here as in the eastern Mediterranean naturally attracted the concern of the Foreign Office and set off alarm bells. Palmerston worried that Mehemet Ali, the viceroy of Egypt, would establish a new state embracing Syria, Egypt and Arabia. Alexandria became a place of French military build-up, and all of a sudden London's concerns mounted: the overland route to Suez was endangered and thus heightened Britain's requirement to keep a larger naval armament in the Mediterranean, and also in the Indian Ocean and its annexes. In addition, the Foreign Office began to court Russia as a counterweight to French designs. These were the background circumstances of the so-called Near Eastern Crisis of 1839–1840.[11]

The Don Pacifico affair was a similar case to the Exmouth in Egypt scenario; it fits the generality. British citizenship, Palmerston said in 1850, had its roots in the Roman pattern. In Romana's time as in Britannia's, the same held true, he said, in words that have become immortal: "As a Roman, in days of old, held himself free from indignity, when he could say *civis Romanus sum*; so also a British subject, in whatever land he might be, shall feel confident that the watchful and strong arm of England will protect him against injustice and wrong."[12]

By this statement, Palmerston had defended his use of the British fleet commanded by Admiral Sir William Parker in establishing a blockade of Piraeus in order to get satisfaction for the claims of two persons – Dr George Finlay and David Pacifico – against the Greek government. In fact, Don Pacifico, as he is sometimes dubbed, was not British. Finlay settled out of court. Pacifico got a portion of his claim from an independent tribunal award.

It is a telling fact, but worth noting here in passing, that Palmerston believed in the efficacy of a naval blockade. And on numerous occasions throughout this period, and after – the Río de la Plata in 1845, Greece in 1850 and Mexico in 1861 – naval force was employed to protect the rights of British and European subjects. Palmerston sent a fleet to re-establish the Queen of Portugal in 1846. He landed troops in Spain to save that country from absolutism. He concluded a convention closing the Bosporus and Dardanelles to ships of all nations in 1841.

> Whenever British subjects are placed in danger, in a situation which is accessible to a British ship of war, thither a British ship of war ought to be and will be ordered, not only to go, but to remain as long as its presence may be required for the protection of British interests.[13]

This was the Palmerstonian dictum and the guide for action in such circumstances. Palmerston was not alone among British statesmen: even that model of British reticence in imperial matters, Gladstone, was not averse to the sending of gunboats or squadrons so as to make the British remit clear. With Lord

Granville, the foreign secretary, he managed a brusque naval threat to compel Turkey to cede Thessaly to Greece. In this instance he was backing Eastern Christians against the Turks.[14] Try as they might to demonstrate how much their views on the use of force differed from those of their political rivals, it is nonetheless true that the use of the Navy as a constabulary, or even the threat of sending a gunboat, squadron or even fleet, was a diplomatic tool that the British used to good effect.

In setting the rules of engagement, Palmerston was prodding the critics and naysayers to action. Many critics came forward to challenge his narrow assumptions. Gladstone, champion of the opponents, had a vision of Europe as a community of Christian peoples possessing equal rights and subject to a code of public law divinely inspired. Gladstone attacked Palmerston's arrogant claim about British rights in the Don Pacifico affair. The British should not be privileged, said Gladstone, and further, there were no privileged castes or nations in contemporary Europe. This was his proclamation. All men and all nations were subject to the same rule of law, and, if any distinctions were to be allowed, they should be associated with the respect due to feeble nations and to the infancy of free institutions. Sir Robert Peel, sometime prime minister, said that Palmerston's policy was not consistent with the dignity and honour of England. Like Gladstone, he held that law and the rule of nations enabling a state of peace to flourish offered the best means of according a good name to Britain in Europe.[15] In these circumstances, Britain was to be a moral force in Europe, and it stood to reason that it would be a moral force everywhere the British flag flew and everywhere a British consul, gunboat or garrison was situated. At least that was the intention, from which practice frequently departed.

Around the rim of the eastern Mediterranean, insurgent forces, and sometimes revolutionary movements, were posing challenges to the old order. This corridor to India had a value of immense significance in British thinking. The security of the Mediterranean, the stability of the Ottoman Empire, the equipoise of Egypt and the control overland to the Red Sea and Arabian Gulf all formed part of an interlocking strategy. And, not least, Russia had to be kept from upsetting the stability of the Ottoman Empire. For this reason, Britain backed the Ottoman Empire for much of the century until such time as new opportunities were taking Constantinople out of the old orbit and old assumptions, and on this change came the reordering of the world, a story for another time, though many have heard of Gallipoli and the Dardanelles already. And in the Indian Ocean and its littorals, British domination there continued to act as a strategic buffer against possible Russian expansion.

Always watched narrowly was Russia. Its continental expansion east and south belied its essentially European character in the community of nations. The Crimean War checked Russian ambitions for two generations. Britain and France, using unparalleled naval forces, sent warships and transports into the

Black Sea. "The command of the sea held by the allied powers was so complete and all-pervading," wrote Admiral Sir Cyprian Bridge, a onetime Director of Naval Intelligence,

> that no one stopped to think what the course of hostilities would have been without it... Not a single allied soldier had been delayed on passage by the hostile fleet; not a single merchant vessel belonging to the allies had been captured by a hostile cruiser. Supplies and reinforcements for the besieging armies were transported to them without escort and with as little risk of interruption as if the operations had been those of profound peace.[16]

At the same time, the Russian state held the Caucasus in fee, stretched out, octopus-like, to the North West frontier, hard against the claims of the East India Company, and grasped even distant Siberia. Kamchatka came under Russia's control, but China was mindful of these encroachments and in 1648 had signed a limiting treaty on Russia's southward progress, making Kiatka a border town and a place of trade. That system existed well into the nineteenth century, and until the collapse of the Celestial Empire. Meanwhile, Britain and China were natural allies against Russian ambitions. It suited such allies to back British policy-makers to keep China strong, although trading with Britain. All the while it was a game of stealth, with agents and travellers working out the destiny of such last toeholds of empire in highest Asia as Lhasa. "The Great Game" was being played out for the control of Tibet and the high mountains and valleys of central Asia. It was in these continental circumstances that British power faced its most intractable difficulties. The British watched the Russian advance towards Persia, Afghanistan and northwestern India with alarm. Afghanistan, covering the best passes into India, served as a buffer state. To keep it out of Russian influence became the announced policy of Whitehall. But a more forward policy developed, despite lessons of 1839 on the difficulties of such an enterprise. So when Russian forces crossed the frontier, the British sent three columns into Afghanistan. The British occupied Kabul and Kandahar, and in the desultory action that followed, peace was eventually restored, the claimant to the Afghan throne, Abdurrahaman, took control, and determined to exclude both the Russians and the British. This was done, and it satisfied British ambitions.

Russian activities towards Afghanistan heightened London's fears of interference with the border tribes of the North-West Frontier. This obliged the British to mount a preventive campaign, otherwise known as the First Anglo-Afghan War of 1839–1842, but with disastrous consequences to British arms. The Second Anglo-Afghan War followed. Thus, by force of arms, the British maintained a peace in the Punjab and on the North-West Frontier against hostile tribes and Russian intrigues. The battles, small affairs mostly, seemed to range over every rock and hill. The human costs were staggering. When viceroy, Curzon, seeking a remedy, devised a strategy to let the mountain tribes govern themselves. This, it was assumed, would allow the British to withdraw forces from advance positions, leaving tribal militias, commanded by Europeans, to keep the peace. It was an idealized solution. On the spot, however, there was a more realistic view. In the opinion of Sir Evelyn Howell, the British resident in Waziristan, the withdrawal policy was merely "setting the poacher to act as gamekeeper".[17]

Turkestan, Afghanistan, Transcaspia, Persia – these names and others speak to many only as "a sense of utter remoteness or a memory of strange vicissitudes and of moribund romance". So wrote that unrepentant imperialist Curzon in 1892, a date near the end of the closure of our era. And to the British reader those spots on the earth's surface and others nearby were indeed the places of antiquarian romance. But to Curzon, sounding the alarm, they were pieces on a chessboard on which was being played out a game for the dominion of the world. He took a swipe at those advocates of British power who saw matters only in terms of blue-water dominance – of ships, sailors and bases that girdled the globe. His countermeasure to all of this was "The Great Game", and then as now it has its advocates and its disciples. Curzon put it this way:

> The future of Great Britain, according to this view, will be decided, not in Europe, not even upon the seas and oceans which are swept by her flag, or in the Greater Britain that has been called into existence by her offspring, but in the continent whence our emigrant stock first came, and to which as conquerors their descendants have returned. Without India the British Empire could not exist.[18]

That the possession of India was the inalienable badge of sovereignty in the East was never in question. British India was the jewel in the crown, and the key to the control of the Indian subcontinent, its water approaches and offshore islands, and its adjacent seas. It was the point of fixation of those concerning themselves with imperial defence. Closely argued treatises on the defence of empire written in the 1890s are full of the soldier's logic that resulted in one essential mandate of policy – that the Khyber Pass must be guarded and the possible approach of the enemy kept constantly in mind.[19] It was a world of spies and agents, of payoffs and kickbacks. The reforming mind of the Englishman might think that no deficiency existed to the immense possibilities of reform in this vast area that included Persia and Afghanistan. But as one authority put it unerringly, "Intrigue, however, is rampant, prejudices are powerful, fanaticism is not extinct, and both Shah and Ministers are caught in the meshes of a system which is characterized by many ingrained vices."[20] How do you fabricate peace in such societal circumstances? Power was the thing to be obtained, and then controlled. The loyalty of tribes was the object of the imperialists.

Here the frontiers were amorphous, and behind every escarpment seemed to crouch a new enemy. The logic of those defining the defences of northwestern India expressed the continental view, just like Curzon, and against this hard-headed logic the blue-water advocates countered with their own. Only when Admiral Mahan vaulted onto the pages of history with his *Influence of Sea Power Upon History* did the Navy have a propagandist. We leave Mahan now but come back to him, as indeed we must, at a later time at the crisis point of *Pax Britannica*. It is fascinating to read Curzon, Mahan's near contemporary, on how the intractable tribes of Central Asia might be brought forward, or "civilized", and we note his insistence that by virtue of the fact that indigenous armies could not be relied on, given tribal strife and internecine rivalry, the ultimate remedy would consist of better communications – postage, roads and bridges, railways and canals, and other means that would induce better administrative practices and centrality of power and influence. Curzon was aware of the immense difficulties of governing such an imponderable land, well beyond the pale of British control, and perhaps his viewpoint reflects that vague hope, never realized, that the benefits of British administration would be revealed in those mountain passes, wastes and deserts that are the characteristic features of Afghanistan.

But there was another scenario that elicited a British response, for the Russians could also come by sea. Since the beginning of Russian sea power, a development credited to Peter the Great, a brown-water strategy had been pursued in St. Petersburg with a preliminary view to gaining full control of rivers (and river boundaries) and estuaries. This was the natural intent of a continental power. Ice-choked river mouths and estuaries were the first objects of Russian sea power control because Russian trade was a hostage to icebound ports. The Black Sea, and the Baltic and Siberian ports all faced this. Thus there existed in Russian statecraft a strong quest for warm-water ports. No greater prize presented itself (i.e. before the Trans Siberian Railway was completed in 1891).

British policy aimed at denying Russian access to the Mediterranean and to deny the Russians the use of the Dardanelles waterway leaving from the Sea of Marmora, past Constantinople and to the eastern Mediterranean. Admiral Sir John Duckworth sailed a fleet through the Dardanelles to Constantinople in 1807, and Admiral Sir Geoffrey Phipps Hornby did the same in 1878. Their effects were rarely of a lasting nature, but the big and compelling moment of this time was what is called the Crimean War. In March 1854, Britain and France entered the war to protect the British corridor to India and the Far East and French spheres of influence in the Near East. The allied navies clashed with the Russian enemy at four locations – the Black Sea, where the Crimea became the major battleground; the Baltic Sea; the White Sea; and the North Pacific Ocean. Its effects showed that Britain would present a powerful force (and bring in an ally – in this case France) in order to block Russian aspirations to the blue Mediterranean sea.

Britain showed its global reach against the continental power of Russia as well as its flexible response by using the China and Pacific stations in combination against the Russians in Kamchatka at Petropavlovsk and also at the mouth of the River Amur in search of elusive Russian vessels (where they found that the Russians had gone to ground, so to speak). The allies landed 700 at Petropavlovsk in 1854, and a heavy cost was paid for poor reconnaissance, faulty planning and bad execution. That the British commander-in-chief, David Price (who is mentioned elsewhere, at page 26) was not up to the task and killed himself was an undoubted factor, but the matter was deeper than that. When the account of the operation reached London, their lordships voiced their displeasure, informing Price's successor that the defeat was

> of a nature which ought to impress upon the officers of H.M. Ships that the utmost discretion is necessary in undertaking expeditions on shore and detaching Seamen and Marines from their ships in the neighborhood of fortified positions of the Enemy, with imperfect knowledge of the Nature of the Country and the force expected to be encountered.[21]

The reprimand failed to recognize the shortage of steam-assisted vessels in the action, and the British and French ships were disadvantaged by lack of mobility. The landing parties had been sent ashore out of necessity, for ships' guns could not be brought to bear. Distant echoes of war were heard on the Northwest Coast of North America, and hospital huts were built at Esquimalt on Vancouver Island in readiness to receive any injured from an intended assault on Petropavlovsk, Kamchatka in 1855. The event did not occur but nonetheless gave strategic value to Vancouver Island and Canada's eventual gateway to the Pacific.

Here, then, was a bold exercise in exerting power during *Pax*. There were many aspects displayed by it. Cooperation with the French had yielded results. The allies wanted to keep the Ottoman Empire strong as a bulwark to Russian ambitions. Their maritime ascendancy demonstrated but could not command what happened on shore any farther than the range of a ship's gun, the energy and stamina of a shore party hauling an artillery fieldpiece, or a gunboat sent upriver on patrol (a dangerous manoeuvre). In short, here was a classic case of a difference in continental compared with maritime strategy. New railways made more effective, and more rapid, the movement of forces, munitions and supplies to distant margins of the empire, and allowed the building of new naval bases. The long arm of British naval reach was a potent force, and one able to pursue the parameters of *Pax*. The eastern Mediterranean remained a problem for the Admiralty, necessarily involving the War Office, particularly in the unwanted scenario of Russia landing forces to take Constantinople from the Black Sea. The British fear was that Russia would seize the Straits and mount a blue-water presence in the Mediterranean, a frightful scenario if made in alliance with France. The Admiralty assumption, backed by plans, was that France's navy based on Toulon could be dealt with in any emergency save a combination of France and Russia.[22]

Put differently, once continental powers – first Russia, then Germany – went "blue water", the old assumptions had to be set aside. The British with suspicion watched the growth of Russian sea power in the late nineteenth century. The telegraph, railway, submarine cables and wireless revolutionized speed of deployment and made instant the preparations for war.

Although Britain was often in the lead in these inventions, their existence, in the hands of old, resurgent enemies and new, ambitious rivals, subverted British authority. There was nothing it could do about it, but it watched the unfolding scenario with increasing alarm. In the circumstances, the British rightly placed great stress on keeping the Persian Gulf from falling into dangerous hands. Curzon, when viceroy, appeared there in the winter of 1903, escorted by the East India Squadron. This broad showing of the flag corroborated the recent statement of Lord Lansdowne in the House of Lords: "I say it without hesitation, we should regard the establishment of a naval base or of a fortified port in the Persian Gulf by any other power as a very grave menace to British interests, and we should certainly resist it with all the means at our disposal." This was accompanied by the sending of trade missions to southeast Persia, the founding of new consulates, and the fostering and support of British commerce. By these means, in the words of Sir Percy Sykes, soldier, scholar and traveller, "British prestige gradually recovered, until the results of the Russo-Japanese struggle modified the policy of Russia in the direction of an understanding with Great Britain."[23]

7
The Indian Ocean, Singapore and the China Seas

From the days of Francis Drake and Thomas Cavendish, the British had been pressing their advantages in the eastern seas, drawn to the spice trade. They did so against great odds. Not only did indigenous rulers, pirates and states pose obstacles, but the pioneer maritime powers of Europe – Portugal, Holland and Spain – seemed always ahead of them. Yet on these distant margins of Europe's influence, the British made significant inroads, one piece at a time. They used their armed military might to do so. It came in two forms: first, the East India Company, with its army and its navy, known as the "Bombay Marine"; and second, the Royal Navy and such units of the British Army as were required from time to time to make the point that Britain was not beholden to any other power, and that the commercial interests of the home islands and overseas places of trade and production had to have equal advantages to those of Britain's rivals. By the time the British had opened China's gates by the end of the first war there, in 1841–1842, they had projected their maritime and amphibious power in a way hitherto undreamed of. As the governor of Hong Kong, Sir John Davis, remarked, the British campaign was "the farthest military enterprise, of the same extent, in the history of the world, surpassing, in that respect, the expeditions of Alexander and Caesar in one hemisphere, and those of Cortes and Pizarro in the other".[1] All of that lay ahead, and the progression came in various stages, all determinants of sea power.

The river of European commerce flowed throughout all of these distant islands. The commercial requirements of British merchants knew no bounds in the late eighteenth century, on into the early nineteenth and after. The power of the City of London, of the shipping interests, of Lloyd's of London and of the East India Company, which pursued its own form of what Vincent Harlow called "the swing to the east",[2] pressed outwards past the Cape of Good Hope, made its ways through the Eastern Archipelago, swept on to China and moved north to Japan. Ultimately it embraced the Pacific Ocean and extended across to Canada and the United States, thereby becoming global. And when steamship lines, cables and then wireless completed the all-red route of British technology and commercial enterprise, the global achievement had been won. But in the early days there was much frustration and many obstacles. From Suez to Aden; beyond to Bombay, Calcutta and Trincomalee; outwards yet again to Singapore; east to Borneo or more prominently north to Hong Kong, the South China Sea; and farther north still to Korea and to Japan, the web of British trade and shipping was extending itself in fits and starts. The whole grand progression when taken altogether, and completed by century's end, seems like one long extension of an arc of British influence along the littoral regions, stretching from Arabia to Japan, but the progression was one of degrees.

At the southern end of the Malay Peninsula stands Singapore, and the wonder of the place was always that it commanded the shortest route between Europe and China. The British had stumbled on it by default almost, for everywhere in these seas the Dutch had stood in their way since the seventeenth century. In the days of sail, shipping had to make the great circuit round the Cape of Good Hope, then head for China via one of two routes – through the Straits of Malacca or the Straits of Sunda. Singapore lay on the short route from Trincomalee or any Indian port, a saving of at least 1,000 miles. When the Suez Canal was cut, the whole stream of European shipping took the short route. Herein lay its magic and its blessing. The coming of steam navigation favoured its progress and gave it an enhanced future.

In addition, Singapore possesses a grand roadstead, and if you were to gaze at it nowadays you would see not a forest of masts but a collection of great ships of the 80,000 ton variety, best seen at night when the twinkling of lights illuminates the vast harbour while the work of container shipping and reshipping goes on without rest. Not only was the Singapore roadstead sheltered but it had fine features of a natural sort between its own coast and the adjacent islands.

To Stanford Raffles, that strange force of *Pax* – ambitious, restless and shy, and an outsider to the affairs of the East India Company, which dominated these seas – Singapore offered many blessings. He would have preferred other locales, but always the Dutch had stood in his way. The Dutch had secured the undisputed mastery of the Eastern Archipelago. A Dutch cruiser was sure to follow any foreign merchantman deviating from the regular China route. Speaking of the Dutch, Raffles wrote to George Canning, then president of the Board of Control: "They are deeply impressed with the recollection of their ancient maritime and commercial grandeur, and would favour any other nation, especially the Americans, to our prejudice." At the time when he wrote, Dutch commercial animosity against British trade was never greater, he said.[3] Raffles never contended that the British should oust the Dutch everywhere, for the task would be as unnecessary as it would be impossible to effect, but he did not discount the requirement that circumstances would lead the British to a more forward view.

In its eastwards progression, the company first concentrated on steamy Penang, an island on the western coast of the Malay Peninsula, but it was an inadequate place quite unfortified, and the Duke of Wellington there in 1796 on inspection reported: "one hostile frigate could insult it".[4] It was now or never, and he regarded Singapore as his last chance of wealth and fortune. "Singapore", he wrote home, "is everything we could desire... With this station alone I would undertake to counteract all the plans of [the Dutch rival] Mynheer; it breaks the spell; and they are not longer the exclusive sovereigns of the Eastern Seas." He regarded it as a child of his own, and had he not studied the Malay people, language and society (for he moved easily among them), he should not have known that such a place existed. Neither the European world nor the Indian had known of it. "What Malta is in the West, that may Singapore become in the East," he forecast unerringly. "It bids fair to be the next port to Calcutta; all we want now is the certainty of permanent possession."[5]

Raffles had been born at sea, in a West Indiaman skippered by his father. He knew all about the plantation trades and slavery, and, counter to those times, he became an early champion of anti-slavery agitation. He entered the East India Company as a clerk at the age of 14. A decade later the shift in world affairs obliged the Board of Control to take measures to strengthen the company's China trade route. Raffles had always thought in naval terms, and he was always searching out possible bases as a means of gathering wealth and projecting power. The Admiralty had given up on the idea of establishing a naval station at Penang, partly as an economy measure and partly to placate the Dutch. Raffles passed by Singapore first in 1811, and it was a swampy, thinly populated island belonging to the sultanate of Jahore. He thought that Singapore could be a central pivot of power. When he first arrived in Singapore he was there on sufferance, for British tenure was uncertain. Acting as a free agent, he often found himself in difficulties with the Board of Control. Nonetheless, by 1826, it had concluded, on the whole, that he was right. All the same, like many another servant of the imperial purpose, his achievements were not fully recognized in his time.

At Singapore, Raffles saw himself as a liberal progressive, a force for good, and what we might amiably call the personification of *Pax*. A new world seemed to open up before him, and he regarded it as his opportunity to embrace more than just commerce and fiscal gain, though that was undoubtedly a point of fixation. He saw in agriculture a way of promoting local wealth and opportunity for the locals. He entertained the local chiefs, explained his new ideas and advanced his own regulations. "There is no radical defect in the character of the common people," he told the directors of the East India Company. "They are alive to the same incentives, have the same feelings, and... would as rapidly advance in civilization as their fellow men, once relieved from the oppression and disabilities under which they labour." He was fighting native feudalism, and so decided to take the more powerful position. "I have assumed", he wrote in 1820 with a touch of feudal remembrance,

> a new character among them, that of Lord Paramount; the chiefs are my barons bold, and the people their vassals. Under this constitution and by the establishment of a right of property in the soil, I am enabled to do wonders; and, if time is only given to persevere in the same course for a few years, I think I shall be able to lay the foundation of a new order of things.

To remove the natives' disabilities was the hardest task, and the slowest. He began with educational institutions, secular and spiritual. Free schools were opened for native children. He sought to encourage instruction in "the useful arts". Missionaries were invited and a Bible society was founded. "I am far from opposing missionaries," he wrote to William Wilberforce, "and the more that come out, the better; but let them be enlightened men, and placed in connexion with the schools, and under due control." He liked the missionaries who arrived, scholars and gentlemen. "Their wives are well calculated to aid their endeavours," but he feared that "they are hardly prepared for the difficulties and privations of missionary life in such a barbarous country as this."[6] He encouraged printing. He sought out the possibility of a college being founded there, with these Eastern Islands forming a branch of the African Institution, an anti-slavery society. He founded the Singapore Institute, intended as a force for spreading education throughout the Malay world. This had formed the brightest thread in his imperial ideal. "Thus", he wrote,

> will all our stations become not only the centres of commerce and its luxuries but of refinement and the liberal arts. If commerce brings wealth to our shores, it is the spirit of literature and philanthropy that teaches us how to employ it for the noblest purposes. It is this that has made Britain go forth among the nations, strong in her native might, to dispense blessings to all around her. If the time shall come when her Empire shall have passed away, those monuments of her virtue will endure when her triumphs have become an empty name. Let it still be the boast of Britain to write her name in characters of light.[7]

He hoped that the British would leave this message for posterity.

Singapore's population in Raffles' time consisted of European merchants, Chinese traders, shopkeepers and coolies, seafaring Arabs, Malays of all sorts from the archipelago, and natives of the soil. He appointed 12 of the leading British merchants as magistrates, and he did so in order that European merchants might not be disadvantaged in the domestic regulation of the settlement. Control the appointments and control the lawmaking, ran his reasoning. Trial by jury was instituted, and the general principles of British law were to be applied to all, without distinction of tribe or nation. Merchant-magistrates, meanwhile, were to initiate regulations of trade. Native headmen were appointed to exercise authority over the native population. He gained revenue other than by trade. He established Singapore on the primary condition of its future prosperity. He declared it a free port, with trade thereof open to ships and vessels of every nation, free of duty, equally and alike to all. It was a masterstroke of policy. "In his actions in Java and at Singapore," writes George Woodcock,

> we see Raffles anticipating the two main directions which British administration was to take during the century of imperial power in Malaya and the China Seas, the creation of a territorial empire largely based on the protection of "independent" local rulers and the parallel creation of a commercial empire based on a freedom of trade in which, thanks to their early start on the industrial revolution, the British would be in a competitively favourable position.[8]

Singapore quickly became the heart of British interests in the Eastern Archipelago. From a little settlement of 5,000 in 1819, it had doubled in population by 1824. In 1826, Penang, Malacca and Singapore were united in the Straits Settlements, under the Government of India. Singapore grew quickly: in 1835 the population stood at 30,000 and by 1860 it was 80,000. Trade had expanded similarly, and whereas in 1840 the exports and imports were valued at £4 million, in 1867 they had reached a value of £10 million, and this was merely the beginning. By an act of Parliament as Singapore – not the Straits Settlements – was constituted a separate government under the authority of the Colonial Office. The old days of East India Company dominance had come to an end. The local government had had a choice in this matter, for there was well-voiced complaint, in the form of a petition to the House of Commons in 1858, of the ignorance expressed at how greatly the Straits Settlements differed from continental India: "the supreme government has almost invariably treated them from an exclusively Indian point of view, and shown a systematic disregard of the wants and wishes of their inhabitants".[9]

By the early twentieth century, Singapore had become one of the greatest ports in the world. In 1924, according to an estimate, its tonnage of shipping "entered and cleared" was almost 22 million tons. Its population was then nearly a 0.5 million. It had outstripped Penang and Malacca. It had become a link in British sea power. "Statesmen may make what use of it they will," wrote one authority, "but it is what Raffles saw it must be, what geography had made it, the Malta of the East."[10] As for Raffles, he was wracked with headaches, and he shipped early for home with antiquities, curiosities and books gathered from the Malay Peninsula. Reaching London, he was feted in a world that he could barely understand, for his fame had preceded him. He was elected president of the Zoological Association, which founded a zoo at Regent's Park, a counterpart to one that he had founded in Singapore. He turned to farming for a while, seeking the repose of the land near Mill Hill, but he died of apoplexy at the age of 45, and was buried in Hendon parish church, though a statue of him stands in Westminster Abbey and a bust at the Lion House at the zoo. However, Singapore is his true memorial, important in and of itself, but a key station of British might and power in eastern seas in those days when British shipping was still predominant.

The rise of this fulcrum of British trade, commerce and mercantile technique had to be achieved against the great Dutch rival. Relief had come with a friendly bargain struck between Britain and Holland, which resolved the nagging difficulties. And by treaty in 1824, Britain retained Singapore but surrendered Bencoolen and all claims in Sumatra. The Dutch gave up Malacca, and while they retained control over the nearby islands and were free to expand and tighten their control over the archipelago, the British had this benefit: they could fall back on continental Malaya and gain the command of the Malacca gate. The British maintained a policy of non-intervention wherever they could. However, administrators in the Malay states were spectators to growing disorder. Turbulent frontiers were worrisome and needed checking. Feuds among Malay chiefs and problems with mass invasion of Chinese miners in the tin areas of the mountainous interior were sources of intractable problems; concurrently, piracy on the Perak coast and clan fights in the Straits of Penang were other matters of turbulence and discord. Solving a pesky problem with the Dutch in a nearby frontier, the British turned to a policy of intervention to protect Perak. Chinese tin miners had come into the state of Perak, and strife between Malays and Chinese, and fights among the Chinese tongs, were the reason the sultan requested the British intervention. There were dynastic problems. The imperial real estate grew. War in Lower Burma led to the annexation of territory; new influence was acquired in Ava, Bangkok and some Malay states. With a nod to future difficulties, the far-seeing Governor Cavanagh in 1863 wrote to his superiors in Calcutta:

> It may be a matter for consideration whether from our position as the paramount power, as well as with reference to the engagements into which we have entered with several of the surrounding states, we have not already in great measure incurred responsibilities which it might be difficult to throw off.[11]

Historians have puzzled over the customary extension of British interests in Southeast Asia, formal as well as informal. Was the guiding rule peace for the purpose of profit? Commercial and strategic reasons predominate in the analysis, with due weight being given to French and German rivalry. Promotion and protection of trade went hand in hand. The Navy did its job. Anti-piracy was routine work. The fervent love of order brought the flag to places of need. British control in the region was linked to this dual requirement. Colonial power secured colonial trade. Fear of foreign intervention or expansion played a customary part in individual cases of expansion. London eyed economic advantages for trade and shipping. And so trade followed the flag and the flag followed trade.[12]

In any event, with Singapore in British hands, that nation was now inside the gate, as it were, with no further barriers to be passed. The prospects lying before the British were glorious. As the eastern gate of India, Singapore became not merely "the next port to Calcutta", as Raffles had imagined. Relatively close to Canton and other Chinese ports, Singapore in British hands now gave the East India Company a mighty advantage in pressing forward the trade to these eastern seas. And being inside the gate, so to speak, meant that that vast island world lying south of the South China Sea became a new focus of British concern for peace and profit. We take the China scenario first, and then revert to the vast island world, reminding ourselves as we do so that these frontiers of influence were concurrent though remarkably different. Once again the Navy was "on station".

Northwards from Singapore lay the China Sea, with its fabled golden prospects. For the previous half-century, "country traders" connected to the East India Company had worked the coast eastwards from the ports of India. They did so mainly in their powerful East Indiamen – well-armed ships of 400 to 800 tons – which the Navy liked to think of as a reserve of shipping in time of need (which indeed was employed periodically). These were independent merchants and mercantile houses that worked within the protection of the charter of the East India Company. They were the means of extending company power beyond formal places of its influence, China being the main target. The company had a growing interest in China, seeking to take out teas in season, and the sale of opium – "foreign mud" the Chinese called it – was the means of opening the gates of commerce to the Celestial Empire. Chinese rules and regulations demanded that payment for teas, porcelains and silks was made in currency, or, as they called it, "cash". The first British maritime fur traders, based on Madras and freighting sea otter pelts from Nootka Sound, Vancouver Island, or Alaska via the Hawaiian Islands, had brought a new form of exchange.[13] Dark and luminous, soft to touch, the sea otter pelt became the ermine of Asia. American traders had the advantage over the British because they did not have to live by the restrictions on British shipping placed by the East India Company and the South Sea Company, which controlled the licensing of British ships between the two great capes. British traders were disadvantaged, therefore, and by the 1820s the trade was fully in American hands. But it did not last, for the sea otter was hunted almost to extinction. Whalers were pressing their searches to the northwest Pacific at this time, and the Japanese islands and the Kamchatka shore became more commonly visited. Still the Japanese Empire was closed to foreign traffic, and bravely resisted any and all Russian attempts, as those of other nations, to breach the protective barrier that surrounded it.

The East India Company remained at the centre of this expansion to China. With resources at home and abroad, all connected with entangling relationships, the company was not only the focal point of Britain's imperial expansion east of Suez and beyond the Cape of Good Hope but it also "forged some of the domestic connections that existed between different elements of Britain's financial, imperial and military power".[14] Dundas at the Board of Control fought valiantly to oblige the East India Company to release its monopoly on British trade in China, and succeeded only by degrees. Vested interests and monopolies with ancient lineage stood in the way. The old South Sea Company held the licensing of commercial shipping between the two great capes. That was ended, as was the East India Company's monopoly of the China trade, by revocation in 1833. Free traders had triumphed once more. Independent traders now joined the older country traders in demanding that the Chinese relax their restrictions on commerce.

Hong Kong differed from Singapore: whereas the Malays, Chinese, Dyaks and others were competing in Singapore, with the Dutch always waiting in the predatory wings, China was a land of warlords and ethnically homogeneous near the coasts. "From time immemorial," wrote the reform-minded editor of the *Chinese Repository* headquartered in Canton, in May 1837, "the Chinese have stood alone. They have been, and still are, an isolated people. This, doubtless, has resulted in part from their own choice, and in part from circumstances more or less beyond their control."[15] Another view comes from the perspicacious Lord Macartney:

> The empire of China is an old, crazy, first rate man-of-war, which a succession of able and vigilant officers has contrived to keep afloat these one hundred and fifty years past, and to overawe their neighbours by her bulk and appearance, but whenever an insufficient man happens to have command upon deck, adieu to the discipline and safety of the ship. She may perhaps not sink outright; she may drift some time as a wreck. And will then be dashed to pieces on the shore; but she can never be rebuilt on the old bottom.[16]

The Chinese countered by trying to suppress the opium traffic, but to no avail. Ships of the Royal Navy were unwelcome visitors along the Manchu's coast. But the East India Company's Select Committee at Canton kept up urgent demands for adequate protection. The Hong merchants became the means of communication between the British and imperial governments. Canton became the opening door. By 1839 a British frigate was always to be found in the waters leading to Canton.

Portugal had been the first foreign empire in the Far East, and at Macao, adjacent to Hong Kong, it had set up a vital entrepôt, for the provisioning and repair of shipping but, more, as a means by which intermittent trade could be carried on into the Pearl River, Canton (Guangzhou). The East India Company, seeing the advantage of Lark's Bay, Macao, as a place for smuggling or, more correctly, trading with the Celestial Empire by special arrangement, anchored two old vessels, laced side by side, to form a storehouse for opium brought from India. The Chinese authorities would allow foreign powers to build factories adjacent to the Strand at Canton, but foreigners, the *Fan Qwai* ("foreign devils"), could only remain during a specified annual trading season. Otherwise they must depart.

The so-called "Opium Wars"[17] followed, from 1840 to 1842, and the issue was really about free trade access and commercial security from the British point of view, one shared with the French, Americans and others. The connection of the British and the Navy with Hong Kong seems to have been a matter of unintended escalation. At first, as Palmerston realized, the opening of trade was entirely a Chinese matter (as his instructions to the British plenipotentiary Sir Henry Pottinger indicate): the British would not presume to rule in China's place. But there were indignities, oppressions, injustices, protests, objections and obfuscations, and British traders complained of ill treatment. They traded principally in opium but the commodity was not the burning issue, only freedom of trade. They wanted legitimate trade, and this the British Government could back and indeed was obliged to back given the spirit of the age.

The British had no intention of establishing a continental empire. In any case, they always preferred to think in terms of islands because these had well-defined territorial limits. They annexed the barren island of Hong Kong in 1841, and soon declared it a Crown colony with a governor and legislature. Sir Henry Pottinger, the first governor, received advice from the colonial secretary in London, Lord Stanley, that inasmuch as Hong Kong was geographically, historically and economically unique, it followed that the technique of controls there would be different from those elsewhere in the empire. Stanley acted on sound advice. Sir James Stephen, the permanent secretary at the Colonial Office, had minuted that Hong Kong was a creature unlike any other colonial estate. He noted: "Methods of proceeding unknown in other British colonies must be followed in Hong Kong, and that the Rules and Regulations ... must in many regards, bend to the exigencies beyond the contemplation of the framers of them."[18] True this was, for Hong Kong was always a creature of British foreign policy backed by the Navy. The British were faced with Chinese hostility to which was coupled disdain at the *Fan Quai*: "these barbarians [the Chinese emperor Tao-kwang said] always look to trade as their chief occupation... It is plain that they are not worth attending to."[19] He was wrong. But he was right in this indirect obligation: the British did not arrive for a noble cause. To liberate China was not their intention.

By the Nanking Treaty of the following year, the four cities that had been captured were declared "treaty ports" – Shanghai, Canton, Ningpo and Amoy. Before long, Foochow was added to the list. Article 3 of the Nanking Treaty exhibited a Chinese appreciation of requirements of British shipping: "It being obviously necessary and desirable that British subjects should have some port at which they may careen and refit their ships when required, and keep stores for that purpose." In these ports the British became the dominant group, the merchants living in special enclaves where extraterritorial rights existed, and consuls and judges provided the means of civil origination. Mere toeholds of empire on the oriental shore, the last of them was not relinquished until 1997. Hong Kong gave power over adjacent waters and rivers. On the rivers the British, backed by the French, gained control in the sense that they backed their enforced rights of trade: this was the issue.

First the pacification, then the policing.[20] At the time when the British established themselves in Hong Kong, the same place was "the headquarters of Chinese robbers and pirates and the centre for smugglers who had no interest in legal procedure".[21] The British set up the customs authority under an inspector general, who arranged the maritime patrol and policing of harbours and rivers, and supplied the steamers – and all to the profit of the Chinese. Captain Sherard Osborn, experienced in steam navigation and illustrious in the Navy on account of other services rendered, managed the new river fleet, putting in place a system of control and self-sustaining income that was eventually to come to an end in the late 1940s. Although this may be regarded as an imperialist power's technique, the Imperial Customs Service, with its ability to raise revenue, was hugely beneficial to the Chinese state, and the process began with the control of Hong Kong in the First China War.

Difficulties and obstructions continued in bays and rivers of trade. Some Chinese, imagining a heroic resistance, blocked a stream of the Canton River known as Fatshan (Foshan) Creek. They made strong preparations for defence. On instructions, Henry Keppel, then a commodore and second in command on the China station, hoisted his flag in the chartered river steamer *Hong Kong*. On 1 June 1857 he delivered an attack on the great accumulation of war junks at Fatshan, and burned about 70 of them. It was a sharp action, much to Keppel's credit and advancement. The British Government, in conjunction with its French opposite, decided on a more extensive pacification.

The Second China War saw severe reverses in 1859 and the sending out of a massive allied force (11,000 British soldiers, 7,000 French, plus naval units) to demand redress. In the following year came the capture of the Taku forts in heavy fighting (seven Victoria Crosses were awarded), and the final capture of Peking. It was a massive military operation involving a great number of transports for the 10,000 troops of the expeditionary force. The French were in support. "The Queen deeply deplores the inevitable loss incidental to the achievement of this great success," Her Majesty's secretary informed the British general commanding, Sir Hope Grant. H. Knollys, who edited Major General Sir Hope Grant's account of the campaign, wrote: "It is scarcely too much to say that the China War of 1860 may be considered the most successful and the best carried out of England's 'little wars,' if, indeed the latter term not be a misnomer." The allies had made no mistakes. "The expense involved was great; but unlike the majority of wars, the consequent return was adequate. We obtained freedom of action for our merchants throughout the whole of the empire." As he saw it, it was a triumph. The British procured protection for the civilized world against the oppression and barbarous outrages of a nation previously accustomed to inflicting damages on strangers. The allies had struck a blow against Chinese pride and were able to exact terms by the Treaty of Peking. On the other hand, and by contrast, these had to be considered:

> Had we, on the other hand, refrained from war, we could not have maintained our position at the several ports where we traded; neither prosperity nor life would have been worth a moment's purchase; the laws of nations would have been habitually set at defiance; and the time would have arrived when we should have been compelled to quit the country altogether – conciliatory measures and efforts to obtain our just demands by negotiation having been interpreted by the Chinese as signs of weakness. We at last, in alliance with the French, we had recourse to arms, the advantages obtained for the civilized world were scarcely less important than those insured for our own interests.[22]

A permanent diplomatic mission to Peking now guarded the commercial and legal privileges acquired by two decades of war.

> By demonstrating, as the navy had done, the maritime power of England, Lord John Russell informed the Admiralty, the rulers and peoples of China were bound to be impressed "with the conviction that their best policy is faithfully to fulfill their Treaty engagements, and to maintain friendly relations with a Power which has at its disposal such ample means for obtaining, in case of need, redress for injuries done to its subjects."[23]

Answering to the aggrieved calls of the British merchants, the Foreign Office had taken the lead in directing the commander-in-chief on the East Indies station to send more frigates, and later strengthened squadrons. But "the Chinese Empire could neither be subdued nor controlled from salt water".[24]

Britain, for all its coercion to obtain rights to trade in the treaty ports, did not seek to be drawn into the continental quagmire. Gerald Graham explains:

> If the rickety throne of the Manchus toppled, Great Britain, jealously watched by European rivals, might face the awful problem of restoring order, or, at the worst, joining in an indecent scramble for a share of the spoils... But no matter how formidable the numbers of the Royal Navy, a *Pax Britannica* required the friendship, or at least the forbearance, of European powers. What happened in China might drastically affect a delicate equilibrium of forces on the other side of the world. A Chinese policy could never be entirely isolated from a European policy. Only Russia was in a position to conduct her foreign relations in two separate compartments, the Asiatic and the European, without one system of foreign relations seriously jeopardizing the other.

When the Treaty of Peking was signed in October 1860, Russia opportunistically annexed a province south of the Amur River, giving a naval port at Vladivostok and making Russia a Pacific power. As the same authority concludes,

> A nation, whose warships had been confirmed by treaty to the Black Sea, and, for many months in the year, by ice in the Baltic, had acquired a maritime stake in the Far East. Not without apprehension did the Mistress of the Seas contemplate the future activities of an Asiatic power, so far removed from immediate European surveillance.[25]

Safeguarding commercial opportunities in the South China Seas formed the central thrust of British energies east of Suez in the middle decades of the nineteenth century, and so prominent are they in their legacies that it might seem that the growth of imperial and foreign interests that began with Hong Kong in 1841 forms the major story. But this is not the case, for another world of British expansion for peace and profit lay eastwards from Singapore. Here the British progression continued: James Brooke was appointed rajah of Sarawak by the former piratical Sultan of Brunei, and, in 1865, Britain recognized its independence. Labuan was ceded to the imperial government by the same sultan and made a Crown colony. Here was another coaling station, this one off the Borneo coast, and a key point of leverage in those seas. The acquisition of bases and the successful prosecution of a war against the pirates in these seas cleared the way for a further extension of British trade and interests in China. The Sultan of Brunei's dominions were purchased by the British North Borneo Company in one of those further examples of late nineteenth-century corporate empire expansion. Kuria Muria Islands were acquired from the imam of Muscat in 1854 as a coaling station, and, three years later, Perim was occupied for similar reasons and also to serve as a cable station. On the Australian route, the Cocos-Keeling Islands were placed under Admiralty control. In 1888 they became part of the Straits Settlements, as did Christmas Island (1889) and Labuan (1905).

Once again, instability on the margins of British interest had led to formal control. The Navy joined the local British authorities in support, as requested. The British North Borneo Company (1881) was "empire on the cheap" and a foretaste of something to come. In 1888, North Borneo, Sarawak and Brunei all became protectorates, closing another chapter in British imperial growth in these seas. A system of indirect rule was developed, in keeping with Malay customs and Muslim needs, but gradually formal rule was effected: the Malay states came into existence in 1896, with inland Kuala Lumpur as the administrative centre. Tin and rubber proved to be powerful economic and financial impulses and hastened the Chinese domination of the population. Interference to stop interracial strife or consolidation for political and administrative efficiency marked the imperial progression, and, by 1909, British hegemony had been established over the Malay Peninsula.[26]

Longer and longer became the Asian coasts needing patrols, protection and survey, and larger and larger the obligations of the commander-in-chief of the East Indies.[27] The need for cruisers was never satisfied. In its actual imperial possessions in the Far East and Southeast Asia, Britain had only a relatively small cluster of territories – the Straits Settlements, Hong Kong and Labuan. Malaya and Borneo were protectorates. Sarawak was ruled by a dynasty of English rajahs, and North Borneo by a chartered company.

Anti-piratical operations also were the daily fare of the Navy in these seas. Captain Henry Keppel (the same as in the Fatshan Creek episode), in aid of Rajah Brooke of Sarawak, took the *Dido* to Borneo to clear waters of the predatory head-hunting Dyaks, for whom piracy was a way of life.[28] For 18 months he undertook the work in upriver operations. On one occasion, sailing in company with the East India Company's steamer *Phegethon*, he destroyed the pirate stronghold together with some 300 prahus. This was an essential step in making these seas safe for all nations. "When he returned twenty years later to the scene of his youthful exploits he wrote an apology for imperialism which is relevant to many other parts of the world," noted Christopher Lloyd in admiration of a naval job well done.[29]

> In 1842 piracy, slavery and head hunting were the order of the day [recalled Keppel]. The sail of a peaceful trader was nowhere to be seen, not even a fisherman's hut along the length of this beautiful coast. Far into the interior the Malays and Dyaks warred on one another. Now, how different! Huts and

> fishing stakes are to be seen all along the coast: the town of Kuching, which on the visit of the *Dido* had scarcely 800 inhabitants, now has a population of over 20,000. At least 250,000 of the aborigines who called themselves warriors are now peaceful traders and cultivators of the soil.[30]

Elsewhere the work of the Navy went on energetically against pirates.[31] Seasoned pirates based on Guangdong made excursions along the Vietnamese coast, the Malay Peninsula and to the Philippines. From the 1820s through to the 1860s they were a powerful force and they captured hundreds of young men and women, selling them into slavery in Siam. In China, Captain Dalrymple Hay, who recounted the experience in his *Suppression of Piracy* (1889), destroyed a notorious fleet of Chinese junks. Actions by the Navy deflected the activities of the Chinese pirates to more southerly locales. Hong Kong remained a pirate arsenal for 20 years after it was acquired. Keppel, now returned as commander-in-chief of the East Indies in 1867, cleared out the creeks and bays. In these actions the British used forward and aggressive policies, and they employed to advantage the gift of steam navigation, experienced gunnery (including rockets) and militant boarding actions.

The British armament in these seas was now formidable – to maintain order and protect trade. The vagaries of weather and climate often dictated ship deployments, and the commercial and diplomatic demands placed on the squadron were as ever-changing as they were demanding. Naval economies could hardly be made here; just the opposite. Benefits in trade brought obligations in defence. In 1864 the China station, based on Hong Kong, was established as separate from the East Indies command. The new command had obligations that stretched north to Korean, Japanese and Russian waters. When taken together with the Australian station and the Pacific station, the administrative reach of the Admiralty, and ships on station, had girdled the globe, all complete by the 1860s and consolidated for the three decades that followed. But in each case the naval armament "on station" would grow with increasing obligations.

Piracy flared up periodically, and shipping companies such as the Peninsular and Oriental Company would demand protection. With direct trade between Britain and China rapidly increasing in the late 1860s, the Foreign Office and the Admiralty were in agreement about the necessity to put down piracy and make sure that there were adequate numbers of a class of vessel suitable for the service. It was all very well to have gunboats and gun vessels in the treaty ports, but that would not suffice to give prominence to the British position in these seas, where the French, Americans, Russians and Dutch were showing considerable naval force. The Admiralty, having conferred with flag officers previously "on station", concluded in 1879 that the general duties of the station ought to be performed by the substitution of larger vessels. At that time, Nathaniel

Barnaby's design for a third-class cruiser, the steel corvettes of the "Comus" class of 2,388 tons, 2,300 horse power (top speed 12.93 knots), and 14 guns with good steam power and full rig, essential for commerce protection across the world, were being built.[32] Accordingly, two were ordered for the China Seas under the rationale that "the occasional visits of these more powerful ships to the several ports would be more efficacious in securing the respect for the flag than the retention of small vessels in various localities". Not least, they would be able to steam against the monsoon, in case of necessity. Gun vessels, with light draft, were retained for the river work. The Admiralty's assessment bears this reassurance:

> their Lordships are of opinion that, under the improved relations with China and the measures now adopted for the suppression of piracy, the duties to be fulfilled in peace time by H.M. naval forces in China, which include the protection of British floating commerce against piratical attacks, the support of H.M. consuls in maintaining discipline amongst the crews of British merchant vessels, and the safeguard of the lives and property of British subjects in various ports, will be at least as efficiently fulfilled as heretofore by the squadron re-organized as proposed, while the strength of H.M. naval forces in Chinese waters will, for war purposes, be materially augmented.[33]

There were calls to Japanese waters, too. The British, on the coat tails of the Americans, breached the Japanese wall at last in the mid-1850s. They did so in keeping with the French, who were aggressive in those seas. The treaty between the United States and Japan was eventually concluded and signed on 31 March 1854. The port of Shimoda was opened for the reception of American ships, which were to be supplied with essentials: wood, water, provisions and coal. In the same year, Admiral Sir James Stirling, commander-in-chief of China, anchored HMS *Winchester* and a squadron in Japanese waters, and concluded a convention with the Japanese. Japan was then in a state of disunity, and Stirling advised the Admiralty in words that seem hardly credible given the sudden subsequent rise of imperial Japan to pre-eminent status that Japan might be taken over by another power, presumably a European or American one. He wrote: "it may with truth be said, whatever Maritime Power may gain preponderant influence in Japan whether by Alliance, Annexation, or Conquest, will be the mistress of the China Seas, and of the Commerce carried on upon them".[34] He urged the Japanese to remain neutral in wartime, fearing that if they did not they would become an object in war, a spoil of war.

British consuls and military advisors followed. At Satsuma Kagoshima, a trader, Richardson, fell victim to Japanese chauvinism, and the Navy's answer, on Foreign Office advice, was to bombard the port, which it did in 1863. The year following, Admiral Augustus L. Kuper, wearing his flag in one of the

Navy's last active 101-gun first-rate warships, led nine British, three French, one American and four Dutch ships in the reduction of Shimonoseki forts and the occupation of Yokohama. Gunboat diplomacy had entered a new phase of strength. Harmonious relations developed thereafter, as Japanese needs for security in the North Pacific world coincided with British needs to promote security on other seas and coasts. Britain dominated Japanese naval development after the Meiji restoration, which subdued the last Satsuma revolt. Japan's consolidation, naval armament and imperial expansion now began with telling consequences, not least a war with China in 1894–1895, and another with Russia in 1904–1905, both of which ended in imperial Japan's further ascendancy to a dominant role in East Asia.[35]

However, the main focal point of British interest in these seas was propping up imperial China, with its hugely important possibilities of trade. In 1888, as part of the review of imperial coaling stations and bases, Hong Kong was designated as a first-class coaling station. As headquarters of the China squadron, it had to be made properly secure with a garrison.[36] Port and dockyard facilities, adequately fortified, added to its value. In the extension of British influence on the coast of China, the Navy was the main instrument of influence. Britain added Kowloon to its colony of Hong Kong. The British organized the Chinese Maritime Customs Service, sending Captain Sherard Osborne and a fleet of steamers to provide patrols of the rivers and harbours. British gunboats policed the rivers of importance, notably the Yangtze. Under Robert Hart, a wizard in administration, the Chinese government grew rich on the imposts of regulated river trade.

The Royal Navy played a unique role in imperial Japan's rise to prominence in the years after the Meiji era, which began in 1868. It helped to train Japanese officers and provided a model for naval education and training. Nelson was a well-known model of a fighting admiral at the imperial Japanese navy's academy, Etajima; naval cadets, including the future Japanese Nelson Togo, were sent to England for training; and many of the ships of the Japanese fleet that fought in the Sino-Japanese War and in the Russo-Japanese War had been constructed in British yards, including Togo's flagship, the pre-dreadnought *Mikasa*. The Japanese government ordered the last vessel to be built in Britain in 1910, and eight years earlier, with the beginning of the manufacture of armour plate, Japan's policy of building its own warships, great and small, was adhered to. However, the British could not control imperial Japan, no matter how influential the military and naval ties that were developed between the two countries after 1868.

Japan demonstrated its naval muscle with a shattering defeat of the Chinese navy in the battle of the Yalu Sea. "master and pupils have just reason to be proud of each other", chirped *The Times* (24 September 1894). The

Japanese naval victory, coupled with a war indemnity, bankrupted the Manchu regime. Now the eastern balance of power tottered precariously, depending on European capital and protection. In 1898, in an arrangement with Japan, the British leased the port of Weihaiwai, as various foreign powers scrambled for influence with the continued weakening of the Chinese Empire. Weihaiwai, it was reasoned, would be a counterweight and challenge to Russia's powerful arsenal and naval establishment, Port Arthur, but it was never more than a coaling station and sanatorium.

It was the crisis in the Chinese Empire that provoked heavier demands by the European powers, similar to France and Britain's interest in the Nile and Egypt. Britain preferred to take an active part. The Boxer Rebellion of 1900 led to the great powers dominating even the capital of the Celestial Empire. The Russians, responding to Japanese conquests, occupied Manchuria. A similar situation had occurred in Egypt, when Arabi's rebellion had led to the British occupation of the country.[37] Turbulence on the distant margins of influence invited a response. The British never stood idly by, worried as they were by the potential advantages gained by their rivals. They thus worked in alliance with other powers. Once the Boxer Rebellion was suppressed, the powers garrisoned Peking under the pretext of protecting their legations. In all of these actions, Britain had been in the forefront. French and US naval forces were welcome partners in the process.

At the opening of the new century the British naval armament in these seas was formidable – six battleships of the fast "Canopus" class, plus various cruisers, destroyers and river gunboats. Headquartered in Hong Kong, the fleet spent most of its time at Weihaiwei, an advantageous watchtower from which to observe the budding rivalry of Japan and Russia, and the rise of German naval power at Tsingtao. From here, too, British warships maintained a "presence" in the waters leading to the throbbing commercial hub of Shanghai.[38] The approach of war between Japan and Russia compelled strict neutrality on the part of British commanders, and the commander-in-chief, Vice-Admiral Sir Gerard Noel, circulated on behalf of the Admiralty rules of engagement "as a precautionary measure against surprise in the presence of either of the belligerents". Soon afterwards the Admiralty reduced the capital ships on station from five battleships to four modern cruisers (which may have been of comparable effectiveness). Noel did not see it this way. Aware of rival armaments in those waters, he considered this reduction an "indignity" to his flag and he protested strongly. He got nowhere with the brittle Admiralty, and his protest brought a rebuff. He returned to England an established opponent of Jacky Fisher, his fleet reorganization and other schemes.[39] Noel was not alone among commanders-in-chief on distant stations crying out for sufficient warships of the appropriate classes so as to make their presence known to foreign rivals.[40]

In point of fact, Britain could not maintain its primacy on every sea and ocean annex; already it was suffering imperial overstretch, with rivals gaining on it daily.

Already, in 1902, had come Britain's alliance with Japan, one of mutual assistance only in its early stages. But then came Japan's defeat of Russia that not only destroyed the imperial Russian navy but also restored the eastern balance of power and halted the Western imperialists' takeover of China. Throughout this process the British maintained their equipoise in these eastern waters. They found in imperial Japan a new means of boosting their sagging fortunes. They concentrated on protecting their powerful commercial positions in Hong Kong and Shanghai. France, the United States and Germany had assisted in this process, and the British leadership had achieved a notable triumph in the most difficult of circumstances. But against this stood imperial Japan, and, although these "old friends" soon became "new enemies", it would take decades before the British would realize that events were beyond their control.[41]

The system of distributing warships among nine foreign stations had been rendered obsolete by changes in strategy and in instruments of war. Advances in wireless telegraphy, torpedoes, torpedo boat destroyers, mines, submarines, guns, armour, steel hulls and steam propulsion – in short, a great advance over the naval equipment of the close of the Crimean War in 1856 – made sea power potentially more effective provided that ships, and especially bases and coaling stations, were available. Mobility was the new requirement. Because its strength at sea remained as essential to Britain's survival as ever – and could serve as a restraining influence on the country's probable enemies – the "new conditions" that Fisher mentioned in his famous recommendation to the Cabinet of October 1904 necessitated a concentration of naval strength in home waters and a reorganization of the squadrons overseas. The China station was renamed the Eastern Fleet, and now included the possibilities of serving the needs of the distant eastern Pacific. As noted, the ships on station were of a different class – fast cruisers. At Esquimalt, the Pacific station ended at sunset on 1 March 1905. And with the resolution of Anglo-American difficulties in such matters as the Yukon–Alaska border, the Bering Sea pelagic seal fishery, the Isthmian canal rights, the Guiana–Venezuela border and Great Lakes naval disarmament, many of the complications built up in the rise to prominence in yesterdays were being put to rest.

While the lights in the Foreign Office burned long and bright as masters and clerks dealt with issue after issue, out on the watery distant margins of influence, admirals and ship captains maintained the British presence as best they could in faltering circumstances. Like Vice-Admiral Gerald Noel in Hong Kong, or his counterpart, Rear-Admiral A.K. Bickford, at Esquimalt, they were disadvantaged, even impoverished, by what the Admiralty could supply in the way of naval units, and they were understandably as angry as they were perplexed by the rapidly changing scene in international affairs.[42] Their lordships balked at the suggestions made by the flag officers at sea that they were being neglected in their needs and that British interests were not being protected. These were cruel reminders of a darkening world – one in which naval capabilities did not match the demanding duties "on station". "Splendid isolation" was quickly coming to an end.

Showing the flag formed an essential feature of the *Pax Britannica*, in colonial or foreign waters, in this case British Columbia in the late nineteenth century. Courtesy: Author's collection

Her Majesty's Ship *Amphion* never fired a gun in anger, but was one of the essential men-of-war engaged in policing the seas and guarding British interests on distant station, in this case the Pacific. Here she leaves Esquimalt, Vancouver Island, British Columbia, on imperial duties. Courtesy: Naval and Military Museum CFB Esquimalt

John Rushworth Jellicoe, later an Admiral of the Fleet, commanded the Grand Fleet at Jutland but most of his time in the Royal Navy had been spent in missions related to sustaining the *Pax*. He was severely injured in the naval brigade advancing on Peking in 1900. Courtesy: Author's collection

Their ship riding safely in Esquimalt Harbour at anchor, some ratings from H.M.S *Amphion* take well-deserved shore exercise in 1890. They were 18,000 sea miles from their homes in the British Isles. On a more formal occasion, the day of the Queen-Empress's Diamond Jubilee, 1897, a naval contingent would be seen swinging up Ludgate Hill. A reporter from the *Daily Mail* thought that they marched "with the steadfast calm of men who have been left aloe with God's wonders at sea." Courtesy: Maritime Museum of British Columbia

H.M.S. *Egeria*, a steam screw sloop of 940 tons measurement, and mounting but four guns, had been built in Pembroke Yard in 1874. Fitted out for surveying duties in 1886 she was exclusively engaged in that service until the early twentieth century. She sailed to British Columbia in 1898 and heroically as well as quietly extended the surveys of men like George Henry Richards and Daniel Pender on that dangerous coast. In history, she lacks the glamour of James Cook's *Endeavour* or George Vancouver's *Discovery* but nonetheless her work was essential to better navigation and commerce in the heady days of *Pax Britannica* and after. Courtesy: Maritime Museum of British Columbia

A summer scene that could be anywhere in a British imperial port or that of a host nation but in this case Esquimalt, British Columbia. Having dropped off her officers for a party with the Admiral commanding these well dressed ratings rest on their oars while the photo is being taken. A boat crew from H.M.S. *Amphion* in the late 1880s. To the left, in the intermediate distance, are the Torpedo Boat Destroyers *Swift* and *Sure*. Beyond them the *Amphion* lies in the left far distance. Courtesy: Maritime Museum of British Columbia

Commander C.W.G. Crawford, second from right, front row, sports a wing back collar and summer trousers and shoes for a garden party ashore with the Admiral. Other officers, all of them citizens of the Seven Seas, take up the imperial pose. A pair of duck-hunting dogs patiently await the command to action. Courtesy: Maritime Museum of British Columbia

The Navy aided British scientific enterprise, and here (in the distance) the *Challenger*, on her great oceanic examination, is at Ireland Island, Bermuda, 1873. Courtesy: National Museum Bermuda

The Floating Dock at Bermuda provided essential service to the Fleet and to merchant shipping. Here in 1900 dockyard workers stand at the bow of their most recent subject of attention. Around the world the Navy needed docks. Most were on solid ground. In the case of Bermuda this was impossible owing to coral rock formations. British engineering could fabricate a floating dock, and this one was towed across the Atlantic and fixed in place. The floating dock at Ireland, Island, Bermuda, presented to naval operations and efficiency. Courtesy: National Museum Bermuda

Gibraltar shown here in the 1930s had been acquired by British blood in an earlier age, and was stoutly kept as guardian of the strait leading to the Mediterranan, and valuable during and long after the *Pax* had fizzled out. Courtesy: Naval and Military Museum CFB Esquimalt

Malta, at one time an orphan, became an essential Britannic daughter of empire, and here welcomes Edward VII and a British squadron, 1909. Courtesy: Maritime Museum Malta

The leading admiral of his age, the highly respected Admiral Sir Michael Culme-Seymour, a superb fleet-handler and a man with geopolitical vision. He saw almost all the seas of the world. After living most of his life at sea in 1896 he came ashore to superintend at Portsmouth. Aide de Camp to Queen Victoria, at her death he was in charge of her coffin. He was later ADC to Edward VII at his coronation. Courtesy: Naval and Military Museum CFB Esquimalt

H.M.S. *Warrior*, the first British seagoing ironclad, laid down in 1859 and completed in 1861, was one of two vessels designed to match French developments at sea. The French had commenced building frigates of great speed with their sides protected by thick metal plates. This rendered it imperative that Britain do likewise, though the Lords Commissioners of the Admiralty, at that time keenly interested in holding down the naval estimates, were obliged to the new construction with great reluctance. The return to power of Palmerston – pre-eminently a Big-Navy man, speeded the process. Courtesy: Maritime Museum of British Columbia

Admiral of the Fleet Sir Geoffrey Phipps Hornby, when captain of the frigate *Tribune*, sailed from China to the Northwest Coast of America to counter United States pretentions on the disputed San Juan Islands, between Vancouver Island and the mainland. Cool heads prevailed, and his conduct was exemplary in the event. His commanding officer, Rear Admiral Robert Lambert Baynes, when he heard that the British governor of Vancouver Island, James Douglas, had wanted to land soldiers and marines and oust the Americans gave the classic comment, "Tut, tut, no, no, the damned fools." Baynes was knighted for his diplomatic skill. Phipps Hornby rose to become one of the great First Sea Lords of the Admiralty. Elsewhere, at mid-century, as in the Hawaiian Islands, California and the Society Islands the British resisted all claims to territorial expansion. Courtesy: Naval and Military Museum CFB Esquimalt

Coal was the fuel that sustained the *Pax* until oil-fired engines were introduced. Here a ship's company, happy to have completed their essential but truly dirty work, pose for the camera. Courtesy: Naval and Military Museum CFB Esquimalt

An essential tool of empire and influence on the distant littorals of the world, among countless islands and hitherto inaccessible passages and bays, the gunboat provided a cheap form of policing and law enforcement. H.M.S. *Forward*, Esquimalt, 1860. Courtesy: Naval and Military Museum CFB Esquimalt

A more potent form of gunboat, the gunvessel, had more powerful engines, larger armament and finer seaworthiness. Dominant in the late 1860s through 1870s, one of the kind was the *Sparrowhawk*. Courtesy: Naval and Military Museum CFB Esquimalt

Projecting power ashore was an essential feature of the *Pax*. Such episodes could get the officers responsible into fearsome difficulties with the Admiralty, who deplored any excursions endangering the ship and weaken its strength. Courtesy: Naval and Military Museum CFB Esquimalt

The introduction of steam transformed the Navy and introduced officers, engineers, oilers, stokers and others to the ship's company. Highly competent in their training and in their work, they oddly introduced a social stratification not always appreciated by the quarterdeck. Courtesy: Naval and Military Museum CFB Esquimalt

Waterborne consul Sir Fairfax Moresby, later an Admiral of the Fleet, fought against piracy and slave trading by negotiating a treaty with the Imam of Muscat. From this treaty grew an influential network of others. Courtesy: Naval and Military Museum CFB Esquimalt

Steam-powered and iron-hulled ships needed repair facilities and docks unimaginable in the age of fighting sail. On the distant margins of influence, such as Esquimalt, vessels such as H.M.S. *Cormorant* needed regular maintenance and, in time of emergency, repairs to damaged hull, propellers or other. Courtesy: Naval and Military Museum CFB Esquimalt

H. B. M. SHIP "WARSPITE" IN GRAVING DOCK AT ESQUIMALT, B. C.

On distant seas, gunboats had given way to gunvessels, then to sloops and then, in this case, to small battleships. Here is H.M.S. *Warspite*, frequently at Esquimalt, here in the graving dock undergoing repairs. Courtesy: Maritime Museum of British Columbia

Anglo-American naval friendship was forged at Bermuda when Vice-Admiral Sir John Fisher (right) met, wined and dined Admiral William Sampson (left) recently triumphant in the Spanish-American War. Courtesy: National Museum Bermuda

The Union Jack is hoisted on 1 November 1884 at New Guinea. From first to last it was naval operation: Commodore James Erskine, Commodore of the Australian Station and flying his flag in H.M.S. *Nelson*, proclaimed the protectorate at the Reverend Mr. Lawes's house, Port Moresby. The proclamation explained the imperial purposes: protection of native interest, prevention of unlawful occupation, establishment of law and order, prevention of bloodshed, establishment of legitimate trade, and possessing themselves of the land – in other words keeping out the Germans. Courtesy: School of Oriental and African Studies

H.M.S. *Kent*, later in the Falklands action, December 1914, against Von Spee's German East Asiatic Squadron, and damaged, lies in Esquimalt harbour circa 1900. Courtesy: Naval and Military Museum CFB Esquimalt

H.M.S. *Iron Duke*, later flagship successively of Admirals Jellicoe and Beatty of the Grand Fleet. A super dreadnought, she was one of four laid down in the 1911 Program. She measured 580 feet overall, 90 feet in width, and drew between 27 and 29 feet depending on load (full load 30,380 tons). Last of the coal-burning British battleships, she was the first all-big-gun ship to carry 6-inch guns as a secondary armament. The purpose, it was said was "to 'hail' on the enemy, if you find him close at hand on a misty day in the North Sea." As it proved, this was an impossibility. Her main armament consisted of ten 13.5 in. guns. Her Parsons engines drove four screws, and she could do 21 knots. Courtesy: Naval and Military Museum CFB Esquimalt

The "soldiers of the sea," Royal Marines of H.M.S. *Sultan* are shown here as forming a boat's crew. Courtesy: Naval and Military Museum CFB Esquimalt

"Rule Britannia, Britannia Rule the Waves" attracted many a lad to join the world's strongest navy to see the world. Courtesy: Naval and Military Museum CFB Esquimalt

8
The Imperial Web in the South Pacific

> You are to protect British interests in the colonies of New South Wales, New Zealand and the Islands adjacent and also to visit or detach a ship to visit the Feejee, Navigators and Friendly Islands, and it will be your object to give to the natives an impression of the power and of the friendly disposition of the British nation and whilst giving due weight to the representatives of the British consuls and missionaries and to strengthen their hand for good, you will repress any tendency to undue interference or encroachments on the rights of the chiefs and natives.

So read the Admiralty's instructions to Captain Fremantle of 18 February 1854, and these were the sort of breezy generalities of the imperial dictum that was to guide a generation or more of British naval officers like Fremantle who at mid-century were sailing half a world away from the home islands and quite out of direct communication with Whitehall. As such, the Captain Freemantles of the age had to read into the future: they had to imagine whether they would receive a note of congratulations or a severe reprimand for whatever actions they took among the islands of the vast Pacific Ocean. Quarterdeck diplomacy was the hallmark of the Victorian Navy, and no place gave it wider scope than the South Pacific, unheralded sphere of empire-making and the European scramble for territorial and strategic advantage.[1]

At the outset of the age it was science that drove the British, save for whaling, sealing and other interests of trade, much of it connected with Latin American ports or China. For the first 15 years after 1815, the myriad island clusters of the Pacific held little fascination for the British. A lack of geographical unity gave the islands and peoples of the Pacific no favourable place in British imperial plans. "Showing the flag" in the Central and South Pacific was only an incidental circumstance of keeping a more narrow watch on the evolving Spanish American republics as far north as Mexico. The same was true of exploring the Bering Sea, where Russians posed as rivals to the British search for the Northwest Passage, as described elsewhere in these pages. The Society Islands were the first to command attention: although missionaries had been sent to Tahiti as early as the 1790s, the commercial prospects of these Pacific islands afforded no opportunities to British investors. The Pacific offered few inducements to British trade and was a business backwater. It is true that whaling interests sought a base in the Galapagos and the Bonin Islands, and surveying expeditions had been sent there and elsewhere with good effect. The Pacific offered a fine field for hunting whales, and here the British competed with the Americans, the French and others. The Hawaiian Islands attracted the liveliest attention, not least because of the immortal Captain Cook's connection with them. He had pointed out the archipelago's essential strategic value. It was a focal point of rivalry and concern by the 1820s but held no attraction for British statesman as a place for permanent empire.

As for the southwestern Pacific, men-of-war were dispatched on surveillance duties only on occasion. In the meantime, New South Wales on the basis of convict origins and later the development of sheep stations had become a secure base for trade, another anchor of empire. Australia's place in what Vincent Harlow called "the swing to the east" has fascinated many historians, and it is now clear that more than just convict settlement lay behind the Botany Bay scheme. Naval stores for British activities in the East Indies is one such meritorious line of fascination to which can be added an interest in trading posts, commercial expansion and strategic position.[2] Sydney offered a convenient port of call for ships destined for or returning from the Pacific Ocean. Settlers, missionaries and traders who ventured to Melanesia and Polynesia used Sydney as their supply base and shipping centre. Missionaries proved to be of importance in the sociopolitical organization of Pacific Islanders, and their actions plus those of the traders, beachcombers, sealers, bootleggers and others induced turbulence – and, much to London's regret, forced the British to take a more active role in showing the flag. Taken together, these were incidental events of an imperial progression. At the outset of our epoch, the Pacific held no unity to official thinking, but rather offered a number of interlocking problems of policing and control. The British desired no empire of the South Pacific, and they fought diligently against any such possibility. Whether they liked it or not, the British were being drawn into the Pacific vortex, and, try though they might, they could not resist its entanglements. It was empire by default.

Governors of New South Wales watched developments in the Pacific Islands with concern, for British subjects were active in the processes of coercion and despoliation, lawlessness and kidnapping. The British had no intention of extending territorial control, but by a statute of 1817 they made it clear that an end had come to any vague claims that British governors enjoyed jurisdiction there though, at the same time, the rule of British law as it related to

British subjects existed throughout this watery waste.[3] It was a sharp denial of territorial expansion, and may now be seen as a vain attempt to counter the propensity to expand formal empire. For a time the policy was effective. New South Wales formed the bridgehead of policies. Beginning with the days of earliest convict settlement at Botany Bay, governors had developed wider imperial visions than merely supervising the local colony, and early on appeals had been made to London to base sloops-of-war in Garden Bay, Sydney, for use in surveillance and police work in the Pacific Islands. Beginning in about 1829, the Admiralty was directing commanders-in-chief on the East Indies and on the South America stations to send frigates and sloops to make occasional, usually annual, calls.

At that point in time of the imperial progression, the disclosure of Pitcairn Island by Captain Beechey of HMS *Blossom* in 1827, and the startling intelligence that the last remaining mutineer of Captain William Bligh's *Bounty*, Alexander Smith, was still alive, drew the attention of the British public to the prospects of the South Pacific.[4] The Navy established a paternalistic watch over the Pitcairn Islanders, and extended the British trusteeship there. Here were some survivors of Jack Tar and his kin. In 1837, Captain Henry William Bruce of HMS *Imogene* left there a salutary reminder to the ex-mutineer residents – this proclamation:

> Captain Bruce recommends to the inhabitants of this Island, and particularly to the three Europeans residing on it, to follow the religious and moral course of life and conduct in which the natives have been instructed and which the word of God points out in the Bible. Captain Bruce will represent to his Superiors the necessity of a person of character and ability being sent from England to preside over the interests of the island, but should his recommendation not be successful the inhabitants may be assured that a ship of war will be ordered to the island to enquire into all complaints, and should any crimes be committed to punish all offenders.[5]

Here was *Pax* in action in miniature circumstances. After at least two naval attempts to find a new home for the Pitcairners, including Tahiti and Norfolk Island, some of them found their way back in 1859, inducing others to follow in 1864. Altogether their story forms the strangest of imperial progressions. A formal colony was proclaimed there, a true oddity of empire – and one that, with Bermuda, the Falklands and a number of others, might justly be called "the limpet colonies".

British naval activity in this ocean consisted primarily of showing the flag and watching for the possibility that rivals would take control of the two great island clusters that seemed to matter in those days – the Society Islands and the Hawaiian Islands. By the close of the 1830s the commander-in-chief of the Pacific was calling for an increased armament for the Pacific because the French and Americans were now in the ascendant in naval power.[6] In the mid-1840s the problem had increased, and the first lord of the Admiralty, Lord Auckland, was stressing British vulnerability there, and calling for a new division to be based at Sydney within the East Indies command. If the French threatened Sydney, it could be helped by ships from both the Pacific and the Cape of Good Hope stations. Here was an attestation of global reach. The Foreign Office needed to remind the Admiralty that Britain had faced similar challenges before, and the state of Anglo-French relations was not at a critical stage. Naval estimates had to be passed by Parliament, and, in these circumstances, heads of departments could not just dream up a heavier armament for the Pacific or any other station for that matter. Parliament, on the advice of the Cabinet, would have to decide these things. Still, bit by bit the number, tonnage and sailors of ships on station rose. In 1846 the commander-in-chief of the Pacific had at his disposal a ship of the line, two large frigates, a handful of corvettes and sloops, and a paddlewheel steamer. In the end it was the French who gained the advantage in the Society Islands, while in the Hawaiian Islands the British declined to take up the possibilities. Religious rivalries played a strong role in both. In Tahiti, Roman Catholic missionaries under the careful assistance of the French navy made decided advances to the disadvantage of the British. In Hawaii, American Congregationalists took firm hold and poisonously portrayed the British in the worst light, manipulating the Hawaiians in the contest for souls and primacy of influence.

Successive commanders-in-chief on the Pacific station, rear admirals Richard Thomas and Sir George Seymour, had their hands tied. Whereas they would gladly have supported intervention in support of British interests in the face of the rivals, they found – in fact, they knew in advance – that the Foreign Office held strongly against the possibility of foreign entanglements. It was one of the recurrent themes of empire-making during *Pax Britannica* that the British Government preferred trade to dominion. Equally important, as we saw earlier (Chapter 5), when the prospect of territorial gain presented itself, the British often backed off and reversed the decisions made on the spot. The view from London was different from that locally. Forbearance was based on sound policies of avoiding tangles, keeping out of wasps' nests and not getting into hot water. This was true for California and especially so for the Hawaiian Islands. Thomas and Seymour, to repeat, knew what the Admiralty and the Foreign Office would accept and what they would deny. In 1843, to cite another case among the Pacific Islands, Captain Toup Nicholas of *Vindictive* urged the taking of the Society Islands but the Foreign Office shot back with this directive to the Admiralty:

> His Lordship directs me to request that you will convey to the Lords Commissioners of the Admiralty his sense of the inexpediency of the Commander of a British man-of-war taking upon himself, without express orders

> from his government, to prejudge the course which they may see fit to pursue, and in so doing to act in such a manner towards a Foreign Power as might induce or involve the two nations in hostilities.[7]

All the same, Palmerston at the Foreign Office did not want the Queen of Tahiti, Pomare, placed in a position of coercion under the French navy or French missionaries, and seemed sufficiently interested in affording protection to ask the Colonial Office its opinion. Back came the quick reply:

> Adverting to the vast territorial extent of the existing Dominions of the British Crown in the Southern Ocean, and to the necessity which has arisen for the extension of Her Majesty's sovereignty to parts of the Islands of New Zealand, and also adverting to the great cost and difficulty inseparable from these undertakings... Lord Normanby,

wrote Sir James Stephen, the permanent undersecretary, "is of opinion that it would be dangerous and impolitic to contract similar obligations towards the Inhabitants of Tahiti."[8] In the circumstances, no colonial accretions occurred under the British crown in the Central Pacific.[9] In Tahiti the British stood aside in favour of the French.

Already the Colonial Office was counselling against imperial overstretch. By 1850 the Admiralty had affirmed its inkling of two sobering, interrelated realizations: that it would soon be impossible to be strong in all places at all times, and that the best way to defend the imperial periphery was to be overwhelmingly powerful in the North Sea. It would take another half-century before these realizations were translated into concrete form. Even so, during that period, officials in the Australian colonies tended to view Royal Navy vessels as colonial assets, and governors and consuls liked to think of the nearby British gun vessel as a personal taxi or marine constabulary. The Australians in the early years enjoyed the privileges that empire afforded without paying the cost. In this regard they had companions in Canada. In 1859 the Australian division had been elevated into an independent station, recognition of the growing importance of trade in those seas and the need to safeguard it. But colonial obligations to the Pacific islands were a necessary adjunct of work, and from these islands came a steady flow of calls for protection and policing. Gradually, individual Australian colonies would come to see the need for colonial navies, though London would make sure that Whitehall's powers were always paramount and unquestioned. The Royal Australian and Royal Canadian navies in the early part of the twentieth century were byproducts of the tug-of-war between imperial and colonial concepts of naval defence, between the inescapable demands of centralization and the forces of local sovereignty.[10]

There existed no pattern of acquisition of territory, save meeting the needs of the day as they arose. Prof. Sir John Manning Ward, who mastered the legal records, argued that the British pursued a policy of minimum intervention in the South Pacific, and what measures they advanced were always those of reluctance and founded more often than not on legal and constitutional practices. This was undeniably true, but even so it did not stop the new Romans from spreading a legal web well in advance of establishing protectorates and acquiring imperial real estate.[11] Formal control came as a last, reluctant resort brought about by compelling circumstances. It was not until the decision was taken in London to take control of the islands of Fiji that the British flag was run up there in 1874.[12] Once again the British administrations fought against annexations, protectorates and more formal means of control.

As a rule, missionaries preferred to be left alone and to work in isolation, free from searching inquiries of imperial amphibious diplomats and lawgivers. Missionaries, not governments, set up the schools, built new communities, established industrial infrastructures and promoted new economies. They liked independence; they demanded protection. Bishop George Selwyn of New Zealand wanted protection from naval powers, British and others. He hoped that the protecting power, Britain being his favourite, would gradually civilize the islands "without attempting to form colonies on them". And again, "He would have for England a ship-of-war having on board a competent official, whose duty would be to visit the different islands and hear and determine cases." There were naval officers whom he knew – Sotheby, Maxwell, Erskine and Home, whom he liked particularly – whom he thought easily entered into the work and carried it on successfully. Yet there were others, unnamed, whom he classified as "naval knights-errant, who, in default of regular war, are ambitious of signalizing their courage by actions worthy only of the buccaneers". Bishop John Patteson's views were similar, and he believed that all that was required was recognition that the islands were attached to British sovereignty and a small man-of-war to keep up the association. His fear was that islands would fall under French, and thus Roman Catholic, sway. Other missionaries wanted nothing to do with gunboats, but their view was not universal. By contrast, the Reverend John Selwyn of the Melanesian mission said that the peoples of the Solomons were "beginning to have the same sort of belief about a small man-of-war that English boys have of a policeman". Missionaries calling for active gunboat intervention were few and far between, and those who found themselves involved in reprisals – bombardments being the worst – soon distanced themselves from the official uses of naval power. Missionaries were faced with various moral dilemmas. They feared being identified with the superior power of the Navy, and oddly, then, the anti-imperialism of the nineteenth-century missionary was inextricably connected to European expansion. By way of summary, it might rightly be said that

> If the missionary frontier in the Pacific in the nineteenth century cannot be seen as a conscious prelude to Empire, there was throughout a strong conviction that Britain was a chosen Protestant nation which had a world calling. The missionaries grew to accept an imperial idea, that Britain alone among the nations had a sense of trusteeship and would prevent exploitation of the peoples she governed.[13]

And missionaries of all stripes had many friends in Britain, from archbishops and lords spiritual to MPs, adherents to missionary societies, anti-slavery bodies and the Aborigines Protection Society. Even children in Sunday Schools knew of the challenges of missionaries in distant lands, and gave their collection money to what was said to be a worthy cause for progress and assistance.

However, incessant warnings from consuls and naval officers, plus appeals from missionaries and traders, describing local difficulties and chaotic circumstances, were hard to ignore. British governments were forced to take notice. The possibility of foreign control reared its ugly head, and thus it was that ultimately Fiji became a Crown colony. Such a thing would have been unheard of a half-century before, but now the British had an island cluster under form of formal empire in the South Pacific and it was now in Polynesia that the French had secured their advantage.

From island to island and archipelago to archipelago, the distances were immense, which explains why sailing frigates and sloops were used so long here, and steam-powered vessels were of little use. Ships making ports of call were far from home, the distance from Valparaiso to Tahiti alone being almost twice the width of the Atlantic. "The Pacific is a desert of waters," mused Captain Sir Henry Byam Martin at a particularly dreary moment during his long passage across a vast oceanic space; "we seem to have sailed out of the inhabited world, & the *Grampus* to have become the Frankenstein of the ocean – a few boatswain birds hooted us as we sailed along".[14] Lacking rapid and regular communication with the Admiralty, or for that matter even with the commander-in-chief on station, the young commanders of gunboats in the South Pacific were obliged to move in physically dangerous and politically unpredictable environments where their training for war was seldom of much use. They did not come armed with anthropologists' reports or ethnographic factums; no such things existed. Instead they were expected to intervene in the complex affairs of places as ethnically different as Tahiti, New Zealand and Fiji at a time when their operational orders were so broadly worded that they provided little or no specific direction as to how Britain's interest might best be advanced. To make matters worse, their superiors were often "utterly confused" as to what the right course of action might be. Thus politically naive naval officers, guided only by their own sense of humanitarian duty and an "innate dislike of disorder and indiscipline", were placed in positions of acute vulnerability and called upon to make limited or far-reaching decisions which might easily expose them to claims for compensation, Foreign Office censure or threats of legal action.[15]

In 1853 the Admiralty requested Foreign Office opinion on the extent to which commanders might exact from Pacific Islanders redress for wrongs done to British subjects in cases of unprovoked and deliberate murder. The law officers of the Crown opined that it was

> extremely difficult to point out the proper line of conduct to be pursued... [but]... where they actually witness the unprovoked commission of murder or any atrocious crime against British subjects they will be justified in peremptorily demanding redress and the punishment of offenders from the Chief or Chiefs to whose jurisdiction the Criminals belong; and, if no reparation can be obtained, in securing and detaining for a reasonable time the persons of such chief or Chiefs and in resorting to hostilities against the natives immediately dependent on the same authority as the Criminals.

But in cases where crimes were merely reported, the difficulty in acting on evidence supplied by survivors had to be undertaken with "the exercise of the utmost caution and forbearance before resorting to any exercise of force whatsoever".[16] Here then were the rules of intervention, the rules for enforcing law. Quarterdeck diplomacy thus required much tact and a good deal of fact-gathering.

Officers combined a keen sense of public duty with a clear-thinking and fair-minded "hands on" approach to policy definition and implementation. To a man they answered to their lordships by a tight chain of command. They had to resist frequent attempts by on-the-spot consuls, governors and high commissioners, notably Sir Arthur Gordon, to appropriate ships of war for consular or even ferry duties. Standing instructions to naval commanders warned against sending naval brigades ashore (and no farther than the range of the guns). The Admiralty held its independence against Colonial Office infractions and Australian colonial meddling, and in the end maintained a degree of autonomy that allowed it to pursue what it did best – minimum intervention by gunboat action. Far from being heavy handed, persons bearing a commission from Her Majesty bore their obligations with a degree of trust that Colonial Office administrators should have admired more than they did. Shooting up native villages in response to depredations against foolish and often interfering European traders, British and otherwise, was the distasteful side of the business. So too was taking hostages and hanging the guilty from the ship's yardarm. Her Majesty's men-of-war, here as elsewhere, were amphibious policemen, and in the early years of the nineteenth century, law and order was administered from the quarterdeck. In this sense, British naval officers were the new Romans, the lawgivers. Naval officers had no anthropologists' reports to guide them. They had little knowledge of native law and order. They tended to disparage indigenous society norms, which they described as savage, especially because they found cannibalism, infanticide, slavery and intertribal warfare at various places in the Pacific Islands. Rather than get involved as rulers (which they never wanted to do, no matter how keen their desire to protect British interests), they preferred a "hands-off" policy. But time and events were overtaking them. They soon found themselves in circumstances beyond their control.

By the 1870s, this had become quite a different story. The Navy played a key role in establishing a protectorate and later a colony in Fiji and in the subsequent protectorate of the Kingdom of Tonga. Civil authority by order in council came with the Western Pacific High Commission's proclamation, and effectively circumscribed the amphibious judicial power of the Navy, but it did little to give the high commissioner much clout without having a marine constabulary at his disposal. Meanwhile, protecting missionaries, watching nefarious liquor peddlers, and checking blackbirders and labour traffickers became the day-to-day work of the Navy. Watching the guano-trade horrors of the Chinca Islands, where Chinese labour was exploited beyond belief, became a regular Navy duty. Reading in-letters to the Admiralty from hard-pressed lieutenants and commanders is a salutary if sad reminder that the Pacific Ocean was hardly that, and that the salubrious climate and swaying palms might hide from view societies in crisis, victims of external and internal strife. A foretaste of the new imperialism was appearing. Did Britain have to shoulder all of the burden of empire? Germany and the United States were making their needs felt. Partnerships were possible, the byproducts of rivalries. Britain formed a mixed commission with France in the New Hebrides. They partitioned New Guinea with Germany. The Cook Islands and Niue they made a British protectorate and later an annexation to New Zealand. Samoa, where there was a tangle with the Germans, Americans and British, was partitioned, but Britain withdrew in favour of exclusive rights in Tonga, which was also New Zealand's focus. It had all begun with the annexation of Fiji. This event in the imperial progression is important in yet another way because it represented a breakthrough in British expansion in the tropics, a step of the 1870s. It foreshadowed other annexations in the interests of peace and social advancement, an accelerating movement that parallels the scramble for Africa by the great powers.

Although historians have stressed that humanitarian considerations propelled the British Government to annex the Fiji Islands, the naval records reveal deeper aspects of the story. As of mid-century, the British had no naval base midway between Cape Horn and Australasia. The Galapagos Islands, examined in 1845, proved to be unsuitable for a number of reasons. Pitcairn Island had no safe anchorage. Choice spots, such as Hawaii and Tahiti, which could easily have been taken, were turned down on account of American and French rivalry, respectively – and British reticence. The increase in steam navigation, however, and in particular the coming of the ironclad in 1869, meant that berthing and coaling needs had to be met. An American admiral concluded that the conversion of the British Navy to ironclads, which could now keep the sea for any length of time, necessitated a great number of scattered bases. The annexation of Fiji thus became imperative.[17] As the hydrographer Admiral John Washington pointed out in warning, Britain did not have an islet or rock across the 7,000 miles between Vancouver Island and Sydney, the extremes of the Pacific. If the French took Fiji, this would add to fear of the capture of ships full of Australian gold voyaging from Melbourne and Sydney to England, he said incredulously. In the circumstances, Admiral Washington urged annexation.[18] The Fijian chiefs favoured this, too, and concluded a provisional cession of the islands to Britain. Under that arrangement the British consul, Pritchard, had procured the enactment of the law, giving to himself, as the nervous foreign secretary Lord John Russell wrote anxiously, "full, unreserved, entire, and supreme authority to govern Fiji and to make what laws you please". This would not do. Accordingly, a Royal Engineer, Colonel W.J. Smythe, was sent to investigate and report. He dodged the issue of annexation but he did point out the military and strategic necessity of having some sort of naval base in the mid-Pacific. Naval opinion on the spot supported him.[19] So did consular viewpoints. Further, by 1873 it was becoming clear that it would be cheaper to annex Fiji and use it as a naval base rather than keep seven ships on patrol duty there against the kidnapping of Kanaka labour that had now developed. It is to this labour problem that we now turn our attention.

In the late 1860s, Australia became involved in the Kanaka trade. Kanakas ("human beings" in Polynesian) – some 67,000 in nearly 40 years – were conveyed to Queensland to work on sugar plantations. Many of the Kanakas had been kidnapped, hence the term blackbirding. They lived wretched lives, and the Anti-Slavery Society sent outraged reports to the London headquarters. This necessarily involved the Navy, and the Admiralty was sent orders from the Foreign Office to deal with kidnapping and other outrages against the natives, including murder. The Admiralty objected (without effect) not only on the grounds that it was unlikely that Navy ships could end the practice but because Queensland legislation could not be challenged. Further, only one warship was available for this duty, and the area to be policed was vast and intractable.

From bitter experience, naval officers learned that they had constantly to be aware of the legal implications of their actions. The regulations for the Navy bearing on the slave trade of the Atlantic or East African waters had little applicability when it came to their efforts to control the labour trade in the Pacific. That body of law was either inadequate or inapplicable to the Pacific setting. The Admiralty frequently despaired of securing convictions in colonial courts. The Admiralty and the Colonial Office were at loggerheads, seeking to define the legal relations between the commander-in-chief on the Australia station and the Western Pacific High Commission.

As Captain George Palmer of HMS *Rosario* would write, it was mission impossible. Palmer received instructions from Commodore Rowley Lambert of the Australia station to determine if vessels under the British flag were active in the nefarious trade and, if so, to take the necessary action. He cruised for thousands of miles, and in doing so found 14 Australian vessels in the traffic. He despaired of Queensland's legislators and officials. The Colonial Office, with this fresh information, notified Governor Sir George Bowen that he was now under close watch: the traffic in islanders was one "in respect of which ... you are under the most serious responsibility". Bowen, we may recall, was the very same who would first use the term *Pax Britannica* publicly, which he did in London in 1886. A committee struck to examine kidnapping issued a whitewashing report. Captain Palmer was outraged that slavery was denied, and he thought the governor erroneous in stating that the indentured Kanakas serving in Queensland had returned there after having visited their island homes. Charges brought by Palmer against schooner captains engaged in kidnapping faced a tough battle in court.

Parliament passed the Pacific Islanders Protection Act of 1872, condemning kidnapping and defining trial procedures. These were steps in the right direction. Whitehall now oversaw the Pacific. But requiring Australian colonial courts to accept native evidence did not effect a great change. Queensland had a mind of its own on imperial matters and, indeed, its own aspirations: in 1883, for instance, when Germany showed signs of getting a toehold in northeastern New Guinea, Queensland's government under Thomas McIlwraith used its small military resources to seize pre-emptively the southeastern coast in the empire's name. "The Empire was appalled at this colonial arrogance," says the Australian writer Thomas Keneally. The fact of the matter was that there, as in other parts of the world, settlers' ambitions to enlarge the Britannic sphere were strong, and they often took energetic and courageous action to run up the Union Jack in places that London did not, and often refused, to acknowledge. From London's point of view it was a matter of command and control, pure and simple, but the patriotism that the empire had generated could not be controlled in the various colonies. A second act established the High Commissioner for the Western Pacific in 1874, with that officer being overseer of all islands of Polynesia and Melanesia that had not already been annexed by other powers. And mightier and larger did that empire grow: in 1893, Tonga, Samoa, the Ellice and Gilbert Islands, the Solomon Islands, eastern New Guinea, and others came within Britain's web.

The Aborigines' Protection Society had never lost the zeal that characterized its founding, and in 1892 it drew attention in Parliament to "a terrible scandal" – that slavery was "perpetuated in islands under the British Flag". The story, first exposed in the prominent *San Francisco Examiner*, and forwarded by a doctor working in British Columbia, contained a recital of a most shocking sort of slave trade carried on between the Gilbert Islands and Guatemala.[20] Embarrassment in international circles was another reason for solving the problem, to say nothing of humanitarian concern and the continued pursuit of the imperial mission against "blackbirding" and other forms of slave-taking and trading.

Accordingly, in 1892, Captain H.M. Davis arrived at Tarawa in the Gilbert Islands in HMS *Royalist* to proclaim a protectorate. "*Pax Britannica* was a phrase perhaps too often used by Imperialists to cover a multitude of sins," wrote Arthur Grimble, a district officer, in his memoir, *A Pattern of Islands*, "but it really meant the dawn of a newer, richer life for the Gilbertise, as the old folk of my day were never tired of acknowledging." *Royalist* interrupted a war between two houses, those of Teabike and Auatabu, who had split the island of Tarawa and on the very eve of the gunboat's arrival were about to settle old scores once and for all. The same informant writes:

> Had *Royalist* arrived a single day later than she did, the House of Teabike would have become by right of conquest, overlords of every square yard of land on Tarawa. But the Royal Navy saved Auatabu alive, and Captain Davis very rightly ordered that land ownership on the island should remain as it had been before the war began.[21]

The would-be victors were thwarted in their scheme, and resentments ensued. The historian wonders how often naval interventions put a stop to native wars, how often blood feuds were stopped up, and how frequently resentments which would have boiled over were sublimated into new orders only to rise at a later time.[22]

Histories of the Pacific Ocean and its peoples contain reports of British naval sloops and steamers making calls, warning recalcitrant chiefs, and pressing local societies and traders to observe customs of civility. It was all in a day's work. But what of the larger scene? Historians looking back on this phenomenal growth of imperial influences – principally British – in these seas are divided as to the form and nature of the coming of the imperial moment. The Navy gave a unity to the Pacific and means of influence in the islands. W.P. Morrell puts it this way: "the advent of a Power which was mistress of the sea and hence of the means of communication between the island groups gave the history of the Pacific Islands a unity it never previously had".[23] Systems of law, order and polity existed before formal control occurred, as anthropologists are quick to point out. But the invaders who came from afar in their armed ships under various competing national flags presented an altogether different scenario. First came the warships, following and protecting trade, and exploring besides; then the missionaries, those engaged in island trading or the plantation labour traffic (which bordered on slavery); and then the consuls, representatives of foreign offices and state departments. It was easy to report situations of violence and cannibalism, and difficult to suppress the ways of intervention.

The exotic islands, with their enchanting bougainvillea and frangipani, their welcoming lagoons, their sparkling atolls and the soothing drumming of the surf on the outer coral ramparts, were bound to prove attractive to the British imperial readership. Missionary accounts offered little vicarious value, naturally, and it would take Somerset Maugham to cast rain shadows over the Polynesian ideal. Naval officers offered a valuable window on that ever-changing and fragile Pacific world, and works such as John Erskine's *Journal of a Cruise in the Islands of the Western Pacific* (1853), Albert Markham's *Cruise of the "Rosario" amongst the New Hebrides* (1873) and John Moresby's *New Guinea and Polynesia ... a Cruise ... of H.M.S. Basilisk* (1876) are but three of a number of fulsome accounts of arrivals and departures, of hopes and dreams, and of vicarious experiences in a world so different from that of city or country life in Britain, or, for that matter, imperial outposts in Canada, Australia, New Zealand and South Africa, all with English readerships. Such works paled in sales in comparison with Robert Louis Stevenson or R.M. Ballantyne. However, looking back on this body of literature now, we sense a constrained method of literary inquiry and storytelling, natural – we might well gather – given the employment of the authors and their hoped-for future advances in the Service where one was bound to mind their Ps and Qs.

Even so, a handful of naval officers used their experiences, backed by their moral zeal, to expose the horrors of the sandalwood trade and the trade in labourers, alikened in the age to slavery. As with the fight against slavery elsewhere (as led by the British), the crusade against slavery in the South Pacific had necessarily to be a naval matter at the sharp end, with the Foreign Office and Parliament responding as best they could to the horror stories recounted from the distant ocean in the form of highly charged rhetoric from missionaries.

British concerns about controlling turbulence in island communities, and about providing peace and stability under the rule of the quarterdeck (then consular law), had brought to an end the long and desperate but untenable resistance to intervention. Here is a good example of how eccentric influences – those of the chaotic outworks of empire – sucked the imperial power into action. Far from the British pushing the case for an imperium, they were obliged to do so by their own volition on the grounds of meeting the needs of the day as they arose. A half-century after they had resisted every opportunity offered, they had become masters of the South Pacific and Oceania. It was a creation of gunboat power and seaborne law and diplomacy.

By the 1880s France, Germany and the United States were exercising naval authority in these waters, Melanesia in particular forming the last phase, so to speak. The British could act in concert with others when circumstances allowed – with Germany in the Solomon Islands, for instance. And after the *Entente Cordiale* was effected, mixed naval commissions were strengthened in the New Hebrides, where deep distrust of Europeans made even more complicated the terror that existed between the forest tribes of the interior and the coastal peoples, many of whom were driven to islets as places of refuge. In 1905 an Anglo-French force from the warships *Pegasus* and *Muerthe* landed at Malekula to quieten marauders. No discussion could take place: a message was received that "the man-of-war was an old woman" and war had been declared on England. In the circumstances, Commander D'Oyley landed a joint force of 160 strong, with a Maxim gun or two, and a nasty scuffle occurred with the loss of some 30 Malekulan lives. Many were taken prisoner then released on good behaviour, but a change was in the wind as the coercive power spread itself. As one historian comments, "A blow had been struck for law and order; but it was high time to pass from punitive expeditions to regular administration."[24]

Better communications were furthering the imperial pulses. By century's end, Oceania had been brought within the worldwide web. Science continued to annihilate distance. Submarine cables stretched from England to the Cape via Madeira, Ascension Island and St Helena. Sierra Leone and the West African colonies were brought closer to London. Strategic demands brought a submarine cable to fruition between the Cape and Australia, with numerous islands along the route joined to the imperial pulse. In the meantime, in Ottawa in 1894, Canadian and Australian politicians in conference had lobbied for a closer commercial link, and the Admiralty and War Office favoured military deployment to the Pacific via the Canadian Pacific Railway and such steamship services that existed. The Canadian engineer Sir Sanford Fleming had urged the adoption of the scheme, even developing the 24-hour clock for the division of the world plus an international dateline. Mobility of force was the key, and rapidity of response was essential. The main worry was Russia, particularly after the Trans Siberian Railway had bridged the great Asian landmass.

The Admiralty had been shifting naval units from Esquimalt to Hong Kong for decades, but when the transpacific submarine cable was completed in 1902, an "all red route" seemed to secure even the most outlying shores of empire. From Bamfield, Vancouver Island, the cable stretched to Fanning and Fiji islands and then to Norfolk Island, and before long, by two branches, to Queensland and to New Zealand, was linked to the whole. In Whitehall, secretaries and undersecretaries fidgeting about imperial defence needs calculated the number of days and hours needed to reinforce the Hong Kong garrison by sending home-based regiments to Halifax, crossing to Vancouver by rail, then sending them forth on Admiralty-subsidized steamers to China. Besides the manifold commercial and social benefits, cable communication had quickened the pulse of empire and facilitated its defence, and the British had a near monopoly on this sort of communication. Wireless, independent of cable communication, gave the British Empire another strategic, commercial and social link. The Pacific Islands were likewise brought into the imperial web, the superstructure of imperial authority as exercised by communications, ending for all time the illusion of a peaceful island paradise. Thus by the time of the outbreak of war in 1914, the empire was embraced by these new communications, which in their own way made more mobile the naval units that provided the sharp end of British sea power.

9
Send a Gunboat!

As the nineteenth century progressed, the Industrial Revolution changed British naval power and made it more effective in inshore and riverine waters. Sail gave way to steam, and the "wooden walls" yielded to iron and steel ships. By the 1840s, paddlewheel gunboats mounting six 32-pounders were serving on distant stations. They proved effective, within their limits of speed and seaworthiness, in those locations where checking piracy, controlling unruly populations such as gold-seekers, and policing native tribes were the requirement. In the early nineteenth century, flag officers on distant stations requisitioned Congreve rockets and 9-pounder fieldguns – the former to terrorize recalcitrants ashore, the latter to be used by shore or landing parties. As the century wore on, Maxim guns came into use, and even armoured trains, for the purposes of coercion and bombardment. For work on rivers, including the Nile, gunboats could be sent out from British ports in parts and then assembled on the spot. The coming of the railways made British control of rivers and lakes an extension of dominance on and over the seas. *Pax* was spread and made more effective by technology.

As early as 1824 we find in the First Burma War the 60-horspeower paddlewheeler *Diana* as the first steam vessel to be employed in war. This shallow-draft boat was under the command of Captain Frederick Marryat, later a novelist of distinction, and she included a Congreve rocket in her armament.[1] Britain still possessed an antiquated fleet. In the late 1840s and early 1850s, most ships in the British fleet did not have steam power. Thus sloops or corvettes, the customary vessels for colonial duties, lacked mobility in the intricate and often uncharted inland waters. Sometimes, in such circumstances, private steamers or tugboats had to come to their assistance. Frequently they had to anchor a good distance from their place of need and send boat parties ashore in the ship's gig, pinnace or steam launch. Most of Her Majesty's ships carried well-drilled Royal Marines, infantry and artillery, who were sent ashore with sailors for limited periods. They were always well equipped with rifles and small arms. The cutlass and boarding pike had not lost their utility. Sometimes naval brigades took howitzers and other field pieces when terrain, vegetation and weather permitted. In the boats they often had Congreve rockets, which were useful for scaring natives ashore or for burning their villages and watercraft.

That there were, at first glance, surprisingly few steam-powered gunboats available in the early 1850s may be attributed to the grinding parsimony of the Treasury and the reluctance of the lords commissioners of the Admiralty. A general hesitancy existed to supplant sail with steam. There was another issue to deal with: steamers needed coal, and coal was expensive and often hard to deliver to the place of intended need in advance of requirements. Sometimes local coal was useful but often it did not meet the specifications of quality of the Service.

The steady rise of industrialization and the need for fast gunboats capable of manoeuvring in shallow, protected waters during the Crimean War signified a change that came over the enforcing of *Pax* in distant waters. Wooden gunboats, such as *Forward* and *Grappler* – whose very names signified advance and aggression – represented this new machine age. Costing £10,000 each, they had been built to fight the Russians in inshore, shallow waters. The war over, they were fitted for urgent service in British Columbia to counter native "threats" and check the possibility of American aggrandizement. They measured 106 feet in length and had a draft (when barnacles and seaweed did not increase it) of 6 feet 6 inches. They had reciprocating engines of 60 nominal horsepower (206–233 hp actually developed) driving screw propellers that gave a service speed of 7.5 knots. They had a fore-and-aft rig that gave adequate speed under sail in suitable winds. They were designed to carry a 68-pound gun on the forecastle, a 32-pound gun aft and two 24-pound howitzers amidships. They had an economical complement of 36–40 officers and ratings. In all, these gunboats constituted a cheap and effective show of power in inshore waters, such as those of British Columbia, and they had long lives.

The term "gunboat" is a euphemism because in addition to the nominal type as just described, there were gun vessels and steam corvettes, both popular after the 1860s. The gun vessels had superior mobility, speed and firepower compared with the gunboats. They had better sea-keeping abilities. In some locales, heavily gunned and powered steam corvettes, such as *Clio*, and steam frigates, such as *Sutlej*, undertook "gunboat actions" in waters that had been surveyed.

The customary technique of the gunboat commander, using British Columbia as a case study, involved the use of force as the last resort. The young lieutenant would wiggle his vessel into a position where its guns could be used to greatest effect. He would parley with the natives, especially the chiefs. He might take chiefs as hostages. He might employ interpreters and send them with police to the shore. He might hire native informants. As a preliminary show of power, he might fire his guns or shoot his rockets[2] at a chosen target. He would set deadlines and demand compliance. In the 1880s he might even show his new searchlights at night. He might flog offenders for petty crimes, such as pilfering. He might seize property, such as canoes, thereby sealing off avenues of escape. However, if a process of escalating pressure was employed without effect, the ultimate arbiter – force – would be used. This might involve destroying villages, fish weirs and canoes, and also killing inhabitants if any remained in the village. If caught and tried, the guilty would be hanged before the assembled tribe, a portable scaffold being made available. In many cases the smouldering ruins of a village and a scattered tribe were the telling testaments of the process of keeping natives "in awe of British power".[3]

At first glance it might seem as if a gunboat commander was his own agent, acting independently. This was not so. On the Northwest Coast of North America, the Royal Navy did not act independently as policemen. Such quarterdeck diplomacy as conducted by officers commanding warships was invariably backed by official sanction. Here, as elsewhere, the mission of British imperialism was to bring peace, order and good government to the areas of British settlement and to carry civilization and Christianity to the uttermost extremities of the earth. The security of British commerce and settlement was made by skilful diplomacy and military influence, most notably by the Navy. The extension of the rule of law was the primary goal of the British Government.[4] The pursuit of law was a British mission: "The true strength of imperialism", the Earl of Carnarvon, Disraeli's colonial secretary, said in 1878, lay in building a powerful and munificent English community and in restoring law, order and liberty in "backward societies", and thereby creating a system "where the light of morality and religion can penetrate into darkest dwelling places".[5] It was more than *noblesse oblige* and extended to a broadening in the social fabric of the British peoples. Nineteenth-century Britons saw it as their mission to extend their authority to the "savage" and to the "uncivilized". British imperial administrators, whether in Whitehall or the wilderness, were married to the concept of law and order, or, to use the time-honoured phrase, "peace, order and good government".

The 1837 House of Commons Committee on Aborigines considered it a national duty "to carry civilization and humanity, peace and good government, and, above all the knowledge of the true God, to the uppermost ends of the earth". This somewhat superior and righteous viewpoint nonetheless expresses a strong strain of thinking held by some colonial administers of the age. One such, the secretary of state for war and the colonies, the third Earl Grey, argued in 1852 that the extermination of less civilized peoples could be averted by the "enforcement of order". Rather than letting natives be destroyed, the imperial mission of civilization and Christianity, he said, was "a high and noble object well worthy of considerable sacrifice on the part of the British people".

If the British voiced a distain of lawlessness among the "uncivilized", they also knew that whites on distant, unorganized frontiers would act in lawless ways. Traders, whalers, gold-seekers, settlers, missionaries, sailors and others were pressing outwards from the home islands to distant frontiers. The acquisitive habits of these persons on the borderlands of civilization, a colonial secretary wrote in 1837, "compelled the strong to encroach on the weak, and the powerful and unprincipled to wrest by force or fraud, from the comparatively feeble and defenceless, wealth or property or dominion, richer pastures, more numerous herds, and a wider range of territory". In these circumstances the British attempted to prevent turbulence on these frontiers – to control indiscriminate, lawless behaviour by whites against one another and against natives.

Faced with the tricky dilemma of letting those persons police themselves or of intervening through means of authority, both civil and military, invariably the British chose to intervene. "If the colonists of European descent", Earl Grey argued in 1852,

> are to be left, unsupported by the power of the mother country, to rely solely on themselves for protection from fierce barbarians with whom they are placed in immediate contact, they must also be left to the unchecked exercise of those severe measures of self-defence which as position of so much danger will naturally dictate. Experience shows that in such circumstances measures of self-defence will degenerate into indiscriminate vengeance, and will lead to the gradual extermination of the less civilized race.

Thus the extension of law and order was inseparable from the concept of native trusteeship. And frequently it led to an extension, despite contrary pressures, of territorial jurisdiction. Yet again the empire grew in size in spite of the general expectation that such growth could be controlled. Colonial governments naturally wanted to determine their own native policies, but seldom did they have the material means to police the frontiers and protect the settlements. Equally important, the oversight provided by the Colonial and War offices served as a check against upstart governors or councils driven by inflamed legislatures who demanded payment in blood for native-committed crimes against persons and property. The collectivity of colonies under the British flag may have been far flung, but it is fascinating for the historian studying the in- and out-letters of the Colonial Office (or for that matter the Foreign Office, War Office or Admiralty) to see the official mind at work. These departments spoke to one another, sought the advice of the law officers of the Crown (which gave rulings and advice about how to proceed in legal ways), and conducted their work in an efficient and rapid way. Because of this, commanding officers on the spot – civil and military – had a very good idea as to what would be accepted policy at home. In the earliest decades of *Pax*, naval officers were guided by instructions so vague as to be of little help in specific crises. Towards the end of the era, not only were standing instructions clearer but also the shared culture of officers commanding, one that had matured by the steady obligations of maritime command during the long years of peace, gave a personification to the Britannic age. Thus the "official mind" of imperialism was exhibited on the frontiers of turbulence.

These commanders and those who sent instructions from home faced, and could expect to face, one crisis after another, for they worked in an external, chaotic world. It has been estimated that on 230 occasions during Victoria's 64-year reign, the British Empire was "at war". These were colonial wars – emergencies, revolts, rebellions, tribal insurgencies, civil strife and more. *Pax* constituted a unique system of global dominance, but strangely this peace of empire was maintained only by "Queen Victoria's Little Wars". Peace, paradoxically, meant war. The high-minded Lord Glenelg, then secretary of state for war and the colonies, put it this way in 1838:

> The great principles of morality are of immutable and universal obligation, and from them are deduced the laws of war... Whether we contend with a civilized or barbarous enemy, the gratuitous aggravation of the horrors of war on the plea of vengeance or retribution, or on any similar grounds, is alike indefensible.[6]

The extension of Her Majesty's dominions by conquest or by cession was diligently to be avoided. But gratuitous aggravations there were in abundance, and many involved the Navy. Parliamentary committees, the Aborigines' Protection Society, various settler societies and the Church Missionary Society (and similar others) took on watchdog roles, looking for heavy-handed actions by the Navy, shore parties or other military units landed from ships. In the circumstances, naval officers were aware of the difficulties that they might face in the overuse of power.

Indeed the Service was not free from searing criticism. When blue jackets and marines clambered ashore in high spirits and with hopeful expectations after weeks and months at sea, they visited bars and brothels. They gambled and drank. They quarrelled and fought. Brawling sailors set no example for good conduct. Shore patrols did not always stop Jack Tar, when filled with spirits, from visiting native villages, molesting native females and creating a general nuisance. Reports of such behaviour did not reach the lords of the Admiralty, nor were they to be found in the pages of the local papers. They were dealt with by officers on the spot, using Admiralty regulations. Occasionally, such as in a missionary account, they appear. And naval surgeon's records of syphilis and other venereal diseases tell of cross-cultural interaction with lethal consequences of an altogether different sort.[7] "It appears to me", remarked Captain George Henry Richards (who features elsewhere in these pages),

> that in the present relations existing between our people and the Indians, it cannot be a matter of surprise if many wrongs are committed on both sides, and my opinion is that the Natives in most instances are the oppressed and injured parties. The white man supplies him with intoxicating spirits under the influence of which most of these uncivilized acts are committed. The white man in too many instances considers himself entitled to demand their wives or their sisters, and if such demand is disputed, to proceed to acts of violence to gain their object.[8]

In these difficult circumstances, the civil power had to be developed: magistrates, government agents, colonial medical personnel and others. Intermediaries were needed, said Richards and other naval officers, to protect the native persons from the unruly actions of settlers who took the law into their own hands. In such circumstances, the commander-in-chief (Rear Admiral Robert Lambert Baynes) might complain to the local governor (James Douglas of Vancouver Island and British Columbia) that "the whole coast is without civil authority". He might call on him to act to rectify the matter, but truth to tell the colonial authority lacked the material strength to do so, and once again the duty fell to the Navy.

In those days the Navy acted under a social compunction based on the public morality of the times. Nowadays this sort of thing would be unacceptable, and press and Parliament would condemn the official use of violence. However, on the distant margins of the empire in the 1860s, gunboat commanders exercised authority as they saw fit, only governed by the instructions that they possessed from a distant governor or what they think London might accept (or find objectionable and liable to scrutiny or censure). Sometimes there were cover-ups by governors at the local level. Captain Nicholas E.B. Turnour employed the steam corvette *Clio* against the Kwakiutl of Vancouver Island, who were accused of murdering whites near Fort Rupert, northern Vancouver Island, a Hudson's Bay Company post. The civilian pilot, hired as interpreter aboard *Clio*, said that it was his opinion that the Indians needed to be taught "a salutary lesson not to play with a man-of-war as they boasted they were doing prior to the shells coming amongst them... They will not forget the *Clio*, however." These Indians were among the toughest on the Northwest Coast, but the same authority said that the whites who knew Indian character were convinced that firm action was necessary in this case: "sharp chastisement" brings effects to the Indians in question and to neighbouring tribes; "kindness and forbearance they cannot understand". The colonial legislature objected to the action, on grounds that it seemed excessive, and demanded explanation. The governor of the day was Captain Arthur Kennedy. As an explanation for his actions, he was wont to say: "It is better to be decidedly wrong than undecidedly right." He had served on the Irish famine commission, and he had previously been governor of Sierra Leone and of Western Australia. Governor Kennedy, who soon acquired a reputation as a soldierly-like man, consulted his executive on the matter, and the decision was made not to produce the files on the incident, leaving the legislature speechless and unable to act. The matter went no farther.

Sometimes the gunboat commander might be the most Christian of fellows and quite willing to assist the Church Missionary Society in its worthy endeavours. Such was the case with Captain James Charles Prevost, who also believed that merely "showing the flag" would suffice to put a stop to piracies. At other times, such a personality might act in the most forthright and energetic way, leaving no doubt as to how he thought Her Majesty's warships should act in the circumstances. Of a slightly different breed was Rear Admiral the Hon. Joseph Denman. He won fame as a fighter against the slave trade in West Africa and became Palmerston's model of a naval officer in actions working close inshore. He became commander-in-chief of the Pacific in 1864. He had 14 ships of various classes at his disposal and the whole eastern half of the Pacific to police. However, the difficulties that developed at Clayoquot, particularly against a native people known as the Ahousat, just north of where Tofino, British Columbia, is today, required bringing in all available resources and firepower.

A cluster of islands, interspersed by deep channels running into the spine of Vancouver Island, formed the landscape. Heavy forests reached up into the hills and mountains beyond. It was a land where strong tribes had developed in consequence of trade, raiding and internecine warfare. Here, not long before, warfare had been a way of life, the last big war being in 1855. To the European mindset, these tribes were brazen in their outlook. "Native outrages" had become numerous, and white offenders had also to be kept in check. A sealing vessel, *Kingfisher*, had been pirated. Governor Kennedy called for aid from the civil power, when the local Indians were showing strong resistance against the paddlewheel sloop *Devastation* under Commander John Pike. The imperial rhetoric is clear. "There could be no future safety for coasters frequenting that part of the island," the governor warned Denman, "if the perpetrators of this diabolical crime are not brought to justice with a view to deter them and afford a warning example to neighbouring tribes." Every effort should be made to capture the suspects, who should then be quickly and effectively punished. "Humanity and sound policy alike demand this." It was time to deal with "these misguided savages".[9]

Employing *Sutlej* in concert with *Devastation*, Denman cleared out all native resistance. Shells and rockets were used as this frontier was sealed. Within a week, Denman was able to report to the Admiralty his success. The pacification was complete. Nine native villages and 64 canoes had been destroyed, and at least 15 Indians had been killed. "The success of this attack," he wrote, "conducted after the fashion of their own tactics, has produced profound discouragement, Chapchah [the leader and a native chief] being in hiding and pursued by his own people, who had abandoned all ideas of resistance and look on him as responsible for all the evils that have befallen him." Governor Kennedy expressed thanks to the Navy for the "forebearing and effective manner" in which the service and punishment had been performed. He confidently maintained that the measure would promote the colony's security, aid its commerce and check the "piratical and bloodthirsty attitudes of the Coast Indians, which have been left too long unpunished". The Supreme Court of the colony, in Victoria, refused to admit native testimony, thus infuriating Denman, who correctly saw that the Navy would lose face. Indeed, according to a local trader and part-time anthropologist, Gilbert Malcolm Sprout, who discussed the matter with the Indians after the incident, the Ahousats believed that they "had gained a victory over the ships, and, in consideration of such a triumph, all the trouble of making new canoes has been forgotten. Chapchah has added to his reputation; he is the great chief who defied and baffled the English on King-George war vessels." The Roman Catholic priest (of the Oblate order), Agustin Brabant, wrote similarly:

> The Indians had not given up their chief to the white man; they had lost their houses, canoes and *Iktas* [i.e. possessions], but these they could and would build again; some of their number were taken prisoner, but were afterwards returned to them ... therefore they claimed a big victory over the man-of-war and big guns.[10]

When reviewing (as was customary in all such circumstance) the concluding report of proceedings sent them by Denman, the lords of the Admiralty had no quarrel with the commander-in-chief's actions. In point of fact, they expressed pleasure at the able and satisfactory manner in which the operations had been conducted. The Colonial Office, apparently considering the matter rather routine, similarly approved the proceedings. Perhaps it reflected its political persuasion because its Liberal successors during Gladstone's first administration did not agree with similar tactics of a punitive expedition taken against another tribe in what is known as "the *John Bright* affair". The local press was mindful of the social costs of these actions. The Victoria newspaper *British Colonist*, in its issue of 12 October 1864, praised the Navy for exhausting every peaceable means before resorting to "extremities" to bring the Indians to terms.

> We have demonstrated our power, we have shown our inflexible determination to carry out the law and to punish the aggressors; let us see that we fail not on the other side – that we leave the Indians no reasonable complaint against us; but carry out our responsibilities toward them by improving their condition, protecting them from injustices on the part of the whites, and, in fact, giving them every legitimate return for the lands of which we have despoiled them.

Denman knew that vessels larger than the *Forward* and *Grappler* needed to be readily available for pacification work on this dangerous shore. The aggressions against British traders had increased "to a formidable account by long continued impunity", he advised the Admiralty, and although the actions he had taken in Clayoquot Sound, west coast Vancouver Island, would prevent their recurrence for some time, it was most desirable that all such cases of murder and piracy should be prosecuted. He thought that a colonial gunboat, commanded by an experienced officer familiar with Indian ways and languages, would suit the requirements.[11] But the colonial authorities did not accept this challenge. Thus it was that the gun vessels *Sparrowhawk, Rocket* and others were sent from England. They had better sea-keeping abilities than the old gunboats, and greater firepower. The ultimate arbiter of empire is the power wielded by the ruler, and in this particular imperial frontier, and in many others like it, the British held the upper hand with their gunboats. They provided the technological advantage, the seaborne variant of Hilaire Belloc's

> Whatever happens we have got
> The Maxim gun, and they have not.

A gun-carrying steamer, as a veteran of the Burma River wars, Colonel W.F.B. Laurie of the Royal Marines, said, was a powerful " 'political persuader,' with fearful instruments of speech, in an age of progress!"[12]

The outrages continued. Whites continued to expand their interests up and down the coast. Mining and forestry was still in its infancy. Church Missionary Society stations were established at the Nass River, the Skeena River, on Haida Gwaii and at Fort Rupert. Liquor vendors pursued a nefarious trade among native peoples. Smallpox, native prostitution and syphilis depleted the native populations, and not until the 1870s was a Canadian Indian agent, a doctor, appointed, though the resources placed at his disposal were virtually nil. Farther north, towards Alaska, and showing no regular pattern, the Indian actions against the whites continued. In its missions the Church Missionary Society served as an excellent example of how pacification could occur without force: its achievements at the new coastal towns of Alert Bay and Metlakahtla, the latter an industrial village, invited many fine comments from naval officers.

These same officers – also travellers, missionaries and government officials – found themselves involved with intractable problems on this same coast. For although the Crown's writ had been extended there, and peace established, quarrels soon developed in the indigenous nations themselves. The native bands had heard of Queen Victoria but they had never seen her, only her representatives. How could the Queen own the land, they wondered? The concept of sovereignty as talked about by the lawmakers and agents, involving as it did title to land, was alien to their way of thinking, and their aboriginal title to land had never been surrendered. So went the popular argument.

Even so, surveyors came and laid down the boundaries of the reserves. Missionaries representing different denominations had brought competition – and introduced division in Indian discussions. It was proven that a missionary made a poor government agent. Well-educated and articulate Indian agents were needed. As the commissioners representing Canada and British Columbia stated in their 1887 report,

> the Indians... probably imagine that they know a great deal and are thoroughly able to say what is good for themselves. So in a way that would not call for particular attention were it not seriously intended, they hold themselves as above and beyond the existing laws which affect them as Indians... To leave them longer to pursue their course unaided, uninstructed, as to the objects and purport of the law, uncontrolled by the civil power, would be fatal to any probability of a future peace.[13]

Even Metlakatla, regarded as a model of a new community, with its clapboard-sided houses, workshops, business practices and brass band, had fallen by the wayside. Factions in that community pitted supporters of the missionary William Duncan against the inveterate older guard of tribal members. Gunboats had been brought in to keep the peace. But in the end, Duncan led his followers north to Annette Island, Alaska, there to found New Metlakahtla, under the careful watch, though from afar, of the London and New York philanthropist Henry Welcome. That the migration had taken place in the year of the Queen-Empresses' Golden Jubilee did not go unnoticed by the press of the day, and the thought that natives previously under Britain's guardianship had got into their canoes and boats and found a new home and shelter in neighbouring American territory attracted comment of horror and disbelief. The Americans had no exemplary Indian policy, as was well known. And it was wondered what had driven the Church Missionary Society's leading missionary on the British Columbia coast to decamp with his charges for foreign parts.[14] Such triumphs as the Church Missionary Society might claim in its publications and pronouncements about raising up savage societies and offering redemption hid from view all of the horrors of acculturation on the frontiers of influence, and all the sweeping aside of existing political and social structures of the indigenous peoples. There is no doubt but that the Navy, in sustaining even nominally the Church Missionary Society and other such missionary societies, aided and abetted the process that First Nations (and their adherents and supporters) rue to this day. Nor did the British Columbia coast stand alone, for by the late 1850s the Church Missionary Society had a complete girdle of missionary stations round the world. That the Northwest Coast had a vibrant and extensive mission field and that there was another across the vast Pacific at Shanghai gave Church Missionary Society leaders cause for hearty thanks, and Captain Prevost, who had come forward to offer his help in conveying the first missionary to British Columbia in the steam corvette *Satellite*, earned a place of honour in Church Missionary Society annals.[15]

Pacification was a work of decades, and not until 1890 had the practitioners completed their task. The Navy based on Esquimalt even answered the appeal of foreign governors in difficulty in the face of native risings or other challenges: it assisted the American authorities in Puget Sound, the Russians in Russian America when a problem arose at Sitka, and the Americans after Alaska had been acquired by the United States in 1867.[16] The pulls to the north on this frontier were not just those of missionaries and gold-seekers, for with them came the need to defend persons and property – and bring law and order to this frontier.

"Indigenous peoples rarely overlooked how it was they came under imperial rule or passed from the dominion of one imperial power to that of another," wrote Nicholas Mansergh when summing up the experience of the empire and the Commonwealth.

> For them the distinctions between settlement, annexation, cession and conquest, with a terminological indifference, were apt to remain, possibly for generations, matters deep in individual and group consciousness. This was a factor of varying but often of profound experience for Empire and for the shaping of the later Commonwealth and one that is by no means always adequately conveyed in imperial historical writings with their brief, passing allusions to the negotiation of treaties, the establishment of protectorates, forays on the frontier and the native wars which pushed outward the boundaries of Empire.

What accounts for this remembrance of times past and of processes of change? In terms of the wider views of a directing imperial policy, these little wars and gunboat actions were small affairs, doubtless. As Mansergh puts it,

> things looked and are remembered differently from the other side of the hill. There, if and when it came to the final test of force, indigenous peoples had

> sometimes numbers but rarely weapons. The possession of the Maxim gun, as Belloc noted with brutal irony in simple verse, made all the difference. But it made all the difference not only in the outcome of the struggle but to the way in which it was then and later regarded. The possessor of the Maxim gun, and his historians, could afford to take a causal view of an episode of colonial history; the victims of it, on the other hand, were more likely to be decimated, dismayed or psychologically overwhelmed in the face of new and unknown instruments of power.[17]

But always there were costs and particularly societal disruptions, even the ends of native communities, bands and languages or dialects. Two anthropologists, writing about the influence of British gunboats on the Northwest Coast, put it this way:

> War had a unifying aspect in making groups come together in tribes and confederacies for greater mutual strength, but it also destroyed people. And those related to both sides in a conflict suffered torn loyalties. War contributed to the plunge in population in the turbulent period after the coming of the Europeans, but it virtually ended about the middle of the 19th century when Vancouver Island became a British colony and Her Majesty's gunboats brought *Pax Britannica* to the Whaling People.[18]

The Navy constituted the cutting edge of an imperial instrument dedicated to establishing the rule of law on behalf of the empire, the young dominion of Canada and the province of British Columbia. The imperial tide had risen so as to lap against every native village. Meanwhile, in England, Oscar Wilde was writing pensively in *Ave Imperatrix*:

> Set in this stormy Northern sea,
> Queen of these restless fields of tide
> England! What shall men say of thee,
> Before whose feet the worlds divide?
> The earth, a brittle globe of glass,
> Lies in the hollow of thy hand,
> And through its heart of crystal pass,
> Like shadows through a twilight land,
> The spears of crimson-suited war,
> The long white-crested waves of fight,
> And all the deadly fires which are
> The torches of the lords of Night.

And England had reason to pause, for the empire was an English product, which changed England itself. And what of the other side of the hill, and of the frontier? These little wars of the frontier, these parades of power – countless in number, puzzlingly insignificant in the amalgam but vitally illuminating in their individual particularities of character, circumstance and place – were episodes of empire whose legacies of distrust and regret linger where Northwest Coast peoples gather still. And many are the white adherents to their cause. The extension of law and order was accomplished by force.

By and large, the young naval commanders and lieutenants who did the bulk of the work were, in fact, *bona fide* justices of the peace, authorized under colonial law. They were more than anything else in that time and place amphibious policemen pursuing policies of minimum intervention and acting in the awkward and inexperienced role of sailor-diplomats. Seldom, if ever, did they act on their own initiative. Responding to requests of the civil authority, they would make a show of power, exact justice by peaceful means if possible, and only by violent measures when necessary. They attempted to check a nefarious liquor trade. They helped to stamp out slavery (there under 10 per cent of the native population) by stopping intertribal marauding. They assisted missionaries, protected shipping, secured settlers and, in general, preserved law and order where and when they could. They were, in short, servants of an imperial cause, guardians of a British peace and, in their own, reluctant way, pathfinders of empire.

For the men who made and carried out the decisions, this type of forest diplomacy must have been distasteful. All too frequently, naval officers have been classified among what the distinguished jurist and parliamentarian Sir William Harcourt called "the warlike classes" – that is, armed agents of empire bullying their way through scrapes with natives and extending British domains in distant places. With few exceptions they were Victorian men of conscience. Some experienced officers, such as Fairfax Moresby and Joseph Denman, could be both high-handed and high-minded. "These wretched creatures", a ship's captain wrote plaintively of his punitive expedition in the Pacific Islands, "have been hunted and worried till it will be long before they settle again... I regret that my whole voyage in these islands has been one of apparently ruthless destruction, but no other course has been possible."[19] Another, Admiral John Moresby, attested in his memoirs some years after the 1853 Cowichan expedition (another Vancouver Island episode of gunboat action) and recalled that as a young gunnery lieutenant the excitement of the event served at the time to suppress any twinge of conscience. Only later did he realize the meaning of the barbarities that he was undertaking for Queen and country. The expedition, he reflected, was "one of the myriad tragedies of the red man's collision with civilization".[20]

"Send a gunboat!" had become a common cry on the British Columbia coast and almost everywhere where British interests were threatened in one way or another. The Foreign Office might ask the Admiralty to browbeat the Manchu or suppress Malay pirates. The Colonial Office might badger their lordships to help a governor or consul in a tight scrape with a foreign foe or an internal enemy. The Archbishop of Canterbury might request aid for a missionary in trouble in Borneo. The British Museum might appeal for protection for harried archaeologists in North Africa. In the same year their lordships received the governor of British Columbia's request to prop up British authority during the Fraser River gold rush, secretaries at the Admiralty had to deal with a flood of correspondence dealing with other requests, all of them granted, from New Zealand, Panama, Kuria Muria Islands, Honduras, Siam, Brazil, Sarawak, Alexandria, Vera Cruz, Morocco and Newfoundland. Such demands seemed incessant, a Foreign Office secretary complained. British agents of empire liked the sense of security supplied by the white ensign. Even in places where no treaty ties bound native to national interests, "claims of humanity" obliged the British to yield assistance.[21]

These demands for "showing the flag", putting down rebellions or intimidating natives meant continual drains on the Treasury in spite of parliamentary objections. In 1871, for instance, half of the naval expenditures went on policing the seas. If economies were to be effected, said the businesslike, penny-pinching first lord of the Admiralty, Goschen, during Gladstone's 1868 administration, overseas squadrons would have to be reduced and fewer duties undertaken for humanity in every corner of the earth. "The fact is", he groaned, "that half our expenditure is not for war service in the strict sense, but keeping the policy of the seas and protecting semi-barbarous and barbarous men against kidnapping and various forms of outrage. Philanthropy decidedly costs money."[22]

Although comparisons are invidious, far more damaging to indigenous populations than the warlike actions of British gunboats was the change brought about by the introduction of diseases that had originated in the Eastern Hemisphere, such as smallpox, malaria, measles and influenza. Alcohol, prostitution and syphilis were supplementary causes of native decline. It has been conservatively estimated that at the time when Euro-Americans began to visit the Northwest Coast in the late 1770s, the native population was around 180,000. A century later only about 35,000 remained.[23] The effect of these diseases on natives reduced the population size, structure, interactions and viability. This onslaught, like the invisible influences of diseases in human history over the centuries, sadly passes without comment by the critics of the imperial process and its results.

10

Anti-Slavery: West Africa and the Americas

Pax brought the gift of peace in places that were accustomed to war but it itself called for the use of force. Africa, a continent of many societies and peoples, posed special problems in certain locales, for it was a place of warlords, and slaves were property captured in war. Whole kingdoms arose from the human pillage. Traffic in slaves by slave-hunters "fermented tribal warfare, destroyed native African culture and agriculture, dispersed peaceful communities, caused unimaginable suffering, destroyed natural immunity to disease and rendered refugees vulnerable to infections they had not previously encountered".[1] It fell to the Navy, as servant of the state, to quell the traffic at sea and on the coasts. This was a central feature of *Pax*. *Pax* was a latter-day consideration in the long history of the African continent, and it had a short life, for once the policing duties of the Navy and the diplomatic pressures brought by the Foreign Office, and even colonial governors ashore, came to an end, control of African societies and principalities passed to other hands. While it lasted, it was a gallant and altruistic attempt to establish freedoms, promote human liberty, and release thousands from bondage ashore and afloat.

Some in Britain thought peace and progress were best brought by missionary enterprise or model farms. Others realized that these schemes would only invite intractable obligations: Africa ought best be left to Africans, ran the argument, and, provided that the British enjoyed freedom of trade, and made that freedom available to all nations, the best benefit for Africa could be achieved. The free flow of goods in and out of the swampy and infested estuaries caught the attention of the policy-makers early in the years of *Pax*, and they adhered to it to the very end. By that time, however, lines in the sand had been drawn, markers put down establishing spheres of influence and protectorates, and indications of the extent of future African states and their capitals had been given. Much has been made of the influence of technology on the reordering of Africa, but one observer of the late *Pax* years, Sir Harry Johnston, said this, with wisdom: "The ease with which the white man... implanted himself in Africa, as governor, exploiter and teacher [was] due more to the work of Missionary Societies than the use of Machine guns..."[2]

There was much moral suasion attached to the campaign against the slave trade. But there was another way of looking at it that did not escape the utilitarian and legal minds of the day: the British effort to secure peace was designed essentially to promote lawful commerce. *Pax* was thus tied to law, and trade was its undeniable vehicle, with the Navy being its necessary advance force and ultimate guardian. In all there were many quarrels about ends and means. The Navy was obliged to shift with the changing requirements of the Foreign Office, which came under pressure from various interests. Humanitarianism cut a wide swathe, and many were the theories about how peace and progress might be extended in the "dark continent". Vacillations of purpose had to be interpreted and dealt with in the boardroom of the Admiralty, and then instructions sent out to the Cape or to Sierra Leone to alert officers commanding of the new requirement. As we will see, the shifting sands had to be crossed. Niall Ferguson comments on the moral suasion that engulfed the British population and obliged the Admiralty to accept the necessary duties of coercion and liberation:

> Here was a measure of the strength of the campaign against the slave trade: that it could mobilize not only legislators to ban the trade, but the Royal Navy to enforce the ban. That the same navy could more or less simultaneously be engaged in opening the ports of China to the Indian opium trade makes clear that the moral impulse for the war against the slave trade did not come from the Admiralty.[3]

Eric Williams in his famous book *Capitalism and Slavery* made the powerful claim that Britain abolished the slave trade because by the late eighteenth century it had become unprofitable.[4] This view has been countered by Seymour Drescher, who says that slavery and thus slave-trading were important in the early nineteenth century for the British economy, a time when the country stood to make significant profits, and that a decline followed the abolition of slavery in 1833.[5] Neither of these views is sacrosanct, and historians will continue to debate the issue of whether interest trumped humanity or vice versa.[6]

During four centuries, ships carried an estimated 10 million persons in bondage from Africa to the Americas.[7] About 60 per cent were transported in the half-century before 1820. Most were shipped to the Caribbean and to Brazil. The Portuguese had been at Benin, a powerful kingdom, as early as 1485. The Dutch and the English soon built factories. The Royal African Company was founded in 1660 as an English trading monopoly; the French West Indies Company followed in 1664; and the Swedes, Dutch, Danish and Brandenburgers were at various places along the shore. The stations had grave problems of disease, dilapidation and maintenance cost, while boredom, drunkenness and brawling were common among the occupiers.[8] The British concentrated on the Gold Coast and confronted the Dutch at Elmina and Axim. Peoples of West Africa – Ibo, Akan, Wolof and Serer, for instance – had stable societies, though of immense differences, and lots of warrior chiefs with soldier-slaves existed, fortified by tax-acquiring techniques. Many societies were hierarchical and undeniably artistic, involving bronze, wood and ivory carvings among others, and lovely fabrics. Some nations did not come under European control till late in the century (Yoruba in 1893), but in Benin there was strong pressure by the British in 1851, and at other times, leading to early annexation (in 1861). In the Akan states of Ashanti and Fanti, where a war for primacy as middlemen in the trade to the coast led to the aggrandizement of the Ashanti, the British eventually intervened to prevent their paramount status. General "All Sir Garnet" Wolseley brought an army there in 1874 with successful though short-term results.[9] Two further expeditions would be sent, and in 1901 the Ashanti kingdom was absorbed into the Gold Coast protectorate.

An ambitions scheme of reform for Africa began with the Sierra Leone Company to set up a factory in Freetown, a place for freed slaves. Those persons who subscribed to the scheme imagined new forms of commerce in agricultural and forest products, nuts, cloths, indigo and various other African wares to be a counterweight to slave-trading at nearby Bruce Island. These investors thought in terms of rivers as conduits of trade opening up even larger watersheds of the interior. These were rivers of empire and of influence. They were waterways and roads by Christians for reconciliation. For half a century this was the message and the hope, and it brought forth persons as various as Hannah More, James Watt, Zachary Macaulay and Thomas Fowell Buxton. The African Association, Thomas Clarkson and Sir Joseph Banks were likewise occupied with it. On the religious side the motive existed to overcome Mohammed. This project faltered and in time the company failed. Even so, it had a lasting influence on the abolition movement, especially on Thomas Clarkson.[10]

The anti-slavery movement continued to gather momentum. Once the Claphamites (or Clapham Sect) turned to the fight against slavery, the matter became one of national importance. The power of the Claphamites cannot be underestimated.[11] From this knot of men sprang most of the Bible societies and almost all of the missionary societies in the world, said Sir James Stephen in 1844. These evangelicals and Quakers, such as the pathologist Thomas Hodgkin, found allies in the Tories. They created a powerful lobby in and out of Parliament that not only changed British politics and forced a reform of British trade in prosperous channels of commerce (shipping, West African commerce, West Indies trade in slaves), but also began a revolution in the form of diplomatic pressure that by the 1860s had completed, or nearly so, circumstances in which trading in slaves had been suppressed. By 1836, Britain had signed treaties with Spain, France, Portugal and Brazil for the suppression of the slave trade. The moral suasion of the British knew no bounds, and the diplomatic persuasion employed by the British was persistent and formidable.

The energy and idealism of the "Saints", powerful in and out of Parliament, had brought results in the form of a colony for repatriated blacks under British control at Sierra Leone, which was landed in 1787. Over the years, this colony, with its capital Freetown, became a place for the reception of freed slaves. Here was a new opportunity for the Church Missionary Society, and some ex-slaves from Bermuda and Nova Scotia were transported there. In 1807, the same year that Parliament abolished the slave trade, the British Government took over control of Freetown from the Royal African Company. Philanthropy and political expediency had trumped the old mercantile system. Naval officers such as John Atkins, James Ramsay and James Prior showed a longstanding interest in the anti-slavery crusade. The most damning indictment of the slave trade came from naval surgeons. They provided much evidence for Wilberforce, Clarkson and the antislavery lobby.[12] Ramsay wanted agricultural colonies to be established as places for slaves in British sugar colonies to be relocated to. Petitioners for parliamentary action included a number of societies, including the Society for Missions to Africa and the East, the parent group of the Church Missionary Society, which worked with older Anglican organizations, the Society for the Promotion of Christian Knowledge and the Society for the Propagation of the Gospel in Foreign Parts. Many of the members had their eyes set on Sierra Leone, the first of the British colonies in West Africa, set up for liberated slaves of the American Revolution and freedom-seekers from Nova Scotia.

By act of Parliament of 1 May 1807, the British slave trade was abolished, and on the eve of this the 300-ton ship *Kitty's Amelia* of Liverpool was cleared for a last voyage. Between 1700 and the year of abolition, ships from Liverpool carried about 1.5 million Africans across the Atlantic. Moreover, about a third to a half of Liverpool's trade was with Africa and the Caribbean. Thus the leaving of Liverpool by *Kitty's Amelia* not only signified the end of an era but also demarked the end of an economy. With some anxiety and passion, her captain, Hugh Crow, wrote sorrowfully in after years "that the traffic in Negros was permitted by that Providence which rules over all, as a necessary evil, and that it ought not to have been done away with to humour the folly of the fancy of a set of people who knew littled or nothing about the subject". To his way of thinking, the philanthropists, through the abolition, had pushed the trade into other hands, where cruelty and disregard for human life was exhibited "to which Englishmen could never bring themselves to resort".[13] Leaving aside the validity of his claims, one thing is certain: one of the "sinews of empire" died with the abolition, and many were the complaints from ship owners and suppliers, who announced that abolition would not only lead to their personal ruination but would weaken the British economy and diminish the carrying trades upon which the profit and power of the realm depended. But once Parliament had acted, and with such resolution and public support, a death knell of the British slave trade had been tolled. The old triangle trade – from British ports to West Africa, across the Middle Passage to the West Indies, then north to Nova Scotia and Newfoundland, then home – with profitable cargoes on each leg of the golden round had come to a staggering halt.

It was in these circumstances that the Navy was tasked with giving support to the new colony and policing the slave trade. The next year, 1808, two warships, *Solebay* and *Derwent*, were sent to this coast.[14] This foreshadowed further obligations and endless headaches for policy-makers and practitioners. Freetown was the only possible place for a station headquarters. An Admiralty court empowered to condemn prizes was set up there. Ashore, at Sierra Leone, the old militia, Goree African Corps, was renamed in 1809 as Royal African Corps. Ten years later its duties were taken over by the West India Regiment (European officers, ex-slave rank and file), which by 1880 was garrisoning Sierra Leone, the Gold Coast, British Honduras and British Guiana, the recruits mainly comprising liberated slaves.[15] Here was another twist of empire. Sierra Leone boasted a commodious and safe harbour, with wood and water, rice and fresh provisions, plus good communications and the best situation on the coast between Gibraltar and the Cape of Good Hope.[16] Even so, Freetown had one of the worst climates on the coast and had a well-earned reputation of being malaria infested. Sailors on shore leave suffered mightily, and with macabre expression they said that ships' standing orders permanently detailed one party "employed digging graves as usual" and another "making coffins until further orders".[17]

Meanwhile, the African Association sent Mungo Park to explore the interior parts of Africa. The British humanitarian movement looked to Africa as a vast field where improvement could be made, and the ending of slavery and the slave trade might be accomplished. The tasks were of inordinate magnitude and invited much sensible pessimism. At the dawn of our period, much had been done. There was talk of redeeming Africa, and even atonement for British sins committed. The crusade grew in popularity in Britain. The British had become not only the practitioners of maritime ascendancy and commercial dominance people of the light. Here is the way one historian puts it:

> the "Saints," by single-minded devotion to one cause through the dark days of war, anti-Jacobism, unpopularity and personal abuse, had achieved the first and hardest step towards the destruction of an evil seemingly indestructible, had wakened the conscience of the British people and planted a humanitarian tradition in the heart of British politics.

A point of no return had been reached.[18]

Once the British stopped their own national commerce in the sordid business, it remained to put a stop to that of the French, Portuguese and Americans. The rhetoric could be high sounding, but implementation came at a high cost. No progress could be made without great effort, naval and diplomatic. Nothing came easily. Abolishing the British slave trade was a victory of principle over national economic interest, and the French were delighted that the British had withdrawn from the trade, which they now saw as more appropriately their own. The French proved the most difficult for the Foreign Office to deal with. Some British merchant shipping continued in the trade under false flags, carrying slaves to Cuba and Brazil. But the British Government tightened the noose, and in 1824, when slaving was declared to be piracy, the crime was punishable by death.[19] The Navy was sent to cruise against pirates and slavers in the Caribbean and off the coast of Brazil, just as it sought to police the trade on the coasts of Africa. In the meantime, in Britain, the Anti-Slavery Society was formed in 1823. Its exalted goal was to abolish slavery in British colonies and dependencies. Backed by evangelical churchmen and the "Saints" who met in the charged atmosphere of Exeter Hall, London, and reinforced by bilateral treaties on the subject (the 1815 peace treaties had had anti-slaving clauses inserted but not enforced), gradually the pressure mounted against slavers on a broad front. "Great Britain alone, in the 1820s, possessed the self-confidence, the righteous arrogance and the naval force to police the seas of the world and to send armed ships in pursuit of sinners," is the way John Parry, historian and former naval officer, describes the new mission.[20] How effective the naval patrols were is doubtful, and some critics dubbed them the "sentimental squadron". Often the ships on patrol were not fast enough to catch the nimble and elusive slavers or pirates. Even so, British naval annals are rich with success stories of slaving vessels captured and of slaves set free. Many were the triumphs in the cause of liberty and freedom that rested in accounts of British naval power.

And what of American commerce and policies during this same time? And how did the Americans respond to British pressure? For one thing, the Americans would never submit to the "right of search" at sea which the British requested of all treaty partners. The British led by example and followed with moral suasion and diplomatic zeal. Alone of the great nations, Britain in the year 1820 mounted a crusade against slave traders, and it would take another 40 years for the Americans to become partners in the same mission. London looked hopefully to Washington. By an act of Congress of 1794, no person could build or fit a vessel for the slave trade. The Treaty of Ghent specified that Britain and the United States would suppress the trade to their "utmost endeavours". Five years passed before Congress, in 1819, authorized the United States Navy to suppress American participation in the African slave trade. In 1820 a further act made slave-trading an act of piracy, a capital crime punishable by death. The effect of these laws was effectively to drive Americans out of the trade and to work through surrogates or miscreants. Merchants as far north as Machias in Maine were named as taking part in the "Black Ivory" trade.[21] That same year saw an African squadron protecting American citizens and property, stopping vessels flying the Stars and Stripes from trading in slaves, and assisting the colony of Liberia, established by the American Colonization Society for freed slaves. After 1823 the American squadron shifted attention to the West Indies, there to suppress piracy (regarded as the greater evil). An American squadron in Africa was no longer maintained on a regular basis until after the Webster–Ashburton Treaty of 1842, in which both parties agreed to maintain squadrons mounting a minimum of 80 guns on West Africa to police the slave trade. Established in 1843, the US Navy's African Squadron had four or five ships only, rarely mounting the requisite armament, and based at Madeira or the Cape Verde Islands, too far north for effective action. Between 1842 and 1850 the haul was but ten suspected slavers, and not until the appointment of Commodore William Inman in 1859 did any zeal infuse the work. In two years he seized 11 of the 24 slave ships captured during the squadron's two-decade existence, and liberated 2,793 of 4,945 blacks freed during the era. The African squadron was called home during the American Civil War, and its duties were taken up by the Royal Navy. The breakthrough African Slave Trade Treaty of 1862 permitted British ships to inspect vessels flying the American flag. This was a British diplomatic triumph over the independent-minded American maritime power. Given the power of the South in the US Cabinet, it was not until the end of the Civil War, and indeed some time thereafter, that the United States joined in the crusade.[22] In short, the bulk of the work rested with the Royal Navy.

Along West Africa's forbidding, dreary coast, maritime authority rested with a handful of ships of the Royal Navy, principally in the suppression of the slave trade and the promotion of legitimate trade. This coast was difficult to police, not least because of its complicated geography. Sailing Directions, issued by the Hydrographic Department, once described the dreaded Bight of Benin as follows: "This coast is forbidding in its aspect, dangerous of approach, repulsive when examined and disgusting when known." Surveying was continued in some places, between spells in the Bight. It was officially recognized that a change of scene and frequent reliefs were needed, for as one commodore observed, "On this coast both mind and body are liable to give way under the dreadful monopoly."[23] Much of the coastline lay in the pestilential tropical rainforest belt, except near Senegal (semidesert), and the Gambia (savanna), while the Niger River delta was characterized by humid jungle swampland, devilishly unhealthy for European crews – "a white man's grave". Winds and currents off this 3000-mile shoreline presented other demands to the squadron, and sooner or later the West Africa station, an offshoot of the Cape of Good Hope station, had three divisions – the Northern, the Bights and the Southern.

By and large the coast was liberated in that order, and in the 1960s the task was completed.

Other nations did not readily follow the British position. Conventions might be signed with countries on such matters as the right of search, but vested interests were formidable and profits from this traffic made the venture worth the risk. Two ways existed of putting down the slave trade: first, by interception on the high seas of vessels carrying slaves, and, second, by destroying the towns or barracoons at the centres where slaves were shipped. Once a slave-carrying vessel reached its destination and unloaded its cargo, it was game over for the Navy and its official backers.

The crusade began three years after the Napoleonic Wars ended. On 19 September 1818, Commodore Sir George Collier received instructions to proceed to the Gulf of Guinea with the frigates *Tartar* and *Inconstant* to protect trade, visit forts and factories, and search for slavers: "You are to use every means in your power to prevent a continuance of the traffic in slaves and to give full effect to the Acts of Parliament in question."[24] The ships provided were undeniably muscular for this kind of work, but were sent as a political exhibition of British intentions and, not least in importance, a warning to other European states. A vice-admiralty court was set up in Sierra Leone, which became the base of British control over a scattering of trading stations from the Gambia to Accra. From this time on, the British stationed a unit of the Navy known as the Preventive Squadron on the coast of West Africa. The command was sometimes separate and sometimes part of the Cape station. However, small obligations soon grew into major responsibilities, forming about a sixth of all ships in commission. By 1850, two dozen ships formed this squadron, the maximum number at any one time "on station". The costs rose to somewhere between £100,000 and £200,000 a year in the 1840s. To compensate for the hazards for those engaged in the suppression of the trade, generous bounties were offered under the Act of 1807, to be distributed among officers and men in accordance with the Prize Regulations. Some of the vessels did well under this scheme, others not so. Thus according to the Naval Bay and Prize Act of 1854, all prize, bounty and salvage money went into a central prize account, and "forthwith be distributed by the Lords of the Admiralty to and amongst the persons entitled thereto, after the same shall have been notified in the *London Gazette*".

Collier's instructions called for him to take his prizes to one of the following Admiralty courts for adjudication: Sierra Leone, Río de Janeiro, Surinam or Havana. It takes little imagination to see what distances were involved, and what cost in time and labour. Collier, who reported on the forts and settlements of the Gold Coast and found them lacking for operational purposes,[25] admired healthy, mountainous Fernando Po (now Bioko) as advantageously situated in relation to the nefarious bights of Benn and Biafra, covering as it did Lagos and the Slave Coast, the Niger delta and the Cameroons. Collier urged its acquisition. Admiralty opinion similarly favoured its acquisition so that the court of adjudication could be shifted there from Sierra Leone.[26] However, the Spanish would not budge. Even so, the Navy kept a depot with a storekeeper there, and the zealous John Beecroft, trader and adventurer, became acting superintendent at Fernando Po and later superintendent. Use of Fernando Po by Anglo-Spanish agreement proved to be valuable to the squadron.

Collier found himself in a bind, for although the anti-slave trade work was a compelling requirement, circumstances beyond his control were obliging him to send ships, boat parties and forces ashore in circumstances where wiser heads had long known that disastrous results would be the only outcome. In the Gambia, British traders wanted to trade further upriver, and, bolstered by the local government and French supporters, a river steamer was requisitioned without success. The traders developed a river basin mentality, and the governor, Findlay, who was sympathetic to their cause, charged that the West African squadron was indifferent to the needs of the Gambia. Collier protested on the grounds that anti-slavery was his first duty. But one of his successors unwisely agreed to the use of HMS *Brisk* 200 miles upriver. The expedition was hastily mounted, and in consequence this misadventure led to Admiralty stricture to keep out of these sorts of situation. Colonial steamers were introduced, and one of them, *Dover*, logged 9,500 miles during 31 passages up and down the river in 1849 alone.[27] In any punitive expeditions, locally raised forces were employed.

Despite every contrary inclination, the Navy got itself embroiled in West Africa, particularly to deal with treats and actions of the Asante. Reinforcing castles and manning guns ashore became the order of the day, and although the British found allies in the Danish, they faced the Dutch at Elmina, who were supplying the Ashanti with guns and ammunition. The climax was reached in 1826, when Colonel Purdon, with regular troops backed by British men-of-war, and in the company of about 12,000 blacks provided by Fante chiefs and others, brought a preventive war to the Asante. The British employed rockets, grape and canister plus field guns, which "made lanes through their columns and did infinite execution". The Asante losses were about 5,000. The toll on British forces was 850 (of the 1,555 troops brought in) and most deaths were from causes related to climate, fever, dysentery, worms, sleeping sickness and malaria.[28] Here was a white man's grave, and a Royal Engineer captain there at the time said that he left the Cape Coast with the memory of "the monthly revels of the men, who being convinced they will not hold out above eleven of twelve months drink to excess whenever they can procure the means, although certain that the day's drink will carry off some of the party". A yellow fever epidemic had broken out there in 1823; the memory of it lingered ominously. British medical officers were poorly trained in tropical medicine or more likely unaware of the causes that wasted the King's soldiers and sailors.

When commissioners were sent to investigate, they vainly concluded that the best thing would be to abandon West Africa altogether. The Colonial Office responded with a suggestion of reducing the number of points of trade and settlement, concentrating force at Cape Coast Castle and at Accra. Lord Fitzroy Somerset said that only naval forces should be kept.

Although the British naval presence on this coast established a form of moral suasion just by showing the flag, it is now clear that these vessels provided no thorough deterrent against the illicit trade in slaves. In fact, many in Parliament doubted the wisdom (and expense in financial and human cost) of this high and noble effort. Naval work needed to be accompanied by diplomacy ashore. Accordingly, in 1849 a consul was appointed, Captain John Beecroft, who was answerable to the Foreign Office so as to carry on the announced policy of five years earlier that the British mission of eradicating slavery would be carried into the rivers – a "forward policy". The main object was the Niger Delta and the centre of influence, Lagos.[29]

In 1835 the Admiralty cut back on the large ships on station there, with their large crews on that unhealthy station, and substituted 10-gun brigs and small steamers, with a complement of 50 men each. So the corvettes and large sloops that customarily carried from 125 to 220 men and boys disappeared from these waters. The change in the composition of the squadron, made during Lord Auckland's time, was judicious, making available larger ships and more men for duties elsewhere. The gun-brigs and steamers, being of much lighter draft, were enabled to stand in closer to shore and discover the lurking-places of the slave raiders.[30]

A commander-in-chief could buoyantly report great successes in the capturing of slave ships and the freeing of slaves, as did Rear Admiral Sir Patrick Campbell in 1838. However, in the next sentence he would bemoan that from all of the information he could gather the traffic continued to be carried on with much perseverance, "and to an equal if not greater extent than at any former period". He could detail the annual increase in both vessels and slaves captured on the station, and that indicated that the number of slave ships visiting the coast to take on slaves was in fact increasing. The vessels visiting the coast were of a superior class to those formerly so employed. The only remedy was to have naval vessels "of the first sailing qualities, possessing capacity for the stowage of provisions and water to a considerable extent, and well supplied by boats, should be exclusively appropriated to this service". However, until other great powers joined in the crusade, Campbell maintained that there could be little chance of complete success.[31] The mindset swung between hope and despair, and while earnest men in Parliament assumed that the Navy could and halt the trade at source, in fact all the time it was increasing.

Ashore, the head men connected with the selling of slaves feared the loss of income attendant to winding up the slave trade. What would they get in return? they rightly asked of British naval commanders. What was in it for them? Captain Craigie of HMS *Bonnetta*, in speaking to Pepple, the King of Bonny (who was accompanied by an interpreter, secretary and his Juju man or high priest), made clear Lord Palmerston's edict about ending the trade. He described the other successful treaties carried out by England with other African princes. Craigie assured the King of Bonny that England dispensed justice, encouraged legal trade, and would continue send merchantmen for palm oil and other products, and that if he applied himself he would grow rich without exporting slaves. He told Pepple that "his mistress [Queen Victoria] was determined to put a stop to it at all hazards". The African king continued to express worry, apprehensive that the end of the slave trade would ruin him and his people. The Juju man pointed out that Spanish ships would come, with attractive possibilities. Craigie persisted. He reminded them that HMS *Scout* had blockaded the river in 1836 and again in 1839, and if necessary he would do the same again. That would stop up the trade. Craigie asked:

> as the English Government always adopt the principle of putting an end to evils by friendly agreements than by compulsion, and as it is that they may be disposed, if your requests are within reasonable limits, to make to you an annual "dash," or remuneration, for a term of years (perhaps five years), how much would you consider to be sufficient?[32]

They finally settled on $4,000 yearly subject to the British Government's agreement. And so it was that the flow of blood was replaced by the flow of gold.

Palmerston, prone to exaggeration on this score, contended that if there was a particularly old, slow-going tub in the Navy, the Admiralty was sure to send it to the coast of Africa to try to catch the fast-sailing American clippers. He also believed that if there was a British naval officer notoriously addicted to drinking, he was sent to a station where rum was the deadly poison. In fact, however, energetic actions by the Navy, partially made possible by the introduction of steam to warships, meant that a closer watch could be made over creeks and river mouths where the barracoons were the lodging houses of the slaves. Commander the Hon. Joseph Denman, son of an abolitionist, Lord Chief Justice Thomas 1st Baron Denman, held a passionate hatred of slavery. Not content to cruise the coast and merely chase slave-carrying ships, in 1840 he had determined to strike hard, totally on his own initiative, and to face the censure of the Admiralty if he failed. At Gallinas River, the most notorious slave station south of Sierre Leone, and now renamed the Kerefe, Captain Denman had showed equal toughness against a Spanish trader, Blanco, and an African king, Siaka, who secreted slaves. Denman and a landing party left their ship, crossed raging surf, secured an island base and meted out punishment against installations of trader and ruler alike. Denman burnt all of the barracoons and he forced the chief to sign an abject treaty of renunciation. In all it was a bold imperial action. He was rewarded by Parliament and promoted to the rank of Captain. Denman had a hand in writing the new instructions, which were placed in the hands of every officer in anti-slavery work.

Denman's success gave Palmerston new hope. "It is like taking a wasp's nest which is more effectual than catching the wasps one by one," he wrote enthusiastically to the first lord of the Admiralty, Minto. From this derived Palmerston's subsequent instructions to the Admiralty that Denman's tactics were to be employed against all piratical slave establishments. Close blockade combined with the destruction of barracoons was the most effective means of suppressing the slave trade.[33] This was the Palmerstonian order. Although such pre-emptive actions and surgical strikes appealed to Palmerston, his successor, Lord Aberdeen, was obliged to have the practice suspended on the advice of the Queen's advocate that such actions against nations with which Britain was not at war were contrary to international law.[34] Aberdeen also regarded peace and the balance of power as ends in themselves, and the means of promoting British power in the outer world. But within accepted limits, a closer watch was to be maintained on inshore slavers.[35] Aberdeen worked to bring France into the anti-slave trade crusade, and to divide responsibilities into select spheres.

Meanwhile, another scheme of intended peace and prosperity was developing; it was doing so from an entirely different perspective from that of the Foreign Office. Seeking to cut off slavery at source was the ambitious intent of the expedition to the Niger River in 1841–1842. The idea was to civilize Africa, doing so by establishing cotton production in West Africa. Thomas Fowell Buxton, previously concerned with the West Indies, was behind it. "One part of our national debt to Africa has already been acknowledged by the emancipation of our colonial slaves," he wrote in 1839, urging atonement for sins committed. "There remains yet, however, a larger debt uncancelled – that of restitution to Africa itself." He continued:

> We have been put in trust with Christianity, – we have been the depositaries of a pure and holy faith, which inculcates the most expanded benevolence, and yet have not only neglected, as a nation, to confer upon Africa any real benefit, but have inflicted upon it a positive evil... Shall we, on whom the lamp of life shines, refuse to disperse her darkness?[36]

Buxton believed that hitherto Britain's policies had been misdirected, both in intent and action – Palmerston's forceful policies and the Navy's actions had made the slave trade into a clandestine one. Buxton was not alone. A litany of "saints" and "dissenters" drove the initiative. It also appealed to the free traders. Some abolitionists opposed it, as did African traders. *The Times* opposed it, too, and the Government proved sympathetic, though the expedition mounted was not authorized by Parliament.

In any event, three vessels were sent, manned equally by Europeans and blacks, the river was entered and a model farm was set up, but fever forced a withdrawal. The next year a relief expedition found the farm beset by tribal warfare, and settlers had enslaved refugees who had flooded into the settlement seeking protection. The whole wild-eyed scheme ended in disaster. However, it served to open the way for explorers, traders and empire-builders who came in its wake.[37] Buxton was broken by the scheme and died not long after. The costs for the Navy were terrible: more personnel were lost during the few months up the Niger than were killed by the climate in the years of cruising.[38]

Palmerston had thought that Buxton's means and methods were madness, for they would have extended annexations. He believed that these "wild and crude" schemes were the opposite of what should have been done. All of the objects sought for by Buxton, he argued, might be attained by private enterprise, and when coupled with negotiations with powers ashore. Palmerston would go on this far: he had been prepared to launch a Niger expedition to negotiate commercial and anti-slave trade treaties with chiefs of the Niger valley and the powerful states of the interior. He would even go so far as to establish a fort upriver, but thoughts of annexation were out of the question.[39] Then he drew the line. Palmerston never changed his mind about legitimate commerce affording the best prospect of ending the slave trade: "the slave trade must first be driven from any place before legitimate commerce and civilization can be firmly established," he advised the third Earl Grey at the Colonial Office in 1849, "for the habits and practices connected with the slave trade render the men who carry on and the African districts in which it is practiced unfit for legitimate commerce and unfit for civilization".[40]

The disastrous Buxton experiment set back attempts to suppress the traffic in slaves and to promote legitimate trade, and a cluster of vocal persons known as "anti-coercionists" sprang up to proclaim that the African Squadron was a criminal waste of men and money. Champion of this group was William Hutt, MP. He thought that a higher authority should look after the moral government of the world. He brought a motion to the House of Commons in 1845 that contained such high rhetoric as "England is annually weeded of its best and bravest in order to carry on this idle and mischievous project of stopping the foreign Slave Trade." He was referring to deaths as a result of pestilence and climate. He thought that the constant international bickering regarding right of search actually "hazards the peace of the world", and the lot of slaves on the Middle Passage was made worse by the Navy's coercive attempts. "I say," he concluded, "withdraw your cruisers; they are far worse than useless for your purpose." Powerful naval officers rose to the defence of the Navy, as did the prime minister, Sir Robert Peel. Palmerston, alerted to the prospect of a reversal of his forward policy and the Navy's longstanding role, prepared to respond, but the vote never occurred because the House of Commons was counted out. However, select committees were struck, the statistics were piled up and all sorts of evidence was gathered. At the end of the day, the anti-coercionists were outflanked. Here's the committee's summary:

> The evidence of all the naval officers, as well as commanders of merchant ships, concurs in stating that north of the Line over a coast of many thousand miles, the Slave Trade, with the exception of a few points in the neighbourhood of Sierra Leone and the Gambia is virtually extinct.

There existed

> fair ground for hoping for ultimate success. Under this head we would venture to recommend that none but the swiftest vessels should be employed; that some of the best Prizes should be converted to the purposes of the service; that steamers should be engaged in watching the intricacies of islands, and the mouths of rivers; and that the system of paying by Headmoney, so unjust to gallant men, or, perhaps, by Bounty at all, should be reconsidered, and possibly be replaced by higher pay and the prospect of promotion.[41]

Given Foreign Office determination and directives, in 1851 the Navy focused on Lagos, where the King of Dahomey, Guezo, a notorious provider of slaves, grew rich on the traffic and dodged attempts to sign a suppression treaty. There were a number of collaborative culprits ashore and inland. "Lagos is near the sea, and on the sea are the ships and cannon of England," Palmerston reminded the Lagos overlord.[42] Naval officers, merchants and missionaries looked to stronger measures than moral suasion. At the Colonial Office, the third Earl Grey opposed the Foreign Office's suggestion to purchase Danish forts and obtain territory in the Gambia to prevent further French expansion there. On moral grounds he thought that the policy of bribing local chiefs with presents of rum, tobacco and cloth to induce good conduct and peaceable behaviour towards the British Government was highly objectionable.[43] But these positions could not stand up against Foreign Office pressure coming from Lagos, and it would take a decade for the British to finally run up the flag ashore there.

Here is how this sordid episode in naval-diplomatic pressure developed. Consul Beecroft kept Palmerston informed of continuing trade in humans, and the latter decisively sent the Admiralty guidance to use its own force as their lordships saw fit. This amounted to a blank cheque. This is how Commodore Henry William Bruce, commander-in-chief of the West Coast of Africa, came to be authorized for an action that was far from perfect in planning and certainly in execution – indeed a horror story in military practice. However, some considerable confusion developed, owing to difficulties in communication, distances being as huge as they were complicating. The British came first in force under Beecroft's urgings. But musketry and gunfire from the shore at Lagos caused considerable and regrettable loss of officers and men. A gunboat went aground. Desperate street-fighting brought casualties. The warships wearily left the river, their mission unaccomplished. Bruce, perhaps to save his skin, and hearing of the particulars, did not approve of the action: it had been done on Beecroft's authority not his. Beecroft received a "bottle" from the Foreign Office. Meanwhile Bruce was making his own plans. Ashore, a succession dispute gave the British an opportune situation, and Palmerston thought that Lagos was a key to controlling the slave trade northwards on the coast.[44] How correct this assumption was may be doubted, but it sufficed for Bruce to take further action – and to send in heavy forces.

The commodore arrived at the lagoons of Lagos in late December in *Penelope*, leading a squadron of four vessels plus the consul's own iron boat. Consultations occurred among the interested parties; plans were made. But once again the Navy found itself in a wasp's nest. Captain H. Lyster of *Penelope* had recommended the course of attack – going past the lines of defence quickly, rounding the point of the island on which Lagos stands, then attacking in force where Koskoko and the slave dealers resided. The vessels made their parade upriver, towing the boats. We can imagine the Union Flag at the mast and the gunboats steaming upriver, dodging sand bars and towing boats filled to the gunwales with bluejackets and marines, weapons and sweeps at the ready. The sailors were dressed in blue frocks, white trousers and straw hats; the Marines wore white frocks, white trousers and white caps – altogether attractive targets for snipers ashore. How many times in the imperial progression had this sort of thing been done before – landing Wolfe's army at Québec, Nelson's river expedition up the river to San Juan in Nicaragua, Worsley's cutting out expedition of American schooners on Lake Huron, other episodes of small boat work, and now this? We can imagine spirits running high under disciplined leadership, for men like Hillyar, Lyster, Eardley-Wilmot and Heath had done this sort of thing before, not here but on some other imperial frontier where water gave way to land. This was their stock in trade during *Pax*.

Taking Christmas Day off as a holy day to be observed, the force proceeded upriver, and there were anxious moments. The landing party is said to have faced fire from 1,500 muskets ashore, but it pressed on. The barracoons, owned by Brazilians, were torched. The stockade was stormed, guns spiked and the place demolished. The force captured and destroyed 36 guns. Lagos had been "reduced" at a cost of 2 officers and 13 men killed, 8 officers and 67 men wounded. The "butcher's bill" gave rise to unfavourable comments in Parliament. Praise came Bruce's way, as it did to six surgeons accompanying the expedition, who did heroic work against the perils of mosquitoes.

"I cannot withhold the expression of my regret for the very severe loss which has attended this achievement," Bruce wrote to the Admiralty, "but in which I trust their Lordships will feel that the dignity of England has been asserted and the honour of the flag gloriously sustained."[45]

The slave traders and their accomplices may have been checked momentarily at Lagos, but they were not stopped entirely. Palmerston minuted 22 April 1860: "trade cannot flourish without security", and if necessary security must be enacted by "the cudgels of a police or the sabres and carbines of a gendarmerie" which would "keep quiet the ill-disposed People whose violence would render trade insecure and thus prevent its operation".[46] Here was the Palmerston dictum. On 25 July 1861 the Navy came again into the lagoon, this time in the form of HMS *Prometheus*. She was under the command of Captain Norman Bedingfeld, who with the local consul, McCrosky, negotiated the new arrangement at the cannon's mouth, by intimidation. This time, though, against the rumblings of the discontented King Docemo, the island of Lagos became a British possession. "The Commander [of *Prometheus*] imposed on me to sign it," he complained, "and if I do not he is ready to fire on the Island of Lagos and destroy it in a twinkling of an eye."[47] Britain ran up the flag at Lagos, got Docemo and others to sign the treaty of suppression of the slave trade, effected legitimate trade, and established a toehold on what in due course became Nigeria. Partly to keep an eye on the French, but mainly to promote legitimate trade, protect colonial interests and stop the slave trade, the West Africa squadron was maintained as a sizeable entity – 20 ships and 2,000 men – in the 1860s.[48]

By 1865 the British were preparing to proclaim an end to the slave trade on the West Africa coast. Commodore A.P. Eardley-Wilmot, the senior naval officer in Sierra Leone, in his summary to the Admiralty listed the views of all officers reporting to him from various ships. The traffic had all but dried up. From Commander F.W. Richards of *Dart*, dated 26 July 1865 in Lagos, he relayed this telling, lugubrious testimony:

> The system of blockade by cruisers at anchor, generally within signal distance of each other, is the most effectual that can be adopted for the prevention of the traffic. But this successful result is obtained at a very great cost to the officers and crews employed upon this service, which is, beyond all question, the most wearisome, monotonous and thoroughly prostrating and dispiriting duty which the crews of Her Majesty's ships have to undergo in any part of the known world.

The commodore added, in appeal: "I must... entreat their Lordships to consider well the necessity of constant reliefs amongst the ships in the Bights Squadron, because I am now convinced, from great experience on this coast, that both the mind and body are liable to give way under the dreadful monotony of the service required...".[49] Here was telling testimony of the debilitating costs of this squadron's work.

British influence now flowed powerfully along the coast, as Palmerston had predicted and the Navy had demonstrated, so that by 1869 it was reaffirmed that the West African slave trade had been suppressed. Steam navigation was advancing imperial desires, exploiting the commercial potential of the river basins, bringing Africa in closer touch with Europe. "It may be of much use to secure a fast friend in the heart of Africa which will now be attainable by steam," minuted H.U. Addington at the Foreign Office.[50] The long and politically complicated task of suppressing the slave trade here at source was nearing its end in these parts, but the Navy was "on station" still, to preserve good order ashore and promote legitimate trade. Gunboats and gun vessels in weary procession continued the dreary work.[51] The trick was to ward off the importunities of European traders who wanted security upstream, far from where the Navy's boat parties should go. No matter the desires for naval economy, maintaining *Pax* in West Africa was costly in money and in men. Attention had already shifted to East Africa (Chapter 11) but the police work continued on the western flanks of the continent, and in the Caribbean and on the coast of Brazil.

Before we close this brief resumé of British naval and diplomatic efforts in anti-slavery work in West Africa, we are reminded that this was a difficult coast for navigation, a dreaded place for malaria, yellow and other fevers, a disadvantageous spot for obtaining fresh water and provisions, and a locale far away from places of rest, repair and relaxation. Hard on ships companies, it was one of the most disliked commands in the Service. Reputedly the officers were unusually prone to drunkenness here and the ships sent were unsuitable. One historian, Leslie Gardiner, sums up this unfortunate view: The West African squadron was

> a task force of out-of-date sloops and frigates, far from the lime-light, from their Lordships' notice and from the modest comports of Channel and Mediterranean warships. This was the station to which the bad hats, the unfortunates and those without interest were banished, to work out their penance and sacrifice their healths and tempers and drop far behind in the belting when the promotion lists were made up.

All of this may be true, and is worthy of examination by an energetic student of history. But of the war against slavery, the critic is perhaps true in this remark of the 60-year campaign against the slave traders: "When finally won it rated no victory parade, general celebration or distribution of honours."[52] Lucky survivors of peacekeeping duties, their spouses and their children know all too well that it is the sharp end war that yields the campaign medals.

There can be no doubt but that Palmerston's policy of using the Navy at source was effective. This was so no matter how often the Navy and the annual naval estimates came under heavy fire at home. Against the key offenders, the Portuguese, in Ambriz Roads and elsewhere, slave importations to Brazil dropped dramatically, and the forceful tactics of the energetic Captain Foote in keeping with Foreign Office instructions made this possible.[53] "It is difficult to convey . . . a full comprehension of the moral effect which a visit from a gun boat has upon the African mind," wrote one governor in West Africa in 1869.[54] Was this mere wishful thinking on the part of the imperialists? On the other side, deviant methods designed to circumvent the naval net were advanced and effective. All of this constituted the precolonial period of African history. The British had withstood almost every propensity to add to the imperial real estate, consolidating only those toeholds that had survived from the late eighteenth and earliest nineteenth centuries. It is true that they ran up the flag at Lagos in 1861; this was a last resort. Prudence and caution constituted the rules of naval engagement, though on occasion local circumstances drove the trident bearers to take action ashore. No rival naval power posed any intervening influence, and it is likely that other nations were pleased that the British were doing the heavy lifting in this regard. Elsewhere, commerce and missionary endeavour was the founding essence of empire, the Navy the essential (and expensive) guardian. Individual corporations, private concerns and, later, chartered companies saw and realized opportunities there. Under the cover of anti-slavery work (in and of itself an imperial mission), the British extended their trade on the coasts and river basins of West Africa. All of this formed a prelude to the partition of Africa.

In the late 1860s the British needed to keep 36 vessels on the West Africa station to do all manner of work. One of them, the gunboat *Fly*, one of the "Beacon" class of 603 tons, with twin screws and carrying a heavy armament, proved to be one of the handy steam vessels. She operated out of Lagos, dealing with the difficult swells of the Guinea current and the dangers of the Lagos bar as required. Men aboard *Fly* saw "the wealthiest of the Rivers of Corruption", the Bonny; they saw the trading hulks at the river estuary; and they saw the barrels of trade oil and the gin bottles lying around.[55] It was a place for mosquitoes and fever, a hellhole where black traders had fought it out for slaving precedence. Champagne was believed to counter malaria but failed to do so. Mary Kingsley and Samuel Ajayi Crowther, the first African Bishop of the Niger, told of the tales of this coast, and it is estimated that 100,000 slaves were shipped from West Africa each year until the Navy and British consuls put a stop to it. But the Navy could not rest. From a more recent perspective we have this observation: "Our basic judgment must be that the continuance of the Slave Trade contributed to the devaluation of human life and liberty; but so too do the wars and coups d'etat which have followed the removal of

European political dominance."[56] Here, as elsewhere, the danger always existed that some unsuspecting naval officer commanding would be drawn into some imbroglio ashore, egged on by the urgent appeal of a consul or a governor. But the days of Commodore Bruce getting into trouble on this score, as at Lagos in 1850, were now long past. Instructions issued to commanders, such as those of 1870, made crystal clear that no intervention ashore was to be made except for the actual protection of British life. No gunboat was to cruise for more than 12 hours steaming by day, only 50 troops could be embarked at any one time, and no rivers were to be navigated upriver until the commander-in-chief gave clearance for the same. Showing the flag still had to be done, but interventions ashore and certainly up previously unpoliced rivers was out of the question, no matter how strong the pleading of a hard-pressed colonial governor.[57] It is worth recalling, as Roger Anstey has put it so eloquently, that behind the political activity of the abolitionists "was a theology of a profoundly dynamic kind". It was one which, "especially through the particular way in which the concept of redemption was worked out and applied, had profound significance both in the development of a theology of anti-slavery, and for future reform".[58] Naval officers and the "lower deck" may not have shared this high-minded and altruistic view, and they may never have thought about redemption or atonement for Britain's past sins, but they carried out their work to the letter, rumbling as they did so. It was one of the greatest missions of *Pax*, carried through to conclusion.

Meanwhile, on the western side of the Atlantic, the work of British warships on anti-slavery and anti-piracy duties was that of catch as catch can. The North America and West Indies station was the principal command directed to stopping the slave trade on the shores of the Americas, and from Halifax and Jamaica cruisers went out on patrol. Smaller bases of operations – Antigua, Barbados and others – made the task easier. A consolidated station as of the year 1836 consisted of 26 ships and 3,106 men, a powerful armament in these American waters. The geographical complications of the West Indies and the Caribbean, including Florida and the Bahamas, the Gulf of Mexico, the coasts of Panama, Venezuela and eastwards to Trinidad and the Orinoco, where the Brazils station took over, were immense. It was a zone of great currents, notably that running north through the Straits of Florida and, of course, the great one that swept easily from West Africa into the vortex of waters where the slavers needed to unload and sell their human cargoes. The northern coast of Cuba was extremely dangerous. Hurricanes were frequent. Hydrographic surveying, the putting down of buoys and the erecting of lighthouses (particularly in the notorious Florida Channel and Grand Bahama Bank) were mandatory steps. One by one the navigational aids were installed, and each time they added to the safety of navigation and made easier American and British cooperation in anti-piracy work. Anti-slave trade work was an onerous duty in the Caribbean, for the places of disembarkation were numerous and invariably out of the way, and for that reason the Navy's squadrons on the western and eastern coasts of Africa attempted to stop the trade "at its source", so to speak.

If the west coast of Africa was "the white man's grave", that of the Caribbean in certain seasons formed a graveyard all of its own. Malaria and yellow fever exacted terrible tolls here, and it would not be until the 1890s that the secrets of these would be determined. Meanwhile, successive admirals on station, and ships captains, scratched their heads as to the cause of yellow fever, the worst offender, and fumigating ships' holds, whitewashing the interior, draining out any stagnant water and other measures were attempted. Eventually it was realized that the best thing to do when "yellow jack" made its appearance was to clear out of port and head for northern climes – Bermuda and Halifax. Even then, Bermuda suffered terribly, not least in 1864. The use of steamers aided the British mission against slavery, but such ships were useless in long chases against the slavers, who had fast Baltimore schooners and other types built in the Chesapeake. The American vessels came south to Cuba fully equipped to take on their human cargoes. These cargoes supplemented the American trade directly from the African slave-dealing coast.

Although, as has been noted, the United States joined the anti-slave trade cause and equated piracy to slaving, departures from the British tactics existed in two forms: first, it was difficult to get convictions of pirates in American courts and, second, American laws drove investors to seek deviant ways in the way of ship ownership and flags of convenience. In addition, the search for speed under sail drove American designers and builders, notably of Baltimore and the Chesapeake, to construct fast schooners and brigs, remarkable vessels that were capable of a speedy getaway. But, as Howard Chapelle, the noted historian of American shipbuilding for this era, commented, the British were no slouches in designing fast vessels capable of overhauling the miscreants. They also took ex-slavers and ex-pirate ships into Her Majesty's service. The loss of vessels in the Caribbean and West Indies was very heavy owing to hurricanes and other storms, navigational hazards, and much inshore cruising in difficult waters. The Navy was able to get convictions in Admiralty courts. Chapelle's satisfactory conclusion is that "The British Navy, operating with the aide of realistic courts, must receive credit for the eventual suppression of piracy as well as of the slave trade. In the process they captured many piratical vessels and took some of the small schooners into naval service in the West Indies."[59]

The last years of the Atlantic slave trade form a story abounding in paradoxes. After 1815 the Royal Navy had policed the Caribbean on anti-piracy duties, a task that it worked in uneasy cooperation with its recent foe, the United States Navy. Beginning in the 1820s, however, under increasing demand from the Foreign Office to put the slavers out of business, ships of the British

Navy did yeoman work. Rear Admiral Sir Charles Rowley made great advances against pirates and slavers, "the principal offenders being scoundrels of Spanish extraction".[60] The trade to Cuba could at one point be said to be extinguished, only to flare up again in astounding proportions in 1860. In the years 1840–1860 some 200,000 slaves were carried to Cuba, and perhaps 7,200 to Puerto Rico. Spanish foreign policy continued to ward off British intrusions. Humanitarian concern about the colony showed no interest in abolishing the institution. The Cuban trade was an American one, in American ships under protection of the Stars and Stripes. The United States Government had declared the trade illegal a half-century before, so it was carried on clandestinely. The British considered a full blockade of the Cuban coast. Tensions with American shipping mounted, and diplomatic files bulged in London and Washington. New York became the centre of the illegal slave trade of Cuba. At Havana, the British consul watched the coming of ships and cargoes with alarm. Sugar was in the ascendant here because Britain's sugar acts had thrown British markets open to all comers. But the last verified landing of slaves on Cuban soil took place in 1870.[61]

From time to time a British sloop-of-war, such as *Frolic*, might drive a slaver ashore on the coast of Brazil or capture a slave-carrying ship and bring her to a port where an Admiralty court might condemn the ship and free the captives. However, in the absence of international agreement, the British Government was unable in the 1820s and 1830s to enforce the abolition of the Brazilian slave trade. Despite the signing of a strengthened anti-slave trade treaty in 1826, which made Brazilian involvement after 1830 the equivalent of piracy, the trade continued. The abolition, always a British demand as a price of international recognition of Brazil's independence and stature among nations, was unpopular in local quarters and led to the abdication of Dom Pedro in 1831.

The illegal slave trade gradually established itself during the mid-1830s, and by the end of that decade as many as 45,000 slaves were illegally being imported annually. Brazilian governments resisted British diplomatic pressure and refused to concede the powers that the Navy needed to suppress the trade. The so-called Palmerston Act unilaterally empowered the Navy to intercept slavers that were flying the Portuguese flag. From time to time the illegal trade revived, but the British never tired in placing diplomatic pressure on the Brazilians. Not until Parliament passed Lord Aberdeen's 1845 act, whereby Britain unilaterally assumed powers to suppress the Brazilian trade, did a change occur. In 1845 the Brazilian slave trade was to be "deemed and treated as piracy". Under this measure the Royal Navy in Brazilian waters employed coercive naval action. It continued its work in 1845–1850, with over 400 slavers being captured and sent to vice-admiralty courts. Final abolition depended on Brazilian governmental will and ability to enforce, and on influential Brazilian opinion. But the diligent student of these matters, Leslie Bethell, states that this act and the naval work of the squadron were "the main factor leading to the effective ending of the trade almost immediately".[62]

In the circumstances, the struggle to suppress the Brazilian slave trade in the 1850s yet again revealed London's persistent and unflinching diplomacy. Brazilian governments and executives might come and go, but representatives of the British Government always had to be contended with. The sight of a British warship in a Brazilian port was an offence to a Brazilian patriot, who naturally had the right to feel that his own government should police the abominable traffic. Like it or not, the Royal Navy was the agent of imperial diplomacy – its long hand of the law. Events reached a crisis in 1850 when British warships, on the instructions from a Foreign Office directive, invaded ports and destroyed Brazilian slave ships. That July the Brazil government acceded to demands in exchange for a promise that the naval actions would be suspended. But the next year a further threat was necessary, and at last the long-delayed Brazilian suppression of the traffic was effected. Brazil had been humiliated by the British naval actions, but the latter were effective and revealed how far the British were prepared to go.[63]

Of the two locales considered in this chapter – West Africa and the Caribbean – the principal focus of suppression was the former. The British sought to cut off the trade at source. At the peak of such suppression efforts, in the mid- and late 1840s, about 15 per cent of British warships in commission and 10 per cent of naval manpower was employed in the task of stopping the flow of slaves to the Americas. At that time the number of slaves shipped from Africa had come to rival in volume and scale that of the eighteenth century. One scholar, David Eltis, remarks that such naval forces committed to the anti-slavery work absorbed a small proportion of British naval strength, which was true. From time to time, as crises developed, ships were sent to other stations – China in 1840 and the Crimea in 1854. There were calls for the withdrawal of the squadron on the grounds of its inefficiencies. Admirals who consulted about the its efficacy were unduly pessimistic but refused to support the considered withdrawal.[64] Palmerston held to the view that the issue was not how many slaves were shipped but how many would have been had British naval efforts not been made.[65] His point is well taken.

The Navy's role in humanitarian work and its inseparability from promoting legitimate trade and the spread of British informal empire was from the Service's point of view one of the least attractive sea duties of the age. It brought little thanks at home and was the subject of derisive comment in the press and in Parliament. It had its detractors, but the Foreign Office stuck with the project of eradicating the slave trade as a British mission, answerable as they were to strong public opinion. By moral suasion and financial obligation, it extended the British mandate to many other nations. This was a British mission on a vast network of international treaties. It was particularly in West African waters that the pursuit of legitimate trade was pressed; while in Caribbean seas the fight also went on against piracy. The cost in human life was large, promotions were slow, and financial prizes and other rewards small.

All of this was going on while in the West Indies and on the Spanish Main, kingdoms of sugar had been built up. Beginning in the seventeenth century, a whole empire of sugar and slaves had been brought into being. From Barbados to Jamaica, then on to the other Windward and Leeward Islands, the planter class had waxed rich on the basis of peace and war. "How are the Sugar Duties?" George III is said to have called from his coach to the Earl of Chatham, knowing full well that Britain's prosperity rested on sugar. Sugar was only as good as slavery in those days, and slavery too was a "sinew of empire". It was far better to add a sugar island to the empire at a peace with France or with Spain than to add some cold northern territory whose chief commodity was beaver.

The triangle trade to Africa made possible the human component for the maintenance and expansion of West Indian plantations. The fruits of war had increased the sugar-producing estate and added to the powerful West India interest in Parliament. The shipping interest of London, Bristol and Liverpool agreed; so did the banks, insurance companies, victuallers, suppliers of charts, purveyors of beer and spirits, and so on.

But the old presuppositions had come under scrutiny when the Clapham Sect and even their precursors began to make noise in Parliament. The absence of war brought stability hitherto unknown, but slave revolts occurred and the Navy came to the rescue of governors, councils and plantation owners. In 1865 a young lieutenant, answering an appeal from Governor Eyre of Jamaica, exceeded all bounds of propriety in helping put down the rebellion in Jamaica, to the everlasting shame of the Senior Service. The ensuing discussion in Parliament and in the press got to the raw essence of the Victorian conscience.[66] It also reinforced the Admiralty's position that minimum intervention ought to continue to be the guiding rule and that naval officers ought to remain wary of being lured into action by overly excited governors, consuls, bankers, missionaries and agents of one sort or another.

The abolition of the slave trade and of slavery did not markedly change the plantation commodity production of sugar. Asian indentured labour filled the gap. The wealth of the West Indies declined and the abolitionists faced ill-placed blame for this downturn. Production increased and profits fell. The old mercantilist logic had disappeared, and a nail had been driven into the old, too long maintained Old Colonial System.

The Navy kept up its beat as policeman. To this was included assorted humanitarian duties because hurricanes, fires, volcanic eruptions, earthquakes and floods played periodic havoc and required disaster relief. Keeping watch on rivals – French, Dutch and Spanish – was integral business to being on constabulary requirements, while cooperation with the United States Navy against piracy strengthened binational cooperation at the same time that American hemispheric interests were in the ascendant. At the end of the century, the old naval bases of Antigua, Barbados and even Jamaica were closed down or retained on a skeletal footing. But the legacies of slavery continued even though the links with Africa trickled out and ended altogether.

11
Treaty-Making and Dhow-Chasing in the Indian Ocean

In addition to protecting the rights of British and European citizens, the policing of piracy was a specifically designated duty of the Navy during *Pax*. Anti-piracy duties, to repeat, were closely intertwined with measures to eradicate slavery and the slave trade. This largely thankless task took the Navy to all seas, for the anti-piracy war was conducted against the likes of Barbary pirates, offending coastal tribes of British Columbia and Brazilian privateers in the Río de la Plata. It was also pressed against pirates in the Malay straits, the China seas and the Pacific islands. In some of these places, piracy could be suppressed. In others, such as the China seas in the 1860s, as one historian concluded unerringly, it "persisted undiminished and unintimidated".[1]

Here our attention is specifically drawn to the Arabian Sea, the Persian Gulf and the waters of East Africa, where the heroic work of the Navy in suppression duties is not as well known as it deserves to be.[2] Hunting pirates was one of those duties of the *Pax* that brought few promotions and little attention at the Board of Admiralty, in Parliament or in the press. It was a workaday affair, largely undramatic in its greatest effect, for it was not a fight against a foreign enemy such as had been the case during the Napoleonic Wars or that against the United States when national honour was at stake. Today as yesterday, readers love to devour works on pirates, and moviemakers have taken their work to the highest form under the general consideration that, as a subject, "pirates are fun". But looking at it from the position of those doing the clean-up work, the hunting of pirates was distinctly unglamorous.[3] A statute of 1825 placed lucrative inducements before officers and men of H.M. warships to eradicate piracy and, indeed, kill pirates – a measure suspended in 1850.[4] It was hard and tedious work, and more often than not it brought little reward. Perhaps in consequence of this, as a subject for historical study, rooting out pirate nests and destroying pirate shipping was an ongoing duty of *Pax* now largely forgotten.[5]

Whereas anti-piracy was an age-old obligation of the Navy, anti-slavery was a newly acquired one of the nineteenth century, particularly after 1815, when naval units could be deployed that hitherto had been solely engaged in belligerent roles. Anti-slavery work, which began as ancillary to anti-piracy in the Indian Ocean and points east, grew in strength and eventually became a crusade. This had the backing of a powerful lobby, as the historian of the Navy in slave-trading suppression in East Africa and the Indian Ocean, Raymond Howell, observed: "While the trade in slaves from West Africa was finally being checked in the 1860s, however, a significant new battle against slavery was developing on the other side of the continent."[6] Here it took major diplomatic moves plus persistent naval pressure over three decades to bring an end to it, or apparently so (for it persisted in smaller currents of activity).

The initial base of operations for the Navy's work in the Indian Ocean and its annexes was the Cape. That location had never been taken from the Dutch for the purposes of anti-piracy and anti-slave trade work, but rather to keep the French from gaining an advantage there. That action of statecraft, based on strategic concerns, had an undeniable secondary advantage in the age of resurgent humanitarian concern. As we will see from the Cape north to the Persian Gulf and the Arabian Sea, British warships spread their influence, also advantaged by the fact that Mauritius had been kept at the 1815 peace, and additional nodes of power, such as Aden, could be acquired as necessary. "The suppression of slave traffic was the child of British policy," writes Captain Philip Colomb in his memoir on slave-catching in the Indian Ocean, and "did not form a leading feature in that of our Indian empire".[7] Colomb pointed out that the Government of India had its hands full with other obligations. The maritime dominion that he was speaking about involved the cooperation of London and Bombay, besides the commander-in-chief on station (the boundaries of which changed with new obligations). Well into the late nineteenth century, India-based units were deployed to East African waters as required in special circumstances, and a strange co-association of imperial interests developed around the Indian Ocean, exercised from a variety of British nodes of power – Cape Town, Durban, Mauritius, Aden, Bombay and Trincomalee.

The first place of concern was the Persian Gulf. In these hot and placid straits, pirates, both Arab and European, infested its waters. They fell upon legitimate traders and peaceful native states, and they were the scourge of those seas. The waters of the Arabian Sea theoretically fell under the management and dominion of the Government of India. After 1809 the Bombay Marine (the Indian Navy after 1830) took up the cause on behalf of the East India Company: the Bombay government was the one most likely to benefit from freedom of the seas. And as the anti-slavery advocates gained influence in Parliament, so, too, did the Admiralty, on the advice of the Foreign Office, and naval officers in the Indian Ocean came to play a role in suppressing the slave trade, which they came to accept (backed by firm legal opinion at home) as a form of piracy.

Once again, Palmerston was in the van: he let it be known that Britain was "the main instrument in the hands of Providence... [it was] vain for these Arabs to endeavour to resist the consummation of that which is written in the Book of Fate".[8]

When the soldier-diplomat Sir John Malcolm sailed into the Persian Gulf in 1800, he was excited by the thought that he was on the scene of the adventures of Sinbad the Sailor. Wondering who inhabited the desolate shores to the south, his servant informed him:

> They are a sect of Wahâbees, and are called Jouassimee [variously spelled]; but God preserve us from them, for they are monsters. Their occupation is piracy, and their delight is murder; and to make it worse, they give you the most pious reasons for every villainy they commit. They abide by the letter of the sacred volume, rejecting any commentaries and traditions. If you are their captive, and offer all you possess your life, they say "No! It is written in the Koran, that it is unlawful to plunder the living, but we are not prohibited in that sacred work from stripping the dead;" so saying, they knock you on the head.

The Joasmi, sometime traders, pearl fishers and pilots, saw the sea as a place of opportunity, and pressures of poverty ashore led them into a wide-ranging business: "the career of the avaricious and voracious rather than the fanatically devout". At the time when Malcolm visited the Persian Gulf, piracy was reaching its height. Tribes competed among one another, and any such peace established between or among them seemed most fragile, observed the assistant resident in the Persian Gulf with regret in 1844. The East India Company was among the first to suffer the sting of pirates who came forth from their concealed retreats, and, given the fact that British merchant shipping and even small cruisers had fallen prey to the pirates, Bombay took it upon itself to arm a fleet, arrange for convoys and take the war to the enemy.[9]

This forward decision was reached after much deliberation by the Government in India, and the British Government at home had always preferred a hands-off policy, being content to let the needs of the day arise. However, the Wahabis and Joasmi were uncontrollable and spread their evil attacks on shipping. They created havoc. Thus a fleet based at Bombay was sent in 1809 in reprisal. It took the Jawasimi base at Ras-el-Khyma and razed its forts to the ground. It burnt or captured upwards of a hundred of the pirates' vessels. Utmost force had been used in this mission; it was a great stroke of policy carried out without reservation or concern for moral questions. Even so, in 1813 the commander-in-chief in the East Indies, Admiral Sir Samuel Hood, came under pressure to send cruisers to the Persian Gulf as a means of protecting seaborne trade, and to capture or destroy any vessels that were suspected of piratical intent. And once again, in 1817, a plan was approved for a full-scale operation against the Joasmi. Cooperating with seven cruisers of the Bombay Marine, a force under Captain J.A. Collier, consisting of a frigate and three sloops-of-war, approached Ras-el-Khyma, which had been rebuilt and refortified after the British storm had devastated it a decade earlier. A large force was landed, fortifications were razed, 30 cruising boats were destroyed and expeditions of pacification were sent to nearby ports. A garrison of sepoys, European troops and a battery of artillery under command of an Arab-speaking officer doing double duty as political agent for Arab tribal matters now maintained the watch ashore.[10] It was an early stage in British occupation in these lands and seas. In 1820 the garrison was moved to Kishm and came under the authority of the Sultan of Oman.

At this stage the British shifted their attention to Mauritius, and ships of the East Indies Station were sent to deal with it, for on that island the French still had slavery. The slaves were brought from East Africa and the Arabian waters. It fell to a young captain, recently "posted", Fairfax Moresby, senior naval officer, Mauritius, to undertake the duty of getting the authorities in Mauritius to understand that a stop was to be put to the infamous trade. Moresby had experience in dealing with native authorities ashore, notably in Morocco, and during the Napoleonic Wars he had acted with commendable capability and bravery. At the peace he was included in the list of those receiving the Companion of the Order of the Bath. In addition, the Emperor of Austria conferred on the young commander the Order of Maria Teresa, carrying with it the hereditary barony of the Austrian Empire.

Like many other officers of this somnolent time he feared inactivity, but Lord Exmouth had provided influence, and so it was that in 1819 Moresby found himself in command of the 26-gun frigate *Menai* and ordered to the Cape station. His first prosaic duty was to act as one of Napoleon's seaguard at St. Helena. HMS *Northumberland* had carried the emperor there, and, in the company of other vessels, landed a guard of 900. The customarily curious Moresby, incidentally, and in opposition to partisan complaints, did not think that the British resident, Sir Hudson Lowe, exceeded his instructions from London with regard to the treatment of the deposed emperor. As long as Napoleon was alive, the principal obligation of the Cape station was to keep watch on St. Helena, thereby preventing any escape or attempted succour by an alien power.[11] When, in 1821, Napoleon died, the station's requirements shifted, and, in the era of anti-piracy and anti-slavery, new requirements presented themselves to the commander-in-chief and the hard-pressed ships of the squadron.

Moresby's next port of call was Simon's Bay, Cape of Good Hope station headquarters, and for the young captain an altogether different assignment in the cause of empire: taking and convoying upwards of 5,000 emigrants east of the

Cape to Algoa Bay, where against great odds they formed the first settlement at Port Elizabeth on that lonely, arid coast. The task was to land safely on the forbidding soil of southeast Africa a large number of British persons with no previous knowledge of roughing it in the bush and hardly a clue as to the urgent task of putting down roots in an alien land.

It was a vast marine operation, unheard of in the annals of British imperial expansion and terribly dwarfed nowadays in the historical literature by the attention given to convict settlement in New South Wales and elsewhere. Still, it was the first attempt at dealing with a burgeoning population at home and exploiting the prospects of a seemingly undeveloped colonial circumstance, newly acquired. Pauperism had increased dramatically in Britain, the economy was in general decline, inflation was rampant and the population was rapidly increasing. The population of Britain in 1821 numbered an astonishing 21 million, of whom about 11.2 million were English, 6.8 million Irish, 2 million Scottish, 0.7 million Welsh and 0.3 million "Army, Navy etc.". Malthus, in the wake of his *Principles of Population* (1798), was urging emigration for the purposes of humanity and good policy. Various emigration societies sprang up. British emigration policy of "shoveling out paupers" was in its infancy, but the Colonial Department of the War Office, headed by Earl Bathurst, turned to the matter with urgency. In 1819, 35,000 persons left British ports, many heading for Upper Canada under arrangements to boost the British settlement on the north shore of the River St Lawrence and the Great Lakes so as to provide better defence against any further American aggression.[12]

However, the Cape Colony scheme was an equally important start and was aimed at settling the new British provinces in southern Africa. In "the Great African Enterprise", as it was called, about a quarter of the emigrants were agriculturalists. Many of the balance were Londoners. The plan called for them not to be thrown together in an unruly mass but to be settled according to a well-thought-out scheme to promote economic self-sufficiency and harmony, something more easily said than done. The farming minority, holding on in the face of hardship and difficulty, became ancestors of the British element in the eastern Cape Colony. Many of the artisans and townspeople, by contrast, gave up the struggle. Meanwhile, missionary activity within the limited area of the Cape Colony pushed the Boers to escape its narrow bounds, and the trekking Boer pressed north in search of the 6,000 acre farm, crossing the Vaal River and setting up an independent republic.

There always existed the danger of armed encounter with indigenous peoples, about which the promoters of this particular settlement knew so little. Of this vast maritime planting of a new society, little has been written. However, Fairfax Moresby's son, himself an admiral, though of a later time, wrote in admiration of his father's work as follows: "he inspired all with his own energy and spirit of order. A canvas city sprang up, and his sagacious regulations held the young colony successfully to its business, whilst the help of the officers and men in the necessary sports and relaxations insured a happy beginning." The Albany settlement, as it is called, was largely a scheme of Scottish settlement uniquely backed by a handsome vote of Parliament. Some 24 ships, each of about 400 tons burthen, took out 3,487 men, women and children from Deptford, Portsmouth, Liverpool, Bristol and, for the Irish, Cork. Few of them had experience in cultivation; most were townspeople. They sailed into a sea of troubles – first to Simonstown and then on to inhospitable Algoa Bay, where the promised land looked bleak, and the raging surf stood as a danger to landing. The land was acidic, the streams unreliable and the water undrinkable. Storms, drought and wheat blight added to the problems. The Xhosa fell upon the cattle of the newly arrived settlers, and troubles with the "Kaffirs" began. There were many misfortunes and disasters, but these need not concern us here because they form a chapter of colonial history, but the fact of the matter is that the settlers found a useful ally in the Navy, which worked in close cooperation with the British administration at the Cape.[13] The governor, Lord Somerset, 46 and with good royal connections but little experience in administration, was strangely hostile to the complaints and needs of the Albany settlers, and eventually a petition arrived on the desk of Earl Bathurst, the colonial secretary, detailing the complaints. A commission of inquiry was sent from Britain, but not before William Wilberforce had been able to advance through Parliament an address to the King against extending slavery to the new Albany settlement. The British reduced the garrison at the Cape under the heading of economy, and they adopted a policy of neglect.[14] After all, they controlled the sea route to India, France could not intervene, and the colonists had to look after their own affairs and keep out of trouble.

The British worried that the Cape would be a further drain on the British Treasury, but the strategic factors overcame all others. All of their advances from Cape Town to the east and north were taken reluctantly. "From the beginning," wrote Sir Keith Hancock,

> the British had to face the same dilemma which had baffled the Dutch. They denied the need for expansion into the hinterland. They denied the white man's right to take land that the black man held. But they were determined to hold the Cape as a bulwark of their trading Empire. Security in this imperial fortress necessitated good order in the colony. And this in turn depended upon good order of the frontier.[15]

For a half-century, British policy in southern Africa vacillated between the "forward school" and the advocates of retrenchment or retirement.[16] The Albany scheme marked the beginning of the forward phase, and many a vacillation of purpose would occur in time, not least because of African migrations and the build-up of African empires, notably that of Shaka Zulu.

The Navy kept watch over the Albany settlement and later found a useful though rather open roadstead in Durban, Natal (now KwaZulu-Natal). Along this coast the Navy began patrols that stretched well northwards where Portugal was the only power of influence on the East Africa shore (and that a faltering one). One empire was beginning to replace another here, and the British showed the flag with increasing regularity and thus effect. And, naturally, the demands on the station increased out of proportion to the resources available to the commander-in-chief.

Moresby next shaped a course for Mauritius, there to check piracy but principally, in a new measure of naval diplomacy, to suppress the slave trade carried on between Africa and the French colonies, and Arab ports about the Persian Gulf. Officers of the Bombay Marine had reported that the main culprits in bringing slaves into the Gulf were the Omani Arabs, who were not covered by treaties. In Zanzibar they were selling slaves to the Portuguese and French, and feeding the illicit slave trade in Mauritius.[17] The progressive forces active in Britain, including the African Association, precursor to the Anti-Slavery Society, had found an ally in the young captain. Moresby's heart was in the anti-slavery movement. "I have heard from several quarters of your generous and indefatigable exertions for the suppression of the slave trade on the eastern side of Africa," wrote William Wilberforce, champion parliamentarian in the cause, "and feel no small gratification in assuring you that your public spirit and philanthropy have obtained for you the respect and regard of many in this country, who consider it an honor to have a countryman thus accredited the name of Briton in a distant land."[18]

Moresby concluded a treaty with the Imam of Muscat, later confirmed by Government, for the suppression of the traffic. He arranged a similar treaty with the King of Madagascar. On 8 January 1820 a general peace was proclaimed, but the British obligation had to be kept up. British vessels remained there, as they also did for a time at Basidu, Qishm Island, to preserve order in the Persian Gulf. There was no turning back on the police work now; it had to be sustained. Under Article VIII the killing of prisoners was forbidden as an act of piracy. Under Article IX "The carrying off of slaves, men, women or children, from the coasts of Africa or elsewhere, and the transporting them in vessels, is plunder and piracy; and the friendly Arabs shall do nothing of this nature." By friendly Arabs, those who had been pacified were meant, and it was assumed that they were prepared to adhere to the treaty's terms. Although there was a tacit understanding that "there shall be a cessation of plunder and piracy, by land and sea", it was understood in political circles that ultimately peace and pacification depended on the forces sent by the Bombay government to the Persian Gulf. Thus was affirmed the policy of having four or five company cruisers, which composed the Gulf squadron "on station".[19]

The first treaty with Sayyid Said of Muscat forbade sale of slaves to Christian nations by the sultan's subjects. It also made punishable the buying of slaves for sale to Christians. A demarcation between religions over slavery had been drawn. It also empowered the British government to place an agent in the sultan's dominions to watch the trade, and to seize Omani vessels that were found carrying slaves to Christian countries.[20]

If it was the Bombay Marine whose duty it was to police these seas, mainly out of self-interest, the Royal Navy was in the lead in the diplomatic effort, bearing instructions and plenipotentiary powers from the Foreign Office and the home government. Moresby was the successful amphibious diplomat, but he also took his turn at the cannon's mouth in dealing with the French, as the following demonstrates. *Menai* lay at anchor in the harbour of Zanzibar when a slaver, *Camilla*, a sleek and beautiful craft much admired for her sailing qualities by the British seamen, and manned by the French, began taking on slaves, with its destination being Mauritius. Moresby climbed aloft, glass in hand, to make sure of his intended prize. He decided that his boats should make a surprise attack that night. Under cover of darkness, the boats set out, and waiting for first light lay in a narrow channel between islands at the harbour entrance. Early streaks of dawn allowed them to see *Camilla* lying under the guns of the fort, and they made for their prey and boarded. The hatches were fastened down, and the skipper, Leroux, was found asleep and then hauled up on deck. As a prize, *Camilla* yielded 140 slaves and 10,000 Spanish dollars. It was a notable event among many, and it showed that despite Moresby's labours elsewhere, the Sultan of Zanzibar was still a force to be reckoned with because he supported the French and kept up a lucrative trade in slaves in order to fatten his own purse. On another occasion, Moresby seized the French slaver *Le Succes*, with 340 slaves aboard, and there were 20,000 more awaiting sale in Zanzibar.[21]

Unlike West Africa, where the European powers engaged in rivalry that led eventually to concessions and partition, East Africa had seen the forestalling of the Europeans by the Swahili Arabs, who had moved south from the shores of the Arabian Sea and pressed as far south as Portuguese places of coastal influence. They worked the ivory and slave trades, which went together – the slaves providing the labour to bring ivory to the coast as the hunting frontier pressed inexorably into the interior. The Arabs established clove plantations on the islands of East Africa, and these depended on slave labour. Zanzibar was the frontier of British India, but the Swahili Arabs dominated it. East Africa is best understood as the economic hinterland of the commercial entrepôt of Zanzibar. Thus it was that in all of its attempts to check slavery and the slave trade, Europe was confronted with the Arab state of Zanzibar.[22] Britain's challenge, in promoting British trade (mainly in cottons) and in abolishing the slave trade, was to turn the Sultan of Zanzibar to the will of the Foreign Office. Making the sultan a collaborator without losing his independence was the trick, and British consuls walked a thin line requiring the greatest degree of care. Making sure that the sultan had his own navy, giving support where required, and cautions and financial inducements when necessary, was the policy. In these early days the Royal Navy was only, at first, an additional factor in the equation. But as the century wore on, and after Moresby's time, its roles became more forceful. The issue was eradicating the slave trade, the Arabs were operating by different rules and the Sultan of Zanzibar's principal source of wealth derived from duties attendant to the slave trade. Senior naval officers, under a scheme of financial inducement, were encouraged to learn Swahili. Interpreters had proved to be unreliable and misleading, hence the desirability of learning the native tongue.

Once again the British were advantaged by geography, and their possession of strategically advantageous was locations of influence acquired by conquest or cession. With anchors of empire at the Cape and in Bombay, and with Mauritius freed from French hands in the recent war, the authorities could deploy warships as required, coordinating activities across an immense oceanic space according to the monsoon season and to intelligence gathered of slaving activities. From the Cape the commander-in-chief deployed a senior naval officer in the Mozambique Channel and another in Mauritius. Working with consuls and governors as required, the duty of ships on station was to look in at harbours and secluded places that were "becoming the resorts of Pirates, Slave Vessels, or dealers, and other lawless or improper characters". Gathering information was an essential duty, as was cruising so as to be able to intercept slave ships. As the French became more amenable to the British lead in anti-slavery work, so, too, did instructions call for cooperating with the French. Indeed, from time to time, combined British and French attacks on slavers' nests were undertaken, as in June 1845.[23] The coast of East Africa was an arduous place to survey, and Captain W.F.W. Owen was presented with surfs, currents, a debilitating climate, the hostility of the natives, and a coast abounding in shoals and innumerable small islands.[24] Owen's survey of 1822–1826 ranks as the greatest single survey carried out. His 300 charts delivered to the Hydrographic Office in triplicate were completed at a cost of lives of two-thirds of the officers and men employed. Here was a malaria coast to be avoided at all costs for inshore work fighting the slave trade. He wrote in passionate tones to the Admiralty about the loss of officers and men, pointing out that such a serious sacrifice in lives would deprive the Navy of half of its efficiency whenever it might become necessary to direct its operations to these regions. The surgeons, he observed, were as much in the dark as to the nature of malaria as if they had never studied medicine at all. Owen was wrong: the cause of malaria had yet to be detected, but his letters were a warning nonetheless.[25]

The British occupation of Aden helped the deployment of naval power. For some time the British had their eye on this ancient stronghold guarding the entrance to the Red Sea. In the 1830s, thought turned to running steamships through the Mediterranean to Egypt, and from the Red Sea to

Bombay. Parliament debated its prospects in 1834. A Commission of Enquiry on Steam Communication with India was struck, and Lord Bentinck made full use of information supplied to him by the Peninsular Steam Navigation Company. The key was Post Office contracts and the closer association of London with Bombay. The Peninsula Company had mastered the steamer runs to Portugal and Spain and, in 1840, to Alexandria, becoming the Peninsula & Oriental Company, with a royal charter. Soon, steamers were placed on the Indian Ocean route, linking Suez and Bombay. Meanwhile, fear of French encroachment existed because Mehemet Ali, the powerful ruler of Egypt, was friendly with Paris. Thus it was that in 1839 the circumstances were such that the British took action, an expedition of the government of Bombay forcibly occupying Aden. It took it ostensibly to check the piratical activities of the locals, but the added benefit was to get a coaling base adjacent to the newly established Suez–Bombay mail steamship service.[26]

Once again we see the expansion of bases of operations as a feature of global reach and security, especially in times of small wars and protracted exercise of showing the flag. Palmerston's attention to the importance of the Red Sea route was predicated on his concern that the independence of the peoples of the coast should not be compromised. He feared French interests there and worried about Ottoman aggrandizement.[27] Via the overland route across Egypt, a mixture of ship management and carriage by canal, river and desert sand passed passengers and mail, supplies and other goods, and even coal for the ships' bunkers on the other side of Suez.[28] In 1870 a British cable ran all the way from Falmouth to Bombay, with only the break across Suez being the missing link in the tentacles of empire. A government mail contract aided the P&O, brought India closer, and increased communications, via the Seychelles, to the East Africa coast and Zanzibar. On 17 November 1869 the first ships steamed through the desert from the Mediterranean to the Gulf of Suez, cutting the unbroken voyage from Europe in half. Although East Africa was off the beaten track from the main link with India, a revolution had occurred. "It was now easier for mails and merchandise, for business-men and tourists, for missionaries and officials, and, at need, for soldiers to play their part in the relationship of Europe with Asia – and with Africa too."[29] And it made British sea power more influential.

Native acceptance of the stipulations of the treaty did not come immediately. Each sheik was required to sign a preliminary agreement. Thus Foreign Office files show an agreement signed by Sheikh Sultan Bin Suggar, the chief of Ras-ool-Khyman, at Shargah on 17 April 1838. He was the war chief of the Joasmi. He agreed to vessels being detained and searched "whenever and wherever they may be fallen in with on the seas by the cruisers" of the British Government – that is, the Bombay Marine or the Royal Navy. He further agreed that these vessels were liable to seizure if it had been ascertained that the crews had carried off – that is, literally, stolen – and embarked slaves.[30]

This preliminary agreement hammered out by quarterdeck diplomacy was followed on by a second a year later. The diplomat's game always shifts from one problem solved to another yet unsolved, and so it was with the naval work of coercion and compliance. This time and so that there could be no misunderstanding as to the areas that the British were policing, the same sheik was requested to sign, which he did, an acceptance of an area defined by a line drawn south from Cape Delgado, passing two degrees seaward of the island of Socotra and ending at Cape Guadel. Within this, all suspected vessels could be detained and searched. They could also be seized except if a vessel entered the area under stress of weather. But now the deal included anti-slavery measures, which were locked into the anti-piracy ones. The sale of males and females whether old or young of the Soomalee (Somali) tribe "shall be considered as piracy". The British were tightening the ring, making sure that the native jurisdiction understood that slaves were to be treated as property that could be seized – and then, of course, freed at some location where recurrence was unlikely. Similar agreements were entered into with three other sheiks along that coast, as the maritime rule of British law was being extended and enforced.[31] From these flowed others: with Trucial Oman in 1838–1839 and again in 1847; with Teheran in 1848 (prohibiting the importation of African slaves and also giving British warships the right of search of incoming vessels); and with Bahrain in 1861. Treaties were not enough: pressure had to be placed continually on old allies, such as Sayyid. The sultan asked for England's consideration of financial compensation for the loss of the trade in human traffic. However, Palmerston at the Foreign Office insisted, as he put it, that his man on the spot, Captain Atkins Hamerton (of whom more presently), "should take every opportunity of impressing on these Arabs that the nations of Europe are destined to put an end to the African S[lave] T[rade], and that Great Britain is the main instrument in the Hands of Providence for the accomplishment of this purpose".[32] Palmerston, here as elsewhere, argued with unbridled optimism that legal commerce would arise when the slave trade was abolished. This, he reasoned, would more than make up for the loss.

In short, the general scheme afoot was to induce every principal sheik to sign a preliminary agreement. This was the necessary first task, which when completed could lead to the next stage of development. It was the work of the inchworm. It took years to establish a maritime protectorate of the Persian Gulf and to enforce *Pax Britannica* even in this confined area. More often than not, quarrels between and among Arab chieftains could be blamed for the continuance of piracy. But soon the British negotiated what has been called the Maritime Truce. Once again there was need and opportunity for expansion, and thus, with the consent of the Gulf-state rulers, it grew into the Treaty of Peace in Perpetuity of May 1853.

This great document went beyond its precursors in one particular way: it gave the British final authority, in its words

> that the "perfect maritime peace" now established for evermore should be watched over and enforced by the British government, that, in fact, in the event of aggression on any one of the parties by sea, the injured tribe should not itself retaliate, but refer the matter to the British authorities in the Gulf.[33]

In other words, the British had established an empire of the seas, and had done so with the agreement of the constituent littoral states. It is a model of early quarterdeck diplomacy and was in its time a remarkable achievement.

In the Persian Gulf and the Red Sea, as in most waters where British interests required succour, Britain's maritime forces, including armed merchantmen, East India Company warships, and sloops, schooners and other light craft, attempted to sweep clean the seas of these corsairs. Here, as elsewhere, the object of British naval captains was to keep free the world's waters for legitimate commerce. Freedom of the seas was the desired end and intervention by the Royal Navy the means. In the case of the Persian Gulf, all nations were believed by the British authorities to be the beneficiaries of this policy and the Maritime Truce. At a later time, Lord Curzon when viceroy of India made clear that the British Raj had an obligation to establish peace and order. "We opened these seas to the ships of all nations," he informed the sheikhs of the Persian Gulf,

> and enabled their flags to fly in peace. We have not destroyed your independence but have preserved it. We are not now going to throw away this century of costly and triumphant enterprise... The peace of these waters will be maintained; your independence will continue to be upheld and the influence of the British Government will remain supreme.[34]

The British put the pirates out of work; they created unemployment, as it were. But the maritime peace achieved by the 1850s afforded great benefit to indigenous and Indian traders, shipbuilders and ship owners.[35] Opportunities for sailors increased similarly, and native chiefs were gingerly led forward through promises of friendship and enhanced legitimate commerce. The beneficiary of the Britannic peace was the aforementioned Sayyid Said, Sultan of Muscat, who resided in Zanzibar. He kept a large fleet of armed vessels of predominantly Western design, and with these he extended his trade throughout the Indian Ocean and the China Seas. In later years, the British supplied a steam yacht for the personal purposes of the sultan; this was another way of engendering loyal support.[36] Friendship cost money; loyalty came at a price.

Zanzibar, capital of the Arab kingdom south of the Equator, was the key post in the trade in East Africa. Sayyid Said, ruler of Muscat, became a merchant-prince of great prominence in East Africa. In 1832 he shifted his capital from Muscat to Zanzibar, and soon raised its commercial power to that of premier port on the coast. "If you play on the flute at Zanzibar," ran the Arab proverb, "everybody as far as the lakes dances."[37] In 1841 Captain Atkins Hamerton of the Bombay Native Infantry arrived as consul for the East India Company. Later, Her Britannic Majesty's consul, he arrived on a political mission to report to the Bombay government on the slave trade as carried on by the imam and other East African chiefs, and to report on French aggressions reputedly in the imam's territories. French and American influence was then in the ascendant, while Britain's lay at a low ebb. Hamerton and the sultan soon became fast associates, with the consul providing the ships that the native ruler needed to exercise his power. Hamerton, similarly, broke into an exclusive American trade monopoly – one concluded in violation of an earlier British one, of 1840.

The diplomatic powers exercised by Hamerton were of undoubted influence, and they won the jealous admiration of the French. So powerful did the British consul become that when the sultan went to visit Muscat in 1854, he insisted that Hamerton remain with the prince, Khalkid, and guide him in state affairs. He "placed his son's hand in mine," Hamerton reported to Bombay,

> and desired him in all difficulties to be guided by my advice and do nothing without consulting me. The Arabs then rose and came and kissed my hand, saying we are now satisfied through the favour of the Almighty and the powerful destiny of Her Majesty Queen Victoria all will go well with us.[38]

Sayyid Said never returned. He died on board HMS *Victoria* on the passage home. To prevent a public demonstration and a palace coup, the dead body was buried secretly. Hamerton put a stop to a suggestion made by an expectant, wealthy Arab chief who imagined this was now his opportunity to grasp power. Hamerton threatened that his head would fall in 24 hours, and he turned him out of the consulate.[39] And thus did Hamerton come into extreme prominence. Visiting missionaries and explorers continued to write glowingly of his good influences. The manner in which he performed his delicate duties as consul won uniform acclaim from those who knew him, not least from the sultan, and on this friendship, and indeed on its influence over native leaders, rested the noted partiality of the imam for all things English. The personal role in extending the intentions of *Pax* was exhibited in Hamerton's life. It fell to others to effect it. In July 1858, Captain Christopher Rigby arrived to continue the work. His championing of anti-slave-trading activities is noted below.

Zanzibar was being drawn inexorably into the links to Suez and thus to the affairs of the Mediterranean and those nations competing for influence in this sector. The canal opened to traffic in 1869, and soon the British Steam Navigation Company ran a monthly service from Zanzibar to link up with the P&O at Aden. The next year the Union Steamship Company opened the route to Durban. Both were under government contract and assumed that this would provide trade and the civilizing influences flowing from it, and would facilitate the suppression of the trade in slaves.[40]

Zanzibar, remarked one cruiser captain, was "the reservoir into which the trickling streams of black blood from the interior flow and are gathered, pending the opening of the sluices which permit its outlet to seaward". By his estimate, 10,000–20,000 slaves passed annually through Zanzibar territory. From there they either found their way to the dominions of the sultan, the interior of Arabia and Persia, or they got "a temporary resting place on the decks of some British man-of-war, to be herded together at the Seychelles, at Bombay, or at Aden".[41] But pending some arrangement that might control the trade at source – it was beyond British measures inasmuch as it was on Portuguese territory – it had to be policed at sea or by such moral suasion and payment as would mollify and satisfy the Sultan of Zanzibar.

In 1856 a headstrong lieutenant in the Indian Army, Richard Burton, who was experienced in intelligence work, sailed from Bombay to explore Equatorial Africa, specifically to solve one of the most pressing geographical puzzles of the times: to locate the sources of the White Nile. The expedition had Royal Geographical Society backing, the tacit consent of the Government of India and the foreknowledge of the Foreign Office. In company went a fellow officer and his eventual rival, Lieutenant John Hanning Speke. Taking a passage in an East India Company ship, they sailed to the Red Sea and the Persian Gulf, then coasted south towards Zanzibar. The party, debilitated by malaria, reached Lake Tanganyika, but regretfully this did not prove to be a source of the Nile. Speke, in an ancillary role, found Lake Ukerewe, which he renamed Lake Victoria, and from native report learned that a large river flowed from the lake's north side. The lake was the source of the Nile. A feud developed between the two explorers. Book contracts, lecturer fees, public acclaim and much else lay in the balance. The quarrel dragged on until 1864 when, just before a debate to settle the matter, Speke was killed by a gunshot wound to his chest. "The charitable say that he shot himself, the uncharitable say that I shot him," said Burton.

Burton seems always able to survive in the most difficult circumstance. With regard to his 1857–1858 explorations, he exceeded mere geographical description. People and places were not enough for him. He took liberties in his report, indicated those sections of the coast that were in need of further hydrographical survey, and presumed to give a situation report on the ill state of British defences in those waters. He also proposed a British agent be appointed for Berberah, for instance, for it would tend to increase trade, be a refuge for shipwrecked persons and "materially assist in civilizing the Somal in the interior".

He also thought a more efficient naval force should be provided at Aden, headquarters of the Red Sea squadron. According to Burton, 35 British merchantmen had arrived and left Jeddah, the port of Mecca, between the end of September and April, from various places in the East – China, Batavia, Singapore, Calcutta, Bombay, the Malabar Coast, the Persian Gulf and East Africa. Their trade was of significance, he said, and he named some of the cargo: rice, sugar, piece goods, planking, pepper and pilgrims. From Persia came dates, tobacco and raw silk, while from Mozambique came ivory, gold dust and other similar costly articles. This increased value of Red Sea traffic, he said, needed increased protection because the slave trade had equal claims on British attention. The trade, he said, was principally in the hands of Arab merchants at Jeddah, who in ships carrying 200 slaves at a time exported them from East Africa to Jeddah and other small ports lying to the south and north of it.

> Our present squadron in the Red Sea consisting of only two sailing vessels, the country boats in the African ports have only to wait till they see the ship pass up or down, and then knowing the passage – a matter of a day – to be clear, to lodge the slaves at their destination.

Burton's recommendation was to supplement fast sailing cruisers with two-screw steamers. These would be small enough to enter every harbour, work steadily along the banks on either shore, and carry English political officers and their native prince allies. He thought that the vessels should be those of the "Flying Fish" class of gunboat, drawing less than 9 feet and sporting four 32-pounders as broadside, and another pair as pivot guns. He concluded that these vessels would gain the full ascendancy in the waters of the Red Sea, and thus "the slave-trade in the Red Sea would soon have received its death-blow, and Eastern Africa its regeneration in our hands".[42]

Burton's problem was that he presumed to give advice, when in fact other persons – naval, military and consular – were better informed. Independent positions were not always welcome at the Foreign Office, under whose control Zanzibar rested. The Admiralty was bound to set aside such recommendations as being unwarranted, and the government and the scientific bodies who had aided the young lieutenant soon distanced themselves from such effrontery and cheek.[43] Burton was the sort of fellow of the Victorian age whom the public could not let down. In 1861 he received the appointment as consul at Fernando Po, and from that advantageous point travelled into West Africa, wrote five books about his wanderings, became a commentator on African customs and rituals, and on the sexual practices of those he observed, and, if that were not enough, translated a number of oriental texts. Consular duties took him to Brazil, Damascus and Trieste. When he died in 1890, aged 69, he had done more to acquaint the English readership with Africa and the Near East than any other person, and except for David Livingstone and Henry Stanley had more strongly fixed the British mindset on African affairs than any story of anti-slavery patrols or the horrors of the middle passage.

Along the flank of East Africa north of Cape Delgado, no ports were under European control, and such influence as Portugal exercised was feeble – an extension of dynastic troubles at home. The coast was not critical to British strategic interests. The volume of British trade with East Africa is difficult to gauge, and only the commerce of Zanzibar was of much value, though the statistics on trade were impossible to assess. British trade was doubtless growing. The main import was cotton goods; the biggest exports being ivory, cloves and slaves – in that order. Some Indian corporations and individuals, or *banyans*, had amassed large fortunes out of East Africa. German, American and French firms traded on the coast as well, but by and large the area was British as a zone of influence, yet nonetheless under the control of the Sultan of Zanzibar.[44] The Colonial Office's knowledge of the great island was limited to the files that it received as copies from the Foreign Office or even the Admiralty. The anti-slavery patrol was a child of the Foreign Office, not the Government of India.

Just as Palmerston opposed the European traffic of West Africa, so did he oppose the Arab traffic of East Africa. Before leaving the Foreign Office in 1841 he wanted to tighten the terms of the treaty with the Sultan of Zanzibar. He wrote to the British consul there:

> You will take every opportunity of impressing upon these Arabs that the nations of Europe are destined to put an end to the African Slave Trade, and that Great Britain is the main instrument in the hand of Providence for the accomplishment of this purpose: that it is vain for these Arabs to endeavour to resist the consummation of that which is written in the book of fate.

Lord John Russell, Lord Derby, Lord Stanley, Gladstone as prime minister, Lord Clarendon and Lord Granville all kept to this line, without failure. In 1849, when Lord John Russell was prime minister, and a consideration was being given to withdrawing the naval patrol, he called a caucus meeting and told members that if such a motion were passed he would resign. The East African trade, as we will see, became the new subject for attack. The government of Bombay had it right in 1861, when it concluded that the facts of the East African Slave Trade "will convince the British Government, which has ever been the chief instrument by which Providence has curbed this inhuman traffic, that its work is not yet completed and that a great evil has still to be encountered and subdued".[45]

David Livingstone, who might well fit the description of a "chariot of fire", drew Britain's attention to the horrors of the East African slave trade. Admiral Beaufort, who met him, thought him a "fine, tough looking, sensible, modest fellow".[46] Palmerston, the prime minister, backed Livingstone's schemes for commercial benefit and moral suasion – legitimate trade would drive out slave traders – and the Foreign Office made Livingstone a consul and sent advice to the hydrographer Admiral John Washington at the Admiralty to supply every means to advance riverine navigation. A river steamer was supplied, and the Navy received instructions to aid Livingstone as circumstances required. Livingstone, who was used to operating on a shoestring budget, was surprised, even alarmed, by the Admiralty's largesse. His connections stretched to Bombay, Aden, Mauritius and the Cape, but increasingly he was dependent on communications coming via the Mediterranean, the Red Sea and Zanzibar. The British imperial links favoured his inland travels and encouraged his further schemes.

In London, Livingstone revealed to the world the horrors of the Portuguese and Arab slave trade in the interior. He antagonized the Portuguese authorities by accusing them of supporting slave trading. However, his sharp critique of the Portuguese resulted in embarrassment to Whitehall, and thus the foreign secretary, Earl Russell, cut the connection. After this he was largely on his own. The alarming news that he spread, though already known to the Navy, was that although the European trade in slaves might be dying, that of the Arabs in East Africa was growing.[47] His appeal for the evangelization of the interior led to the founding of the Universities' Mission to Central Africa of 1858–1859, which established itself on the Zambezi. In 1862 it was removed to Zanzibar. For Livingstone's 1858 Zambezi expedition, the steam launch *Ma Robert* was constructed in parts and assembled at the point of need, and now the power of steam speeded the missionary progress in search of rivers, trading partners and villages brought into the imperial web. Livingstone made other journeys, to Lake Tanganyika and the River Lualaha, which he thought mistakenly to be the Upper Nile. He died in 1873, his multiple illnesses too much for him, and with the bitter knowledge that the slave trade still flourished. But he had lit a fire under the crusaders against slavery in this area, and his influence, and theirs, brought renewed Foreign Office zeal to the anti-slavery cause and brought increased force and determination to the slave patrols of the Navy. His remains were buried in the central nave of Westminster Abbey. His iconic status, built upon extraordinary travels and exploring journeys, his legendary encounter with Henry Morton Stanley from the *New York Herald* who went to find the all-but disappeared and possibly dead Scot, and his belief that commercial development for Africa went hand in hand with conversion to Christianity have given him a special place in the history of the British Empire. Not only did he fuel the "scramble for Africa" but, by conjoining commerce and Christianity, he shaped European activity in Africa for many years afterwards.

Watching over Livingstone's travels and expeditions was but one duty of the Navy in these seas. An early episode is an indication of this, and it speaks of the missionary explorer's humanity. Writing to the Rev. Dr Tidman in 1856 about future operations, Livingstone reported that HM brigantine *Dart* had called at the port of Quilimane several times in order to offer him a passage homeward, but on the last occasion her commander, the officer of marines, and five seamen were lost on the dangerous bar at the river mouth.

> This very event threw a cold shade over all the joy I might otherwise have experienced on reaching the Eastern Coast. I felt as if it would have been easier for me to have died for them than to hear the thought of so many being cut off from all the joys of life in generously attempting to render me a service.

Some time later a British cruiser arrived as promised and took him to the Cape, for connections home – a far better course than going via a Portuguese trader or Arab vessel (the only alternatives) to some trading point on the "overland route to India".[48]

As of 1870 the East Indies station included Burma, Mauritius and the east coast of Africa. The usual round of work for a cruiser on patrol was to leave Simons Bay in midwinter, pass up the Mozambique Channel and call at Zanzibar, then cross the Indian Ocean to Trincomalee, the naval headquarters, there to rendezvous with the commander-in-chief, refit and resupply as required, then await new orders. The viceroy of India, for instance, might wish to visit Rangoon and Moulmein in British Burma, and a man-of-war would be provided as the transport, sailing from Calcutta and beating up under sail against the northeast monsoon. Arriving in the Hooghly River, his excellency the viceroy would be received on board then conveyed to the intended place. In 1871, HMS *Glasgow*, a frigate, carried the viceroy of India, Earl of Mayo, to this location, and at Moulmein on the Burma coast was given a wonderful display of elephants stacking timber.

Next it was on to the Andaman Islands, and a call at Port Blair, the penal settlement for India, where the most serious cases were sent. At Port Blair, after a period of close confinement and hard work, such convicts of good report, be they male or female, were allowed a certain amount of liberty. They might even be allowed to marry and work a small agricultural holding. On the occasion of this visit, the imperialists failed to take adequate precautions.

Danger lurked ever near in such locales. Lieutenant Arthur Moore takes up the story:

> A picnic was proposed by the Viceroy on Mount Harriet above the part for married convicts and in the afternoon he landed to see if it was suitable. It was getting dusk when he and his party arrived at the small pier that was rather long, a convict Shere Ali rushed through the party and jumping on the

> Viceroy's back, stabbed him twice. The convict was secured, and Lord Mayo was conveyed on board the steam barge and expired in a few minutes.[49]

A court was assembled aboard ship the next day. The accused was found guilty and on shore was hanged. The ship's company painted the vessel grey, with yards topped, gaffs drooped and other signs of mourning. The ship sailed for Calcutta. The viceroy's coffin was placed on display in the Throne Room at Government House, and after lying in state for some days it was taken back aboard *Glasgow*. The vessel sailed for Suez, the coffin was taken home to Britain and the new viceroy, Lord Northbrook, with his military secretary, Major Evelyn Baring, afterwards Earl Cromer (famous for the Anglo-Egyptian arrangements later in the century), embarked at the transshipment point and was conveyed to Bombay via Aden. Lord Northbrook landed with the usual honours, and so the Raj continued.

This murder of the viceroy was an event that was unusual in the history of British activities in the Indian Ocean; the workaday world of the Navy soon returned to police work of the usual sort. The ports on the east coast of Africa were regularly visited as part of slave-trade suppression. The traffic in slaves on the east coast of Africa remained astonishingly active and this despite the continuing efforts that continued to be made for its repression.[50] The always overtaxed squadron undertook the challenge, and there were never enough men-of-war to keep up the great watch that was required to cruise for suspicious dhows. Thus steam launches and, above all, open boats were used, the men at the oars for long days, several in succession. It was miserable, and for a time the Admiralty arranged to have kroomen, so successful in the West African inshore and riverine work of slave-trade suppression, employed in East Africa, but this gave way to the employment of East Africa natives, who were less highly regarded by the Navy. Bounties were introduced to encourage the taking of dhows, but the Treasury discounted the tonnage of the vessels captured, thereby cutting back on the prize money given. In all, it was wearisome, and it is hard to say that the slave trade there was fully brought to a conclusion. The introduction of steam made the work more effective, and the design of certain warships that were useful for this sort of task aided the process. Even so, the costs to officers and men were considerable, for operating inshore in mosquito-infested waters was very demanding. Here was a world for extraordinary naval activity. Boats would be left by the mother ship for the labour of weeks in the rivers and on the coast. Paddle-box boats and rowed gigs would venture upriver, spying out dhows and slaving vessels. When going upriver, extra rum was added to a concoction of quinine, so as to dull the dreadful taste of the latter. Boats crews got ragingly high on this concoction but malaria made no claims here. Naval supplies had been deposited in a metal tank on an offshore island; and to this the crews would repair for resupply, sleeping in tents. Once back aboard ship, the men could bathe in the water well between the paddlewheels, safe from voracious sharks.[51]

In the early 1860s, naval architects turned their attention, on Admiralty guidance, to new types of warship used for extending *Pax Britannica*. The gunboats and gun vessels so important to success in the years after the Crimean War – and by this time dispatched around the world in places of need – also revealed the possibilities of certain vessels to be used for certain types of cruising. One of these, which began to appear in 1866, was the steam sloop. This design featured a wooden, ram-bowed hull, which was rather experimental at the time; it led to the composite, ram-bow corvette with timber and iron-cross beamed construction that was stronger and more efficient. Besides the new hull design, the steam sloop carried two swivel 7-inch, 6.5 ton guns, which were good for coastal and inshore work. Four vessels were launched of this class, and all had long use in the anti-slavery campaign on the East Africa coast. They were *Dryad*, *Nymphe*, *Vestal* and *Daphne*, launched from Pembroke, Wales, and noted for their long and effective service in that line of work.[52] Altogether they wove a spider's web – a coordinated attack on the Zanzibar slave trade and the elusive coastal commerce.

In July 1871, given evidence that at least 10,000 slaves a year were being shipped out of East Africa, and likely through Zanzibar, the Foreign Office decided that more drastic measures would have to be taken there. The Government sought a mandate from the House of Commons. A select committee was appointed

> to inquire into the whole question of the Slave Trade on the East Coast of Africa, into the increased and increasing amount of that traffic, the particulars of existing Treaties and Agreements with the Sultan of Zanzibar upon the subject, and the possibility of putting an end entirely to the traffic in slaves by sea.

Among the advisors were Rear Admiral C.R. Hillyar and Admiral Sir Leopold Heath, who had successively commanded the patrolling squadron in the previous five years, and Captain Colomb, who had served in it from 1868 to 1870. The admirals agreed that the patrol squadron should be reinforced to at least 10 or 12 ships. A complete blockade of the coast, though suggested by the governor of Bombay, the influential Sir Bartle Frere, and others, was deemed impractical. A depot ship should be kept in Zanzibar, the consul should have his own yacht so that he could regularly visit ports along the coast, all patrol ships should be steam corvettes, or gunboats, and equipped with steam launches for work inshore, smokeless fuel should be used, and good interpreters should be provided – these were the main recommendations on the naval side. With these improvements, this policy of restricting the slave traffic would have a good chance of success, it was agreed. Territorial annexation was ruled out.[53]

In Zanzibar, always closely watched, there was still a public slave market in the early 1870s. "We often saw the slaves put up for auction and sold to Arabs for domestic service or for labour on plantations." So wrote Lieutenant Moore, who added,

> They were captured originally far inland by Arab raiders, and used as porters for the conveyance of ivory to the coast, and then put on board sailing dhows or for transport to Zanzibar and markets in the Persian Gulf. We could take the dhows at sea, but had no authority over the Sultan of Zanzibar and the slave market, but on one of our visits, Sir Bartle Frere arrived and made a treaty with the Sultan and later the cathedral of the Universities' Mission was built on the site of the slave market.[54]

The climate here was very debilitating, and members of the mission looked pale and exhausted, opined Moore, there again 30 years later as an admiral. By contrast, the French, accustomed to drinking a little wine, were in much better shape. In a daring move, Moore sent the mission a barrel of pontac, a red wine made at the Cape.

> When I called, fearing their disapproval, I asked diffidently: 'Is it peace?' They laughed and thanked me, and gave me a sample of their work: a baby's cap of calico, sewn in red and white sections with a tassled cord to tie under the chin. With it was a paper inscribed "To the Great Father Admiral."[55]

The slave market in Zanzibar horrified naval officers and disgusted sailors. In Coupland's words, "What the average British seamen thought of it may be inferred from the fact that it was considered dangerous to allow the crews of the patrolling squadron to go ashore at Zanzibar lest they should be tempted 'to make a clearance' of the market."[56]

The commerce of Zanzibar depended on the finances of Indian traders, or *banyans*, who now found themselves in difficulty because of the British proscription. A supplementary anti-slave-trade treaty of 1876 extended controls to the coastal zone, but the rise in the clove trade brought an increased demand for slaves.[57] It cannot be said that the British were powerless to deal with the problem, only that local circumstances outstripped any diplomatic or military attempts to check the trade. On land, the British were helpless unless they intervened and took control ashore. This they were opposed to, and they stood by their unannounced policy. To make more effective their naval patrols, the Admiralty sent out the old two-decker *London* to Zanzibar in 1874. She served as hospital, prison, factory, victualling yard, depot and man-of-war – an immovable "stone frigate". She had a large number of boats, many of which were steam-powered. Each had a strong crew and was well armed. Along with an interpreter and provisioned for as many as 42 days, these went forth on their relentless quest for slavers.

For a young lieutenant or an aspiring midshipman, being in command of a small boat on detached service from a man-of-war spelled some interesting hours in what is called "dhow-chasing". Here, expert boat-handling was required and a tactical knowledge suitable for dealing with equally expert native sailors. There were long hours and days on this sort of assignment. The dhows preferred to work during the southwest monsoon, when they could make, they hoped, an escape. In such circumstances the boat had to cruise in rough weather and rain. In spite of exposure and constant wet, the crew had better health than those lying off Zanzibar. The Arabs were expert at handling their dhows. "It was exciting work, maneuvering to overtake them on the windward side, to force them to heave to."[58]

Hardly an aspect of the Arab slave trade found favour with those intelligent naval officers – Colomb, Devereaux and Sulivan – who wrote accounts of their experience about the work from Mozambique to Madagascar and Bourbon.[59] In an era when British eyes were beginning to be fixed on the East African slave trade, doubtless given added attention by David Livingstone's graphic testimonies and the informed British public's reactions, these memoirs of service told more than the official in-letters that were the workaday story of slave-trade suppression and came from the pens of outraged commanders-in-chief or senior naval officers.

These naval officers were eyewitnesses to human misery and degradation. The traffic and those who controlled and ran it abhorred them. The unimaginable crowding of the slaves between decks horrified them. Piratical crews cut the slaves' throats in advance of capture, or ran the dhow ashore and let the property swim for land. At the Zanzibar market, exhibits of sunken chests, protruding eyes and knotted limbs brought feelings of disgust and nausea. Devereaux would like to have employed a few midshipmen with a blackthorn each to clear the market of "those vile Arabs". Children and women in slavery brought forth outrages from Sulivan, while the first British consul, Atkins Hamerton, shared the revulsion of the naval officers to the Zanzibar slave market. "They are in such a wretched state from starvation and disease that they are sometimes not considered worth landing, and are allowed to expire in the boats to save the duty of the dollar a head."[60]

The business was hazardous. Sir John Kirk, consult-general in Zanzibar, told of how Captain Brownrigg, RN, of *London*, the guard ship in Zanzibar, left his ship in a steam pinnace with ten men, to inspect his boats that were then cruising off Pemba Island, north of Zanzibar. He chanced upon a large dhow jammed full of slaves and coming out from Pemba. It flew French colours, and Brownrigg determined to verify her nationality, but without taking the precautionary measure of arming the crew. The Arab crew of 25 fired into the pinnace, then boarded her, and killed Brownrigg and others, driving many overboard. Brownrigg's last moments are described by William Laird Clowes, the Victorian historian, as follows:

> Brownrigg alone offered serious resistance. He seized a rifle, shot one of his assailants, and, standing in the stern sheets with the clubbed weapon, held out manfully in spite of twenty wounds, two at least of which would have been mortal. Nor did he desist until he fell shot through the heart.

Three British sailors shared his fate; three others were wounded. The Arabs let the boat drift, and the survivors, managing to recover the craft, took her back to *London*. The dhow, having disposed of its human freight, was eventually captured. News of the tragedy, and of Brownrigg's personal courage, reached Parliament and was subject to discussion in *The Times*, which much regretted the lack of precaution. "Captain Brownrigg died, not only as an Englishman, but as the bravest of Englishmen. It is to be regretted that precautions were not taken whereby we might have been spared the loss of so gallant an officer."[61]

Proper precautions called to place the boat to windward of the dhow, then order "prepare to board" when the men would arm and go to their stations. The always-essential interpreter would shout to the dhow to send its crew forward, which would have been low and flush decked (the aft section being high with a poop). Half of the men would then cover the fore part, a couple the after part, and having had the dhow sail lowered, the boat would be run alongside and boarded, and a search undertaken. His coxswain with his drawn cutlass might accompany the lieutenant. At first, no slaves might be found, but on a relentless search, slaves would be found crammed together. They would all be taken ashore. The various missions cared for these young persons and taught them to earn a living, as it was impossible to return them to Central Africa. Similar precautions had to be taken by landing parties ashore.

Many are the success stories of dhow-chasing in the Indian Ocean. The corvette *Briton* captured ten slave dhows by means of boats between May 1884 and July 1887. The steam sloops *Reindeer* and *Kingfisher* took about the same number during the same period. But always sharp reminders came home to those doing the work that "the scoundrels who conducted the abominable traffic were not always willing to be suppressed without hard fighting". So it was in the case of *Turquoise*, cruising off Pemba in May 1887. Despite receiving a volley of musketry and fire from the pinnace's 9-pounder, the dhow bore boldly down on the pinnace. "Prepare to resist boarders! Stand to them, my lads!" barked the young lieutenant Frederick Fogarty Fegen, and when the Arabs boarded, the gallant lieutenant shot two with his revolver and ran a third through with his sword. Fegen, though badly wounded, continued to fire his revolver. Three bluejackets were cut down and others were injured until the dhow, having lost nine, sheered off. But the Navy continued the attack, and the pinnace and dinghy drove the dhow ashore, where it capsized. The Arabs, now ashore, opened fire, all the while covering the retreat of their friends. The gun of the pinnace peppered the musketeers. Some 33 slaves were liberated from the dhow (20 others had drowned). One bluejacket was mortally wounded and three others were put out of action. Fegen was invalided home, "but enjoyed the satisfaction, on his arrival, of finding that he had been specially promoted [to commander] for his bravery".[62]

Such were the incidental cases of the price of Admiralty of the age. Small boat actions, undertaken in conditions of unbearable heat and scorching sun, often on diminished rations and with daily rum rations running short, were the order of the day. The story is told that on one occasion, with all provisions gone, the boat party lived on a handful of rice and a pint of water. "Never shall I forget the joy that I felt on seeing the dear old ship heave in sight!" wrote one sailor. "I think, if I were a captain," mused one officer some years later, "I should consider the lives of twenty men far more valuable than all the slave dhows in the Mozambique at £5. 10s. Per ton."[63] "It was tedious work rowing up-stream, elbowing past mangrove thickets under clouds of mosquitos, or drifting for hours near the coast without a breadth of wind and under a piercing sun," writes Gerald Graham about the Navy's work in East Africa and the Indian Ocean.

> It could be frightening work, fighting a gale off the coast, hove-to for days at a time waiting for a spell of moderate weather to fetch the rendezvous, or, with close-reefed mainsail, reeling before the charging ridges that advanced rank upon rank with the menacing power of an avalanche. North Sea fishermen learned to take such troubles in their stride, and somehow managed to cook a meal or find their bunks even with the decks awash and the mast swinging fore and aft like a clock's pendulum. But most of the seamen in cutter, gig, whaler, or pinnace were not fishermen but men-of-war recruits, and this was not the life they had anticipated when they watched the big frigates rolling in the swell outside Portsmouth harbour.[64]

But, still, there was lots of excitement as compensation and a chance to see the world. There was the thrill of the chase leading to armed combat and, if lucky enough to survive, prize money. Steam, doubtless, was making the work easier, but still the lower deck, often without notice or reward, did the heavy lifting of anti-slavery work. The deadly enemy was the mosquito.

Relief came at last to the ship's company when, after four years, the ship's commission ended. Another vessel would provide the relief at Aden, and in the case of Lieutenant Moore and his ship they were able to sail for England, calling at Malta after passing through the Suez Canal, and at Gibraltar, that legendary imperial rock. This, then, formed the regular naval routine in these seas in the late nineteenth century, and the opening of the Suez Canal had extended the efficiency of ships on station, avoided long passages back to the Cape of Good Hope and the long Atlantic passage home. The Indian Ocean was increasingly becoming more of an extension of the Mediterranean, with Suez the mid-shipment point, as it were, and Aden a new anchor of empire. Suez had been purchased by Britain, a decision governed by Disraeli's own peculiar concept of empire. It was, as the historian Leland H. Jenks put it, an example of making "foreign investment a veritable weapon of British foreign policy".[65] Perhaps, if Gladstone had been in power, the khedive of Egypt's offer of shares would have been refused. But the purchase of the shares went ahead, and was a precondition for a series of events whereby Britain became "an Egyptian government", as Gladstone, with sombre irony said, in 1884.[66]

As for East Africa, resistance to formal empire on the continent remained strong. Robinson and Gallagher put it this way: "A handful of enthusiasts for imperial expansion in tropical Africa by themselves could no more make an imperialist summer in the late Eighteen seventies than they could in the Eighteen forties and Eighteen fifties."[67] No amount of reasoning or moral preaching could lead to a policy of intervention there. The Foreign Office was dead set against it. If private enterprise could do it, then well and good. Conservatives and Liberals alike fought against any commitment embroiling the nation in future troubles. As the viceroy of India, Lord Ripon, put it, the British should "avoid implicating ourselves in matters over which we could exercise no real influence without an expenditure of money and a display of strength out of all proportion to the advantages to be gained".[68] The limits of humanitarian intervention had been reached, and the costs were mounting, drawing the fire of the press and Parliament. On the eve of the discovery of gold and diamonds in southern Africa, the British had developed a clear mindset: they would work to eradicate the slave trade by a process of minimum intervention, which was the work of the Royal Navy. It was a seaborne operation, not a land-based one. Establishing treaties with sheiks of the Red Sea and Arabian Sea, or with the Sultan of Zanzibar, was the technique of statecraft. It was only when this order of affairs broke down with the demands that turbulent frontiers necessitated that *Pax* in this part of the world became compromised, and the limits of naval influence on affairs ashore had been reached. But the early, preliminary chapters in the suppression of the east coast of Africa slave trade had been completed. The allies had been put in place, or silenced by treaties and arrangements to encourage loyalty. These were essential benefits to the British Foreign Office as it now began to consider how international rivalry would test the British pre-eminence on the East African coast. From the Arabian Sea and the Persian Gulf south to Zanzibar and then Cape Town, the British naval presence was supreme, but it could not in and of itself direct the course of empire ashore.

12
Darkening Horizons

It was a world in which the sun never seemed to set on the British Empire. The 1880s were the years of *Pax Britannica*'s finest influence, the years in which persons such as Sir George Bowen (as we saw in Chapter 1) could talk about the magnificence of the Britannic achievement. Still, these years marked the beginnings of its feared decline. But throughout the age of *Pax Britannica*, Britain and the empire were never without testy and jealous rivals. Such rivalry had driven colonial expansion. The course of history since 1815 gave assurance, perhaps falsely, that upstart rivals could be dealt with, managed even, and from time to time smaller wars had been fought to maintain British primacy. The Crimean War is the boldest example, and in numerous cases merely raising fleets and deploying squadrons and battalions had served the purpose, always in alliance with adroit diplomacy. In the Americas the challenge came from the United States. The French and Russians proved to be the most contentious challengers in the eastern Mediterranean, though never in combination. Portugal's strength had waned, as had Holland's. Spain's strength was still exercised in Cuba, the Philippines and elsewhere, its resurgent power of the late nineteenth century posed no particular difficulty to Britain though crossed directly over the course of the rising naval power and global ambitions of the United States. Since 1815 the technique of deploying regiments to British North America and beefing up the squadrons at Halifax and Esquimalt had proved to be a useful counterpart when faced with American "manifest destiny".[1] Germany, forged in federation in 1871 under Bismarck, and fresh from victory over France, might turn its attention overseas, and indeed was doing so incrementally in various ways, chiefly in trade, but as of yet posed no great challenge to Britain. Imperial Japan after 1868 offered a new contender for influence in East Asia, while Russia had ambitions to develop itself into a Pacific power, assuming a railway could be built across the great Eurasian landmass.

The adaptation of the steam engine to transcontinental and transoceanic transport had created an entirely different world – and in a surprisingly short period of time. Submarine cables had begun to link continents – the Atlantic crossed in 1868 – and the tentacles of business communication were secured by government contracts, and in this field of endeavour the British were unsurprisingly the dominant nation. The terrestrial globe had indeed contracted, and in 1873 Jules Verne's *Around the World in Eighty Days* celebrated the conquest of distance in delightful, magical style. The world began to be looked at as smaller, and the chancelleries of Europe fixed attention more specifically on those parts not yet acquired. The British tried valiantly to stand aside from this. They held to their policy of informal rule, and, as long as their naval supremacy allowed them to control the perceived belligerent or acquisitive activities of their rivals, they would stick to that policy. Under this mantra, the export of British capital continued without restriction, still more powerfully than that of other nations. The flow of capital was slowing, it is true, but still in advance of French and German rivals.

Technology was driving great changes in the nature of sea power and the deployment of naval units. A growing imperial estate had to be protected against incipient rivals. At the same time, commercial interests at home sought preferable and protected markets abroad. From the mid-century, chancellors of the Exchequer had been faced with an awkward dilemma: how to lower tariffs and duties in the interest of free trade versus how to provide protection for trade and colonial interests. This last was made all the more complicated by the technological revolution in hulls, armour, armament and propulsion that was driving up naval estimates to hitherto unheard of heights. In 1845, Sir Robert Peel, the prime minister (who oversaw the great budgets of his ministry), asked for an increase in naval expenditures. This was hardly in keeping with the Pacific outlook of orthodox free trade. C.R. Fay, the economic historian, explains:

> But how could he avoid it: with the China War but recently concluded, with Afghanistan the graveyard of a recent British disaster, with France on the alert in the Mediterranean, West Africa and the Pacific, with the Dutch and English settlers at blows in Natal, with the Argentine rent by civil turmoil to the great prejudice of British commerce, and with the steamship presenting a new demand for naval outlay – for those steam boats which were so important in running down pirates and slavers?[2]

At mid-century, Sir Robert Peel made his plea for a £1 million increase in the naval estimates so as to provide protection for an extended colonial empire and growing commerce, for new naval stations on the coast of Africa, in the Pacific and in China seas, plus the need to maintain "a respectable steam navy suitable to a peace establishment". These were the requirements of the new age, and the spirit of Palmerston had entered a new phase. The obligations of *Pax* increased with each successive year and did so at an exponential rate.

A compelling argument directing the course of politics in Westminster and Whitehall was free trade. The chief proponents, Richard Cobden and John Bright, both MPs, were pacifists who saw channels of commerce as pathways of peace. Even so, and out of necessity, they advanced the causes of having a Navy to protect seaborne commerce. Peace for the purpose of profit was their motif. If necessary, said Cobden in 1860, £1 million should be spent to maintain a clear superiority over France at sea. At the same time, these free trade advocates rigorously opposed colonies and colonial expansion. Colonies, if self-regulating, should be self-defending. "Cut the painter" became their useful call; cut off the life support from home and the colonies will survive or melt away. Colonies were a millstone around the necks of mother England. In 1862, a parliamentary committee enunciated principles for allocating defence responsibilities between Britain and the colonies:

> That this house (while fully recognizing the claims of all portions of the British Empire to imperial aid in their protection against perils arising from the consequences of imperial policy) is of the opinion that colonies exercising the rights of self-government ought to undertake the main responsibility of providing for heir own internal order and security and ought to assist in their own external defence.

From it flowed the ideals and policies of Gladstone, who first became prime minister in 1868 and dominated, whether in or out of office, the pacifistic position down to 1893 (when he left office, having resigned because of the naval estimates, which he had fought so hard to control). Cobden linked his economic thought and hatred of war with the possession of empire. He was not alone, but others held a different view. For instance, Joseph Hume, a radical free trader, vehemently defended British actions in the First China War of 1840 and the Punjab War in 1849. Many were the views of the free traders with regard to trade protection and imperial expansion (under the heading of "free trade imperialism"), but the intention was the greatest benefit for the least obligation. As an MP put it in the Corn Law debates in 1846, free trade was the "beneficent principle by which foreign nations would become valuable colonies to us, without imposing on us the responsibility of governing them".[3]

Gladstone, as said, had his eye on the stability of Europe. He believed that Britain could be an example to Europe in the world of international law. He found foreign affairs uncongenial. He had distrust for martial types. He did not show disdain for the Navy, realizing that it was an essential instrument of value to European progress. Rather, he objected to its costs and he deplored the Admiralty's importunate calls for more naval units and more men. A first lord of the Admiralty might point out that there was hopefully "a never to be repeated demand upon our naval force... from Vancouver's Isle to the river Plate [and] from the West Indies to China". Indeed, if any certainty existed as to the demands placed on the Admiralty for naval force, the board would be relieved of much embarrassment; however, the calls were "always sudden & foreseen".[4] He showed disinterestedness in matters of imperial and colonial defence, a viewpoint that can be followed through to the Liberal administration of Sir Henry Campbell Bannerman, who took office in 1902. By contrast, the Conservatives were much more defence-minded. Whether in power under Disraeli or active in parliamentary committees dealing with such matters, they tended to show a more marked interest in military and naval matters – and in Britain's preparedness. Gladstone hated imperial adventures. He did not think that the empire was the foundation of Britain's greatness; rather it was, with all of its continual difficulties and doubtless future demands on British resources, a claim on the energies and abilities of the British people.

> There is no precedent [he declared in the opening speech of his Midlothian campaign on 25 November 1879] in human history for the formation like the British Empire. A small island at one extremity of the globe peoples the whole earth with its colonies. Not satisfied with that, it goes among the ancient races of Asia and subjects two hundred and forty millions of men to its rule. Along with all this it disseminates over the world commerce such as no imagination ever conceived in former times and such as no poet ever painted. And all this had to do with the strength that lies within the narrow limits of these shores. Not a strength that I disparage; on the contrary, I wish to dissipate if I can the idle dreams of those who are always telling you that the strength of England depends, sometimes they say upon its prestige, sometimes they say upon extending its Empire, or upon what it possesses beyond these shores. Rely upon it the strength of Great Britain and Ireland is within the United Kingdom.

Remarking on the same state of affairs from the distant point of a century later, A.J.P. Taylor wrote about the uniqueness of the British Empire until about 1880: "It encompassed the globe. Its white communities were growing in population and resources. British control of India seemed unshakable. All this rested on command of the Seas, the *Pax Britannica*."[5] News of the armed peace of empire came back to the motherlands to haunt ministers of the Crown and to fuel the fires of complaint. Gladstone was fully aware of this. So was every secretary of state for the colonies. Members and secretaries of the Aborigines' Protection Society would address impassioned letters to the Colonial Office and to the British press, calling for fair practices against Maori, Aborigines or Bantus.

Trusteeship in which *Pax* was at the centre by the 1880s had become a political creed of thousands, and trusteeship was seen as an essential part of British duty on and over the seas. It was embraced in the ideas of imperialism, besides matters of profit and trade, security and defence, anti-piracy and anti-slavery. Writing of imperialism as a credo, A.P. Thornton puts it this way:

> In the last generation of the Victorian era, many men thought they had found just such an idea. It became their faith, that it was the role of the British Empire to lead the world in the arts of civilization, to bring light to the dark places, to teach the true political method, to nourish and to protect the liberal tradition. It was to act as trustee for the weak, and bring arrogance low. It was to represent in itself the highest aims of human society. It was to command, and deserve, a status and prestige shared by no other. It was to captivate the imagination and hold fast the allegiance of the million by the propagation of peculiar myths – one among which was the figure of Queen Victoria herself, who became depersonalised, an idea: the idea of the Great White Queen. While encouraging and making profit from the spirit of adventure, it was nevertheless to promote the interests of peace and commerce. While it was to gain its greatest trophies in war, it was to find its main task in serving the ends of justice, law and order. It was an idea that moved, an idea that expanded, an idea that had to continue to move and to expand in order to retain its vitality and its virtue.[6]

But the idea of imperialism, or the high imperialism of this age, with all of its hopes and expectations, carried all of the legacies of yesteryear – all of the mistakes and all of the difficulties lined up against the signal successes, many won by the sword or preserved by the gunboat. Since the 1840s, British ministries had laboured with the problem of colonial defence, and the mounting costs and obligations of the same. Safeguarding the borders of the British North American provinces was one matter.[7] The withdrawal of garrisons from Canada in 1871 had encouraged the confederation movement there on the necessity of self-defence. Dealing with the Maori was another. New Zealand, however, was the scene of a protracted war in 1860–1872, and the costs borne by imperial and colonial governments were extensive. Colonial collective identity arose on the basis of colonial military abilities (lauded by some as better than the British ones).[8] On the South African frontier the border disputes continued, notably in Natal. Bermuda's defences needed upgrading and those at the Cape similarly. Not only were there matters of colonial security and peace, order and good government in the settlement colonies, but an entirely new imperative of the steam age was protecting British seaborne trade. When Gladstone took office in 1868, Edward Cardwell, instructed to cut costs and obligations, turned his attention to colonial defence. By this time John Colomb was pointing out the centrality of coal to imperial defence and commerce protection. The volume and value of seaborne trade passing the Cape was such that concern was raised as to its protection, assuming the Suez Canal unusable. Questions were raised as to the inadequacy of the Navy in units and types of ship, and discussion was now entered into regarding the matter of fast, armed merchantmen. The War Office demonstrated a strong interest in coastal defence, and in the case of South Australia, Jervois suggested that a warship be stationed there for that purpose. This was acted on.

In fact, as of 1880, the British Empire was the only one of its kind in the world. It was oceanic and it was global. It consisted of self-governing dominions, colonies and dependencies, and it was studded by garrisoned bases as "anchors of empire" and linked together by British seaborne trade, British merchant shipping, the Royal Navy and a stupendous communications network. "The character of the British Empire will be found by tracing its distribution over the world." So wrote Dilke and Wilkinson in their classic work *Imperial Defence* (1892). As commentators on the then state of affairs, they had instructive observations to make of an analytical kind, potent warnings to British parliamentarians and statesmen of the day:

> British settlements and British authority are planted at intervals all along the coast of Africa; they are dotted all round the shores of the Indian Ocean. Most of the islands, great and small, are covered by the British flag. Even where strong and civilized Powers, as old or older than the English nation, might seem able to secure their coasts from the salt-water incrustation, British influence has penetrated. On both coasts of Europe the small islands are or have been British. The Englishman has sat down at the gates of the Celestial Empire. Where two seas meet, or where a double coastline makes a land peculiarly accessible to influences from the sea, this sea-borne energy seems more than usually potent. Witness the long possession of Gibraltar and the steady progress of British power in India and in South Africa. It is as though the sea had been saturated with British influence, and had deposited it along all the unprotected portion of its margin.[9]

The ethos of the age was imperial, and the vision worldwide. "Just as the Royal Navy remained supreme largely by virtue of its own swagger, so the proclamation of empire possessed the virtue of a decree, and made people think it must be binding." So writes Jan Morris with delightful perspective, to which she added:

> The mystique of it all, the legend of blood, crown, sacrifice, formed a sort of ju-ju. The red looked ingrained on the map, as though it had been stained there in some arcane ritual, and the vast spaces of Greater Britain were like a

field of perpetual youth, where future generations of Britons would forever be regenerated.[10] But how would it be held together in a form of permanence that the edifice seemed to demand? How could the Admiralty maintain the connections in times of stress? How could the Colonial Office manage the edifice in the face of local discontent or local wars? How could the Foreign Office deal with the rivals on the frontiers so far away?

Some at home, and still others abroad, looked on the self-governing portions of the empire as the basis for some sort of Greater Britain. An association known as the Imperial Federation League (founded in 1884) took up the call for closer union of the British possessions overseas and of the mother country. An all-empire central parliament would control defence, trade and foreign policy. The tendency was to strengthen London's interests but this had little support in the dominions and colonies. "Englishmen overseas," explains Nicholas Mansergh, "though somewhat divided in mind were for the most part preoccupied not with building up a common nationality or a single state but with the development of the distinct and separate political identities of their own territories, on the basis not of one but of several states or nations."[11] Indeed, the concept of federation, made into propaganda by some, served only to promote an alternative to it. At the same time, concepts of a closer union of Britain with the United States emerged and much press attention was given to it, without any resulting concrete development. However, the tendency suggested a closer cooperation between the Royal Navy and the US Navy, and the Spanish-American War (discussed in Chapter 13) brought the two powers closer together, diminishing longstanding distrust that had arisen in consequence of the War of 1812 and that had been strengthened by occasional flare-ups in Anglo-American relations, notably the *Trent* crisis.

The dominions, colonies and dependencies had a stake in their own defence but tended to look to the mother country for sustenance and protection. Queen Victoria's Jubilee in 1887, for instance, offered a golden opportunity (one not lost) for discussion in London on matters of imperial affairs, for many of the public men of overseas governments were present. The prime minister did not miss the opportunity for a chat under the general heading that "there is on all sides a growing desire to draw closer in every practicable way the bonds which unite the various parts of the Empire". Lord Salisbury said that the empire, "which yields to none – it is, perhaps, superior to all – in its greatness" possessed a peculiarity which set it aside from other empires – "a want of continuity; it is separated into parts by large stretches of ocean; and what we are here for today is to see how far we must acquiesce in the conditions which that separation causes, how far we can obliterate them by agreement and organization".

Dispersion of British peoples overseas meant a commonality of interests, but such a vast spectacle of empire was founded not on force but on consent. Salisbury hinted that in future years the business conducted in 1887 might seem "prosaic", which indeed it was. But that event of the Jubilee year was to be repeated on occasion as circumstances required (and has a legacy in the regular Commonwealth Conferences). At the time, defence was the chief issue, and the Australasian colonies promised to contribute to the support of a strengthened naval force for the Western Pacific. More coaling stations were to be arranged, but imperial federation was not discussed, the colonial tide running against it.[12]

When, in response to the Russian war scare of 1879, a defence committee was struck under the chairmanship of the colonial secretary, Lord Carnarvon, colonial representatives were not appointed. However, notable personalities, such as Sir Henry Parkes of New South Wales and Sir John A. Macdonald from Canada, testified before it, taking the view that no common system of defence could be established and that it was better to trust to a patriotic response in the circumstances of crisis. This first systematic survey of British defence needs on a global scale emphasized three interlocking matters: first, the sea communications of empire; second, the necessity of their security; and, third, the contributions that colonies might make, chiefly in port facilities and coaling stations. It was admitted that the cost of the Navy needed to be borne by the mother country for the foreseeable future, but noted that the colonies had the capacity to take greater shares of the burdens of the future. The commission recognized that new alignments on the world stage were demanding a greater concern with global security, a process that was shifting attention away from local defence matters of particular colonies or outposts of imperial defence.[13]

It is a mistake to say that the Admiralty showed complacency with regard to matters of imperial defence, as demonstrated in its response to the Carnarvon Commission. "Secure in its status as guardian of the *Pax Britannica* and trading on the reputation that Nelson's exploits had conferred, it maintained an attitude of insularity which was a far greater potential determinant in the age of steam than it had been in that of sail." The Navy did not want to be drawn into an interdepartmental squabble. The Admiralty did provide a report on military possessions overseas and instructed commanders-in-chief overseas to cooperate with the commission's inquires; otherwise "it maintained its silent tradition".[14] That is only half of the story. Part of the reason for the Admiralty's indifference to imperial defence is that it was distancing itself from responsibilities of colonial defence. It had been a longstanding though hardly well-broadcast policy of the Admiralty that it could provide protection for trade and shipping. By contrast, and apart from the defence of bases, the Admiralty made clear that it had no general obligation to defend colonies. The local or immediate defence of colonies was the responsibility of the Army or locally trained forces in those colonies, and the scale of defences required demanded sufficiency to resist attacks by squadrons, or single ships. General naval operations would look after attacks from larger enemy forces, the surest shield of the Navy in contributing to the defence of the empire as a whole.[15]

At a conference in Whitehall with the War Office, the Admiralty would not budge on this point:

> the Naval Members desire to place on record their opinion that the safety of all our garrisoned ports abroad should be independent of the Navy, beyond its well understood duty of keeping touch with and engaging the enemy's fleet, which would keep Her Majesty's ships fully occupied in a maritime war... It would be unwise to throw upon the Navy, when war is probable, the duty of protecting such places until they are fully garrisoned, and of conveying to a number of widely scattered points small bodies of troops, a duty which could be performed with ease and certainty in time of peace. In this expression of opinion the other members entirely agree.[16]

Towards the end of the years of *Pax*, and after, the Admiralty saw imperial defence differently, and it saw it as one of protecting seaborne trade. The Navy shied away from any requirement to protect colonies. The base was to serve the squadron, not the opposite. The sea was a broad common, as Mahan had decreed. Thus their lordships saw any division of sea authority between and among dominions and self-governing colonies as hazardous to the general health of naval mastery. It is true that the Colonial Naval Defence Act of 1865 authorized the commissioning of colonial warships and the raising of colonial personnel. The intent was to allow colonies to build and maintain vessels for colonial defence, shore-based fortifications then being proclaimed by the War Office as essential for the security of colonies and trade. However, no colony was in a situation of being able to construct large warships, and, in any event, suitable dockyards were few and far between. In 1867 the Colony of Victoria commissioned a sloop, the germ of the future Royal Australian Navy. The vessel was used in the Maori Wars. In Canada, some of the colonies had revenue and fisheries patrol vessels, and these are regarded as the origin of what later became the Royal Canadian Navy.[17] But no general strategy linked the imperial outworks, for the Navy provided the ties that bound the whole together, aided and abetted by a global communications system that was increasingly advantaged by the revolution in electricity – telegraph, submarine cables and wireless. Right until the end of the era, the Admiralty clung to view that there was one ocean and one naval ensign to uphold the imperial requirements. It may have been a noble position but it could not last, and the Admiralty was caught by its own logic. It could serve the parent British state; it could not, and would not, serve the growing power and independence of the dominions and colonies.

The Navy thought in terms of oceans and sea commands, of sea areas of dominating control, the whole tied together with a logic resembling a domino thesis – how the fall of one would affect the fall of others. Keeping safe the Mediterranean corridor of links between the North Atlantic and the Indian Ocean was a central task, but coupled with it was this intractable difficulty: how to create stability in lands adjacent to the Suez route. More and more we are realizing that it was domestic troubles ashore – rivalries among contending powers – that forced the imperialists to show their hand and take action to secure their interests. Always there existed the problems of unstable frontiers. In these matters the Navy was disadvantaged, save for sending the occasional landing party, equipping a gunboat for distant river travel, or even manning an armoured train. As the century moved towards its close, so did the Navy find itself more engaged ashore. Africa came calling.

When Egyptian rebels – in fact, a motley array of Sudanese and Fellaheen gathered under the banners of the upstart colonel Arabi – threatened the security there, British forces were able to overthrow them through a decisive victory in the field. The plan of the campaign hinged upon naval primacy, on which the army of invasion could absolutely depend. The bombardment of Alexandria in 1882 was a purely naval incident, and by it came the destruction of menacing batteries bearing on the harbour. Then troops were landed to save the city from destruction. This episode had a far-reaching influence on subsequent British army operations. From transports, soldiers were landed in considerable numbers at Alexandria. Subsequently, Lord Wolseley's army enjoyed liberty of action thanks to locally exercised maritime command. Then came the triumph of British arms at Tel-el-Kebir, an episode that demonstrated the power of the empire's amphibious strength. There were lessons learnt, as the authority Colonel Charles Callwell described:

> Huge armies are not always essential for maritime expeditions against the dominions even of a powerful foe... The suddenness with which such blows can be delivered goes far... to compensate for deficiency of numbers. And the security of retreat will often justify the undertaking of such enterprises with bodies of troops which are insignificant and paltry as compared with the hosts which the enemy calculates on ordinarily putting in the field.

Whereas some might cite pure technological advantage as the key to victory, the Egyptian campaign and aftermath demonstrated that overall advantage in sea power, with mobility and psychological influence projected ashore, can defeat a vastly superior force. Gunfire from the great pre-dreadnoughts and the armoured train cars ashore caused fearful excitement that "tended to rivet the attention of Arabi and his myrmidons". In the end, the power of the khedive upon the Nile was restored at minimal cost to the expeditionary force.[18]

One professor of African history, G.A. Sanderson, writing about the eve of the Partition of Africa, nicely defines the British position with regard to the rivals this way:

> British manufacturers and merchants, thanks to their half-century lead in industrialization and their expert knowledge of the requirements and functioning of overseas markets, were in the 1870s still able in most commodities to out-trade and undersell their commercial competitors; and this not only in Britain's vast overseas possessions, but in the markets of Latin America, East Asia and coastal Africa – in fact, wherever free trade prevailed, or could be caused to prevail by the guns of British warships. Only in the comparatively limited colonial holdings of other powers could the keen edge of British competition be blunted by discriminatory tariffs and other restrictions. The obvious solution for these powers was to add to their colonial holdings; but after 1815 British naval hegemony was very effectively used (and nowhere more effectively than on the African coasts) to discourage annexations that would create new quasi-monopolistic trading enclaves for other powers. This system of 'informal empire', whereby British sea-power safeguarded and even created the conditions of free trade which guaranteed Britain's economic preponderance, was usually in British eyes clearly preferable to formal possession, with its attendant expense and responsibilities.[19]

In the circumstances, it was far better for British statesmen and their advisors to think in terms of preventing others from "staking out claims". This was particularly true of tropical Africa, where the greater profitability of informal empire could obtain. But other powers found themselves squeezed out of this scenario, and considerations of formal possession began to be vouched in the 1870s. They grew in that decade. Railways were being built into the interior from South Africa, into the Sudan, and into Senegal and Niger. The dreams of "railroad empires" indicated that the interior of continents would become less isolated. In 1876 the British colonial secretary, Lord Carnarvon, had decided that the British could not stand idly by. "We cannot," he wrote, "admit rivals in the East or even the central parts of Africa . . . To a considerable extent, if not entirely, we must be prepared to apply a sort of Munro [Monroe] doctrine for much of Africa."[20]

Carnarvon's fears were not unfounded. If the British circumstance, or state of affairs, had been largely unopposed as of 1880, it had changed dramatically by the end of that decade. Beginning in about 1890, international relations entered a state of flux in which new issues were modifying traditional enmities. Gradually the Triple Alliance had emerged, of Germany, Austria-Hungary and Italy, and against this was pitted the Franco-Russian Alliance. Suspicion and hostility became a constant state of affairs in the chancelleries of Europe, and it both fed militarism and promoted further attempts at imperial advantage in distant locales. France wanted the return of Alsace-Lorraine while Italy wanted elbow room in the Mediterranean. Russia distrusted the Austrians in the Balkans. The Ottoman Empire moved towards decrepitude. There were deadlocks of all sorts, and in these circumstances imperial enterprise and rivalries in Africa and East Asia dominated world politics.

In 1890 a tidy agreement between Germany and Britain resolved festering difficulties in Africa. Among its many provisions was that Germany acquired the area between Mozambique and the British "sphere", German East Africa. Lines in the sand had been drawn at last. British chartered companies, props of empire there, now gave way to formal colonial control. As for Zanzibar, Bismarck would dearly have liked to have acquired it, but the British finally got title to it, at the same time as Britain handed the fortified island of Heligoland to Germany. "What we have we hold," had been Queen Victoria's dictum, but all of this was changing late in the century. Heligoland was seen as a liability. The Kaiser, Wilhelm II, was especially anxious to secure Heligoland because without it the Kiel Canal would be useless to Germany in time of war. The Germans promptly set about fortifying it, as they did other watchtowers on the North Sea, such as Dune. In 1895 came the completion of the Kiel Canal, giving Germany access to the North Sea for the great warships of the age. It was time for some British repositioning as well and, in 1903, Britain established a naval base at Rosyth. Before very long it was casting eyes at a lonely, landlocked sheet of water in the Orkney Islands called Scapa Flow, a well-sheltered anchorage of strategic importance in the great wars of the twentieth century.

The Germans had got Heligoland at last, and Zanzibar had come into British hands, a signal event in the partition of Africa and a fateful development in British policy, which had always sought independence of action and moral suasion in East African waters. The British protectorate over Zanzibar was proclaimed in the presence of a British consul and Vice-Admiral Sir Edward Fremantle, commander-in-chief of the East Indies, and the Union Jack and the sultan's flag were hoisted side by side. The Foreign Office now assumed direct control. The Navy was used as a coercive force when a pretender to the sultanate made a bid for power, and a force of six cruisers in the harbour had a salutary effect. From 1893 to 1896, when the matter reached its climax, the Navy was a constant watchdog over the shifting sands of the sultanate. But when the pretender, Seyyid Khaled, seized the palace, the guns of the warships (under the direction of Rear Admiral Rawson) opened fire, and landing parties of bluejackets and marines secured their objectives with small cost to themselves.[21] The protectorate had been sustained by naval force. A collateral effect of this Anglo-German agreement was that the Kaiser's cruisers, based at Dar-Es-Salam, now joined with their British counterparts in the anti-slavery patrols.

France eyed this new association of her old and dreaded rivals Britain and Germany with growing concern. For the balance of the decade, through the Fashoda crisis and the Anglo-Boer War, British relations with that power were on tenterhooks. A combustible scenario might lead to an unwelcome war. Only time awaited such a circumstance. A near firestorm developed in Anglo-French relations with regard to Siam in 1893, because the British sent the gunboat *Linnet* to lie at Bangkok, on Menam River, so as to be on the spot to protect British lives and property in the growing emergency. It was a classic triangle. Siam was then a weak state; France, seeking an indemnity for alleged damage, intended to intervene; and "we waxed chivalrous", as Sir Edward Grey, then a parliamentary secretary for foreign affairs, put it. The French used their vessels to enact a so-called "pacific blockade" of the river mouth, a position that the British protested because blockade could only be effected in wartime. Telegrams passed thick and fast. In the heat of the moment, a French gunboat at the river mouth turned its guns on the British cruiser *Pallas* (under Captain Angus MacLeod), a gross insult that would in naval etiquette have justified the captain of the British ship in firing on the French ship. MacLeod's prudence and coolness "averted a most regrettable conflict".[22] An apology was demanded. The French required that *Linnet* leave Bangkok. The British would not oblige. War seemed imminent, but then the Siamese conceded to the French demands and the whole matter ceased to have any importance. It had, in London, seemed like a deliberate French challenge and that war would occur. "It was reported in the Foreign Office," said Grey, "that the telegrams had been shown to the German Emperor, who was then visiting Queen Victoria on his yacht at Cowes, and that he had expressed with evident satisfaction the opinion that there was no way out of the incident but war."[23]

The international naval rivalry that developed during those years was directly related to the rivalry among various imperial nations seeking concessions, protectorates, colonies, resources and strategic bases. The so-called "new imperialism" had immense influence on naval build-ups, and vice versa. The Caribbean, Southeast Asia, the Chinese Empire – all were subjects of concern and interest, but none got so much attention as Africa, which now acquired enhanced strategic value. The scramble for Africa marked the next phase of these rivalries, and it became increasingly difficult for Whitehall to avoid extending its formal influence in East Africa. By the mid-1890s, British policy turned on whether British East Africa and Uganda should become definitely British possessions. Should a railway to Uganda be laid down? The Foreign Office sought to maintain a distinct friendship with the other great powers but would not sign a distinct agreement. Once Germany and France entered more aggressively into the rivalry, the British seemed obliged to intervene, along the lines of the old model, so as to protect their own interests there. The control of the Nile became a fixation for Lord Salisbury, not because he wanted it but because of the domestic difficulties inherent in that country and rival, local claimants to power. Meanwhile, Cecil Rhodes' ambitions alarmed the Portuguese. France had its eyes on Fashoda. General Marchand's expedition crossed lands where British claims existed. A show of British force and diplomacy solved that problem. The Anglo-Boer War was the climax of these rivalries as well as a crisis in Southern Africa among the British colonies and the Boer Republics. The route to India was threatened, and the security requirements had to be upheld.

In the circumstances, and as was required, naval forces were increased at the Cape, in the Mediterranean and in the Indian Ocean. Nothing was lost or given away, and the pressure against the slave traders continued. The naval landing parties went ashore as required – to deal with the Zulu in 1879–1880, to secure Alexandria in 1882, to occupy the town of Suez on the Red Sea coast of Egypt, to do similarly at Port Said and Ismailia, and to control the Suez Canal and nearby railways. Various naval detachments were deployed on the lower Nile, and a naval brigade commanded by Lord Charles Beresford undertook major operations in an attempt to rescue Gordon at Khartoum and later to secure the Sudan. The naval contribution to this war seldom receives its due in the literature, and in Brackenbury's *The River Column* (London, 1885) it is scarcely mentioned. However, Laird Clowes, the ranking naval historian of the late nineteenth century (and one doing heroic duty in that line when these events went largely unchronicled), did not forget to give the basic details.[24]

One is struck in reading the account of how mobile naval power was ashore and afloat so late in the century, as steam navigation and railways were allowing the faster delivery of forces in the field. Naval brigades were put together from six or seven warships, and then deployed inland, often at considerable sacrifice. The Admiralty hated such missions, but the political pressure for action was great; besides, as of yet there was no rivalry on the seas to challenge Britain's authority. It was natural, therefore, to send such naval force ashore, no matter how strangely out of their own element the officers and men must have felt. Still, great reputations were made ashore – in armoured trains, for instance – and not a few naval officers and men came home bemedalled from their trials ashore in the service of Queen and country. Maxim guns, rifles and pistols, field artillery, rockets, boarding pikes and cutlasses were still part of the essential kit of the imperial marine arm. After defeating the Mahdist forces in 1898 using Egyptian troops and money, the British kept control of this dependency until 1924, using collaborators and supporters who were agreeable to their purposes.

> It was the crisis in Egyptian government provoked by heavier collaborative demands, rather than rivalry in Europe, which first set Britain and France competing for the advantage under the new arrangements; and the lack of reliable Egyptian collaborators, rather than fear of France or any increased interest in Egypt, which brought the redcoats onto the Suez Canal in 1882 and kept them there until 1956.[25]

It may be noted that by the General Act of Brussels of 1890, the European powers that were interested in Africa committed themselves to act against slavery: "not precisely to end it, but at least to place the pursuit of liberty in Africa on the agenda of Europe's civilizing mission". This had been the British position now widely adopted. The will of Europe to rule Africa lasted a mere two generations, says one authority, and thus the commitment to end slavery in Africa and end the slave trade generally has not been sustained, in our times.

> At the time of writing [1997, says the same authority] a slave trade in children seems to survive in Nigeria, and newspaper reports are frequent of the incidence of slavery in Mauritius where, despite the abolition of the institution at least three times, most recently in 1980, 90,000 black Africans are said to live as full-time slaves to Arab masters: precisely whence the Portuguese, in 1441, first carried black slaves away to a remote northern destination.[26]

This is a chilly reminder of the difficulties of suppressing the slave trade. It does not call into question the combined determination of "the Saints", Parliament, the Foreign Office, the Colonial Office and the Admiralty to eradicate the nefarious trade at its height. What it does is to point out that the suppression of such a trade requires political and moral desire and commitment, unending diplomatic zeal, and the means to police the trade and to watch for further violations. Lessons learned from Royal Navy actions in these distant and dangerous seas come down to us over the long years, and they invite the inquiry of nations, separately and in alliance, as to the means of eradication. Even nowadays it is a moral obligation based on the acceptance of the rights of individuals to have liberty and freedom.

Other than in slave treaties, successive British governments declined long-term commitments in international affairs, though they would commit to colonial campaigns to secure their interests or keep others from gaining an advantage of significance. That is why they had fought so hard to campaign in East Africa and in the Sudan. But they preferred a state of affairs where they could be the brokers or possess independence of action. Gladstone hated any such imperial involvement, which was prejudicial to British interests in such quagmires and equally damaging to a state of equilibrium and justice in European affairs. Other British statesmen were turning to the United States as the new means of keeping a global, maritime peace. In all, the making of British policy was well defined. It was to avoid complications and commitments that were hazardous to British interests – in other words, to preserve freedom of action. Salisbury, who was both prime minister and foreign secretary from 1886 to 1892 and again from 1895 to 1902, was rather ingenuous when he declared: "British policy is to drift lazily downstream, occasionally putting out a boathook to avoid a collision." He disliked the rigidity of the Bismarckian system of alliances, described above, and in this state of affairs he was prepared to cooperate with other nations to preserve peace in the Mediterranean, the Pacific and East Asia. If that meant a joint blockade of Venezuela with a foreign navy, or policing the Pacific Islands High Commission in concert with the German and American navies, that was fine. These were small but important measures to maintain British ascendancy elsewhere in the face of mounting challenges.

The actions of foreign rivals forced on an essentially conservative Admiralty the necessity of change. New powers had emerged in the struggle for overseas colonies, bases and markets. Rivals to Britain's empire had acquired bases of repair and supply, beachheads of trade and commerce, railways and entrances to interoceanic canals. Britain's once comfortable lead in bases – Castlereagh's 1816 keys to security of trade and military protection – was shrinking fast. And in guns and gunnery at sea, not always did Britain's position rank first. In gunnery, for example, French gunnery and shells of the 1860s brought their lordships to rapt attention. In fighting ships alone, despite continental rivalry, Britain's lead had been maintained from the 1870s onwards. But a remarkable ascendancy in French naval construction had alarmed the press and Parliament. Naval "scares" were easy to generate. The issues were debatable but the final results were never in doubt: Britain required a navy superior to all others.

One flurry of press activity merited the closest attention of those in or close to the seats of power, including the shipping, banking, investment and manufacturing sectors of the imperial economy. In the *Pall Mall Gazette*, week by week beginning 15 September 1884, journalist W.T. Stead, taking cues from Captain John Fisher (later first sea lord), warned in his "What is the Truth about The Navy?" articles of how (and in what ways – armour, guns, speed) Britain was losing its primacy. Stead was a Liberal who backed free trade. Like Richard Cobden, notoriously a critic of expensive armed services, he held the view that the strong necessity existed to maintain superiority over the French at sea. Free trade demanded safe seas for the passage of British ships and cargo. British naval spending had decreased in contrast with that of other nations, but British merchant shipping, growth of trade and the value of national wealth had all increased. He brought forth pages and pages of statistics and details on ships, armament, armoured protection and speed. Why was the Navy neglected and shortchanged? Stead also thought in global terms and about the sinews of British power. He laid out the growing nature of the formal British Empire, where territorial obligations existed that involved the White Ensign:

> Since 1868 we have annexed Fiji in the Pacific, established a protectorate over one-half of New Guinea and one-third of Borneo, besides establishing a quasi police supervision over all the islands of the Southern Seas. We have extended our sovereignty in the Malay Peninsula, and have pushed our garrison on the northwest of India to Quetta and beyond to Pishin, on the road

> to Candahar. In South Africa we have annexed Basutoland, and one-third of Zululand, to say nothing of the shadowy suzerainty over the Transvaal. On the west we have annexed the whole coast of the Orange River to the Cunene, excepting Angra Pequena. We have just annexed the delta of the Niger; we doubled our possessions on the Gold Coast by taking over Elmina and the Dutch forts; and we have extended the chain of our custom houses from Sierra Leone to Liberia. In the Mediterranean we have occupied Cyprus and made ourselves supreme in Egypt. British marines hold Suakin and a British general is Governor of the Soudan. In the other hemisphere our responsibilities have been nominally rather than actually extended by the formal incorporation of what used to be the Hudson's Bay Company possessions in the northwest. All round the world, therefore, we have more to guard and more to do than we had in 1868 ... [27]

Stead's was a powerful, if alarmist, indictment of the government, indeed of ministries since 1868. There was little rebuttal; indeed, there was almost uniform agreement that something had to be done in these desperate circumstances. The charges were exaggerated.[28] However, one retired admiral, Gardiner Fishbourne, thought Stead's stream of articles were entirely fair, but he added that he thought that they had underestimated the danger. The Navy's job resembled that of the constabulary on a grand scale, its work that of police action designed to protect the weak and repress crime. "This is the clear duty of Government, and for which the sword is given to them by God."[29]

The arguments were picked up by Lord Brassey, noted yachtsman and a civil lord of the Admiralty, who, in successive issues of his *Naval Annual*, of 1886 and 1887, quoted the French extensively as to their strategic innovations in sea power, using the new weapon of naval war, the torpedo. The press was alive to the circumstances of British imperial reverses and naval challenges. Difficulties – including humiliations in Egypt, the Sudan, scrambles in Africa and the Pacific, the Penjdeh incident that brought new war with Russia – all highlighted the state of British preparedness for war and often gave out stark warnings.[30]

These warnings pushed the Admiralty into action, though the first lord of the day, Lord Northbrook, held to the opinion that inasmuch as hull design and weaponry were changing rapidly, it would be better to have a "go slow" policy than to build ships that would soon be outdated. His point was valid, but it could not last for long. In the meantime, the political pressures increased for a suitable naval rearmament. To watch on foreign naval build-ups, the Naval Intelligence Department was formed in 1886 and the Admiralty issued instructions to that new department regarding "preparation for war".

Under terms of the famous Naval Defence Act of 1889, the Navy was made theoretically superior to the combination of the fleets of any two European powers. Thus it bore the label the "two-power standard". In defending this new policy, Lord Dunraven, the first lord, identified the key requirements of naval paramountcy for Britain: "the defences of the Empire, the safeguarding of the trade of the national and imperial commerce, are really the foreign policies of this country".[31] As with Dunraven, so with Castlereagh three generations before. Imperial defence was vital, ran the logic, and indeed was inseparable from national defence. But what share would the dominions take in their own defence? Would they share the imperial global dream as lawgivers and preservers of peace, or would they look to their own moats, content to defend themselves against encroachments? From London came the desire to coordinate and centralize, to keep the idea of one empire and one fleet alive. The dominions for all their desire for autonomy were part and parcel of the whole reorganization of the naval and military services in the years that closed the era when Britain alone was perceived as being mistress of the seas. However, a central problem remained – one called "the Britannic question" by many, including its noted scholar, Richard Jebb, an expert on the history and development of colonial and imperial conferences. As the German naval threat became more visible, and the challenges to British profit and power more real, so too did Jebb seek to define the issues – issues that he contended (and this was affirmed by many) were central to the survival of Britain and the empire. He pointed out that circumstances of imperial growth had produced two kinds of imperialism: the one was the British view with all of its great power needs; the other was the colonial view with its requirements to recognize local needs. The conflicting impulses were British ascendancy and Britannic equality, or a difference between the centralizers and the autonomists. The former he thought could lead to imperial federation, the latter to Britannic alliance. It was the former that won out in the end, and it was Canada's resistance to a centralized Navy under Admiralty control in peacetime (no question was raised about the Admiralty's necessary control in wartime) that put paid to the concept of imperial federation, though Sir Robert Borden's Naval Bill of 1913 (which failed to carry in the Canadian Senate and thus became a dead letter) gave powerful possibilities to that concept.[32]

In 1896, George Goshen, the first lord of the Admiralty, had used the term "splendid isolation" for the first time in Britain. "We have stood alone in that which is called isolation – our splendid isolation, as one of our colonial friends was good enough to call it." He was referring to the usage by Sir George Foster, a Canadian politician, in a speech in the House of Commons, Ottawa, in January 1896.[33] As Goschen was aware, when presenting the annual naval estimates, justification had to be given for the rise in intended naval expenditures. Worried about the extent to which Britain stood isolated in a hostile world, he called for an increase of nearly 11 per cent for 1896–1997. That costs of naval primacy were escalating is given by the fact that they had risen nearly 22 per cent from

1893–1894 to the year following, and then by 13.5 per cent in 1895–1896.[34] For the past 50 years, said the colonial secretary, Joseph Chamberlain, the policy of the country had been "strict isolation. We have had no allies. I am afraid we have had no friends ... ".[35] He feared a combination of great powers and therefore posed this possibility so as to avoid any possible conflict that might early arise: closer bonds of amity with "our kinsmen across the Atlantic ... terrible as war may be, even war itself would be cheaply purchased if in a great and noble cause the Stars and Stripes and the Union Jack should wave together over an Anglo-Saxon alliance".[36] Salisbury's policies, concluded Chamberlain, had allowed the two powers to understand themselves better than at any time before. This was a correct assessment.

British naval primacy was facing serious contenders, a recurrent theme in these last chapters. Chief among these was the German navy and the surging German merchant marine. German cruisers and gunboats began to "show the flag" in places hitherto undreamed of to the British way of thinking. The arrival of Germany in the affairs of the Persian Gulf after the turn of the century presented another challenge, for that water was regarded as a "British lake" against a variety of challenges. Germany joined Russia, the Ottoman Empire and France there, and even smaller states – Italy, the United States and Portugal – played minor roles. But the "lake" was no lake at all but rather an international waterway in an era of increasing imperial rivalries and diplomatic difficulties.[37] It was natural in the circumstances for the Foreign Office to think of Germany as less of a threat than France or Russia, and a combination of the last two was the worrying scenario that had led to the "two-power standard".

13
The Lion and the Eagle

In 1898, the very year difficulties were building with the Boer Republics concerning paramountcy in southern Africa, a new ally in the guise of a neutral power presented itself to Britain and its sagging fortunes. The United States, victorious in war over Spain, suddenly appeared as a global power; at the same time, it removed from the board an older, decrepit one. This turn of fortune favoured the British, particularly the Admiralty, and although at the time the full fruits of an American victory could not be imagined, it soon became apparent that another important chapter had been entered into in Anglo-American relations. No formal alliance could be vouchsafed, so awkward were the political and historical differences of the two powers; but a sharing of global interests in trade and foreign relations dictated accommodation. That same decade marked a surge of American maritime activity along the Atlantic seaboard, to Europe, and to the Far East. "[Few] noticed that this American commerce was largely a free ride on the coat-tails of the *Pax Britannica*, the near dominant British world-wide naval hegemony," observed the American student of maritime strategy Rear Admiral J.C. Wylie. And he continued: "This was not altruism. Britain... found it convenient to support the American Monroe Doctrine because that held in check French or Spanish exploitation of the Americas."[1]

The change in affairs brought on by the results of the Spanish-American War had, understandably, not been foreseen by the British. In the many years leading up to it, the British had kept a sizeable naval armament in the Caribbean. For instance, in 1891 the squadron consisted of a powerful ironclad as flagship, four composite-built corvettes, three steam sloops, four gunboats and half-a-dozen vessels of smaller classes, including a "mosquito fleet" of torpedo boat destroyers. All told there were 14 ships with a total tonnage of 27,000, and 2,700 personnel.[2] The investment in infrastructure ashore had been prodigious, not least in armaments and fortifications – the concrete and steel of imperial infrastructure – designed to protect ports from fitful raids by the imagined enemy. A fortune had been spent in the land-based accompaniment of British naval hegemony in these seas.[3] How long was this to be sustained?

On 14 August 1897, the Admiralty appointed Vice Admiral Sir John Fisher to be commander-in-chief of the North America and West Indies Station, instructing him to proceed to Portsmouth. There he was to hoist his flag aboard the battleship HMS *Renown* on the 24th, then sail for Halifax, the station headquarters. *Renown* was of shallow draft, designed to transit the Suez Canal if a speedy reinforcement of the China squadron was required. Global demands required mobility of the naval force and flexibility in possible deployment. Nothing in Fisher's abilities, character or personality had made him particularly eligible for the appointment; the fact was that he was on the waiting list for such a sea assignment. This was his first command of a "foreign station". Doubtless their lordships were pleased to be sending him to this one, with its many important duties and nagging concerns, and the appointment was sure to be full of interest if not amusement. The palmy days of *Pax Britannia* continued uninterruptedly, and, if Fisher had his way, would continue forever. The best guardian of the world's peace, he said often enough, rested on a strong Royal Navy. One senior admiral, writing to Fisher by way of congratulations, said that his fellow officer and friend had well earned the comparative ease of the new appointment but would still have a future before him when it was over.[4]

Renown sailed as intended, experiencing force 8 headwinds nearly the whole passage, and the ship, reported Fisher, "behaved exceedingly well and proved herself to be an excellent Atlantic sea boat".[5] Fisher, we now know, had influenced her design, for when in the post as director of Naval Ordnance and then again as controller, he favoured evolution of a certain ship design intended for distant service on the China and Pacific stations. Fisher convinced the Director of Naval Construction, Sir William White, that what was required was "the lightest big gun and the biggest secondary gun." He wanted something close to uniform armament. In consequence, the *Renown* mounted four 10-inch guns and ten 6-inch quickfirers. Fisher was much enamoured by this fast but lightly armed battleship. Others did not think so, and only six of the class were constructed.[6] In any event, Fisher arrived at Halifax on 13 September and assumed command.

Thus began an assignment that was to engage Fisher's attention in more ways than one. Historians have tended to dismiss this chapter in Jacky Fisher's life as little more than an American adventure or interlude, one of little moment in the long and volcanic life of this future admiral of the fleet who would revolutionize the Royal Navy in the first decade of the twentieth century. Arthur Marder, his strongest admirer, says that this appointment was an "uneventful command", and perhaps it was, relatively speaking.[7] But make no mistake: at this juncture the station had many demanding problems and much unfinished business with regard to international affairs and rival claims. Wars were brewing in the Caribbean and in South Africa; France and Britain were vying for authority in Africa in what became the Fashoda dispute and crisis of 1898; and Germany had ambitions on the coasts of South America. Rivalry for concessions to build an isthmian canal persisted. The French continued to haggle with the British about fishing rights in Newfoundland and Labrador. An Anglo-American dispute festered over the supposed demilitarization of the Great Lakes, where the United States was flexing its muscles and causing the Canadians much concern. Gold was discovered in the Yukon in 1896, prompting the Alaska boundary crisis, an Anglo-American irritant involving Canada. Humanitarian matters also presented themselves: sheltering refugees from Haiti being one such, dealing with disasters from volcanoes and hurricanes another. These problems can only be referred to in passing because they do not comprise the main theme here.

One by one, however, these festering problems of empire and imperial rivalry were blessedly solved. The Fashoda crisis, which ended to Britain's advantage, closed a great chapter of imperial rivalries in Africa and inaugurated a new era of understanding between Britain and France. Attendant to this, the Anglo-French *entente cordiale* of 1904 led to speedy resolution of the Newfoundland fisheries differences and had beneficial repercussions elsewhere. All the while, these powers and the United States watched with alarm the rising German interest in bases, concessions and territories overseas, and such incidents as showing the flag in concert against German pretensions in Venezuela reflected a desire to band together in the face of a new and potentially aggressive rival.

Fisher's vast and complicated command stretched south from the 55th degree of north latitude to the coast of South America to Cape Orange, the northern extremity of Brazil, and then eastward by the parallel of the latitude of Cape Orange, while on the west it was defined by the shores of the United States and on the east by the 36th degree of west longitude. Fisher was familiar with the round of duties on this station because almost two decades before he had been there as flag captain to Vice Admiral Sir Leopold McClintock in HMS *Northampton*.[8] From the fog banks and ice floes of its northern reaches south through the Gulf Stream, the Bermuda Triangle and the Sargasso sea then south again to the tropical waters and marshes of the mosquito, where malaria, dengue fever and yellow fever had exacted their own price of Admiralty, captains of ships on station conducted quarterdeck diplomacy as best they could in the environmental circumstances, shifting to northern waters in the summer months and reversing the process in the winter, dodging hurricanes and Atlantic storms as required. In their in-letters to the Admiralty since 1815, and what might be claimed to be the beginning of *Pax Britannica*, British admirals and captains had complained vigorously of the want of naval units in number and strength for the numerous duties of an extended station. Other stations were in the same situation but economy ruled in the policing of a global empire with its global British shipping. Even so, from time to time, when emergencies were faced, such as in the Oregon boundary crisis of 1844–1846 or the *Trent* crisis of 1862, their lordships would boost the station's naval armament, responding as the needs of the day arose. Flexibility marked the British response, while all the while the annual naval estimates had to have parliamentary approval and more than one first lord of the Admiralty resigned or threatened resignation. At the time of Fisher's appointment, George Goshen held that supreme appointment. At the Foreign Office was Lord Salisbury, the secretary of state, who had great faith in Fisher's abilities, naval and diplomatic, and who, a few years later, was to send him as naval representative of the British delegation to the conference at The Hague.

At the time of Fisher's appointment, 11 vessels of various types, in addition to *Renown*, served the duties of the station plus six gunboats and gun vessels. There was a commodore based in Jamaica, and a senior naval officer for the Barbados division; there was also a senior naval officer for Newfoundland, who watched over the affairs of the Gulf of St. Lawrence, including tetchy relations with the French islands St. Pierre and Miquelon. The size of lobster traps and rights of drying cod on stages on the French shore of Newfoundland were intractable problems facing the officer commanding there. The telegraph and the submarine cable made the deployment of warships more effective, the Admiralty insisting on being kept in close touch with affairs overseas. Fisher kept up his own communications network for the eastern flank of North America. He remained in contact with importunate colonial governors in Newfoundland, Bermuda, Jamaica, Barbados and elsewhere, and likewise with the governor general of Canada, the local authorities in the British North American provinces then working towards closer connections, and the prime minister of Canada, Sir Wilfrid Laurier. But Fisher kept his distance from the local authorities, and on more than one occasion, though of a later date, he complained about "the old women of Halifax of both sexes" who constantly appealed for naval help. Canadians, Fisher thought, should mend their fences and learn to live with the Americans. In point of fact, during this same time, when the Yukon and Alaskan gold rushes were in process and the Bering Sea pelagic sealing difficulties were continuing, a general understanding was being met between London and Washington, with Ottawa being the interested party; and thus when the Alaska Boundary dispute was resolved, in 1898, this cleared the way for the further resolution of water boundaries issues between Canada and the United States. In short, during the years when Fisher was "on station", many urgent problems were being resolved, though obviously these did not eventuate at the same time. But Fisher saw in Bermuda a focal point of naval power, and he was much impressed with the floating dock, and the repair and storage facilities there. The Navy might depart from other bases in the Western Hemisphere but Bermuda was to be left alone. You might run down the fleet as occasion warranted but you would not abandon the base to its fate.

In those days, all eyes settled on Spain's sagging authority in Cuba. Besides the social matters of which slavery was crucial, the strategic issue commanded all. Cuba was the key, for it commanded the approaches to the future isthmian canal. Alfred Thayer Mahan, who in consequence of his *Influence of Sea Power Upon History*, published in 1890, seven years before Fisher arrived in American waters, was at that precise date stressing the importance of Samoa, Hawaii and the Caribbean for the protection of a naval communication to the Isthmian canal. This last, once constructed, would be critical to the defences of the two American coasts and domination of the Pacific.[9] The United States expressed concern that Germany, with its search for a base in the West Indies as also the Galapagos, with some sort of fulcrum along the coast of Costa Rica, Colombia and Venezuela, might be posed within striking distance of the Panama Canal. It was under circumstances such as these that John Hay would invoke the Monroe Doctrine, and the dynamic President Theodore Roosevelt is said to have threatened to send an American fleet if Germany intervened.

Fisher was a commanding force when on station, well known in the foreign navies that he encountered. Within the service and as a believer in strict discipline, and with a reputation for unpredictable behaviour, he was a person to be watched and feared. He had acquired great power from his several battles ashore in gunnery and torpedo development and training, and he was by no means an easy officer to serve under, though many found him agreeable and pleasant, even great fun.

> I still have a vivid recollection of the awe which the "great man" inspired whilst on board; not that he did any of us any harm, but he had such a terrific face and jaw, rather like a tiger, and he prowled around with the steady rhythmical tread of a panther,

recalled Captain the Hon. Bingham, VC, who had served with him on that station. "The quarter-deck shook, and all hands shook with it. The word was passed from mouth to mouth when he came on deck. 'Look out, here comes Jack.' Everyone then stood terribly to attention, while the great one passed on and away."[10] But he took a great interest in the welfare of younger officers and midshipmen, and at the admiral's house in Bermuda he and Lady Fisher were known to turn it into a pleasant place of rest and rehabilitation.

Cuban affairs were coming to a crisis. The insurgents had begun their action in 1895. Alone among the great powers, Britain was sympathetic to the American position with regard to Cuba. British warships were always on the alert in the run-up to hostilities and throughout the Spanish-American War of 1898. American statesmen were to record their gratitude to the British for their maintenance of strict neutrality. This stance allowed the United States to use its navy and army without let or hindrance. While the US Navy blockaded Havana, Royal Navy vessels, such as *Talbot* under Captain Gamble, were able to visit it three times to fetch distressed British subjects who wished to leave. An American press boat hounded the outward-bound *Talbot* for news ashore, but the ship's company was fallen in, all ports closed, and no answer of any kind was given. Near Matanzas an American gunboat fired a shot across the bow, so as to heave the British ship to and get it out of the way, but rather than it being a blank it was an actual shell. When challenged, an apology was given: that the gun's crew had made a mistake. Later, a picture appeared in a New York paper showing the projectile falling into the water on the port side of *Talbot*. Years later it was learnt by the British officer that the American had fired a shot to bring the ship to because he had no blank.[11] These are the tight circumstances that British warships found themselves in.

Fisher learned with pleasure, and perhaps with envy, of Admiral William Sampson's victory over the Spanish fleet in Santiago Bay. Sampson was invited by Fisher to bring his fleet to Bermuda on 4 July, and this was accepted. There exists a fine illustration of Fisher's *Renown* and Sampson's flagship *New York* riding safely at anchor in near proximity in Grassy Bay, Bermuda.[12] *Renown*'s band played American patriotic airs as the US ships sailed into these waters for the first time since the War of 1812. There was much to celebrate, for the American victory over Spain had given the United States a worldwide empire. American interests might now be seen marching hand in hand with those of the British. The old order had given way to something new. The Admiralty was perhaps the first in the world to realize this great and fundamental shift, and instructed Fisher (as he later said) to invite Sampson and the American fleet to Bermuda. As far as "courtesy calls" are concerned, this may well have been the most important in naval chronicles.

Fisher hosted a banquet for Sampson, his staff and senior officers at Admiralty House, which looking down and across to the two fleets at anchor in repose. It was on this occasion that Fisher proposed his toast to Admiral Sampson's health, and the health of the United States. Nothing happened; there was no reply. "He never said a word," Fisher recalled later, absolutely dumbfounded at the lack of response from his American opposite. Seconds passed, perhaps a minute. Fisher takes up the story: "Eventually one of his Officers went up and whispered something in his ear. I sent the wine round, and the Admiral then got up, and made the best speech I ever heard. All he said was: 'It was a d___d fine old hen that hatched the American Eagle!' "[13] And that was it. No other record is known about the encounter of these two admirals, or of the event at Admiralty House in Bermuda.

Who was this fellow who was slow to rise in response to his gracious host? William Thomas Sampson, of Fisher's age, was born in Palymyra, New York, of northern Irish ancestry. Like Fisher he had a keen interest in torpedoes and guns, and he was for a time chief of the Ordinance Bureau. Sampson would have liked to have attacked Havana directly but, brought to task by the navy board, on the declaration of war on 21 April 1898, he sailed from Key West with 26 vessels to blockade Cuban ports. Sampson had a genius for blockade, much to the Naval Department's anxiety, and in the end Rear Admiral Winfield Scott Schley made the more aggressive attack on the Spanish force under Admiral Cervera. The politics of this episode do not lie here for our concern, but Sampson's message that "The fleet under my command offers the nation as a Fourth of July present the whole of Cervera's fleet" brought derisive comment from the press. Sampson's sea career ended in October 1899.[14] Reticent in nature, he gave an initial impression of coldness. Press correspondents disliked his abrupt manner.[15] He thought that the Monroe Doctrine should be enforced by material means. Unlike Fisher, who was invariably jabbering, his American opposite was quite the reverse: he was taciturn. Of greater interest, perhaps, is his health as a factor in leadership. When he died on 6 May 1902, the cause specified was paresis. A faltering memory and being speechless in front of his host seems a natural explanation of naval leadership experiencing ill health. He said few words, but those he issued in Bermuda have echoed down the years, and we return to them near the close of our story.

The Fashoda crisis – the clash of British and French ambitions to control the sources of the Nile – was then coming to a boil. Fisher had taken care to find out as much as he could about French dispositions, and the matter that concerned him most, given the secret advice provided by Commodore Bourke, the senior naval officer in Newfoundland, was that British submarine cables ran near, or sometimes through, St. Pierre. His worry was that if war should occur, his connections to the wider word would be cut off and his ability to communicate with Canada, Bermuda or the West Indies severed. The files bulge greatly on this issue.[16] Far more attention has been given to Fisher's immediate scheme (the details of which have never been found and perhaps were never more than a wide idea) to attack the French at Miquelon, Îles des Saintes and other French West Indies islands, and to free the French army officer Alfred Dreyfus, who had been imprisoned on spurious charges of espionage at Devil's Island, French Guiana. There Fisher planned to cut the cable to France, and then land Dreyfus secretly on French soil, there to spread dissension. Fisher had worked up a plan of troops, transport and escort vessels, including five cruisers and five smaller vessels, earmarked for the enterprise. From the Admiralty files we now know that Fisher's plans for the mobilization of gunboats and the troopship *Malabar* at Bermuda exist, ready for sail in 24 hours notice, and to carry 1,000 troops, fieldguns, horses, ammunition and provisions. Understandably, no military objective is specified.[17] Fisher, it is said, decided to sail *Renown* to the Mediterranean so as to fight the real war there if it eventuated, but that never transpired either. His appointment to the British delegation to The Hague occurred at that time. Fisher always gave others the impression that he was spoiling for a fight with the French (and later the Germans), and with regard to the Fashoda crisis he is on record as saying to a friend: "One ought not to wish for war, I suppose, but it was a pity it could not have come off just now, when I think we should have made rather a good job of it!"[18]

Fisher's appointment to The Hague Conference in May 1899 was received on 23 March in Bermuda. Coupled with it was cheery news that he would be appointed commander-in-chief of the Mediterranean at the next vacancy. He was to take *Renown* with him. He wrote to his daughter that if war came it would be either a peerage or burial in Westminster Abbey. "You also will appreciate what a terrible wrench it is to give up 18 months on this lovely station! Particularly as I don't like the Mediterranean!"[19] Fisher duly made his appearance at The Hague. There he met Admiral Mahan, the US naval representative. In the councils, Fisher showed belligerent instincts, opposing all measures of naval arms control, contending then, as always, that in wartime controlling the means of violence was idiocy. The British Government had every confidence in Fisher at The Hague, but no seriousness seems to have been given at the time to advancing views for international accord.

As the twentieth-century opened, the British had experienced a revolution in their dispositions in North America, the West Indies and the Caribbean. The Caribbean was fast becoming an American lake. Various coaling stations acquired by the United States even before the Spanish-American War allowed for the better projection of American naval power. Under Theodore Roosevelt, the US Navy became a bluewater battleship fleet dedicated to eliminating foreign rivals in the Caribbean and protecting both seaboards. It was not designed to compete with the Royal Navy but rather to complement it. Roosevelt established fleet bases at Culebra off Puerto Rico and Guantanamo Bay, Cuba. He consciously courted British favour. The Americans, adopting Mahan's view about geographical pivots, were looking progressively outward. This was reflected in discussions in the British Foreign Office, which show the incontestable duality of existing considerations about the future: on the one hand, apprehensions were uttered about the drawbacks that the British would face given the expansion of the United States Navy and its necessary addition of coaling stations; on the other, much support was given by way of acquiescence to American ambitions. As time passed, and it took two decades to accomplish the change, the Foreign Office was prepared to see the United States (with all of its assertiveness) as a partner, not a competitor.[20] Arthur Balfour, then at the Foreign Office, held the root conviction that the Anglo-American peoples must stand together. He turned "cold neutrality into friendship towards the United States".[21] On land he was the counterpart to Fisher afloat.

The hinge of fate had turned here, one of colossal consequence to the peace that would obtain between the two powers. This revolution in disposition cleared the way for those actions in international law that would give the Americans a free hand, all the while allowing the British to maintain their positions in the West Indies and the Caribbean. So much had changed in 50 years, for in 1850 the famous Bulwer–Clayton Convention was signed by Britain and the United States. It provided that neither power should ever obtain or maintain for itself any exclusive control of any canal connecting the two oceans, or erect fortifications protecting it. The older British logic that the construction of a canal across the isthmus would impair the country's maritime superiority, increase the responsibilities of the Navy, and aid the development of rivals to Britain's mercantile marine had been blown apart by the United States' triumph over Spain and the sudden acquisition of Cuba, Puerto Rico and the Philippines. American sovereignty had been extended in Hawaii. But by the second Hay–Pauncefote Treaty of 1901, the United States was given a blank cheque to construct what became the Panama Canal. It was settled that the canal should be "free and open to the vessels of commerce and of war of all nations... on terms of entire equality". Whatever independence or self-determination the nearby local republics held was now mortgaged to the foreign policy of the United States. The Caribbean, no longer a *cul de sac*, was now seen as an artery, and in London and Washington worry existed that new powers, notably Germany, would attain new footholds and naval stations, thereby threatening respective British and American communications and interests. In Whitehall, for instance, military strategists concluded that the American build-up in power and influence might pose certain risks.[22]

This same turn of the tide in the affairs of the Caribbean allowed a gradual reduction in British naval units and personnel in the Western Hemisphere. The late war had demonstrated the value of cables and cable communication. It had also revealed that mere control of the ocean surface was not enough. The rapid deployment of units of naval war rested on fast instructions and on the availability of coal. Smaller colliers, those under 4,000 tons, had proved to be the best. Fixed bases were less valuable than the mobility of support functions providing resupply and nourishment. Military planners who read the lessons of the war remarked that it had been a "coal and cable" war.[23] Intelligence-gathering by Americans (including spies), sloppy Spanish message-handling and aggressive journalists favourable to the press were all factors that explained that the control of communications was a central feature in the outcome of the war. There were many lessons to be learnt here, as Vice Admiral Philip H. Colomb, RN, a lecturer in naval strategy and tactics at the Royal Naval College in Greenwich, noted in his third (1899) edition of *Naval Warfare, Its Ruling Principles and Practice Historically Treated*.[24] The principal maritime powers with colonial possession awakened to the fact that cables affected commercial strategy and military dispositions. American experts watched with alarm British advances in submarine cables that added round-the-world power. "England's sea-power is not alone measured by the number, character, and tonnage of her warships," remarked a captain in the US Signal Corps in 1901, "it is immensely increased by the system of exclusively controlled submarine cable network, which at present forms four-fifths of all the cables of the world, woven like a spider's web to include all her principal colonies, fortified posts, and coaling stations."[25] True it was that although cable communication was only 50 years old, at the beginning of the new century the British Empire was already bound together by one great system of intelligence transmission. And such capabilities made more flexile and more immediate its means of naval force and diplomatic influence.

Although it might be imagined that the British had relinquished to the United States the key to their maritime empire in these seas, the mobility of the British naval force could still have an effect in these waters. When Fisher came to the Admiralty as first sea lord for Trafalgar Day 1904, his so-called Fisher Reforms, duly effected, called for a revolution in British armed deployments overseas, the reduction of bases, the changes of overseas stations, and the withdrawal of ships that were ineffective and out of date. A cruising squadron based at Devonport (and linked necessarily to Gibraltar) now served the eastern flank of the Americas. The British kept Bermuda, though on a reduced level, as their watchtower in the western Atlantic but passed Halifax to the Canadians (as they did Esquimalt on the Pacific station); they also closed Port Royal in Jamaica. The dockyard was closed and reduced to a "cadre" in 1905, after the existence of practically two-and-a-half centuries. The port guardship, HMS *Urgent*, was removed in 1903 and, to the shame of the British Navy, ended her days as a coal hulk in Boston harbour.[26] Other smaller bases – St. Lucia, Barbados and Antigua – had long since been closed. Fisher's argument about this was that communications had made possible these adjustments and that naval power was more mobile than ever before. And lying behind his thinking was that the British had a new partner in maintaining British and other interests in the Americas: the United States.[27] But driving the diplomatic agenda was the rise of imperial Germany's navy under Admiral von Tirpitz, already referred to, and the alarming announcements of the shipbuilding plans which, when coupled with imperial ambitions overseas, spelt a new, and perhaps the last, threat to *Pax Britannica*. The United States was fully aware of this new threat. As early as 1902, Roosevelt, now president, had warned the Kaiser that the US Government would not stand idly by if the Germans took any action regarding the acquisition of territories in West Indian waters.[28]

By and large, however, then or afterwards, no issue could upset the equilibrium demonstrated in Anglo-American affairs, though union or reunion was out of the question. The prospect of an alliance never grew beyond mere talk.

Naval officers were obliged to maintain strict neutrality with regard to their opposites, and when Commander William Sims of the US Navy spoke at the Guildhall, London, in 1910 and forecast Anglo-American unity in any future large-scale war, his remarks reverberated from Berlin to Washington.[29] In the audience was Fisher, and from this encounter and others the admiral formed a high opinion of the American officer. Sims outlived the difficulties that nearly ended his budding career. In 1917 he returned as the senior naval representative of the United States and an advisor to the Admiralty.

A distant echo of the Fisher and Sims encounter of 1910 could be heard after the First World War in the charming story of how Fisher had coaxed from Admiral Sampson those famous words of 4 July 1899 about the links of the British and United States navies attaining a new lease of life. In May 1919 the secretary of the United States Navy, Josephus Daniels, who, along with William Jennings Bryan, was the chief representative of the populist tradition in the administration of Woodrow Wilson, arrived in London. Daniels, an apostle of peace and a publisher, had seen his country go from peace to war, and through all the battle and the breeze, the cut and thrust of war, had seen how freedom of the seas was a concept worth fighting for. He had visited distant Scapa Flow, where he found the Royal Navy men not reconciled to the end of the war. They still wanted to deliver a crushing blow to the enemy. Now he was in London with all of its imperial trappings, where the American Luncheon Club was to fete him at the Savoy. His speech about the new responsibilities of the republic may have caught some by surprise, and it received widespread attention at home and abroad. The United States, he said, had accepted new responsibilities for world peace and world conditions when it entered the war. These it could not escape if it would, and would not if it could. "So far as my country is concerned," he continued, "our desire is that this cooperation should never stop. Our traditions are yours, and no Englishman has more claim to Runnymede than I."[30] A new era had dawned.

Among the 250 guests was Jacky Fisher, who rose to a standing ovation. The old admiral, well past his prime, though never at a loss for words, gave a reply to the toast given to him personally. He took his time, savouring every moment. He recounted that he had been in the United States for a week (the same duration that Daniels had been in Britain, which brought laughter), that his son had married the daughter of a prominent Philadelphia family, that he had driven those long American roads, and that King Edward VII was his only true friend when he was making his seismic naval reforms. He concluded by discussing the event of 1899 in Bermuda, when Admiral Sampson had issued his famous words. Fisher said that he had been directed by the lords of the Admiralty to host the dinner in question at Admiralty House, Bermuda. He said it was the best thing that ever happened to him. He recounted his toast to Sampson: "I proposed his health and turned on as much hot air as I could, but the beggar never said a word." Seconds went by, the port was passed once more and then the American admiral made his response. It had brought great laughter and applause at the time and now, it did so once again, at the Savoy.

Then, as if in a slight and kindly reminder given to Mr Secretary Daniels, he proceeded to recount how so many years ago he had told the first lord of the Admiralty, Goshen, that do what you might, you ought not to play fast and loose with the Navy and its expenditures, for at the end of the day it was that which counted most in the security and wellbeing of the state and its interests. It was a resounding speech: vintage Fisher.

Although the press reported the precise wording incorrectly, Fisher followed up immediately with a letter to *The Times* (7 May 1919), and the letter was published under the correct one: "A Fine Old Hen That Hatched the American Eagle." To this he added his own concluding words:

> Somehow the war has been won beyond the dreams of Nelson. The enemy's Fleet (so full of perturbations to our most eminent experts!) not annihilated in battle, as his custom was, but locked up in Scapa Flow without a massacre, and the German Army so splendid (at the eleventh hour even!) vanished!

Fisher never resisted the chance to have the last word. A year later he was dead. A funeral service, said to be second only in size to that of Fisher's great friend Edward VII, was held in Westminster Abbey. Greeting the naval party that brought the coffin to the west end entrance were several uniformed US Naval officers, lined up at attention and paying their respects. They were the only foreigners to take up such a position among those of their Royal Navy counterparts.

Looking back over the last few decades leading up to the First World War, it can be seen how Britain had no desire to maintain any predominant interest in the Caribbean. The sole objects were those of protecting trade and investment, and of ensuring the preservation of sovereignty, law and order in British West Indian territories and on continental shores. Policing foreign – that is, non-American – encroachments could now be a duty met by the United States Navy and Marine Corps. Sufficient anchors of American empire now existed between Florida and Panama to maintain the influence of the Stars and Stripes, and provided that Britain assumed no hostile stance, such a happy state of co-association would likely remain. And remain it did, for never again would tempers flare over the control of swamplands and potential corridors of transport; no quarrels would arise over would-be coaling stations or safe harbours. That the British were to extract themselves from such a colossal island empire so quickly and so peacefully may be marvelled at. For, after all, they had kept up a grand Caribbean design, "the Western Design" of Cromwell, over three centuries and more. To find it being run more conveniently by a new Western power and one derived from Britannic origins must have caused statesmen on both sides of the Atlantic to scratch their heads in wonderment at the thought of one empire replacing another. Such things even inspired thoughts of Anglo-American union. Later we would realize that it was all part of what could be, and should be, called the Anglo-American succession.

14

The Trident Bearers: The Navy as Britannia's Instrument

The closing years of *Pax Britannica* were marked by long shadows over the imperial scene and darkening clouds forming on the horizon. The story of the rise of the imperial Germany navy with Wilhelm II's support and under the energetic building programme of Admiral von Tirpitz has often been told, and has already been alluded to in these pages. Less well known but of signal importance was the rise of German commerce on the seas, and a realization at the British Admiralty that in order to win a rapid victory in any future war with Germany, a plan would be needed to wage economic warfare on an unprecedented scale.[1] Dealing with German commerce raiders would be one thing; establishing an effective blockade would be another. Bringing the High Seas Fleet to account would be a primary task of British fleet units, while dealing with "fitful raids" by enemy cruiser squadrons would be equally necessary. By October 1901 the first lord of the Admiralty, the Earl of Selborne, had recognized the implications, for the calculations regarding British naval supremacy now hinged more than ever on relations with France and Russia, with whom permanent peaceful accommodations would have to be made.[2] In the circumstances, the selection of a new second sea lord who would soon rise to the top professional spot in the Service became one of urgency.

The British Cabinet needed the right man. They chose Sir John Fisher, whom we have already seen as a promoter of Anglo-American naval accord in the wake of the Spanish-American War. Before he was appointed second sea lord, many questions were asked in the inner circles of the Admiralty. In the end, the volcanic reformer was brought into the higher echelons of influence. His arrival in June 1902 allowed for consideration of the revolutionary Selborne Scheme on the entry, training and employment of officers and men of the Navy and the Royal Marines. This and other measures for readying the Navy for possible war have been studied many times. No matter how cool and calculating the British position for increased readiness in shipbuilding, dockyard expansion, officer education and training, lower deck expansion and much else, the truth is that this was being done against a double political shift, at home and in Germany.

The Admiralty held to the view of concentration of force as the best means of maintaining command of the sea. Decisive battle was expected, and thus the centralization of the British fleet to deal with such an eventuality was key. "The importance which attaches to the command of the sea lies in the control which it gives over sea communications," declared the Admiralty's memorandum on imperial defence presented to the Colonial Conference of 1902. "To any naval Power the destruction of the fleet of the enemy must always be the great object aimed at", and, in undoubted reference to the scattered possessions and components of the British Empire, the same document noted: "It is immaterial where the great battle is fought, but wherever it may take place the result will be felt throughout the world." In other words, the victor would be able to gather all of the fruits of victory, all of the outlying bases of authority, plus the shipping and commerce of the seas, and likewise have the capability of prosecuting such overseas campaigns as those in the Iberian Peninsula or South Africa of yesteryear. All depended, therefore, on the British fleet being able to deal with the hostile forces which it is liable to meet. The British fleet must therefore be strong where it was likely to meet the enemy contender.[3] Such a policy was therefore fair warning duly given that something was in the wind concerning the then current policy of the Admiralty to maintain distant stations on all seas, with a naval armament on each that was sufficient to undertake the protection of British interests (or otherwise being capable of reinforcement in emergency). The Admiralty did not spell out at the time the intention of fleet reorganization and ending the showing of the flag on distant stations. It was not slight of hand; it was just not mentioned. In the circumstances, the dominions and colonies were then not sufficiently aware of the German naval threat. Certainly they did not complain against such an Admiralty policy statement, but the underlying text must have been to prepare for the possible reality of dealing with some prominent enemy at sea. All parties adopted the general principles of the 1902 policy, and Australia asked for a clearer statement of Admiralty purposes, these to be given at the 1907 Imperial Conference. All looked well in theory:

> That a single Imperial Navy under one control is the most efficient and economical means of maintaining the "pax Britannica" on the high seas is now generally admitted and at first sight it would seem desirable that all parts of the Empire should contribute a just proportion of the cost of upkeep of the ships, and supply the due quota of the men required to man them.

These were the views of an Admiralty official. But all sorts of complications existed as to how the bills would be apportioned; and, in addition, London realized that many differences existed in the self-governing parts of the empire concerning abilities and willingness to make such contributions to the imperial fleet. The project had some life through 1909, and, as late as 1914, Churchill was still trying to keep it alive.[4]

In Britain, the Conservative government gave way to the Liberals in 1906 under Sir Henry Campbell-Bannerman, who was soon succeeded by Herbert Asquith. That administration was dominated by persons (other than Winston Churchill) who were invariably pacifistic and trenchantly opposed to large military and naval estimates. Irish affairs ranked as a major concern along with labour strife and depression; the suffragette movement was a preoccupation of parliamentarians. Getting acceptance for rising naval estimates posed a difficult job for the first lord of the Admiralty and the Cabinet, for it was an age of austerity. In the circumstances, the artful Fisher was obliged to advise his superiors that such new and expensive warships as the "Dreadnought" battleships or the "Invincible" battle-cruisers were examples of getting more firepower for less money than other types of ship, many of which could be scrapped as too slow to fight or even to flee from a potential enemy.

The other contingency, working itself out at the very same time, was the increasing power of the wild and increasingly dangerous Kaiser. In the years since the iron Bismarck, the German people had been seized by a hubris that argued (along Hegelian lines) that the state was affirmed by war and that it was the result of preparations for war successfully carried out. Germany's imperialism – its place in the sun – came at a time of Britannic overstretch, and financial circumstances in which a fight was going on between guns and butter. That battle was fought out in Cabinet discussions at Downing Street. These were years of increasing Anglo-German rivalry, for these two powers were searching for the trade and industry of the world, and the Germans were playing "catch-up" in seaborne trade. The growth of their merchant marine and consular service was prodigious, reflecting their vast industrial capacity. German armed merchant cruisers and great ocean liners became an appreciable threat, obliging the Admiralty to develop the battle-cruiser of the "Invincible" class with capabilities of speed and armament, though not of armour, to track them down and destroy them.[5] There were other factors, and the investigative journalists on visits to Germany marvelled at the organization and capabilities of the German industry and military capacities then growing. The consolidation of the German Empire after 1871 and the notion that the state would be strengthened by corporate integrity and war only fuelled the imaginations of the Germans for *Weltpolitik*. Envious of the British – who had built an overseas empire and a network of trade and commerce under entirely different prospects and intentions (on liberal democratic and free-trade principles) – Germany marched quickly under Bismarck's imperialism, in leading the field in the naval race with Britain (one that it did not win), and in doing so spurred the role of the radical right, and contributed to the origins of the war of 1914.[6]

The Jameson Raid, though ill-starred to the British ministry, was a signal to Berlin that it did not have sufficient sea power capable of intervening in a war in support of Kruger and the Transvaal. Moreover, the Anglo-Boer War proved the feckless capabilities that Germany had in the naval line, feckless because it could not act even had the German ministry decided on military action. In other words, the boiling difficulties of southern Africa could only see Germany as a bystander, which was an intolerable position.

The Royal Navy – and none too soon – was becoming a reinvigorated "blue-water" concern, with even more powerful ships (in armament and armour, range and speed) than ever before. Naval architects and contractors were pressing ahead with new designs, with Britain a surging force in the naval armaments race. It is true that other powers – the United States, Germany and Italy – were making formidable advances in ship design, not least in the capital ship category, leading commentators to remark that the famed "Dreadnought" class of 1906 was not so unique after all: the Americans and Italians had equally innovative plans. But the real difficulty, as has been expressed by many historians and students of strategy and international affairs of the era, lay in terms of personnel, and specifically officers.

The Navy was unprepared for war in the sense that it had not seen a fleet engagement of any magnitude since Trafalgar. The Nelsonic legacy weighed heavily on the shoulders of Britannia. The undoubted triumph of 1805 and the long years of hegemony had a corrosive effect. Naval duties were now of a prosaic sort. War was far from the minds of admirals of the late Victorian and Edwardian eras. "I don't think we thought very much about war with a big W," mused one such flag officer, in retrospect. "We looked on the Navy more as a World Police Force than as a warlike institution," and again: "We considered that our job was to safeguard law and order throughout the world – safeguard civilization, put out fires onshore, and act as guide, philosopher and friend to the merchant ships of all the nations."[7] "Ships hardly ever assembled together in harbour," recalled another, who knew from first hand the Far East and Pacific stations at the close of the century, "and practically never cruised together as a squadron. British men-of-war might spend a year without seeing one another. The Flagship generally cruised along some coastline so as to be near a telegraph line, but most of the rest were scattered far and wide." The list of duties was long: patrolling the Bering Sea to protect sealers or observing the convention with the United States; protecting British interests during the frequent revolutions in the Latin American states; investigating a boundary dispute in the South Seas; burning Chinese junks that were interfering with treaty provisions or British concessions; and teaching a cannibal chief or an Arabian potentate a lesson. To these duties were added quelling mutinies in merchantmen, rescuing earthquake victims and rounding up rebellious tribesmen.[8]

Not the least among the results of the half-century of gunboat diplomacy was the effect on the morale of the service itself, for this was not war with a capital "W" but the day-to-day work of a worldwide marine constabulary. "The humanitarian argument had other ramifications," explains historian Arthur Marder:

> Mahan had said that the surest pledge of peace was an England strong at sea. If England did not retain naval supremacy {so it was reasoned}, it would place undue temptation in the way of nations to break the peace, and would be, as [Admiral Lord Charles] Beresford phrased it, "as culpable (but on a much larger scale) as a tradesman who displayed his wares unguarded and unwatched on the public pavement to throw temptation in the way of less fortunate people than himself."[9]

The spirit of the age, in naval terms, was to provide a sense of security and strength to the home islands, to the empire overseas, and to the trade which was the lifeblood of the whole national and imperial enterprise. The press, aware of the growing danger posed by rivals, made clear to the reading public the main issues. As *The Observer* of 18 July 1909, put it,

> Without the supremacy of the British Navy the best security for the world's peace and advancement would be gone. Nothing would be so likely as the passing of sea-power from our hands to bring about another of those long ages of conflict and returning barbarism which have thrown back civilization before and wasted nations.

Unless a powerful fleet existed, Britain would have to depend on an alliance that might involve the nation in matters in which there was little interest. Isolation, although still "splendid", demanded a preponderant navy. In the circumstances it was big ship time. Marder explains:

> The spirit of the age was a very powerful, if only derivative, force underlying naval expansion. Imperialism and militarism, the two inseparables, were the root causes of the governing emotions of Europe – jealousy, suspicion, fear, hatred, and undeclared war. It was a period of armed distrust. Every power feared an attack and armed itself to the utmost of its resources. The steadily mounting outlay on artillery, ironclads, and quick-firers was supposed to afford security. "*Si Vis Pachem, Para Bellum*" was the militaristic watchword in all countries.[10]

And the Board of Admiralty knew that it was the two-power standard of strength, established in 1889, which had without doubt been largely instrumental in preserving the peace of Europe for the last two decades.[11]

As the century came to an end, the Admiralty was already bound on a course of replacing its "Kingfishers" and "Ringdoves", its "Sparrowhawks" and "Pheasants", with capital ships and cruisers that were more appropriate to meeting the military threat of rival nations closer to home. The time had arrived, the foreign secretary, Lord Rosebery, said, when Britain could no longer "afford to be the Knight Errant of the World, careering about to address grievances and help the weak".[12]

Rosebery's stricture, coming as it did from a Liberal imperialist, was but one voice from an experienced parliamentarian and office holder who was concerned about the rising costs of acting as world policeman. Technology was driving the change, too, and new means of communication – electric telegraph, submarine cable and wireless – were making British naval might more mobile, and more easily able to meet the day's needs as they arose. The naval revolution in military affairs, which admirals such as John Fisher, Percy Scott, A.K. Wilson and Prince Louis Battenberg understood, was encouraging the centralization of planning and administration. Britain was the centre of the world system of communications and the Admiralty was at the heart of it all. In this scenario, one made more frightening with the rise of German naval power after 1900 (the old rivals France and Russia now extinguished by arrangements and later formal treaties), the belligerent was fast supplanting the philanthropic. Echoes could still be heard about the beneficent and humanitarian influence exercised by the Navy. British sea power had been used as the servant of mankind: the slave trade had been destroyed; piracy suppressed; and law and order throughout the world safeguarded. As *The Observer* of 18 October 1909 put it in a heady warning,

> Without the supremacy of the British Navy the best security of the world's peace and advancement would be gone. Nothing would be so likely as the passing of sea-power from our hands to bring about those long ages of conflict and returning barbarism which have thrown back civilization before and wasted nations.

When Fisher arrived at the Admiralty in October 1904 as first sea lord, the reorganization of the distant stations was speeded up, dockyards were transferred to dominion auspices, and new cruising squadrons at Devonport, Gibraltar and China were developed. Economy was in the wind, but more important in the calculus of imperial defence was concentrating force against the prospect of war in European and Mediterranean waters. To some degree this did violence to the old doctrinal saying that "the sea is one". Fisher employed it: "the whole principle of sea fighting is to be free to go anywhere with every d___d thing the Navy possesses".[13] The proof of this mobility was demonstrated in the Battle of the Falkland Islands in December 1914, when two battle-cruisers were dispatched from Devonport to annihilate the successful cruising squadron of

Admiral Graf von Spee, putting an end to his sea-raiding and the damaging of allied communications infrastructure. By the same token, the tragic episode of the Battle of Coronel which preceded it, in which a British squadron fell prey to von Spee's superior force, showed the ill wisdom of keeping a mixed bag of cruisers unsupported by sufficiently fast and mobile firepower protecting trade off the west coast of South America.

When the swarm of sloops, corvettes and gunboats of questionable fighting value was withdrawn from their distant locales by Fisher's dictatorial measure, something like a social revolution albeit of a minor sort occurred in the empire. No longer were consuls cheered up by those ships patrolling local waters; no longer were merchants feeling the security that a gunboat exhibiting the flag lent to affairs ashore. The old peacetime routines of the peacetime navy, which had brought tennis and golf, cricket and dancing, to the scenes of empire – and boosted the spectacle of empire – were swept away. The social heartbeat of a community had always pounded a little faster when the Navy was in port. Not only was local business promoted but also the social scene had always been more vibrant, and certainly more promising to aspiring daughters and their hopeful parents. Admiral B.M. Chambers reflected that the larger ports of call still witnessed ships wearing the White Ensign calling probably for longer periods, "and probably no one is much the worse for the change, unless it be the girls at the smaller outposts who more rarely get a chance of flirtation with 'those charming naval officers' ".[14] In Victoria as in Halifax, steam went out of the social scene when the old sloops-of-war were withdrawn, and the local press proclaimed that England was derelict in its imperial duties. The story could be repeated in Sydney, Capetown, Bermuda, Wellington and elsewhere.

But still, in later years, there existed the need for a single ship to show the flag and carry out all manner of duties in so doing. In actuality, and of necessity, the British were obliged to cling to the practice of gunboat diplomacy almost as long as the empire continued, as well as after, and used warships as shows of force against recalcitrant Pacific Islanders as late as the 1940s. In 1947, ships of the Royal Navy and the Royal Australian Navy were employed to check "Marching Rule", a quasi-nationalist movement in the Solomon Islands involving terrorism and robbery.[15] The principle of these operations remained the same: enforce law and order through the threatened use of legalized state violence.

In these years leading up to the outbreak of war with Germany, the onrush of technical developments pressed the Royal Navy into challenges that were previously unheard of. Steam turbines, more formidable guns, loading mechanisms for guns, mechanical computing devices, ever-increasing tonnage and more spelt what historian Rob Davison has described as a means of confronting many long-cherished beliefs and sensitive social and political issues. The Service and its officers dealt with fundamental changes in professional requirements. Cultural and social values underwent a transformation in the run-up to the First

World War. The Navy became an industrial workplace.[16] In the circumstances, officers had to get their hands dirty. The culture of command changed from the old days of the sailing ship. Naturally, the social reformers came to the fore – Fisher, Beresford, Corbett and others. But there were tensions, too, and many irreconcilable issues existed. Engineering officers never were fully embraced by executive officers, and even to this day, social stratification exists in navies.

"We had competent administrators, good experts of every description, unequalled navigators, good disciplinarians, fine sea-officers, brave and devoted hearts: but at the outset of the conflict we had more captains of ships than captains of war." So wrote Churchill in reference to the Navy in the years immediately before the First World War.[17] The overall truth of these assertions may be questioned; however, the incidental details, plus surviving anecdotal evidence, point out the deficiencies. It must be kept in mind that the Navy at sea had not fought a major battle since 1805. Had the Navy been lulled into a false sense of invincibility following Trafalgar and been so long engaged in maritime police work on a grand scale that its warlike zeal had disappeared?[18] No matter how mentally prepared officers might have been in 1914, they had little experience of war against European rivals. Experts in gunboat operations they certainly were, and sticklers for protocol and regulations similarly. But as fighting admirals they were deficient in experience, and this was the oddity of *Pax Britannica*, for naval power had created that maritime supremacy that was the characteristic of the age, but that same pre-eminence and predominance had removed its practitioners from the sharp end of naval battle.

Prof. Marder, noted adjudicator of British and German naval rivalry, described the Royal Navy of the closing years of the nineteenth century as "in certain respects a drowsy, inefficient, moth-eaten organization".[19] That seems a harsh criticism, but his rival, Stephen Roskill (writing of the time when the Royal Marines officer Maurice Hankey joined the Mediterranean fleet in 1900), could quarrel little with this appraisal. Sailing into Malta's Valetta harbour was always an inspiration as well as an historical remembrance of a world still existing. Roskill, who had sailed into this port himself, puts it this way:

> Many young officers of those days on arriving in Malta, or for that matter any naval base or overseas garrison town of the colonial Empire, confined their leisure activities to the English club and the sports club with its golf course, race track and polo grounds, and took no trouble whatever to get to know the indigenous people. The narrowness and snobbery of such men, and too often their women-folk as well, sowed seeds of hatred which were to a bitter harvest in the mid-20th century.[20]

Still, Hankey did not like the English colonial society that he met in Malta, and thinking "the specimens of English society here... most objectionable; they

[are] not only all asses, but they are all very silly, jabbering, empty-headed, ugly, conceited asses", he determined to avoid society altogether.[21]

Hankey deplored that warlike efficiency in the Service was not what it should have been and remarked on the excessive importance placed on "spit and polish".[22] The defects were widespread and deep-seated, comments the reformist-minded Roskill. He explained:

> They derived from nearly a century of unchallenged supremacy, from the contempt of the ruling class (which provided the great majority of senior naval officers) for the new technology, of which they were very largely ignorant, from a rooted conservatism which was automatically resistant to changes which did not conform to a largely outworn "tradition", and from an exclusive educational system based on birth and wealth rather than on ability. Though the Navy was of course merely a microcosm of late-Victorian society, which was still largely based on rule by a hereditary aristocracy, the conditions of sea service and the hierarchic naval command structure tended to produce even greater resistance to change and innovation afloat than on shore.[23]

It may be observed that when Britain and the British Empire faced its utmost dangers, beginning with the Anglo-Boer War and continuing in increasing levels of anxiety to the outbreak of war in 1914, the call went out from London for the outworks of empire to come to the aid of the whole. Many of these calls fell on deaf ears.

In the immediate years preceding 1914, when *Pax Britannica* was at its height in terms of sea power and financial strength, the security assured by the whole made possible for the dominions – Canada, Australia, New Zealand and South Africa – to concentrate almost wholly on their internal development. External policies were regarded as merely subsidiary to this. Their intimate associations with the great world power with its worldwide commitments and requirements naturally made them dependent on sea power and the free flow of goods across the oceans. This was a cosy arrangement, though it was not taken for granted. It spurred imperial loyalty under the heading of "One life, one flag, one fleet, one throne. Britons hold your own!" Even so, it did not result in voluntary contributions to the overarching power of British warships and bases, except for raising local garrisons and manning local patrol boats. Imperial trade advantages and immigration schemes increased the ties of kinship and were good for business. In the years after the South African War, the empire grew in strength and in number. The British did not seek to control any local autonomy and had no interest in hindering any development in responsible government. In fact, in South Africa, for instance, they engineered the peace and put in place the new federal system, in doing so allowing local interests to cooperate with others. A general harmony existed among the dominions in such intergovernmental arrangements as they had, though most dominions preferred to communicate with others via London. When they and their representatives were brought together at colonial and then imperial conferences they often eyed each other warily, as keen as cats. They had been brought together by the course of history; apart from the ties to the Crown and to London, however, they were champions and masters in their own houses and lands. They liked it that way. They were on the alert for imperial coercion or even subversion from a sister dominion.

German naval armament set up the new clarion call of the British Empire after the South African War. As early as 1902, at the Colonial Conference, the secretary of state for the Colonial Office, Joseph Chamberlain, appealed thus, echoing a phrase of Matthew Arnold: "The weary Titan staggers under the vast orb of his fate. We have borne the burden for many years. We think it is time that our children should assist us to support it." The dominions and the colonies had rallied to the side of the mother country in the Boer War. Would they do so again in response to Chamberlain's new appeal? They could supply manpower in abundance and could supply horses and horse artillery, but could they supply the money for shipbuilding and even ships themselves? No. The building and arming of ships is a formidable business in terms of expertise, to say nothing of expense.

None of the dominions had the material capabilities of laying down a steel-hulled dreadnought, and even the construction of a light cruiser would have to be done in home yards. Any battle-cruiser built for Australia would have to be built in a British yard.[24] Canada might consider funding three dreadnoughts but these would have had to be built in British yards. But the Admiralty could compensate by granting the construction of smaller vessels in Canadian yards – a quid pro quo in the construction line which would satisfy those in Parliament who worried about the financial equation. Some dominions responded more willingly than others. Some saw a trap; others a necessary badge of citizenship. Australia, New Zealand, the Cape, Natal and Newfoundland made contributions – but not Canada. Chamberlain had misjudged the moment. His scheme for tariff reform, so as to compete with foreign powers, was a bungled attempt, for the principles of free trade ruled uncontested. His views of imperial federation and cooperation overstretched the realities of the colonial societies that formed the empire. Thus in 1902, Canada's answer, as given by Prime Minister Sir Wilfrid Laurier, was bluntly: "If you want our aid, call us to your councils."[25] A tone of desperation sounded in Chamberlain's appeal, but it counted for nothing with the autonomous-minded Laurier. He was sufficiently devious to avoid accepting any imitations that might come his way. Each of the dominions and self-governing colonies had its own response to Chamberlain's call. Their collective response was bound to be difficult because they could not speak of one accord. Once their heads came together around the imperial conference table they were always eyeing each other like nervous cats, as one wag put it, and unanimity was never agreed on.

The empire was, in the views of one, "a political fact, but only a phrase, an influence, or a sentiment". The empire was less a unified whole than, as Adam Smith had put it unerringly in 1776, "the project of an empire". In a sense the empire was a mental construct that had fired the imaginations of Britons at home and abroad. At home the construct was always reluctantly held. The English were perhaps the slowest to realize this. The Canadians understood it implicitly but were too polite to give a hard-core answer. Meanwhile, preparations for military and naval capacities continued at home and abroad, and questions of interchangeability of weapons, standards of drill, chains of command and others all progressed rather remarkably – and imperial defence of another order.

The Admiralty tended to regard the empire as an essential unity. The main concern was to have central and unified control on and over the seas. For this reason the Admiralty refused to have any dominion or colonial ships of a naval type fly under any other than the White Ensign, and fought for the uniformity of command right through the 1920s. The lords of the Admiralty clung to old ways with tenacity. They were right to do so because the trade and commerce of empire, and the safety of the seas, required a system of safeguards that needed a central command. The whole network of imperial communications spoke the language of Whitehall, and that network had been put in place for good reason, not least the security of messages (diplomatic, military and commercial) that passed out over the globe and returned home again. Territorial and other militia regiments and reserves were established; the process of militarism went down into the towns and villages of Britain. Drill halls were thrown up and cadet corps established. None of this could stop the advance of war, for it was other nations that were setting the agendas, and in the end the war that began in 1914 was set off by the assassination of an heir to the throne in a continental empire far away from London. That immediate cause of war was based on nationalism of the Serbs; oddly, it had less to do with the Kaiser's wish for a great fleet or an imperial place in the sun. The war at sea – 1914–1918 – came in any case, owing to commitments and promises to allies, and continental challenges to maritime dominance, the latter the result of *Pax Britannica*. Germany's quest for power at sea meant that Germany and Britain could not be friends, and by the same token it meant that Britain would court friendship with two ancient rivals: France and Russia. Britain entered the war with great friends but the power that would have made improbable a world war, Germany, was by definition antagonistic to British prerequisites of security. Ever since the Anglo-Boer War a conviction had risen in Berlin that sea power was the condition of world power. No matter the decline in international morality, the search for naval bases and the scramble for overseas territories, a perverse faith was created in Germany that a powerful navy was an obligatory means to world power.[26]

In London there could be no disagreement of opinion about the foreign policy of empire being indivisible. The rationale, as Sir Edward Grey, the foreign secretary, pressed on the dominions and colonies at the 1907 Imperial Conference was that the foreign policy was based on naval issues and the British command at sea. The logic was indubitably about maritime security. This was the essential thing. It necessitated unity of command. If war were declared, the empire would be at war. The question as to whether the dominions, such as Canada, Newfoundland, Australia and New Zealand, would fight against an enemy rested only with regard to degree and under whose control that contribution in men, guns and butter be made. The Admiralty was on the side of the Foreign Office, and did not wish for the diminishing of the Royal Navy by various sub-Britannic navies. "One life, one flag, one fleet, one throne": this was the mantra. Herein lay one of the great difficulties of the age, never satisfactorily resolved. The Dominions and colonies could sense the urgency of the arguments put forward by the foreign secretary and the Admiralty. The local Navy Leagues and Sea Cadet Corps sensed the urgency. Far more difficult was to get support in the individual legislatures for direct or indirect contributions to naval capabilities that were essential to imperial purposes, including local defence. Pride in the Britannic achievement was one thing; contributing to its welfare was quite another.

Throughout the long century of *Pax*, and particularly during the last half, new rivals had been presenting themselves. Rivals to Britain's global reach had acquired islands and coastal enclaves, and erected bases of repair and supply, beachheads of trade and commerce, and railways and entrances to interoceanic canals. In the circumstances, the advantages of Castlereagh's 1816 keys to security of trade and military advantage seemed to be shrinking fast. But the British had countered with new bases, and these in particular were advantageous to the development of dominion navies and naval capabilities: Esquimalt, British Columbia; Sydney, Australia; Wellington, New Zealand; and Simons Bay, South Africa. These were directly advantageous to the global reach of the Britannic edifice, and they augmented the essential nodes of power built up in Bermuda, Halifax, Trincomalee, Aden, Singapore, Hong Kong and elsewhere.

The crimson tide of kinship was of immense value in the coming struggle against the Central Powers and in support of France and Belgium in the First World War. The naval services of the dominions and self-governing colonies gave undoubted support, moral and material, to the same causes of keeping the seas safe for those who pass on their lawful occasions (and for denying imperial Germany's quest to grab the trident of Neptune, as the Kaiser had proclaimed). The search for autonomy by dominion and colonial navies was a natural pursuit, for self-defence had always been promoted by the Dominion and Colonial offices as commensurate with self-government. In the circumstances, however, the Admiralty rose to challenge this assumption, worried as their lordships were by the division of authority between the Admiralty on the one hand and local naval boards on the other. The closer war came, the greater the worry. Britannia might have willing daughters but there was always the worry about the curfew.

"England has been described as the Mother of Parliaments. With almost equal fitness she may be called a Mother of Navies."[27] The Commonwealth Naval Forces were created in 1901, the precursor to the Royal Australian Navy; the Canadian Naval Service (later the Royal Canadian Navy) was established in 1910; and the Royal New Zealand Navy was set up in 1941. South African and Indian navies, and others besides, found their parentage in the Royal Navy. And beyond the bounds of empire, services like the imperial Japanese Navy and the Chilean Navy owed much to the legacy provided by the Nelsonic tradition, British strategy and tactics, and British armament, propulsion and armour. British-built warships not only served in the Royal Navy and the dominion navies; they had been taken into most of the world's navies save for those of France, Italy, the United States and Germany. As of 1914, Britain was the principal supplier of the world's dreadnoughts. The key for British statesmen was to make sure that Britain had the predominant number for its own strategic purposes. Thus dreadnoughts destined for Brazil or for the Ottoman Empire found their way into the hands of the Royal Navy – insurance policies, so to speak, in the dreadnought race with imperial Germany and its allies.

Right to the eve of the First World War, British strategists and statesmen kept their eye on what was happening on salt water. "There are two ways in which England may be afflicted. The one by invasion . . . the other by impeachment of our Trades . . . ". This was Sir Walter Raleigh speaking from an earlier era. Even so, the same rationale held true. Trade protection became a burning issue at the Admiralty in the late nineteenth century, and the rise of German seaborne raiding capacity, in armed merchant cruisers and liners, posed a major threat that the Admiralty responded to, chiefly in the design and development of the battle-cruiser. Britain was dependent on foodstuffs, munitions, industrial raw materials and global communications. If trade were halted, Britain could not maintain its industries, feed the population or equip its armies.

As of August 1914 the Royal Navy still possessed an uncontested preponderance at sea. Britain and the empire held the trident of the seas. That strangely curious interlude in world affairs, *Pax*, was fast drawing to a close. On nearly every sea and ocean, Britain possessed coaling stations, bases, refitting yards and drydocks, reprovisioning places and sometimes naval hospitals – the anchors of empire. On nearly every coastline if Britain did not boast cruisers or gunboats, they could soon be there – enforcing the country's mandate of the freedom of the seas. And even if those overseas fleets had been reduced in number rather savagely in the course of the previous few years, reorganized cruiser squadrons still showed the pirates, the slave traders and Britain's testy rivals that Britain and the empire intended to keep the peace of the seas. Seaborne trade, the lifeblood of empire, needed to be protected. "It will be obvious to everyone," *The Times* said by way of urgent reminder, "that in a scattered and oceanic Empire united by the highway of the sea this highway must be safe, for if it is not neither goods nor troops can pass along it in security, and consequently neither commerce for war can be conducted with success."[28] Although, in the corridors of power in Westminster and Whitehall, politicians, strategists and bureaucrats might sternly debate the question of future British naval and military obligations in future wars and police actions, there was never any discussion of yielding to a foreign power the sceptre of the seas.

15

Recessional: The End of *Pax Britannica* and the American Inheritance

With proud thanksgiving, a mother for her children,
England mourns for her dead across the sea.
Flesh of her flesh they were, spirit of her spirit,
Fallen in the cause of the free.
Solemn the drums thrill: Death august and royal

Sings sorrow up into immortal spheres.
There is music in the midst of desolation
And a glory that shines upon our tears.
As the stars that shall be bright when we are dust,

Moving in marches upon the heavenly plain,
As the stars that are starry in the time of our darkness,
To the end, to the end, they remain

Laurence Binyon, "For the Fallen"

The termination of *Pax* came with the end of so-called Splendid Isolation and its fateful replacement, the Continental Commitment. That is the comfortable view from our times. Apart from these British-centric reasons, a more powerful explanation comes in the form of the German threat and the unleashing of German power on and over the seas coincident with the events of August 1914. The course of events lay beyond the control of the British Empire once the British Cabinet made the fateful commitment to give an ultimatum to Germany that the independence of Belgium must be respected. A history of the great and tragic conflict that was the ruin of Europe and set in train a whole host of misery, death, revolution, and social and intellectual discord lies outside this book. The naval history of the First World War does not belong in these pages. However, once the dogs of war were unleashed, the Kaiser's navy enjoyed great success before collapsing in revolution. It raided English towns, attacked British merchant shipping in distant seas, engaged the Grand Fleet at

Jutland and nearly won, and mounted a formidable U-boat campaign that was so effective that in early 1917 the first sea lord, Admiral Sir John Jellicoe, held the view that the British could not hang on much longer – though a reversal of fortunes came with the introduction of convoys and the later assistance of US naval units. That time had marked the greatest peril faced by the British Empire.

Throughout, the British never lost command of the seas. The outlying ramparts of influence proved immensely advantageous, as did the cable and wireless systems that bound the whole together; seaborne commerce, the lifeblood of empire, was sustained despite heavy losses to Germany cruisers and U-boats. In many ways the British Empire was stronger in consequence of the war. In time of need the solidarity had been effected so as to bring about the end results, but the costs had been enormous, and the experience of war would forever change how empire was viewed from near and from far.

Von Tirpitz had miscalculated in assuming that the rapid expansion of the German navy could serve its desired purpose in challenging British world influence. All it did was awaken British feelings that were centuries old, and chief among these was that Britain would gather every resource possible, would gather all allies to its side, and would even ruin itself financially so as to keep the dominion of the seas. Maritime power would be brought to bear, as it had in the time of the contender Napoleon, to contain continental power. No matter what the cost, no matter how long the struggle, Britain would continue. Von Tirpitz had been wrong about the need for colonies; it was bases that mattered. He was wrong about monopolizing trade, for free trade was what counted. And he was wrong about creating a great fleet capable of containing what amounted to the Grand Fleet. German propaganda, which could be matched by Fleet Street, fanned the flames of certain war. The British were not blameless. Their navalists called for more dreadnought battleships and cruisers. But one thing was certain: Britain could and did outbuild the German navy. It did so at formidable cost to the British taxpayer. It has never been entirely clear what Germany hoped to gain, for it could not dominate at sea as well as dominate on land. It could not be supreme in both, just as the British could not win on the Continent. The great Anglo-German rivalry in the building of dreadnoughts, particularly in the measures begun by Britain in 1909–1910, then countered by Germany, and repeated again by both sides in later years leading to and through the beginning of the war, served to intensify fear. The insecurity of the two powers increased, the British were driven into an alliance with France – a fateful necessity – and by August 1914 the ancient British freedom of action which had been the hallmark of British policy for the previous 100 years, and indeed before that, had been destroyed. The German miscalculation had elicited the British response, and that response had spelt in its own way disaster.

The German threat at sea was entirely removed by November 1918, the fleet in revolution and the nation in ruins. Events on the Western Front had seen to that. Unconditional surrender was ordered by the German high command. Peace was effected by the Armistice. Now a new challenge came to what was the remnant of *Pax Britannica*. At the close of the First World War, the Navy's obligations to protect seaborne commerce remained, and thus came the shrill cry from the Service for more cruisers. The White Ensign, wrote Captain Augustus Agar, signified law and order on the seas while at the same time the Red Duster indicated trade and the exchange of goods. "Together the flags were symbols of peace, progress and integrity in business matters. Our ships did not come, as others had before them, to foster tribal warfare, pillage villages and carry off loot, leaving behind a trail of misery, with fear lest the visit be repeated." The Navy acted as traffic cop on the sealanes and in the ports of the world, he noted. But the societies with which the British came into contact in this era wanted protection. As he said, "They reasoned rightly that under British rule they would live in peace with their neighbours, instead of a continual dread of strife; and if they were set upon or interfered with by others without just cause, retribution and justice would soon follow."[1] But more than just protecting legal trade was required. The acquisition of new colonies and others under League of Nations trusteeship arrangements increased obligations. This was a new obligation for formal empire and promoting the crimson ties of kinship. Showing the flag continued as policy. One officer on the North America and West Indies station has left this statement of promoting the crimson ties that bound the empire in the 1920s:

> For the next two years our activities were to extend from Trinidad in the south to Newfoundland and the St. Lawrence in the North, with Bermuda as headquarters. We were to convey the spirit of Empire to these colonies, to show the White Ensign, that emblem of Britain's far flung Navy, to these pioneers of British trade and commerce, and to make them realize that if they couldn't visit the Homeland for long intervals, the Homeland's Emissaries could visit them. And how they did welcome us! When our two years would end, a new crew would come out and relieve us; and so the cementing of these bonds of kindredship, of loyalty and of love of Britain would go on forever and ever Amen![2]

In June 1918 the Board of Admiralty tabled at the Imperial War Conference its policy calling for a single empire navy and an "Imperial Naval Authority". To the dominions this was dynamite. Modification followed. The Admiralty mission to the self-governing dominions made by Admiral of the Fleet Lord Jellicoe in 1919–1920 had one clear intent: to encourage naval capabilities in the dominions and to promote intra-imperial cooperation and coordination. Wherever he went he was enthusiastically received during his tour of empire.

The results of his investigations into naval defence included the formation of a naval base at Singapore and establishment of the Royal Indian Navy and a New Zealand naval division. These had far-reaching effects. But in other respects such naval unity as Jellicoe and the Admiralty would like to retain under the White Ensign and central command was already being subverted by events and the results of the costs of the recent war. Already the lure of autonomous action was driving the separate responses of Canada and Australia, in particular, while New Zealand resisted any influence likely to weaken the imperial naval link. The dominions were touchy about their newly acquired autonomy, won at considerable sacrifice on the battlefields of France, Flanders and Gallipoli. They were not to be pushed around by London. As early as the Imperial War Conference in March 1917, the Admiralty had come in for severe criticism by representatives of Australia and New Zealand. The premier of New Zealand, Sir Joseph Ward, charged that the Admiralty had defaulted on earlier promises to maintain sufficient naval units in the Pacific to meet the needs of the day. The idealism of the early interwar years encouraged self-governing members of what became known as the British Commonwealth of Nations to believe that there would be no more major wars and that the League of Nations could preserve the peace. This was largely the Canadian view. Ward, however, wanted their lordships to advance a new scheme for post-war security in the Pacific and argued for the possibility of a British Pacific fleet or some sort of coordinated dominions naval force. The Australians had always provided more in the way of naval units in support of committed strategic requirements than either New Zealand or Canada. The many unresolved, indeed irreconcilable, issues in intra-imperial relations of this era weakened the imperial stance, giving a window of opportunity to resurgent Nazi Germany, and made all the more difficult a response to contain Hitler's quest for continental power.[3] Meanwhile, in 1919, the British Cabinet had invoked the "Ten-Year Rule": an assumption that war would not recur for at least a decade, and military expenditures were trimmed to the bone, while at the same time units of the Army and Royal Air Force were stationed from Mesopotamia to Singapore.

Jellicoe recognized that the empire's strategic focus ought now to be on the Pacific, given imperial Japan's rise in naval might and East Asian influence. At the Admiralty, his views were seen as exaggerated, though they are now seen as correct.[4] In the Far East, the twilight of *Pax Britannica* was difficult to discern by those "on station", or by those who did the business of the British Empire and its commerce there. "To many a young Englishman who went east in 1930 it seemed as though the empire would never end, as though the lordly relation in which his race stood to the native peoples of the Far East would continue into the indefinite vagueness of the future."[5] This view is not far off the mark. But the key date in the imperial recessional in these waters had long since past, and this was 1902, when Britain signed the treaty of alliance with Japan. This first such undertaking towards another power in the new era demonstrated Britain's concern for its eastern rather than its European interests.[6] The arrangement allowed the withdrawal of the Far Eastern fleet. This left the country's interests protected by smaller vessels and small garrisons at a time of the growing power of imperial Japan and burgeoning Chinese nationalism. In 1930 the British, under the influence of American statecraft, relinquished their almost forgotten imperial outpost at Weihaiwei, though by agreement the Navy received continued access to Liukungtao, the naval base.[7] Weihaiwei was no longer a British hostage to fortune.

After the Washington Naval Treaty of 1922, neither successive British governments nor, for very long, the Admiralty held the illusion that Britain would still be able to engage Japan successfully at sea. The United States now had naval parity with Britain and was fast building a new navy in which air power would have a central place in operations. War Plan Orange, first issued in the 1890s and since modified through "rainbow plans", called for new strategic thinking about how to deal with imperial Japan's rise to hegemony in its "East Asia Co-Prosperity Scheme". It would take another decade for the British, well into the 1930s, to realize the impossibility of checking Japan's naval and military might. Even so, there were warning signs. "The Japs lull us to sleep," the commander-in-chief in China, Admiral Sir Frederic Dreyer, told the first sea lord, Chatfield, on 19 August 1933. He continued: "one day when the moment is propitious they will cut our throats – because their policy cannot tolerate one having the position in the Western Pacific which we require".[8] Lord Hankey, secretary of the Committee of Imperial Defence, told the prime minister, Stanley Baldwin, that British armed services might be able to mount tattoos and Navy Days but were incapable of imperial defence. Other (but more sinister) indications of the recessional were apparent. Imperial Japan now acted independently of British interests, the alliance having been abrogated by the British in 1921. Japan began working towards what was presumptuously called The East Asia Co-Prosperity Scheme, another name for naked imperialism and military aggrandizement. The appallingly horrific incidents of Japan's aggressions on the Chinese mainland, notably at Nanking, before the Second World War, are well known and have no place in this narrative. British naval power was circumscribed by British foreign policy and cabinet action, and a hitherto unheard-of policy of Whitehall was adopted in the hasty search for peace and order in the wake of the recent global war. Assured that all German warships had been surrendered and that German U-boats were unlawful, the Admiralty turned to the protection of seaborne trade as its principal duty. This was a global obligation. In the circumstances, new arrangements could be entertained with other great powers. But Anglo-American cooperation with regard to the Pacific was non-existent, and it was not until December 1940 that emergency discussions were held between Britain, the United States and the Netherlands (which had extensive territorial holdings and trade in Southeast Asia). By this time France had been knocked out of the war, and the triple axis of Germany, Italy and imperial Japan had been forged.

For some time now, from 1919 down to 1939, the illusion of *Pax Britannica* had been maintained even if naval primacy needed to be suspended or shared. How long could this bluff be sustained? The post-war treaties hobbled Britain – that is, the international legal constraints that independently accompanied the financial disasters that had been beset upon the nation and its trade by the previous war. Any oil sanctions to be imposed against Italy during the Ethiopian crisis would be borne by the Navy. But the cable of British imperial defence was drawn so tight that the fear existed that this new problem would snap the whole. By terms of the Washington Treaty, the British agreed to naval parity with the United States. By this measure came tacit acknowledgement that the British were no longer sole arbiters of the sea. No longer was Britain the first strategic power of the world, and the long recessional commenced, teasing out the illusion of permanence for as long as possible.

However, looked at from a fresh angle, we see a new co-association emerging, with the Royal Navy and the US Navy maintaining the dominant roles in global influence – the British in the Mediterranean and North Sea (with global interests in empire and trade); the Americans powerful in the North Atlantic, the Caribbean, the Americas and, of special importance, the Pacific. "The *Pax Britannica* was over," commented historian Christopher Lloyd. "The supremacy of the British battle fleet, and even of the battleship itself, was now a thing of the past." New mechanisms of war – air power and submarine power – had entered into the picture, resulting in a transformation of naval warfare into something entirely different. The Washington treaties demonstrated the geopolitical revolution.

> Britannia no longer ruled the waves unchallenged, not because she had been defeated at sea but because the strain imposed by the war had so weakened her that she was compelled by economic factors to resign herself to a position of parity, if not subordination. The flag was dipped: it was not hauled down. Henceforth the trident of Neptune was to pass into the joint guardianship of the English-speaking peoples.[9]

The course of history brings together strange bedfellows; it links in awkward alliance nations that had long been enemies, nations that had taken separate courses in their individual development that had been demanded by circumstances. The United States had been born in revolution, and had thrown off the ties of kinship, acquiring independence from Britain in 1783. It had fought Britain again in the War of 1812 and threatened its colonies in what was later called Canada. There was no love lost between these countries, but the Spanish American War had brought them closer together. Britain was the only non-belligerent power to remain neutral in its opinions about United States actions. The relations of admirals Fisher and Sampson augured well for future cooperation. The winds of change were blowing hard, and in London and Washington, senior naval personnel were quick to take advantage: the rise of imperial Germany and imperial Japan had brought them diplomatically closer. In his *Influence of Sea Power upon History, 1660–1783*, Mahan had given practical expression to the importance of predominant sea power in the affairs of nations. Mahan contended that a multinational consortium was needed to defend international trade. A cordial Anglo-American understanding, though not a formal alliance between the two nations, would serve American purposes. At the time when Mahan was writing, the maritime purposes of the two states were complementary. Mahan saw the rising German naval threat in terms of its effect on Anglo-American naval relations rather than in respect of the strategic concerns of either Britain or the United States.[10] This co-association of naval and strategic interests thus has important implications for alliance maritime strategy in the abstract, and interesting applications later in 1917–1918 and in the years of the North Atlantic Treaty Organization. He was lauded in Britain – even though the British knew that what he proclaimed was but an announcement of the fact that they already knew an affirmation as it were. Mahan had said that sea power was the basis of world power. Secretaries of the Navy could not proclaim this publicly, but they held the concept close to their hearts. Despite the claims of the airpower enthusiasts, the free use of the seas as a broad common is the best assurance of global security.

In the First World War, American sea power, despite many strains along the way between the Navy Department and the Admiralty, in 1917 provided massive support for a beleaguered dreadnought fleet and strengthened the means of protecting seaborne trade and military operations across the sea.[11] In 1917 the United States declared war against Germany, and the US Navy was sent to the European theatre serving with the Navy in a number of capacities. Keeping the freedom of the seas was the essential reason. The Queenstown patrol, the central duty of which was guarding convoys against U-boats, actually witnessed American warships serving under a British admiral, a strange and unheard of disposition that was inconceivable to many.[12] The teamwork was of mighty importance to countering the U-boat threat.

The British fleet might still be all-powerful and dominant but had begun to decline in relation to that of other nations. Indeed, the United States was familiar with the challenges to British naval primacy. "In explaining this development, Mahan had drawn the conclusion," wrote Captain Tracy B. Kittredge of the US Navy, in his official naval study on naval cooperation during the Second World War,

> that the United States must develop naval power as the basis for its future national defense, but should cooperate with Britain in establishing and

maintaining Anglo-American sea power and control of the seas to assure the heritage of the "Pax Britannica," which the Royal Navy was no longer able to guarantee alone, as the basis of world peace and of a stable and just world order.[13]

This was the goal, understated and seldom publicly proclaimed. Public opinion would never have allowed any public pronouncement. Because of technical advances, the broad Atlantic Ocean was fast shrinking to the narrow dimensions of the English Channel. All the same, in the United States the administration kept its eye on Latin American states and security, and a "policy of the good neighbour" led for a time to the rejection of the technique of armed intervention. German investment, commercial penetration and diplomacy in Latin America were watched with alarm in Washington. In his address to Congress on 4 January 1939, President Roosevelt made clear (in preparation for a large increase in armed forces expenses) that his country might rightly decline to intervene with arms to prevent acts of aggression, but it must be prepared to defend itself and its interests. The old lesson that probability of attack was decreased, he said, by the assurance of an ever-ready defence. Not only were armed forces and defences needed but the organization and location of key facilities were needed so that they could be immediately utilized and rapidly expanded so as to meet the needs of the day. This is essentially the reasoning of Castlreagh of more than a century before. By agreement, Canada was added to the American security perimeter in 1938 and with no stir in the United States whatsoever. The bounds of the Western Hemisphere were being toughened, and to this position, Britain and the British Empire at large could have no objection, only welcome relief in the circumstances.

From September 1939 to December 1941, Britain and the empire, along with its allies, were at war with Germany and Italy. For Britain in particular, these were months of lonely peril. Questions of security of the seas, the safeguarding of war materiel and essential supplies, and the safe passage of armies all became worrisome issues of major magnitude. Once again, sea power dominance became the issue of British survival. "The cooperation of the United States Navy with the Royal Navy in assuring the supremacy of Anglo-American sea power 1940–1945 was a further expression of the prophetic doctrine defined a half century earlier," wrote Kittredge, who added that "The effective combined American-British partnership, in winning and maintaining command of the sea in World War II, was in conformity with traditions of national policy and naval power repeatedly manifested after 1890."[14] In all it was a remarkable partnership, for at the outset much of it had to be sustained in ways so that the inquiring press could be kept at bay. Britain and the empire were at war; the United States and its territories were not. The British needed destroyers, torpedo boats, flying boats, rifles and much else. The Americans needed air and sea bases so as to be better able to safeguard and police the eastern flank of North America and the Caribbean. The Americans, particularly President Franklin Delano Roosevelt, wanted assurance that the British would not scuttle their fleet but that its units would find a safe haven in empire ports or American harbours. Churchill provided every assurance.

In 1940, Churchill, then prime minister, pointed out to President Roosevelt the perilous position in which the United States would find itself if Hitler mastered Europe and controlled its navies and ports. The Royal Navy urgently needed destroyers to hunt U-boats, and Churchill offered long-term leases of bases in North American and West Indian waters in return. The Newfoundland and Canadian governments were consulted, and those of certain West Indian colonies too. The Destroyers for Bases pact was effected, the destroyers delivered and the United States then established naval and air bases in Newfoundland, Labrador, Bermuda, the Bahamas, Antigua, St. Lucia, Trinidad and British Guiana. Here was what might be called "succession empire" – informal and unannounced, the work of "allies of a kind". Jonathan and John Bull seemed reconciled at last. In Parliament, Churchill spoke of the affairs of the British, and the United States having become "somewhat mixed up together in some of their affairs for mutual and general advantage".[15] It was easy to read between the lines. "I am very glad that the army, air, and naval frontiers of the United States have been advanced along a wide arc into the Atlantic Ocean," said Churchill, "and this will enable them to take danger by the throat while it is still hundreds of miles away from their homeland."[16]

Of the role of personalities in history there can be no doubt, and the combination of Churchill and Roosevelt makes for compelling interest. To review, Churchill was delighted because, as he said, "the worth of every destroyer that you can spare to us is measured in rubies"; Roosevelt (fulfilling demands from the Navy Department) got what was wanted: bases on a 99-year lease stretching along that long arc from Labrador and Newfoundland to British Guiana, including Bermuda. The emphasis, he told a press conference by way of careful calculation, was on the acquisition of bases "for the protection of this Hemisphere, and I think that is all there is to say".[17] These were the first steps. They were immediately followed by schemes for convoy support, a communications network, intelligence sharing, anti-submarine patrols and much else. Roosevelt did this without going to Congress, and the public saw that new naval bases were surely a greater asset than 50 old destroyers. Roosevelt told the Canadian prime minister, Mackenzie King, at Ogdensburg, New York, that Churchill had given adequate assurance, indeed a pledge, that he would under no circumstances surrender the British fleet to the Germans.[18] Thus was the Anglo-American "naval union" brought about. The German challenge had mandated it. Naturally drawn into the scenario was the vitally important Canadian military contributions, naval and air. It would take some years to finish the job, difficult as the German and Italian navies were in the Atlantic and

Mediterranean seas (plus encounters in distant seas) and the imperial Japanese Navy in Asia-Pacific waters. But that which Churchill and Roosevelt worked up in that profitable time known as "the phoney war" was central to the final outcome. The statecraft, most of it conducted behind the scenes, that made this possible is of compelling interest, not least because the survival of democracy itself hung in the balance.

In Chinese waters, where there was always much potential friction, the Royal Navy stayed on in circumstances that were constrained by international treaty and Foreign Office directions. The gunboats toiled alongside those of the United States Navy in the Yangtze in observation of international agreements – and protecting trade and investment of the foreign states. Elsewhere, one by one, near settlements where British traders, missionaries and administrators lived, the gunboats were quietly withdrawn. In 1927, Britain relinquished its concessions at Amoy, Hankow, Kiukiang and Chinkiang. In other locations, notably Nanking and Shanghai, settlements were formed by the amalgamation of former British and American concessions. The Yangtse River was the last to see the British enforcement of treaty rights; ten British gunboats were on the inland waters as of 1939 but the Japanese imperial tide was rising fast, bringing the war to the Asiatic mainland. The Japanese brought humiliating pressure against the British concession in Tientsin.[19] At the Admiralty and from the flagships on station, the worry arose that getting reinforcements to the Far East when the crisis, as foreseen, occurred would be entirely problematic: British maritime control of the Indian Ocean was by no means secure, while beyond Singapore the situation presented a scenario of hopelessness. Imperial overstretch had raised its ugly head. Admiral Sir Roger Backhouse, first sea lord, made clear that 1938 would be a bad year: "The fact of the matter is that we cannot be strong everywhere. Things have been allowed to go back too far... Things will be very different at the end of 1941."[20] He was overly optimistic, and already events were overtaking the Admiralty and the defence committees. The last remaining British gunboat on the river, *Peterel*, a veteran fixture in the reach of the river at Shanghai, was sunk by fire from a Japanese destroyer and gunboat. The date was 8 December 1941. London's reasoned appeals to the Japanese, bearing as they did the Foreign Office's undeniable logic that Shanghai had unique status as an international port, were dismissed by the Japanese commander, who said: "Our countries are at war." Shanghai, old centre of the British network, came under siege, and only Hong Kong, the watchtower for Shanghai, remained in British administrative hands. Thus did the last of the British gunboats on the great river end the 100 years of British naval diplomacy there.

It was now only in the lower reaches of the Yangtze that the Navy doggedly maintained its presence, such vessels operating from hitherto but now endangered Hong Kong. Loss of the battleship *Prince of Wales* and battle-cruiser

Repulse, sunk by imperial Japanese naval land-based bombers and torpedo-carrying aircraft on 10 December 1941, signified the collapse of British naval might in those seas. The British garrison in Hong Kong was a hostage to fortune and it fell to the Japanese Army in 1942. And just as Hong Kong was the key to Shanghai, so was Singapore the key to the whole of the eastern seas. Singapore was surrendered to Japan in February 1942, with 40,000 Australian and imperial troops made prisoner. An epoch in British expansion and projection of power had come to a crashing end. The Dutch and French suffered similarly on land and sea in the region, with only the United States, Australia and New Zealand holding out against the rise of the imperial Japanese tide. It would take the might of the United States armed forces, along with those of the allies, to reverse this state of affairs and end the Japanese Empire's blatant aggressions and ill-conceived intentions. In 1944 the Admiralty commenced plans to revive its sagging strategic presence in these seas, and it put together a multi-aircraft-carrier task force to cooperate with the United States Navy in the final reduction and defeat of Japan. The chain of British bases aided the process but was no challenge to the mobility and strength given to the American allies by the sea logistics train, and the ships under Sir Bruce Fraser, the commander-in-chief, were much dependent on American sustenance and the fully cooperative work of ships in Commonwealth navies.[21] Now it was ex-imperial and ex-colonial forces propping up British naval influence, not the other way round.

Pax Britannica was suspended in eastern seas by the progress of the war. By August 1945, plans were being made to regain lost territories and re-establish order. The supreme commander of South East Asia, Admiral Lord Mountbatten, directed these affairs in conformity with American guidance, notably the domineering influence of General MacArthur. From Trincomalee, British naval, air and army forces moved east, and Penang then Singapore were regained. West was meeting East once again: at Singapore, the Japanese officers complained that their British officers who came to sign the documents of recontrol were two hours late, which prompted the British to reply: "We do not keep Tokyo time here." Meanwhile a British task force was formed up at Subic Bay, with its destination being Hong Kong. The whole came under the Admiralty, but

> the susceptibilities of General Chiang Kai-shek, the difficulties produced by General MacArthur's order [that no landings or surrender documents were to be signed until the main surrender ceremonies in Tokyo Bay], and American reluctance to involve themselves in any way in the recovery of a British colonial territory necessitated a long interchange of messages before the matter was settled.[22]

The British fleet – really a Commonwealth task force – under Rear Admiral Cecil Harcourt took up station outside Hong Kong harbour on 30 August 1945, with an entirely different intent than that shown by the old gunboats of the mid-nineteenth century. Liberation not conquest was in the wind. Now the fleet had come to repossess the colony from the Japanese occupiers.

The ships took up position according to their instructions. The time-honoured customs were observed. Battle ensigns flew from the appropriate yards. The admiral's pennant was there for all to see, indicative of the chain of command, and the respective obligations and duties that all commanders and their subordinates knew from long experience. The guns were at the ready, every man to his station. Countless had been the cases of such, or similar, expeditions in times past. Now the task force sailed to liberate Hong Kong and restore the peace. Other matters were in the wind: the Americans did not want to see a resurgence of British imperial authority and the Chinese Communists were up to mischief, seeking opportunity.

Minesweepers had duly been sent ahead to do their painstaking and dangerous work, and to sweep clear the channels of approach. Anti-piracy patrols had been implemented, too. Harcourt flew his flag in *Indomitable*, and the rest of the fleet consisted of another battleship plus two cruisers, four destroyers, a submarine depot ship and flotilla, eight Australian corvettes led by HMAS *Mildura*, and the Canadian armed merchant cruiser HMCS *Prince Robert*. The Japanese commanders soon handed over their swords to Admiral Harcourt, and an air of normality soon returned to the city-state and to its military outposts on the frontier.

After the peace the British returned to observe the treaties in Chinese waters. They were there as neutrals under treaty rights. British gunboats returned to the Yangtze in 1945. Against the rise of the Kuomintang, all treaty port concessions were threatened and abandoned. In 1949 the sloop *Amethyst*, last of the British "gunboats", was trapped in the river for three months in unbearable circumstances of heat, mosquitos and high winds, diminishing fuel and food supplies. On 20 April, while proceeding to Nanking, Communist guns opened fire on her. The trick was to extract herself from the grips of the Chinese People's Liberation Army, whose local officer, Colonel Kang, in tortuous negotiations that exhibited Chinese high-handedness and intransigence, had insisted that the British had "invaded". In fact the British were neutral, as the British commanding officer, Lieutenant Commander J.S. Kerans, insisted. The impasse continued. For three months *Amethyst* lay under the constant watch of shore batteries. Only a rush for freedom could end the matter. She eventually made her daring escape down the river on the night of 30/31 July. The British withdrew *Amethyst*, and also *London*, *Consort*, *Black Swan* and a Sunderland flying boat (medical personnel and supplies), to Hong Kong.

The Yangtze incident, legendary in British film and in telejournalism, heralded the lowering of the Bamboo Curtain.[23] The Naval Service Medal with the bar "Yangtze" was awarded to the various ships' companies and to the air crew of the flying boat.[24] Officers and men were lauded for their seasoned fortitude in the face of the most difficult circumstances. *Amethyst* called at many a port of empire en route home – Singapore, Penang, Colombo, Aden, Port Said, Malta and Gibraltar: "What a voyage, everywhere a wonderful reception. Race or creed forgotten, Black, Yellow or White all gave us the same welcome." Finally the ship reached that ancient of harbours, Plymouth. Of the reception accorded them there, "This was the finest of them all," noted Coxswain Leslie Frank, who won the Distinguished Service Medal for outstanding courage, skill and devotion to duty, "homely, spontaneous of own people, all united once again – With 'Drake's Drum' to welcome us home again".[25]

Reviewing the matter in a memorandum to the ship's company, Kerans said that 1949 marked a year that none of them would ever forget. He pointed out that incidents such as the Yangtze in peace are extremely rare, and *Amethyst*'s stay in the Yangtze Kiang had no parallel in history.

> The fact that everyone from the oldest to the youngest faced the situation with poise and equanimity was indeed salutary, and my greatest asset. The spirit of leadership and devotion to duty was fully exemplified by officers and senior ratings; this after all is the fundamental basis of our training and the essence of everything that the Royal Navy has stood for in the past and stands for in the present and the future.

He concluded, writing from his sick bed in Royal Naval Hospital, Plymouth: "Our prayers were answered, and escape was achieved without loss of life and serious damage. FAITH is not the least of the lessons to be learnt when in adversity."[26]

The British had clung on mightily to their obligations there. Protecting British interests, political and commercial, had always been the basis of their presence in these waters. But it was time to go, the tide of Chinese Communist sentiment flowing strongly against them. It was the end of the imperial twilight on these seas, and only interminable anti-piracy duties would be carried on in the South China Seas and the critically important straits connecting the Indian Ocean and the Pacific. Intriguingly, however, the banking and commercial systems set up by the British, notably the Hong Kong and Shanghai Banking Corporation, so key to the imperial progression of the nineteenth century, remained and grew to global dominance. Newspapers, universities, colleges, schools, missionary societies, country and golf clubs continued, though under new guises.

The British imperial presence in China had always depended on sea power and such forces as the Navy could project ashore. To some degree, also, it had rested on Chinese compliance and even cooperation – established by peace if possible, by force if necessary. *Pax* here was always about trade and about protecting business and legal concessions that had been wrung from the Chinese. It had no further ambitions. The work had been tedious and without any expectation of thanks being rendered. Standing orders for officers commanding Her Majesty's ships had as their principal intent the protection of British nationals, their ships and property. Chasing pirates was purely an incidental obligation. With regard to dealing with rioting or other forms of violence, action as envisaged fell into three categories: protective action (by landing of armed parties to preserve the lives and property of British subjects), retaliatory action (to fire on ships that had opened fire on ships flying the British flag), and punitive action (measures taken as a result of an outrage where the lives and property of British subjects had actually suffered deliberate destruction; a bombardment carried out under the authority of the commander-in-chief might be the result). Wherever possible the naval officer on the spot would act in concert with the local British consul; the authorization of the Chinese government was never assumed or considered.

In the circumstances, however, officers and men of the Navy had often acted independently of Foreign Office expectations; indeed, that was the nature of local command in distant circumstances. One case will suffice to illuminate this. With regard to an episode that occurred in 1926, when Chinese pilots were demanding exorbitant fees, and with the river falling quickly, the commander of HMS *Tarantula*, Commander J.V.P. Fitzgerald, placed his ship in the river so as to halt all shipping. He made his point successfully and the river was opened to traffic. In the House of Commons a member asked: "Is there any precedent for Naval Officers using their discretion in relation to foreign powers in this way without reference to the Government at home?" The Foreign Secretary of the day gave this forthright reply: "There is plenty of precedent for the use of their discretion by Naval Officers. Happily for the British Empire and the peace of the world they have shown themselves very capable of using their discretion."[27]

Modern British imperial and naval history shows that although 1914 marks the end of *Pax Britannica*, British power continued thereafter on a global scale. But the dynamics of national influence on a worldwide basis according to the rules of the game, as largely laid down by the British in their unique moment of power, were not present after the First World War. All too soon the world's stage had aspiring new actors and new directors. Gone were the days of undoubted naval superiority and diplomatic freedom of initiative that had been hallmarks of the years 1815–1914. The true era of *Pax Britannica* was no more; only the illusion remained, and the fast-fading memories. For some years thereafter, certain episodes might occur that resembled the interventionist activities of the pre-1914 epoch. However, these did not bear witness to the full dynamics of Britain's overall supremacy in the 1815–1914 era.

In the course of decolonization which swept the world in the aftermath of the Second World War, and in which the origins had long before begun,

Britain chose not to defend the concept of empire. It was time to go, one to lay down the burdens. London's tendency was to advance with the changing times. The dissolution of the empire occurred quickly, and with the support of statesmen and office-holders in London. One crisis followed another in quick succession. Burma opted for independence free of any post-imperial connection. Self-sustaining regimes were put in place with the hope that permanence and stability, as well as social viability, would be the results beneficial to the emerging Commonwealth. The British disengaged from India in a spirit of goodwill. One by one the dependencies were made into places where a new flag and a new identity were created, and after Ghana and Nigeria the process increased in speed. In coastal states, new navies were created and based on older connections with the Royal Navy – the Royal Indian Navy owing its origins to the Bombay Marine. Old anchors of British influence became bases for new localized navies that were important for local security and anti-piracy work. The largest of the world empires was among the quickest to liquidate. Only Portugal, the oldest, was tardier in the process. Macau, Portugal's last holdout in Asia, was handed to China in 1999, closing the Vasco da Gama era of Asian history.

In the recessional from empire, Britain had chosen not to defend the concept of empire as worthy in and of itself; rather, all mention of imperial mission and colonial development vanished from public relations' statements. It was time to play by new rules. But Britain had not chosen Europe wholeheartedly either. Britain actually joined the European Community in support of the commonality of interests. Perhaps the European solution was Britain's way of extending power and influence in another way than absolute power and independence of action. There was no attempt in these late days of retaining empire as anything more than a reassuring illusion, a rallying point based on past glories. Eventually the Harold Macmillan government took the position that the choice of Europe was not only wise; it was essential for Britain to survive. The goal of imperial power was not replaced by economic strength.[28] And even once in Europe, and a member of the European Community, doubts persisted in Britain concerning the benefits of membership, and chief among the complaints was that concerning the European Community's rules and regulations, a blearing list of new requirements, dos and don'ts, that were yet another layer of regulation on an already heavily regulated country. Britain kept its currency and reordered it by a process of making a pound equal to 100 pence, casting sovereigns, half-crowns, shillings and thrupenny bits to the wind. But the Bank of Scotland retained its fundamental separateness. Lloyd's continued as the master player in the world's insurance business, and the wealth of Britain continued to rise in the finance, insurance and banking sectors. It might have seemed to an unknowing observer that the dissolution of the empire and the decline of Britain were well in progress, but in fact the creation of wealth through the City of London's interest and global capacity continued to advance. Profit and power were being acquired in a new way, for a new time.

The process of European integration was offset by the continuance of British association with the North Atlantic Treaty Organization and the essential alliance with the United States. Britain's geographical position athwart the European continent, its dependence on overseas trade, its central power in finance and insurance made it global still, even as it turned from empire almost in a post-modern way. The flag-waving was kept for ceremonial purposes, or for cheering on the forces for the retaking of South Georgia and the Falkland Islands. As long as national purposes were ensured, the territories and dependencies could pass to other hands. Securing "British interests" remained the byword, just as it had in the days of Palmerston, Disraeli and Salisbury, to name a few. Naturally there was a tendency to want to exert influence in the councils of the world, and there was always a tendency to want to send a gunboat, a detachment of troops or a squadron, but invariably such action had to be undertaken on a multilateral basis. The Falklands War was an exception to this, prompted by foolish action by Argentina against British sovereign territory.

"While the Empire existed," wrote Thornton,

> the British could with justice and reason claim that they had a responsible role in the world; and as their reluctant but definite stand against Nazi Germany proved, they could also claim that the concept of "British interests," which it was Britain's duty to defend, defended also the general welfare of the world at large.

And thus it was that the process of decolonization signified not just the dismantling of the apparatus of imperial administration: "In depriving the world of the *pax Britannica* it has also deprived Britain herself of her long-standing assumptions about her own position."[29] And British society at home had been transformed beyond all recognition from that at the close of the Napoleonic and 1812 wars. The long years of peace had been of salutary benefit to British profit and power. The great maritime achievement on a global scale would not be seen again. All of a sudden the catastrophic struggle in the two world wars had sent the Britannic world spinning, dislodging fundamental values along the way, bringing in new and uncertain purposes. The social revolution alone changed the imperial purpose. Writing in 1951, Churchill said: "During this first half of this terrible twentieth century all values and proportions have been changed to a degree which would make the picture of British society, as it now manifests itself, very strange and startling to those who had their heyday in the Victorian era."[30] Simon Winchester, in his widely read *Outposts: Journeys to the Surviving Relics of the British Empire*, has it correct when he says that the imperial ethos never had much to do with global domination. But in the making and running of the empire, the British had exhibited a divine right, a mission: "our success in all this grand endeavour came in no small part because we cared". The British had managed the imperial estate with close attention to detail. There is no doubt but that London sent out the best: "We managed the Empire with men and women of compassion and skill, energy and intellect, and something of a romantic dream about them."[31]

We have seen that imperial overstretch in times of financial challenge and rival threats was a cause of a response known as "the fear of falling". "Make me mightier yet" may have been the call in the song "Rule, Britannia!", but no hope of this existed even in the run-up to the First World War, when the new priorities were being set as to the size of the Navy and the growth of the Army. No wonder these two services were at loggerheads over ways and means, and interservice cooperation was virtually non-existent, each of the services thinking that the other was in desperate need of reform.

Being overcommitted invites these challenges and these arguments, and it makes the conduct of a successful foreign policy all the more difficult. An American historian and an expert in public affairs, Jeremi Suri, author of *Liberty's Surest Guardian: American Nation-Building from the Founders to Obama*, puts the contemporary American problem in these sharp terms: "Perpetual crisis management contributes to confusion, waste and overall ineffectiveness. To reestablish focus, the [American] nation needs clear and disciplined priorities. To reestablish leadership, the nation needs the courage to say it will do some things well, while practicing self-restraint everywhere else." Preventing bad things from getting worse is not a viable policy, he says, at a time when the credibility of the dollar as the world's de facto reserve currency is threatened. "Washington," he says, "has good reasons to care about other issues, from nation-building and human rights to climate change and energy security. But economic constraints and bitter partisanship make success on those issues unlikely. What is required right now is a return to basics."[32] The recent recession and debt crisis have shaken the old assumptions. A national debt out of control, inability to raise new revenues, high unemployment over a long period, lack of stimulation for growth, rivals to nuclear armaments and the ascendancy of China, which makes the United States a debtor and a dependent nation, reduce American power by subverting national independence in decision-making. This is the greatest challenge since 1776 and has never been faced by the United States in all its modern history. Terrorism stalks the airports, bridges and ports; homeland security adds to domestic worries; civil rights are curtailed; the true rights of citizens now have limits, except for the constitutional right of a citizen to bear arms. The unstable and apparently unregulated nature of American public finance and credit will invite discussion from professionals in that field, but in doing so some of them will recall the days when Britain held the financial assets of the world, was the principal shipping nation with the greatest carrying trade, had global commercial and banking reach, boasted the highest credit rating and had a close association between the City of London and government offices in Whitehall. "In all things, profit and power ought jointly to be considered," warned that scion of the East India Company, Sir Josiah Child. Throughout the years of *Pax Britannica*, the British had kept that maxim in close observation. That rule of thumb still existed in 1914.

Prof. Michael Lewis, who taught a generation of officers at the Royal Naval College in Greenwich, was mindful in the 1960s of how British naval power was facing some of its greatest challenges. He was equally aware of how little the general public knew about the previous obligations of the Navy in times of peace. Fascinated by the milieu in which the Navy operated, he turned his attention to the social history of the organization, the first to do so. In discussing the period 1815–1914, and particularly the earlier years, he made some poignant observations:

> *Pax Britannica*! Over much of the world today the very phrase has become a reproach, scarcely decent to mention. People scorn it; deride it as "arrant imperialism," based upon self-seeking and hypocrisy. But was it? Was it hypocritical to chart the oceans of the world for the benefit of the world? Was it selfish to make the pirate's trade not worth the candle; to break the slave trade, with all its revolting cruelties which were turning a whole continent into so many parcels of helpless slaves... The prime instrument of the *Pax Britannica* was the Royal Navy, its ships and its men.[33]

A prominent British journalist, F.A. Voight, writing in the early years of the Cold War, observed that England had always been respectful of the rights of small nations. This was based on the conscious respect for the rule of law and, by extension, its moral influence in the world. Moreover, as an island power off the European mainland, it depended on overseas communications and bases for trade and security.[34] Guarding the sea routes and protecting the independence of small nations remained the essential goal. In the two world wars, Britain had responded to the continental challenges of its opponents that threatened small states or allies, while during the Cold War the not inconsiderable material capabilities of the Royal Navy provided a link in the Atlantic system of immense value. But since 1989 that, too, has passed away, and the dimensions and benefits of *Pax Britannica* seem even more remote. Sagging British naval fortunes in ships and sailors mark a steady decline, and as early as 1982 that decline afforded Argentina an opportunity not to be missed to capture the Malvinas (Falkland Islands), invoking a British response by deploying forces previously committed to the North Atlantic Treaty Organization commands to what it had classified as an "out of area concern". The Falkland Islands and South

Georgia – British sovereign territory – were repossessed as a further payment to the price of Admiralty.

Paul Kennedy, noted adjudicator of the rise and fall of nations and empires, has explained that the vacuum created by Britain's passing from power, plus the favourable economic and strategical position that the United States possessed, meant that the United States "having become number one, it could no longer contain itself within its own shores, or even its own hemisphere". The United States had committed itself to the reordering of Germany and Japan, and deployed forces in numbers as required. "But while it alarmed the likes of Churchill and attracted isolated Republicans," he writes,

> it proved impossible to turn the clock back. Like the British after 1815, the Americans in their turn found their informal influence in various lands hardening into something more formal – and more entangling; like the British, too, they found "new frontiers of insecurity" whenever they wanted to draw the line. The "Pax Americana" had come of age.[35]

But already a great shift in world affairs has happened to upset this new *Pax*. Just as the First World War ruined empires and reconstituted the British Empire in many ways previously unimagined, so too the treaties that brought a reordering of the world in the early 1920s called for new obligations, and later a great rearmament to deal with Nazi Germany, Mussolini's Italy and Hirohito's Japan. In the case of the United States in recent years, the reordering of the Warsaw Pact, the fall of the Soviet Union, the reconstitution of a united Germany under the European Union – all of these and more meant new obligations and adjustments for a *Pax Americana*.

Balance-of-power policy-making is now dead. Asymmetrical warfare is the norm. External terrorist threats and actions now invoke American military and political responses, as Afghanistan and even Pakistan come to feel the might of the American armed services under presidential control and Congress's will. These are not affairs like Palmerston's Don Pacifico imbroglio. The responses are far from an empire of consent of the governed, but extensive, invariably unilateral, police actions against peoples far away in which the United States has no intention of establishing a local peace save to protect its own homeland interests. Sometimes allies are in consent and give aid. They pick and choose as they like. Meanwhile, guarding the seven seas by American sea power was, and is, a different requirement faithfully pursued, though sea-to-shore missile capability gave an inland reach never known in the age of *Pax Britannica*. Hardly an issue of a highly respectable American newspaper escapes discussion of these issues. Fear of falling is in the wind, and of moral collapse, too. Imperial overstretch is one issue of concern. Going to war with deadly drone strikes over far horizons is another. Exercising force with restraint is yet one more.

The new Romans of our time have force disproportionate to their numbers, and probably guns and ammunition out of all proportion to their world requirements. But already the seeds of collapse are apparent: as Mahan had said, financial stability at home was one of the essential features of having great sea power, and as earth-shaking fiscal crises have shown in Wall Street and on Capitol Hill, the descent into chaos though not imminent may not be as far away as American politicians, statesmen and pressmen discuss on a regular basis. Profit and power need to be jointly considered, and the United States is increasingly a debtor nation, with Saudi Arabia and the People's Republic of China increasingly being its creditors, and Canada its foreign energy supplier. In his critique of Kennedy's *Rise and Fall of the Great Powers*, the economic historian W.W. Rostow made some useful observations that nicely frame the arguments with which our study concludes:

> The answer for the United States at this historical interval, when its relative power and influence, while diminished, still transcends by far that of any other power, is, in a sense, to pursue on a wider basis the policy Britain should have pursued towards Europe after 1945; that is, to move forward with others to give institutional substance to the profound common interests that suffuse the Pacific Basin and tame forehandedly the tensions which exist or might emerge; to move similarly in the new spirit of authentic partnership within the western hemisphere; to tighten the ties of partnership within the Atlantic community; and to hold out to the Soviet Union [*Vide* Russia] a vision of a soft landing from the Cold War.[36]

In the years and decades ahead, many will ponder if the United States and its allies on and over the seas can maintain a *Pax Americana*.

> Like its predecessors of Minos, Athens, Rome, Venice, Holland and Britain, the United States found itself the only surviving maritime power capable of maintaining order on the seas, enforcing international law, and leading multinational efforts to check piracy (especially hijacking at sea and in the air) and smuggling (arms and drugs) and in promoting weather reporting and rescue at sea. By its formidable military strength at sea and in the air the United States has balanced the continental powers of Russia and China and policed the oceans of the world.

That was Clark Reynolds, noted American naval historian of air power in 1985, almost a generation ago.[37] To a large degree, the North Atlantic Treaty Organization provided a new arrangement for *Pax Americana* to succeed *Pax Britannica*, and even to this day the interdependence of Britain and the United States in matters naval and maritime, not least in nuclear policy, warheads and propulsion, reflect the complementary nature of their sea power missions. The European Community presents a form of continental stability that the British worked so hard to keep in place but failed to maintain with the rise of the Kaiser's Germany. Its strength remains a pillar of peace to the world. But beyond Europe, out on the margins of its influence through the eastern Mediterranean, through the Red and Arabian seas, up through the passes of Pakistan and into Afghanistan, across through the Islamic republics that once formed part of the Soviet Union, and then into China with its unresolved border difficulties with Taiwan, Russia and Japan the tensions continue. China's muscular buildup, naval and military, in Chinese seas and the international waters of East Asia and a substantial naval and military build-up in China and the waters of East Asia loom as the newest challenge to peace on a worldwide basis. Britain abandoned its primacy in Asian waters in order to deal with the German challenge in home waters. The American position is rather different, for from its own home continent-island and possessing superior tools of war, its sharp-end capabilities are undeniable. But great powers are by their very nature reactive, responding as the needs of the day arise to the chaotic challenges brought to their attention in the wider world.

In conclusion, the age of *Pax Britannica* showed four characteristic features:

- predominant military power as expressed in its naval instrument and mobile regiments capable of imperial policing and security;
- economic and financial power on an increasingly global scale, backed by the credit of the British Government and Parliament;
- an adapting trade policy that went from mercantilism in 1815 to free trade and then to fair trade protectionism in 1914;
- increasing imperial responsibilities of a truly global empire, a state of affairs modified, even strengthened, by consolidation of new federations or unions overseas – Canada, Australia, New Zealand and South Africa.

Links between the City of London and Whitehall remained close and tightly managed on both sides. The British developed a habit of authority, one with export value. There was an official mind of British imperialism. In the Cabinet offices, the Admiralty and the War Office, the same intention was pursued – to maintain the profit and power of the British state. The well-honed British ministerial system of individual departments having command of their own matters under purview, plus the typical discussion of a particular matter under consideration and then the final agreement as expressed by the political head, had immense credibility. Departments interacted with each other, and there were undeniable tensions and rivalries. In the later years of *Pax*, the interdepartmental cooperation sagged under overwhelming pressure of time and events. The old Victorian system, sustained with hardly any reform during the

Edwardian age, became increasingly overloaded. A cloud of despair descended during the Edwardian period in the face of new uncertainties and a lack of clear vision about the ways and means of maintaining primacy. With great powers, the fear of falling is a necessary corollary of a state under pressure. No wonder the British had cause for worry: they held global power, advantageous to themselves – of that there was undeniable evidence; but they also had responsibility for its freedom and security, the protection of seaborne trade and the preservation of the interests of the smaller nations. The formal empire was in a period of great shifts. The changing circumstances between the Boer War and the opening of the First World War posed insurmountable problems to the individual departments, and interservice planning proved faulty. A number of years would pass before a well-oiled high command would develop at the centre of empire, but then not altogether successfully. The arrival of the dominions at the Imperial War Council or at the Imperial War Conference further complicated the problem of imperial management.

The First World War ended so many empires – German, Russian, Austro-Hungarian, and Ottoman – and it changed the British Empire beyond all recognition. The British were perhaps the last to realize the extent of change: the habit of authority, perfected by so many years of acting alone as the parent state, died a lingering death. In many respects the British were unprepared for what happened so suddenly in 1914, with such tragic costs to the European order and to humanity at large.

Long will the fingers be pointed accusingly at the Admiralty and its plans to deal with the German Navy. And an additional factor of influence was the growing reliance of the United States as a partner in the management of world affairs. There existed an affinity of interests here that neither party could vouchsafe openly. American support for the British imperial fabric could not be publically pronounced, for it ran counter to historical principles. British acceptance could not be proclaimed openly on account of the humiliating dependence that American finance and military power gave to the whole system of world security.[38] The maritime and naval preoccupations of both in protecting trade and sovereign interests blended into a harmonious whole, though it was never proclaimed.

At the same time the age had seen the on again, off again rivalry with France. *Pax* could be obtained in the years after the defeat of Napoleon. That was the necessary precondition, and once achieved all of the earlier quests for commercial growth and political stability could once again be pursued, as indeed they were. The victory of the Navy at Trafalgar gave Britain a decisive superiority in naval power over any conceivable combination of rivals. All the same, since 1815, Britain had had to contemplate the nasty possibility of a Continent controlled by a single aggressive power. That was the dreaded scenario (and it eventually arose in 1914 and in 1939). With the advantage possessed by the ring of sea power that stretched outwards from the British Isles, encircled Europe and the Middle East, extended across the Atlantic into the Caribbean and to the Pacific, and also stretched eastwards from the Cape of Good Hope and the Suez Canal outwards to Hong Kong and the North Pacific, the system to protect settlers, trade and other "British interests" was guarded by the fleet. But it was vulnerable because it was so vast, lying athwart so many places of danger and uncertainty. The success of the preying U-boat, the perfection of the torpedo and the coming of the military aeroplane increased the nightmare scenario. The risks seemed to rise with each and every new year. Overseas trade, colonial development and British merchant shipping brought immense wealth to British investors, bankers and insurance companies. The profits of the age were matched by means of military might. Profit and power went hand in hand. Both grew from 1815 to 1914, but other powers came forward with greater strength and speed towards the latter quarter of that age, with some indications from Germany and the United States of earlier advances. France was an ally in the Crimean War only because Russia was the enemy, and France was resurgent again in the 1890s and later became a British ally because of the necessity of checking German intentions of dominating the Continent and expanding to global power. Russia became a British ally in consequence of France's position. Japan became a British ally owing to the need to check Russian ambitions in East Asia. British policy made quick work of being on side with the new naval powers, imperial Japan and the United States. They could not contain Germany despite many peaceful overtures. The British Empire was being outflanked, and there was nothing that the British could do about it, nor, for that matter, the self-governing dominions. The prospect of a lasting friendship with Japan vanished totally when Japan broke solemn promises under the covenant of the League of Nations. Australia, New Zealand and Canada grew nervous, and they were not alone. In 1935 the Admiralty had advised the Foreign Office that the Navy could not fight Italy and imperial Japan at the same time, a telling factor, for it revealed that all along the route from Gibraltar to Hong Kong, and past Singapore, the old logic of a self-contained, self-defending empire had vanished. Britain made a vain promise to Australia and New Zealand that a main fleet would be dispatched to Singapore in time of need. Even that capability could not be shifted from the Atlantic and the Mediterranean when the time came.

The speed of these changes was rapid, the whole a flurry of late activity during the long afternoon of British supremacy. War came upon the British Empire in an unexpected flourish. British sea power could control Germany on the seas, but it was powerless to act beyond the range of the guns of its warships. In all of the diplomatic developments, the British Foreign Office was the key player, not the Royal Navy. The latter was merely the tool of the British state. The Foreign Office called the tune. It gathered the information and sifted it; it shaped the treaty-making process; and it formulated what became the British imperial war plan. The peace of Europe was the essential thing, and the well-thought-out position of Gladstone was everywhere in evidence in the actions of Sir Edward Grey, the foreign secretary, in the run-up to the outbreak of the war in 1914. The Continental Commitment was the result of the *entente cordiale*. This was an expedient in the last and failing years to hold up *Pax*. It could not be expected to work without material help from the armed services. The formidable power of imperial Germany brought down the whole edifice. The strain on the British imperial system and the British Empire was too great in the face of the enemy's strength. While historians will continue to seek explanations as to why the British system of global influence faltered, they had better realize that circumstances were rapidly spiralling out of control in early 1914. The enduring thought is that no matter how certain statesmen are about how the outside world may be controlled by statecraft backed by military power, the chaotic external players on the world stage, even runaway states with uniquely potent weapons and backed by zealous leaders with uncertain dispositions, pose a great danger to Europe's peace and that of the world.

British statesmen of the age of *Pax Britannica* were well informed by their knowledge of ancient and modern history. They were familiar with the scenarios of the rise and fall of empires. They trusted that theirs would continue. They did not trust to the past. They had not been born in revolution; rather the reverse. All the same, they lived in the present and for the immediate future. They were conscious of budgets and naval estimates that had to be voted for by Parliament. Economy of operations was a watchword of the age. Accountability for every shot and shell fired was the order of the day, duly observed. That secretaries and undersecretaries held their appointments for lengthy periods, despite the workloads, speaks of the continuities of policy. Of all the statesmen who held the ring, a few stand out: Castlereagh because he understood bases as anchors of empire and influence; Palmerston because he understood that the fleet, the gunboat and, if necessary, the landing party of sailors and marines were the best ways to back up British demands and long-range intentions; Gladstone because he worried about the financial obligations of naval and military power in the face of increasing worldwide obligations; Salisbury because he preached Splendid Isolation and saw it vanish; and Grey because, against all odds, he sought to avoid the catastrophe that came when imperial Germany sought to dominate Europe. Understandable variations in policies and preferences existed in the pronouncements and actions of these men. But looked at altogether there is a centrality of thinking. They had inherited a vast imperial edifice that had been built up over many centuries, notably during the years of Queen Anne, and they were largely favoured by the absence of a continental threat, except that in Grey's years at the Foreign Office the unravelling of the old order was quick. The First World War came upon Britain and the

British Empire like a vast storm coming all of a sudden into view. Nothing in the previous 100 years had prepared them for this. In fact, the conflagration was something that none of the great powers could have imagined. Armageddon, as Jacky Fisher had advertised, had come to be, and he was not far off the date he said it would come to pass.

With regard to imperial expansion, the above makes clear that the British Empire was not acquired in a fit of absentmindedness but in the long and incremental process of seeking and enhancing security. Turbulent frontiers brought the response of officials on the spot, all reviewed by London. Some acquisitions were annulled, the properties being returned to the local authority, with some regret on both sides of the equation. Keeping foreign rivals that were a threat, real or imagined, was always part of the consideration. Statesmen, secretaries and undersecretaries found themselves forced into circumstances that required action. They were reluctant imperialists. The same was true of admirals and captains afloat, and many are the cases in which distasteful actions were taken against what were regarded as recalcitrant persons ashore.

Anti-piracy and anti-slavery duties carried out by the Navy had little attraction to those who were on patrol. The work was dangerous because it was conducted in tropical waters where disease, poor water and boat work of an exposed nature took its toll on mind and body. The task was part of "heaven's command" and came in response to the power of the abolitionists who had vaulted into prominence in Britain. It was undeniably a crusade, but the fact of the matter is that the work of the Navy had to be teamed up with the work of the Foreign Office. Getting the compliance of other powers proved to be difficult. The actual use of force against difficult Brazil brought the slave trade there to an end. This was the last chapter of the long story. No historian of the Navy and the slave trade has claimed that the Navy ended the slave trade, and rightly so: the challenge was too difficult and there were too many ways that the deviants could use to carry out their nefarious deeds. In Parliament the futility of the work was expressed; some naval officers felt similarly. But it was carried out. Parliament and the press demanded it, as did all Christian denominations in Britain, not least the Quakers and the evangelical Anglicans. By the same token, the Navy responded to the needs of the state in support of missionaries in distant fields of endeavour. Many naval officers promoted the missionary cause but they did so privately. Many of them were members of temperance societies ashore and afloat. That naval officers were invariably members of the Church of England gave a unity of religious purpose to the Service, but this was always of an unstated and private nature. The Navy did the work of the Crown and the state, not the Church.

Independence of action by naval officers was a feature of the age. The man on the spot had to determine, given the evidence available, what the response should be. He would be mindful of what their lordships would or would not approve. He had to keep in mind also what the Foreign Office, the Cabinet and Parliament would accept. Because the corporate mindset of the officer corps was so well developed by tradition, training, example and experience, we find that naval officers acted with care and always with proportionate response to the circumstances. There is no denying that nowadays the shelling of native villages and the destruction of native canoes, the despoliation of native fields and places of shelter, and the deaths of innocent men, women and children ashore are unacceptable by any standards of civilized warfare. At that time, and in that age, the practitioners of gunboat diplomacy were mindful of the moral imperatives. The laws of war, therefore, derived from the circumstances of cross-cultural relations. The historian stands back from all of this with feelings of sadness and sorrow. Pacification was designed to bring peace, law and order; it was the repugnant last resort. The new Romans carried the banners of their forefathers. Those who do so today do likewise.

The historian in reviewing the dynamics of policy-making during *Pax Britannica* is struck by the stolid British reserve and restraint, a reluctance to intervene and, more, willingness out of necessity to leave well alone as the peoples of the world, in all their varieties and all their circumstances, endured their own march of progress or decline. It bears repeating in our own time that those who pursue a *Pax Americana* are ruled by circumstances largely not of their own choosing and certainly not of their own ability to change or correct. And yet the idea of peace established by armed force still persists, and the light still burns bright of a world in which the majestic holders of such power could bring universal peace to humankind. This biography of an idea has many chapters yet to be written, but the brightest of them was that of *Pax Britannica*, and we may never see its like again.

Notes

Prologue

1. Note: Admiralty (Adm.), Board of Trade (B.T.), Colonial Office (C.O.), Foreign Office (F.O.) and War Office (W.O.) documents are in the National Archives, Kew, Surrey, England (T.N.A.).
   Peter Ackroyd, *Thames: Sacred River* (London: Chatto & Windus, 2007), 187.
2. Joseph Conrad, "London River: The Great Artery of England" (1904), quoted ibid. 198–199.
3. Ibid., 209–210.
4. Joseph Conrad, *Heart of Darkness and The Secret Sharer* ([1910] New York: New American Library, 1950), 66–67.
5. Bernard Bailyn, *Voyagers to the West: Emigration to America on the Eve of the Revolution* (London: I.B. Tauris, 1986).
6. I.K. Steele, *Politics of Colonial Policy: The Board of Trade in Colonial Administration, 1686–1720* (Oxford: Oxford University Press, 1968), 4–8.
7. See Chapter 3, *Oxford History of the British Empire*, Volume 2.
8. J. Child, *A New Discourse of Trade* (2nd ed. London, 1694), 114–115; see also Charles H. Wilson, *Profit and Power: A Study of England and the Dutch Wars* (London: Longmans Green, 1957), 1.
9. D.A. Low, "Rule Britannia. Subjects and Empire: The Oxford History of the British Empire", *Modern Asian Studies*, 36, 2 (2002): 491–511, especially 500–501.
10. I owe this observation to D.A. Low in Canberra, 2002.
11. Quoted C.A. Bayly, *Atlas of the British Empire: The Rise and Fall of the Greatest Empire the World Has Ever Known* (London: Hamlyn, 1989), 90.
12. *Oxford History of the British Empire*, 2, Chapter.8.
13. *Oxford History of the British Empire*, 2, Chapter. 9; see also D.A. Low, "Rule Britannia. Subjects and Empire: *The Oxford History of the British Empire*", *Modern Asian Studies*, 36, 2 (2002): 492–493.
14. Thomas Arne set it to music.
15. Quoted in preface to Christopher Lloyd, *The Nation and the Navy: A History of Naval Life and Policy* (London: Cresset, 1954).
16. Quoted in Lord Esher's "Memoranda by Sir John Fisher, 1903–4", ESHR 7/3, Churchill Archives Centre, Cambridge.
17. Alfred T. Mahan, *Sea Power in Its Relation to the War of 1812* (2 vols.; Boston, Little, Brown, 1905), 2: 118.
18. Quoted in Harold Temperley, *The Foreign Policy of Canning, 1822–1827* (London, 1927), 463.
19. Quoted, *The Cambridge History of British Foreign Policy*, 3: 9–10. See also J.F.C. Fuller, *The Decisive Battles of the Western World and Their Influence upon History* (vol. 3 London: Eyre & Spottiswoode, 1963), 326.

1 Defining *Pax Britannica*

1. A.P. Thornton, *For the File on Empire: Essays and Reviews* (London: Macmillan, 1968), 381.
2. More correctly, as of 1815, Upper Canada (later Ontario), Lower Canada (the Province of Quebec), New Brunswick, Prince Edward Island and Nova Scotia. Labrador was an administrative appendage of Newfoundland. The Dominion of Canada was brought into being by imperial legislation, 1867, British Columbia joining the union in 1871.
3. H.W. Richmond, "Some Elements in Imperial Naval Defence", *Naval Review*, 21 (1933), 447.
4. Brian Tunstall, "Imperial Defence, 1815–1870", *Cambridge History of the British Empire, Volume 2* (Cambridge: Cambridge University Press, 1940), 808–809.
5. Hansard, 1st ser., XXXII, 1104.
6. Charles Webster, *The Foreign Policy of Castlereagh, 1812–1815* (London, 1931). Castlereagh's Memorandum on the Maritime Peace, 1815, is printed in Charles Webster, *British Diplomacy, 1813–1815* (London: G. Bell, 1921), 127.
7. Here I am guided by John H. Parry, *Trade and Dominion: the European Overseas Empires in the Eighteenth Century* (New York: Praeger, 1971), 329–337.
8. Cyprian Bridge, *Sea-Power and Other Studies* (London: Smith Elder, 1910), 63.
9. Anon, "Thalassarchie", *Encyclopédie*, 7 January 1765, in ibid., 63 (my translation).
10. *Naval Chronicle*, 32: 243.
11. Herbert Richmond, *Statesmen and Sea Power* (Oxford: Clarendon, 1946), 258.
12. John Briggs, *Naval Administrations, 1827–1892: The Experience of 65 Years* (London: Sampson, Low, Marston, 1897), 23.
13. Raymond Flower and Michael Wynn Jones, *Lloyd's of London* (rev. ed. London: Lloyds of London Press, 1983), 85.
14. John Barrow, *A Description of Pitcairn's Island and Its Inhabitants* ([1831] New York: Haskell House, 1972), 244–245.
15. Quoted, Andrew Lambert, "The Shield of Empire, 1815–1895", in Richard Hill, ed., *The Oxford Illustrated History of the Royal Navy* (Oxford: Oxford University Press, 1995), 162.
16. Henry Kissinger, *Diplomacy* (New York: Simon & Schuster, 1994).
17. Huskisson, Gladstone and similar views on the benefits of empire are analysed in A.G.L. Shaw, "British Attitudes to the Colonies, ca. 1820–1850", *Journal of British Studies*, 9, 1 (September 1969), 83.
18. Hansard, 3rd ser., 86: 1165–1167 (25 May 1846).
19. George R. Mellor, *British Imperial Trusteeship, 1783–1850* (London: Faber & Faber, 1951).
20. Margery Perham, *Colonial Reckoning: The Reith Lectures 1961* (London, 1963), 79.
21. Ibid., 79–80. *Report of the Select Committee on Aborigines* (1837: reprint, London, 1837), 7, 425.
22. Arthur Grimble, *A Pattern of Islands* (London: Reprint Society, 1954), 11–12.
23. John S. Galbraith, *Crown and Charter: The Early Years of the British South Africa Company* (Berkeley: University of California Press, 1974), 310–311.
24. Raymond F. Betts, "Allusions to Rome in British Imperialist Thought in the late Nineteenth and Early Twentieth Centuries", *Victorian Studies*, 15 (1971), 149–159.
25. S.J. Owen, "The Stability of Our Indian Empire", *Contemporary Review*, 31 (1878), 517. I owe this reference to Christopher Hagerman.

26. Published in the Britain and the World Series, Palgrave Macmillan, 2013.
27. *Journal of the Royal United Service Institution*, 30, 146 (1886), 837–861.
28. A.J.P. Taylor, *The Struggle for Mastery in Europe, 1848–1918* ([1954] Oxford: Oxford University Press, 1977), 235.
29. Hagerman, *op.cit.*
30. See Stanley Lane-Poole, ed., *Thirty Years of Colonial Government from the Dispatches and Letters of the Rt Hon Sir G.F. Bowen* (2 vols; London, 1889). Entry on Bowen in *Oxford Dictionary of National Biography*.
31. *Journal of the Royal United Service Institution*, 30, 46 (May 1886), 865.
32. For a discussion of this and related issues, Trevor Reese, *History of the Royal Commonwealth Society, 1868–1968* (London: Oxford University Press, 1969), 66–70.
33. J. Chamberlain, "The True Conception of Empire, 31 March 1897", in William Jennings Bryan, ed., *The World's Famous Orations* (10 vols.; New York: Funk and Wagnalls, 1906), 5, 184–191.
34. *Transactions of the Aborigines' Protection Society, 1890–1896*, new ser., 4, 1 (1896), 1.
35. Charles Wentworth Dilke and Spenser Wilkinson, *Imperial Defence* (rev. ed.; London: Archibald Constable, 1897), 35.

2 Empire of the Seas

1. Cyprian Bridge, *Sea-Power and Other Studies* (London: Smith Elder, 1910), 51–52. Andrew D. Lambert, *The Crimean War: British Grand Strategy against Russia, 1853–1856* (Manchester: University of Manchester Press, 1990) gives more specifics about maritime strategy and the defeat of Russia. The Ottoman Empire was the beneficiary.
2. The reference is to Christopher Cradock in Geoffrey Bennett, *Coronel and Falklands* (London: Pan, 1967), 15.
3. C.J. Bartlett, *Great Britain and Sea Power, 1815–1853* (Oxford: Clarendon, 1963); also Gerald S. Graham, *The Politics of Naval Supremacy: Studies in British Maritime Ascendancy* (Cambridge: Cambridge University Press, 1965), 108–110.
4. See "Ships on Overseas Stations, 1821–1900," in John Beeler (ed.) *British Naval Policy in the Gladstone-Disraeli Era, 1866–1880* (Stanford: Stanford University Press, 1997), 26–27, a comprehensive accounting on five-year intervals, with useful notes about station names, divisions and consolidations.
5. Much of what follows derives from Michael Lewis, *The Navy in Transition: A Social History, 1814–1864* (London: Hodder and Stoughton, 1965), and by the same, *A Social History of the Navy, 1793–1815* ([1960] London: Chatham, 2004).
6. Report of the Admiralty Committee on the System of Training Naval Cadets on Board HMS Britannia, *Parliamentary Papers*, v. 15 (1875), 347.
7. Theodore Ropp, *The Development of a Modern Navy: French Naval Policy, 1871–1904* (Annapolis, Naval Institute Press, 1987), 44.
8. E. Marjorie Moore, *Adventure in the Royal Navy: The Life and Letters of Admiral Sir Arthur William Moore* (Liverpool: privately printed, 1964), 17. Reforms in the cadet training ship *Britannia* may be followed in Commander E.P. Statham, *The Story of the "Britannia" the Training Ship for Naval Cadets with Some Account of Previous Methods of Naval Education, and of the New Scheme of 1903* (London: Cassell, 1904).
9. Frederic C. Dreyer, *The Sea Heritage: A Study of Maritime Warfare* (London: Museum Press, 1955), 26–27.
10. The reader's attention is drawn to the novels of Frederick Marryat as excellent accounts of stories (and scrapes) of sailors, ashore and afloat.

11. B.R. Haydon's autobiography, quoted in [Marion Coates], *Sea Sequel* (London: Nonesuch, 1935), 269.
12. Captain R. Burridge of the flagship *President* concluded that Price's action in shooting himself was a result of "intense mental anxiety". Burridge to Commodore Sir Frederick Nicolson, 30 August 1854, Cap N52, Adm. 1/5631.
13. Beeler, *British Naval Policy*, 102–103.
14. Leslie Gardiner, *The British Admiralty* (Edinburgh: William Blackwood, 1968), 313.
15. Geoffrey L. Lowis, *Fabulous Admirals and Some Naval Fragments* (London: Putnam, 1957), 11.
16. John Winton, *Jellicoe* (London: Michael Joseph, 1981) is a good introduction, but see also A. Temple Paterson, *Jellicoe* (London: Macmillan, 1969). On the *Victoria-Camperdown* collision and problems of communications at sea during manoeuvres (or in battle), see Andrew Gordon, *The Rules of the Game: Jutland and British Naval Command* (Annapolis: Naval Institute Press, 1996), especially 155–294.
17. For a recent analysis, see Denver Brunsman, *The Evil Necessity: British Naval Impressment in the Eighteenth-Century Atlantic World* (Charlottesville: University of Virginia Press, 2013).
18. David Phillipson, *Band of Brothers: Boy Seamen in the Royal Navy, 1800–1956* (Annapolis: Naval Institute Press, 1996), 13.
19. Ibid., 3.
20. Ibid., 4.
21. See, for an introduction, Denver Brunsman, *The Evil Necessity: British Naval Impressment in the Eighteenth-Century Atlantic World* (Charlottesville: University of Virginia Press, 2013), 249–251.
22. Phillipson, *Band of Brothers*, 14.
23. Richmond, *Statesmen and Sea Power*, 258–259.
24. Quoted, Phillipson, *Band of Brothers*, 22.
25. H.G. Ward to Vice Admiral James Dacres, 23 May 1848, Adm. 123/2, TNA.
26. Ibid.
27. Information from Eugene Rasor, 16 October 2011. For more details, see Eugene L. Rasor, *Reform in the Royal Navy: A Social History of the Lower Deck, 1850 to 1880* (Hamden, Conn.: Archon Books, 1976).
28. Phillipson, *Band of Brothers*, 49.
29. Arnold Wilson, *SW Persia: A Political Officers Diary, 1907–1914* (London: Oxford, 1941), 208.
30. Memorandum by the First Lord of the Admiralty, 12 January 1914, copy, T 1/11598/25942, TNA.

3 Anchors of Empire

1. Roger Willock, *Bulwark of Empire, Bermuda's Fortified Naval Base* (2nd ed.; Bermuda: Bermuda Maritime Museum Press, 1988), 83.
2. G.S. Graham, *The Politics of Naval Supremacy: Studies in British Maritime Ascendancy* (Cambridge: Cambridge University Press, 1965), 116.
3. Jonathan Coad, *Historic Architecture of the Royal Navy: An Introduction* (London: Victor Gollancz, 1983), 15.
4. On Esquimalt, international rivalry pressures, strategic shifts and technological changes mandating a new base there, see Barry Gough, *The Royal Navy and the Northwest Coast of North America, 1810–1914: A Study of British Maritime Ascendancy* (Vancouver: UBC Press, 1971).

5. See Ian Stranack, *The Andrew and the Onions: The Story of the Royal Navy in Bermuda, 1795–1975* (2nd ed., Bermuda: Bermuda Maritime Museum Press, 1990).
6. Algernon Aspinall, *Pocket Guide to the West Indies* (new and rev. ed.; London: Sifton, Praed, 1935).
7. Richard Cotter, Purser, RN, *Sketches of Bermuda, or Somer's Islands* (London, 1822), 66.
8. R.M. Martin, *British Colonial Library, Volume 4* (London, 1850), 229.
9. Quoted in James Morris, *Heaven's Command* (1973), 27.
10. William Frith Williams, *An Historical and Statistical Account of the Bermudas, from Their Discovery to the Present Time* (London, 1848), vi.
11. Quoted, Julian Gwyn, *Ashore and Afloat: The British Navy and the Halifax Yard before 1820* (Ottawa: University of Ottawa Press, 2004), 145.
12. American policy and naval activities in regard to Bermuda may be traced in William S. Dudley et al. eds., *The Naval War of 1812: A Documentary History* (Washington, DC: GPO. 3 vols. to date, 1985).
13. Stranack, *The Andrew and the Onions*, 4.
14. Here I have drawn heavily on George S. Ritchie, *The Admiralty Chart: British Naval Hydrography in the Nineteenth Century* (new ed.; Edinburgh, Pentland, 1995), 108–110.
15. See Gwyn, *Ashore and Afloat*, 145–148, 220–228.
16. The paternalism of the British Government has been demonstrated. See Gertrude Carmichael, *History of the West Indian Islands of Trinidad and Tobago, 1498–1900* (London: Alvin Redman, 1961), 136.
17. Each colony of the British Empire was formed of special circumstances, though there existed model templates as to the types of colony. Trinidad and Tobago had a mixed European population (Spanish, French and English) and was in need of labour for development. The Colonial Office, battered by long battles with the planter class in other West Indian colonies, did not want an extension of this kind of influence to Trinidad and Tobago. Nor did it want, on the grounds of the power exerted by the anti-slavery lobby, to extend slavery. Eventually, indentured labour from India was resorted to. The important thing here is that the Crown maintained its dominating power. Eric Williams, *History of the People of Trinidad and Tobago* (London: André Deutch, 1964), 51–85.
18. Willock, *Bulwark of Empire*, 86. Colonel F. Whittingham, *Bermuda, a Colony, a Fortress, and a Prison; or, Eighteen Months [1855–56]* (London, 1857), appendix (contains an account of the yellow fever epidemics in Bermuda).
19. H.C. Wilkinson, *Bermuda from Sail to Steam: A History of the Island from 1784 to 1901* (2 vols. 1973), 2:454.
20. H.J. Webb, *Narrative of the Voyage of H.M. Floating Dock "Bermuda" from England to Bermuda* (London, 1870).
21. Two battleships of the Lord Nelson class, the *Lord Nelson* and *Agamemnon*, were 16,500 tons, nominal measurement. Launched 1906, completed 1908. The *Dreadnought* was 17,900 tons, nominal measurement.
22. Edward Harris, *Great Guns of Bermuda: A Guide to the Principal Forts of the Bermuda Islands* (n.p. Bermuda Maritime Museum Assn., 1987), 11. Documented spying activities 1842–1852 (letters and drawings by officers of the US Army Corps of Engineers) are to be found in United States Archives. Ibid.
23. Brian Arthur, *How Britain Won the War of 1812: The Royal Navy's Blockades of the United States, 1812–1815* (Woodbridge: Boydell Press, 2011). Among her various valuable studies on privateering, see Faye Kert, "Cruising in Colonial Waters: The Organization of North American Privateering in the War of 1812", in David Starkey,

et al. eds., *Pirates & Privateers: New Perspectives on the War on Trade in the 18th and 19th Centuries* (Exeter: University of Exeter Press, 1977).

24. *Castlereagh Correspondence*, 5: 29–30; quoted in Sir Herbert Richmond, *Statesmen and Sea Power* (London: Oxford University Press, 1946), 340.
25. Admiral Sir Anthony Hopkins to J.A. Fisher, 27 August 1897, FISR 1/19, 30, Churchill Archives Centre, Cambridge.
26. Robin W. Winks, "William Jervois", *Dictionary of Canadian Biography*, 12 (Toronto: University of Toronto Press, 1990). Available online.
27. Reports Upon Leaving Command by Vice-Admirals Sir Houston Stewart, 1860, Sir Alexander Milne, 1864, and Sir James Hope, 1867 are in Adm. 128/114.
28. *Brassey's Naval Annual, 1889–9*, 705.
29. Quoted in Lance C Buhl, "Maintaining 'An American Navy' 1865–1889", in Kenneth J. Hagan, ed., *In Peace and War: Interpretations of American Naval History, 1775–1984* (2nd ed., Westport, Ct.: Greenwood, 1984), 155.
30. M.H. Ludington and Geoffrey Osborn, *The Royal Mail Steam Packets to Bermuda and the Bahamas, 1842–1859* (London: Robson Lowe, 1971).
31. Dilke and Wilkinson, *Imperial Defence*, 33–34.
32. Quoted, Peter Padfield, *Rule Britannia: The Victorian and Edwardian Navy* (London: Routledge & Kegan Paul, 1981), 4.
33. R.B. Pugh, *Records of the Colonial and Dominion Offices* (London: HMSO, 1964), 8. This work explains the new administrative requirements of this enhanced, diversified empire, the particulars of which are not the concern of this book.

4 Surveying the Seas, Expanding the Empire of Science

1. Laurence Kirwan, *White Road: A Survey of Polar Exploration* (London: Hollis & Carter, 1959).
2. Herman R. Friis, ed., *The Pacific Basin: A History of its Geographical Exploration* (New York: American Geographical Society, 1967), 221–255, especially, 250.
3. Memorandum of 24 May 1830, proposing founding the Geographical Society. Quoted in ibid., 74–75.
4. John Barrow, *Voyages of Discovery and Research within the Arctic Regions, from the Year 1818 to the Present Time* (London: J. Murray, 1846), 12; Christopher Lloyd, *Mr. Barrow of the Admiralty: a Life of Sir John Barrow* (London: Collins, 1970), chapters 7 and 8.
5. [Alman] *A Letter to John Barrow . . . on the Late Extraordinary and Unexpected Hyperborean Discoveries* (London: privately printed, 1826), 44–46.
6. R. Vesey Hamilton, ed., *Journals and Letters of Sir T. Byam Martin, vol I* (London: Navy Records Society, 1903), 115.
7. Ibid.
8. For a brief description of this unfortunate expedition, see Fergus Fleming, *Barrow's Boys* (New York: Atlantic Monthly Press, 1998), 13–27.
9. Barrow, *Voyages of Discovery*, viii.
10. William Laird Clowes, *The Royal Navy, a History, vol. 6* (London: Low Marston, 1901), 517.
11. John Franklin, *Voyage to the Polar Sea*, 319; Barrow, *Voyages of Discovery*, 17–18.
12. Quoted by James P. Delgado, in John Franklin, *Narrative of a Journey to the Shores of the Polar Sea in the Years 1819–20–21–22* (Vancouver: Douglas & McIntyre, 2000), 20.
13. A useful survey, containing an extensive bibliography, is Ann Savours, "The British Admiralty and the Arctic, 1773–1876," *Pôle Nord* (1983), 153–167. The North West

Company (before 1821) and the Hudson's Bay Company assisted in the quest for the Northwest Passage. See P.D. Baird, *Expeditions to the Canadian Arctic* (n.p., n.d.), reprinted from *The Beaver*, March, June and September 1949.

14. Maurice Hodgson, quoted in Franklin, *Journey to the Polar Sea* (reprint, 2000), 19.
15. See Trevor Levere, *Science and the Canadian Arctic: A Century of Exploration, 1818–1918* (Cambridge: Cambridge University Press, 1993).
16. Robert Falcon Scott, "Introduction to 1908 Edition of Franklin," *Journey to the Polar Sea* (reprint, 2000), 22.
17. L. S. Dawson, *Memoirs of Hydrography* ([1885] London: Cornmarket, 1969), 48.
18. T. Hurd, memorandum on the state of hydrography, 7 May 1814, enclosure in Hurd to Secretary of the Admiralty, 12 October 1816; quoted in Vice-Admiral Sir Archibald Day, *The Admiralty Hydrographic Service, 1795–1919* (London: HMSO, 1967), 27–29. See also George S. Ritchie, *The Admiralty Chart: British Naval Hydrography in the Nineteenth Century* (new ed.; Edinburgh: Pentland Press, 1995), 115–116. This new edition contains an important introduction by Andrew David.
19. List of Admiralty Ships Employed on Missions of Discovery, etc., 1669–1860, R. 3/34, 5–19, TNA. For various expeditions, notably of the Navy and often in conjunction with the Hudson's Bay Company, see A. Cooke and Clive Holland, *Exploration of Northern Canada, 500–1920; A Chronology* (Toronto: History Press, 1978). Also, John Caswell, "Sponsors of Canadian Arctic Exploration, III, 1800–1839," *The Beaver*, 300 (1969), 26–33.
20. Quoted in Day, Admiralty *Hydrographic Service*, 357.
21. This, and discussion of Hawaiian annexation and freedom of access to ports, may be followed in Gough, *Royal Navy and the Northwest Coast*, 29–49.
22. Among other sources, see Richard A. Pierce, *Russia's Hawaiian Adventure, 1815–1818* (Berkeley and Los Angeles: University of California Press, 1965), 26.
23. S. B. Okun, *The Russian-American Company*, trans. Carl Ginsburg (Cambridge, MA: Harvard University Press, 1951), chapters 6 and 7.
24. Quoted in Kirwan, *Polar Exploration*, 77.
25. Sir John Pelly to Lord John Russell, 6 February 1841, Barrow to Stephen 11 February 1841, and Stephen to Sir John Pelly, 16 February 1841, C.O. 42/485.
26. For the revival of British Arctic exploration in the early years of *Pax Britannica*, see M.J. Ross, *Polar Pioneers: John Ross and James Clark Ross* (Montreal: McGill-Queen's University Press, 1994), 23–33.
27. See Harold W.V. Temperley, *Foreign Policy of Canning, 1822–1827* (London: G. Bell, 1925), 104–105, and, most importantly, John S. Galbraith, *The Hudson's Bay Company as an Imperial Factor, 1821–1869* (Berkeley and Los Angeles: University of California Press, 1957), 133 and n. 62.
28. Barry M. Gough, ed., *To the Arctic and Pacific with Beechey: The Journal of Lieutenant George Peard of H.M.S. "Blosson," 1825–1825* (Cambridge: Hakluyt Society, 1973).
29. See the narrative of the *Bounty* as gathered by Peard, in ibid., 80–95.
30. Alfred Friendly, *Beaufort of the Admiralty: The Life of Sir Francis Beaufort, 1774–1857* (London: Hutchinson, 1977), 129.
31. Mary Blewitt, *Surveys of the Seas* (London: MacGibbon and Kee, 1957); quoted in ibid., 247.
32. Philip Parker King, *Narrative of the Survey of the Intertropical and Western Coasts of Australia* (London: John Murray, 1832).
33. Friendly, *Beaufort of the Admiralty*, 252.
34. Ibid.
35. Ritchie, *The Admiralty Chart*, 189.

36. Many are published in James Colnett, *A Voyage to the South Atlantic and Round Cape Horn into the Pacific Ocean* (London, 1798).
37. George Basalla, "The Voyage of the *Beagle* without Darwin," *Mariner's Mirror*, 49 (1963), 42–48. Also, Keith S. Thomson, *HMS Beagle: The Ship that Changed the Course of History* (London: Orion, 2003).
38. Friendly, *Beaufort of the Admiralty*, 299, prints the correspondence.
39. On this, see Peter Nichols, *Evolution's Captain: The Dark Fate of the Man Who Sailed Charles Darwin Around the World* (New York: HarperCollins, 2003). Also, H.E.L. Mellersh, *FitzRoy of the Beagle* (London: Rupert Hart-Davis, 1968). Also, Alan Moorehead, *Darwin and the Beagle* (London: Hamish Hamilton, 1969).
40. E. Belcher to Rear Admiral C.B.H. Ross, 17 December 1839, from San Blas, copy, F.O. 204/67, fols. 512–516.
41. On the *Sulphur* and *Starling* surveying voyage, see Gough, *Royal Navy and the Northwest Coast*, 43, 45–48.
42. Friendly, *Beaufort of the Admiralty*, 254.
43. Ibid., 255.
44. I agree with Fleming's view that many doubts were raised about the veracity of Rae's evidence, which was largely (as far as I can determine) unsupported by other data. Rae felt slighted, oddly, and wanted more attention than he got. Still, he was awarded £10,000 for his share in ascertaining Franklin's fate. Captain Robert McClure received an equal amount. The Admiralty seems to have been pleased to have at last wound up the prize-hunting business. Fleming, *Barrow's Boys*, 410, 411, 429 and 440. A study of how the Admiralty determined who would receive what in the prize-money stakes would make for interesting reading, if ever undertaken.
45. Andrew Lambert, *The Gates of Hell: Sir John Franklin's Tragic Quest for the North West Passage* (New Haven: Yale University Press, 2009).
46. Much has been written about Franklin and will be so in the future. He was an outstanding naval officer, and his third expedition has best been described by the classic one not to be ignored: Richard J. Cyriax, *Sir John Franklin's Last Expedition: The Franklin Expedition, a Chapter in the History of the Royal Navy* ([1939] Plaistow, West Sussex: the Arctic Press, 1997).
47. David Murphy, *The Arctic Fox: Francis Leopold McClintock, Discoverer of the Fate of Franklin* (Toronto: Dundurn, 2004), 177–178.
48. Somehow he received £5,000 for his information but never got the big prize of £20,000 that he thought was his due.
49. See R.L. Richards, "John Rae," *Dictionary of Canadian Biography*, v. 12, 876–79.
50. See "Sketch Map of Eastern Newfoundland" showing supposed position of the iceberg, 1851. MPI/320(1), TNA.
51. F.W. Beechey, "Presidential Address for 1856", *Proceedings of the Royal Geographical Society*, 26 (1856), ccviii–1x.
52. Quoted, Hugh Wallace, *The Navy, the Company, and Richard King: British Exploration in the Canadian Arctic, 1829–1860* (Montreal: McGill-Queen's University Press, 1980), 13.
53. A.G.N. Wyatt, *Charting the Seas in Peace and War* (London: HMSO, 1947); quoted, Friendly, *Beaufort of the Admiralty*, 248.
54. Minute by G. Goshen, 25 November 1872, in Day, *Admiralty Hydrographic Service*, 85.
55. Richards, minute of 25 November 1872, and Admiral Dacres, minute of same date, in ibid.
56. Dawson, *Memoirs of Hydrography*, 137.

57. See the entry on him, and related entries, in John T. Walbran, *British Columbia Coast Names, 1592–1906: To Which Are Added a Few Names in Adjacent United States Territory, Their Origin and History* ([1909] Vancouver: J.J. Douglas, 1971), 421–422.
58. Jane Samson, "An Empire of Science: The Voyage of HMS *Herald*, 1845–1851," in Alan Frost and Jane Samson eds., *Pacific Empires: Essays in Honour of Glyndwr Williams* (Melbourne: Melbourne University Press, 1999), 74–75.
59. R.J.B. Knight, "John Lort Stokes and the New Zealand Survey, 1848–1851," in Frost and Sampson ed., *Pacific Empires*, 87–99.
60. Quoted, ibid., 96.
61. Stokes to Gladstone, 15 July 1851, and the reply, 30 August 1851, STK 52, NMM.
62. Eric Linklater, *The Voyage of the Challenger* (London: Penguin, 1972).
63. David Howarth, *Sovereign of the Seas: the Story of British Sea Power* (London: Collins, 1974), 326.
64. The rise of Germany as a commercial, maritime and, above all, naval power has been dealt with by a host of historians. For an excellent brief survey, see Paul G. Halpern, *A Naval History of World War I* (Annapolis: Naval Institute Press, 1994), 1–20. See also, among other studies, Volker R. Berghahn, *Germany and the Approach of War in 1914* (New York: St. Martin's Press, 1973) and Gary E. Weir, *Building the Kaiser's Navy: The Imperial Naval Office and German Industry in the von Tirpitz Era, 1890–1919* (Annapolis: Naval Institute Press, 1992).
65. Selborne letter, 31 October 1901, in D. George Boyce, ed., *The Crisis of British Power: The Imperial and Naval Papers of the Second Earl of Selborne, 1895–1910* (London: Historian's Press, 1990), 136.
66. A. von Tirpitz, *My Memoirs* (2 vols.; London: Hurst & Blackett, 1919), 1:67.
67. Day, *Admiralty Hydrographic Service*, 208–209.
68. Ibid., 251–252.

5 Informal and Formal Empires in the Americas

1. The treaty is known as Clayton–Bulwer (1850).
2. Jerry Bannister, *The Rule of the Admirals: Law, Custom, and Naval Government in Newfoundland, 1699–1832* (Toronto: University of Toronto Press, 2003).
3. Herman Merivale, *Lectures on Colonization and Colonies* (2nd ed. London: Longman, Green, Longman and Roberts, 1861), vi–vii.
4. Paul Knaplund, *James Stephen and the British Colonial System, 1813–1847* (Madison: University of Wisconsin Press, 1953), 91–93.
5. A. G. L. Shaw, ed., *Great Britain and the Colonies, 1815–1865* (London: Methuen, 1970), 2.
6. John Gallagher and R.E. Robinson, "The Imperialism of Free Trade", *Economic History Review*, 2nd series, 6 (1953), 1–15.
7. Albert H. Imlah, *Economic Elements in the "Pax Britannica"* (Cambridge, MA: Harvard University Press, 1958), 186.
8. Paul Kennedy, *The Rise of Anglo-German Antagonism, 1860–1914* (London: George Allen & Unwin, 1982), 5.
9. J. Blankett to E. Nepean, 25 January 1795, in Vincent Harlow and Frederick Madden, eds., *British Colonial Developments, 1774–1834: Select Documents* (Oxford: Clarendon, 1953), 19–21.
10. On this point, see Oliver Macdonagh, "The Anti-Imperialism of Free Trade", *Economic History Review*, 2nd series, 14 (1961).

11. J.W. Croker to H.U. Addington, 6 March 1846, Addington to Croker, 6 March 1846, F.O. 5/460.
12. See the important Abraham P. Nasatir and Gary Elwyn Monell, comps., *British Activities in California and the Pacific Coast of North America to 1860: An Archival Guide* (San Diego: San Diego State University Press, 1990).
13. Robert Erwin Johnson, *Thence Round Cape Horn: The Story of United States Forces on Pacific Station, 1818–1923* (Annapolis: United States Naval Institute, 1963), 1, 6, 79.
14. T. Jefferson to T. Leiper, June 1815, in Dorothy K. Coveney and W.H. Mendlicott, eds., *The Lion's Tail: An Anthology of Criticism and Abuse* (London: Constable, 1971), 177.
15. Gough, *Royal Navy and the Northwest Coast*, 8–28, and, for more extensive treatment, by the same author, *Fortune's a River: The Collision of Empires in Northwest America* (Madeira Park, BC: Harbour Publishing, 2007), 303–41.
16. Barry Gough, *Fighting Sail on Lake Huron and Georgian Bay: The War of 1812 and Its Aftermath* (Annapolis: Naval Institute Press, 2002), 122–36.
17. George Raudzens, *The British Ordnance Department and Canada's Canals, 1815–1855* (Waterloo: Wilfrid Laurier University Press, 1979).
18. Regis A. Courtemanche, *No Need of Glory: The British Navy in American Waters, 1860–1864* (Annapolis: Naval Institute Press, 1977) for discussion. See especially 175.
19. R. A. Humphreys, ed., *British Consular Reports on the Trade and Politics of Latin America, 1824–1826* (London: Camden Society, 1940), viii–ix. For further particulars, see D.C.M. Platt, *Finance, Trade and Politics in British Foreign Policy, 1815–1914* (Oxford: Clarendon, 1968), 322–23. Principal: in-letters to the Admiralty are printed in Gerald S. Graham and R.A. Humphreys, eds., *The Navy and South America, 1807–1823: Correspondence of the Commanders-in-Chief on the South American Station* (London: Navy Records Society, 1962).
20. Michael Barratt Brown, *The Economics of Imperialism* (Harmondsworth: Penguin, 1974), 170.
21. Quoted in Dexter Perkins, *The Monroe Doctrine, 1823–1826* (Cambridge: Harvard University Press, 1932), 154.
22. Charles K. Webster, *Britain and the Independence of Latin America* (2 vols. London, Oxford University Press, 1938), 1: 11.
23. Quoted in Neville Thompson, *Earl Bathurst and the British Empire* (Barnsley: Leo Cooper, 1999), 147.
24. John Barrow, *A Voyage to Cochinchina* [1806] (reprint, Kuala Lumpur: Oxford University Press, 1975), 134. Barrow, who saw Río, devotes three chapters to Brazil.
25. Rudy Bauss, "Río de Janeiro: Strategic Base for the Global Designs of the British Royal Navy, 1777–1815", in Craig L. Symonds, ed., *New Aspects of Naval History* (Annapolis: Naval Institute Press, 1981), 75–89.
26. Instructions to Rear Admiral Sir William Sidney Smith, 25 January 1808, Adm. 2/1365; also, Canning to Admiralty, 25 December 1807, secret, Adm. 1/4206.
27. Brian Vale, *Independence or Death! British Sailors and Brazilian Independence, 1822–25* (London: Tauris, 1996).
28. Rear Admiral Sir T. Baker to Captain W. Waldegrave, [?] April 1831, Adm. 1/35.
29. Baker to Secretary of the Admiralty, 14 June 1831, and Admiralty minute of 16 August 1831, Adm. 1/36.

30. Service career details from Graham and Humphreys, *Navy and South America*, 158; see also Bowles to Manley Dixon, 11 April 1814, enclosed in Dixon to J. Croker, 16 April 1816, Adm. 1/22, and Bowles to C. Wood, 27 July 1838, Adm. 1/1568, CapB 174.
31. Platt, *Finance, Trade and Politics*, 322–23; John F. Cady, *Foreign Interventions in the Río de la Plata, 1838–50* (Philadelphia: University of Pennsylvania Press, 1929); and Henry S. Ferns, *Britain and Argentina in the Nineteenth Century* (Oxford: Clarendon, 1960).
32. Graham and Humphreys, *Navy and South America*, xxxiv.
33. Special instructions to Captains... Pacific, 25 January 1858, Adm.1/5694, Y192.
34. Barry Gough, *The Falkland Islands/Malvinas: The Contest for Empire in the South Atlantic* (London: Athlone, 1992). Despite my heroic attempts to write a neutral history of this subject, I discovered that my reviewers were invariably inspired by anti-imperial motives. I learned how difficult must have been Sisyphus's calling.
35. Discussion of Foreign Office and Admiralty positions on reasserting authority are given in ibid., 85–94.
36. The key documents are Palmerston to Admiralty, 30 August 1832, Adm.1/4249, and Admiralty reply of the next day, FO 6/499. Onslow's instructions, 28 November 1832, are in Adm.1/40; his report on proceedings, 19 January, is in Adm.1/2276.
37. A.J. Coles to B. Gough, 2 July 1982, author's files. The modern account may be followed in Lawrence Freedman, *The Official History of the Falklands Campaign* (2 vols. London: Routledge, 2005), and a review of the same by Bernard Porter, "Palmerstonian," *London Review of Books*, 20 October 2005.
38. David Cordingly, *Cochrane: The Real Master and Commander* (London: Bloomsbury, 2007); Brian Vale, *The Audacious Admiral Cochrane: The True Life of a Naval Legend* (London: Conway, 2004).
39. Quoted, Ibid., 290.
40. Jorge Ortiz-Sotelo, "Peru and the British Naval Station (1808–1839)", PhD thesis, University of St Andrews, 1993.
41. All particulars of these regulations, which changed over time, are set forth in Barry Gough, "Specie Conveyance from the West Coast of Mexico in British Warships c. 1820–1870: An Aspect of the *Pax Britannica*", *Mariner's Mirror*, 69, 4 (November 1983): 419–433.
42. T. Byam Martin to R. Barrie, 5 April 1822, Navy Office, Barrie papers, SPC Ms, FC441.B3 A4 1967, Royal Military College of Canada, Kingston, Ontario.
43. Ibid., xi.
44. H.W. Bruce to Rear-Admiral Ross, 10 May 1839, Adm. 1/587, CapB 100.
45. Briggs, *Naval Administrations*, 29–30.
46. For sources, see Barry Gough, "HMS *America* on the North Pacific Coast", *Oregon Historical Quarterly*, 70, 4 (December 1969): 292–311.
47. Gough, *Royal Navy and the Northwest Coast*, 80–81. And, by the same author, "Specie Conveyance," 425–426.
48. Lieutenant T. Dawes, Journal of HMS *America*, JOD/42, MS 57/055, 107, NMM.
49. Briggs, *Naval Administrations*, 175.
50. A.E. Ekoko, "British Naval Policy in the South Atlantic," *Mariner's Mirror*, 66 (1980): 209–23.
51. I owe this insight to Prof. Ronald C. Newton, Simon Fraser University.
52. For further discussion, see Barry Gough, "Profit and Power: Informal Empire, the Navy and Latin America", in Raymond E. Dumett, ed., *Gentlemanly Capitalism and British Imperialism: The New Debate on Empire* (London: Longman, 1999), 69–81.

6 Challenges of Europe, the Mediterranean and the Black Sea

1. John Bew, *Castlereagh: Enlightenment, War and Tyranny* (London: Quercus, 2011), 454.
2. Harold Temperley, *England and the Near East: The Crimea* (London: Longmans Green, 1936), 61.
3. H. Palmerston, *Opinions and Policy of the Right Honourable Viscount Palmerston* ([1852] New York: Kraus, 1972), 132, 198, 246–49.
4. Conrad Thake, *William Scamp (1801–1872): An Architect of the British Admiralty in Malta* (Malta: Midsea Books, 2011). See also the review of same by Jonathan Coad, *Mariner's Mirror*, 98, 3 (August 2012): 377–78.
5. G.H. Francis, *Opinions and Policy of Lord Palmerston* (London, 1952), 413.
6. Robert Holland, *Blue-Water Empire: The British in the Mediterranean Since 1800* (London: Allen Lane/Penguin Press, 2012). This is not a work of maritime history, and its greatest contribution is its examination of British rule in an odd collection of towns, islands and protectorates.
7. Paul Johnson, *The Birth of the Modern: World Society, 1815–1830* (New York: HarperCollins, 1991), 692–701. Instructions and naval correspondence in Lady Bourchier, *Life of Admiral Sir Edward Codrington* (2 vols: London, 1873).
8. Palmerston's correspondence may be followed in Minto papers, National Maritime Museum. Christopher Lloyd, *Nation and the Navy: a History of Naval Life and Policy* (London: Cresset, 1961), 232.
9. Bartlett, *Great Britain and Sea Power*, viii–ix.
10. C. Northcote Parkinson, *Edward Pellew, Viscount Exmouth, Admiral of the Red* (London: Methuen, 1934), 419–72.
11. Graham, *Politics of Naval Supremacy*, 67–72.
12. Hansard, 3d ser, CXII, 25 June 1850; See also A.P. Thornton, *The Imperial Idea and Its Enemies: A Study in British Power* (2nd ed. London: Macmillan, 1985), 2–4.
13. Palmerston, quoted in Gregory Haines, *Gunboats on the Great River* (London: Macdonald and Jane's, 1976), vi.
14. See Agatha Ramm, ed., *The Political Correspondence of Mr. Granville and Lord Granville, 1868–76* (London, 1952) and *1876–86* (2 vols. London, 1962).
15. John Morley, *Life of William Ewart Gladstone* (3 vols. London: Macmillan, 1903), 1, 368–70. See also Philip Magnus, *Gladstone, a Biography* (London: John Murray, 1954), 95.
16. Bridge, *Sea-Power and Other Studies*, 229.
17. Victoria Schofield, *Every Rock, Every Hill: The Plain Tale of the North-East Frontier and Afghanistan* (London: Buchan and Enright, 1984), 150.
18. George N. Curzon, *Persia and the Persian Question* (2 vols. London: Longmans, Green, 1892), 1:4.
19. For a statement of the centrality of the northwestern passes of British India to the defence of the British Empire against Russian advance, see Dilke and Wilkinson, *Imperial Defence*, 88–109.
20. This was Curzon again. Ibid., 432.
21. Admiralty minute, 6 December 1854, Cap N52, Adm.1/5631. Commodore Nicolson's report, 19 September 1854, in the same document cluster, was a careful report on proceedings designed to protect all concerned. For discussion, Gough, *Royal Navy and the Northwest Coast*, 108–30.
22. Arthur J. Marder, *The Anatomy of British Sea Power: A History of British Naval Policy in the Pre-Dreadnought Era, 1880–1905* (New York: Alfred A. Knopf, 1940), 144–73.

23. Percy Sykes, *A History of Persia* (2nd ed. 2 vols. London: Macmillan, 1921), 2:380.

7 The Indian Ocean, Singapore and the China Seas

1. Quoted, Gerald S. Graham, *The China Station: War and Diplomacy, 1830–1860* (Oxford: Oxford University Press, 1978), viii.
2. Vincent T. Harlow, *The Founding of the Second British Empire, 1763–1793* (2 vols. London: Longmans, Green, 1952–1964).
3. Raffles, Memorandum submitted to G. Canning, Add. MSS. 31237, f.243; also, *Cambridge History of the British Empire*, 2: 598.
4. Maurice Collis, *Raffles* (London: Faber & Faber, 1966), 26.
5. Quotations from Reginald Coupland, *Raffles, 1781–1826* (Oxford: Oxford University Press, 1926), 101.
6. Ibid, 104.
7. Ibid., 113.
8. George Woodcock, *The British in the Far East* (New York: Athenaeum, 1969), 56.
9. Quoted, *Cambridge History of the British Empire*, 2: 614.
10. Coupland, *Raffles*, 127.
11. Cavanagh to Sec. to the Government of India, 31 December 1863, quoted in Nicholas Tarling, *British Policy in the Malay Peninsula and Archipelago, 1824–1871* (Kuala Lumpur, Oxford University Press, 1969), 78.
12. C.N. Parkinson, *British Intervention in Malaya, 1867–1877* (Singapore: University of Malaya Press, 1960), xv; cf. C.D. Cowan, *Nineteenth Century Malaya* (London: Oxford University Press, 1961); for historiographical reviews, see E. Chew, "Reasons for British Intervention in Malaya: Review and Reconsideration", *Journal of Southeast Asian History*, 6, 1 (March 1965), 81–93, and Damodar R. SarDesai, "British Expansion in Southeast Asia: the Imperialism of Trade in the Nineteenth Century", in Roger D. Long, ed., *The Man on the Spot: Essays in British Empire History* (Westport: Greenwood, 1995), 1–20.
13. Barry Gough, "India-based Expeditions of Trade and Discovery in the North Pacific in the late Eighteenth Century", *Geographical Journal*, 155, 2 (1989), 215–223.
14. H.V. Bowen, The *Business of Empire: The East India Company and Imperial Britain, 1756–1833* (Cambridge: Cambridge University Press, 2006), 28–29.
15. *Chinese Repository*, 6, 1 (May 1837), 1.
16. Quoted, Frank Welsh, *A History of Hong Kong* (London: HarperCollins, 1993), 33.
17. " 'Opium war' was 'a question-begging epithet' ", wrote Samuel Couling, editor of *Encyclopedia Sinica* (1917), 410, "and had unfortunately passed into current use." His more extensive treatment of "Opium and the Opium Question China" is given in ibid. 405–410.
18. J. Stephen, minute of 3 June 1843, C.O. 129/3; Welsh, *History of Hong Kong*, 7; Jan Morris, *Hong Kong* (New York: Random House, 1988), 235.
19. Quoted Roger Pelissier, *Awakening of China, 1793–1949* (New York: Putnam, 1967), 90; see also Welsh, *History of Hong Kong*, 1.
20. One scholar who has looked at the Admiralty papers stresses that the purpose of British warships was far from belligerent.

    > The Board of Admiralty wished the captains and commanders to be impressed with their responsibilities for the promotion of peace with the Chinese people.

> They laid emphasis on the respect due to Chinese authorities and populace, their usages and institutions. They expected naval officers to study Chinese wishes and feelings in order to preserve amicable relations 'with so peculiar a country as China where actions indifferent in themselves and which among European nations would lead to little or no inconvenience, might produce an impression highly unfavorable to the British character and destructive of that wholesome influence which it is so important should attach in China to everything connected with Great Britain.' This instruction remained constant from 1846 through 1869.

Grace Fox, *British Admirals and Chinese Pirates, 1832–1869* (Westport: Hyperion, 1940), 59–60, quoting Instructions to Admiral Inglefield, 3 August 1846, Article 2, Adm.13/3.

21. Ibid. 38.
22. James Hope Grant, *Incident in The War in China* (London, 1860), 224–225.
23. Russell to Admiralty, 10 November 1860, Adm. 1/5745. Graham, *The China Station*, 406.
24. Graham, *The China Station*, 419.
25. Ibid., 421.
26. D.G.E. Hall, *A History of South-East Asia* (2nd ed.; London: Macmillan, 1964), 521–532.
27. Details of the East Indies' station limits before and after the key reorganization year of 1844 are found in Graham, *China Station*, 423.
28. Henry Keppel, *The Expedition to Borneo of H.M.S. Dido for the Suppression of Piracy* (3rd ed. of 1847; reprint, London: Frank Cass, 1968), 2: 48–64 and elsewhere. For similar episodes of this critical period, see Tim Travers, *Pirates: A History* (Stroud: Tempus, 2007), 257–260; see also Harriette McDougall, *Sketches of Our Life at Sarawak* (London: SPCK, 1882).
29. Christopher Lloyd, *Nation and Navy* (London: Cresset Press, 1961), 229.
30. Ibid. Henry Keppel, *A Sailor's Life under Four Sovereigns* (3 vols. London, 1899); *The Times*, 18 January 1904. L.G.C. Laughton (rev. Andrew Lambert), "Keppel, Sir Henry", *Oxford Dictionary of National Biography*.
31. See the recent study by Robert J. Antony, "Turbulent Waters: Sea Raiding in Early Modern East Asia," *Mariner's Mirror*, 91, 1 (February 2013), 23–38, especially 30–31; for Malaya, see Nicholas Tarling, *Piracy and Politics in the Malay World: A Study of British Imperialism in Nineteenth Century South-East Asia* (Melbourne: Melbourne University Press, 1963).
32. David Lyon and Rif Winfield, *The Sail & Steam Navy List: All the Ships of the Royal Navy 1815–1889* (London: Chatham, 2004), 272–273.
33. Admiralty to Foreign Office, 21 July 1879, Adm.1/6485, S.208.
34. J. Stirling to Admiralty, 27 October 1854, Adm.1/5657, S.10.
35. For a survey of these developments and imperial rivalries, see Clark Reynolds, *Command of the Sea: The History and Strategy of Maritime Empires* (New York: William Morrow, 1974), 421–426.
36. Donald M. Schurman, *Imperial Defence, 1868–1887*, ed. John Beeler (London, Frank Cass, 2000), 111.
37. Ronald Robinson, "Non-European Foundations of European Imperialism", in Roger Owen and R.B. Sutcliffe, eds., *Studies in the Theory of Imperialism* (London: Longman, 1972), 132.

38. Here I have drawn on Richard Hill, " 'A Difficult Person to Tackle': Admiral of the Fleet Sir Gerard Noel", *Mariner's Mirror*, 98, 4 (November 2012), 491.
39. Ibid., 492–493.
40. See Gough, *Royal Navy and the Northwest Coast*, 235–236.
41. Arthur J. Marder, *Old Friends, New Enemies: The Royal Navy and the Imperial Japanese Navy, Volume 1: Strategic Illusions, 1936–1941* (London: Oxford University Press, 1981).
42. Gough, *Royal Navy and the Northwest Coast*, 235–239.

8 The Imperial Web in the South Pacific

1. Admiralty instructions dated 18 February 1854 to Captain Fremantle, Adm. 2/1697.
2. For a beginning, see Ged Martin, ed., *The Founding of Australia: The Argument about Australia's Origins* (Sydney: Hale & Iremonger, 1978). The naval stores and related arguments are advanced by Alan Frost; for counter positions, see David Mackay, *A Place of Exile: The Settlement of New South Wales* (Melbourne: Oxford University Press, 1985). For related views on commercial policy, see Margaret Steven, *Trade, Tactics and Territory* (Melbourne: Melbourne University Press, 1983).
3. John M. Ward, *British Policy in the South Pacific, 1786–1893* (Sydney: Australian Publishing, 1948), 39–41.
4. *Blossom* was on detached service (for exploration duties) and did not form part of the Pacific station's allocation of ships.
5. Bruce to Commodore Sulivan, 2 January 1838, Adm.1/1586, Cap B159.
6. Rear Admiral Ross to C. Wood, 23 January 1839, Adm.1/52.
7. H. Addington to Admiralty, 19 August 1843, F.O. 58/23. On Toup Nicholas's actions in support of the British Consul, see Ward, *British Policy in the South Pacific*, 70–71.
8. Pritchard to Palmerston, 9 November 1838, Palmerston's minute of 16 July 1839, Stephen to Fox-Strangways, 1 August 1839, and Palmerston to Pritchard, 9 September 1839, F.O. 58/15; see also W.P. Morrell, *Britain in the Pacific Islands* (Oxford: Clarendon, 1960), 72–73.
9. For discussion of imperial rivalries for Hawaii, see Gough, *Royal Navy and the Northwest Coast*, 34–41.
10. Information from James A. Boutilier.
11. Ward, *British Policy in the South Pacific*.
12. Morrell, *Britain in the Pacific Islands*, 117–170, 361–399.
13. Neil Gunson, in Jane Samson, ed., *British Imperial Strategies in the Pacific, 1750–1900* (Aldershot: Ashgate, 2003), 276–278.
14. Sir Henry Byam Martin, *Grampus* journal, 28 July 1846, Martin Papers, Add. MSS 41472, British Library.
15. John Bach, *Australia Station: A History of the Royal Navy in the South West Pacific, 1821–1913* (Kensington, NSW: University of New South Wales University Press, 1965), 34, 56. Additional information from James A. Boutilier.
16. Sir J. Harding et al., Report to the Earl of Clarendon (F.O.), 28 July 1853, F.O. 83/2314, 188–189. Also in Clive Parry, comp., *Law Officers' Opinions to the Foreign Office, 1793–1860* (Westmead, Hants: Gregg International Publications, 1970), v. 51, 140–143.
17. *Congressional Record*, 44th Congress, 1st session, vol. LV, pt. 2, 6 March 1876, 1489. Cited in John I. Brookes, *International Rivalry in the Pacific Islands, 1840–1875* (Berkeley and Los Angeles: University of California Press, 1941), 379–380, 391.
18. Report of J. Washington on Fiji Islands, 12 March 1859, copy, in Adm.1/5721.

19. For reports and interdepartmental discussion, see "Correspondence re: Fiji Islands," *Parliamentary Papers*, 1862, XXVI, Cmd.2995.
20. G.F. Bodington to Sir J. Whitwell Pearse, MP, 24 October 1892, Aborigines' Protection Society manuscripts, C52/23, Rhodes House Library, Oxford.
21. Morrell, *Britain in the Pacific Islands*, 247.
22. Visiting the Republic of South Africa in the years after apartheid's end, I had perhaps naively believed that peace and reconciliation would come to the tribes and to the various communities. I was distressed to read about old scores being settled in intertribal or intervillage conflict in communities such as Richmond, Natal, the Pietermaritzburg and Durban, with newspapers reporting almost daily on murders and "cleansings". There were many old scores to settle. I wonder how often in the post-imperial experience this sort of thing happens. We know that the Irish Civil War that followed Partition there was far more violent than the Easter Rising and its aftermath. The Partition of India is another example of ethnic tensions released with the end of Britannic dominance.
23. Morrell, *Britain and the Pacific Islands*, 1.
24. Ibid., 355.

9 Send a Gunboat!

1. Dreyer, *Sea Heritage*, 43.
2. The Hale 24-pounder rocket was standard issue in the Victorian navy (high-pressure gas in the tail, generated by internal combustion). Hardly accurate, they "produced an awe-inspiring effect on bush tribes, to whom the prolonged and diabolical howl as they soared overhead almost suggested the wail of the last trumpet in the sky". George A. Ballard, "War Rockets in the Mid-Victorian Fleet," *Mariner's Mirror*, 31 (1945), 174.
3. This chapter draws on Barry Gough, *Gunboat Frontier: British Maritime Authority and Northwest Coast Indians, 1846–1890* (Vancouver: UBC Press, 1984).
4. W. Ross Johnston, *Sovereignty and Protection: A Study of British Jurisdictional Imperialism in the Late Nineteenth Century* (Durham, NC: Duke University Press, 1973), 13–16.
5. Quoted in C.C. Eldridge, *England's Mission: The Imperial Idea in the Age of Gladstone and Disraeli, 1868–1880* (London: Macmillan, 1973), xv–xvi.
6. Glenelg to Benjamin D'Urban, 26 December 1835, C.O. 49/28. For discussion of Glenelg's bolt from the blue, see Mellor, *British Imperial Trusteeship*, 249–251.
7. Ibid., 76.
8. Extract of a letter from G.H. Richards, 21 August 1859, enclosure in Rear Admiral R.L. Baynes to Governor J. Douglas, 26 August 1859, F1212a 24, Archives of British Columbia. For further discussion, see Gough, *Gunboat Frontier*, 79–81.
9. A.E. Kennedy to Rear Admiral Denman, 27 September 1864, in Adm. 1/5878, Y133.
10. Charles Moser, *Reminiscences of the West Coast of Vancouver Island* (Victoria: Acme, 1926), 190.
11. Denman to Admiralty, 19 October 1864, Adm. 1/5878, Y165.
12. W.F.B. Laurie, *Our Burma Wars and Relations with Burma* (London, 1880), 109; quoted in Daniel R. Headrick, *The Tools of Empire: Technology and European Imperialism in the Nineteenth Century* (New York: Oxford University Press, 1982), 54.
13. Joint statement of Clement Cornwall (Government of Canada) and J.J. Planta (British Columbia), 30 November 1887, in *Papers Relating to the Commission Appointed to Enquire into the State and Condition of the Indians of the Northwest Coast of*

British Columbia (Victoria, BC: Provincial Secretary's Office, 1888; reprinted Toronto: Canadiana House, 1979), 11.

14. Eugene Stock, *The History of the Church Missionary Society* (4 vols. London: Church Missionary Society, 1899–1916), 4, 383–388.
15. Ibid., 2, 614.
16. Gough, *Gunboat Frontier*, 148–158. Hudson's Bay Company steamers were employed, on request, in Puget Sound. Ibid., 58–59.
17. Nicholas Mansergh, *The Commonwealth Experience* (New York: Praeger, 1969), 10.
18. Eugene Arima and Alan Hoover, *The Whaling People of the West Coast of Vancouver Island and Cape Flattery* (Victoria: Royal BC Museum, 2011), 148.
19. Quoted in Antony Preston and John Major, *Send a Gunboat! A Study of the Gunboat and its Role in British Policy* (London: Longmans, 1967), 8.
20. Moresby, *Two Admirals*, 107.
21. Preston and Major, *Send a Gunboat!* 37–38.
22. Quoted in C.J. Bartlett, "The Mid-Victorian Reappraisal of Naval Policy," in Kenneth Bourne and D.C. Watt, eds., *Studies in International History: Essays Presented to W. Norton Medlicott* (London: Longmans, 1967), 205.
23. For an introduction, including a discussion of censuses, see Robert Boyd, *The Coming of the Sprit of Pestilence: Introduced Infectious Diseases and Population Decline among Northwest Coast Indians, 1774–1874* (Vancouver: UBC Press, 1999).

10 Anti-Slavery: West Africa and the Americas

1. James Watt, "Sea Surgeons and Slave Ships: A Nineteenth Century Exercise in Life-Saving", *Transactions of the Medical Society of London*, 104 (1987–1988), 130.
2. Quoted, E.A. Ayandele, *The Missionary Impact on Modern Nigeria, 1842–1914* (London: Longmans, 1966), 28.
3. Niall Ferguson, *Empire: The Rise and Demise of the British World Order and the Lessons for Global Power* (New York: Basic Books, 2002), 98.
4. Eric Williams, *Capitalism and Slavery* (Chapel Hill: University of North Carolina Press, 1944).
5. Seymour Drescher, *Econocide: British Slavery on the Eve of Abolition* (Pittsburg: University of Pittsburg Press, 1977).
6. A review of the literature is in Selwyn Carrington, "The State of the Debate on the Role of Capitalism in the Ending of the Slave System", *Journal of Caribbean History*, 22, 1–2 (1988), 20–41; reprinted in Verene Shepherd and Hilary McD. Beckles, *Caribbean Slavery in the Atlantic World: A Student Reader* (Oxford: James Currie, 2000), 1031–1041.
7. Philip D. Curtin, *The Atlantic Slave Trade, a Census* (Madison: University of Wisconsin Press, 1969), 265.
8. Arnold W. Lawrence, *Trade Castles and Forts of West Africa* (Stanford: Stanford University Press, 1964).
9. John Keegan, "The Ashanti Campaign 1873–1874", in Brian Bond, ed., *Victorian Military Campaigns* (London: Hutchinson, 1967).
10. Christopher Fyfe, *A History of Sierre Leone* (Oxford: Oxford University Press, 1962).
11. Georg Otto Trevelyan, *The Life and Letters of Lord Macaulay* (2 vols in one: New York: Harper & Brothers, 1874), 1: 74, where Stephen is quoted at length.

12. Watt, "Sea Surgeons and Slave Ships", 130–148. This study also examines the role of naval surgeons in anti-slavery efforts in the nineteenth century, the efforts of Dr W.B. Blaikie being particularly notable.
13. George Francis Dow, *Slave Ships & Slaving* (reprint, Toronto: Coles, 1980), 181. Additional details from Merseyside Museum, Liverpool.
14. Paul Mbaeyi, *British Military and Naval Forces in West African History, 1907–1874* (New York: NOK Publishers, 1978), 16.
15. Alfred Burdon Ellis, *History of the First West India Regiment* (London: Chapman and Hall, 1885).
16. Mbaeyi, *British Military and Naval Forces*, 62–63.
17. John Winton, *An Illustrated History of the Royal Navy* (London: Salamander, 2000), 106.
18. Reginald Coupland, in J. Holland Rose, A. P. Newton and E. A. Benians, eds, *Cambridge History of the British Empire* (8 vols. Cambridge: Cambridge University Press, 1929–1959), 2: 216.
19. John Parry, *Trade and Dominion: The European Overseas Empires in the Eighteenth Century* (London: Cardinal, 1974), 431.
20. Ibid., 432.
21. Howard I. Chapelle, *The Search for Speed Under Sail* (London: George Allen & Unwin, 1968), 299.
22. Among other sources, George M. Brooke, Jr., "The Role of the United States Navy in the Suppression of the African Slave Trade", *American Neptune*, 21 (1961): 28–41; Alan R. Booth, "The United States African Squadron, 1843–1851", *Boston University Papers in African History* (Boston, 1964); Judd S. Harman, "Marriage of Convenience: the United States Navy in Africa, 1820–1847", *American Neptune*, 32 (1972), 264–274; and A. H. Foote, *The African Squadron* (1855).
23. From P.W. Brock, HMS *Rocket* dossier, 4, Maritime Museum of British Columbia, Victoria (copy in National Maritime Museum).
24. Christopher Lloyd, *The Navy and the Slave Trade: The Suppression of the African Slave Trade in the Nineteenth Century* (London: Longmans Green, 1949), 57.
25. His Gold Coast report 1821 is in WEL/10, National Maritime Museum, Greenwich.
26. J. Barrow to J. Hay, 27 September 1830, C.O. 82/3.
27. Mbaeyi, *British Military and Naval Forces*, 84–85. The episode and related aspects may be followed in W.O. 1/573 and 488.
28. Elliott to J. Croker, 11 November 1826, C.O. 267/76.
29. Ronald Robinson and John Gallagher with Alice Denny, *Africa and the Victorians: the Climax of Imperialism* (New York: Anchor, 1968), 34.
30. Briggs, *Naval Administrations*, 55.
31. P. Campbell to C. Wood, 28 April 1838, Adm. 7/604, no. 8 (Admiralty miscellanea).
32. Conference on board Her Majesty's ship *Bonnetta*, 11 March 1839, *Parliamentary Papers*, LXIV, "Papers Relating to Engagements Entered into by King Pepple and the Chiefs of the Bonny" [970], 2–3. Also, Jane Samson, ed., *The British Empire* (Oxford: Oxford University Press, 2001), 129–130.
33. Palmerston to Minto, 25 February 1841, Minto papers, NMM, and same to same, 1 June and 28 July 1841, F.O. 84/384.
34. Lloyd, *The Navy and the Slave Trade: the Suppression of the African Slave Trade in the Nineteenth Century* (London: Longmans Green, 1949).
35. Aberdeen's instructions, 14 December 1842, Aberdeen papers, Add MSS 40453, British Library. Here and elsewhere, particularly in this chapter, I have relied on R.J. Gavin, "Palmerston's Policy towards East and West Africa, 1830–1865,"

unpublished PhD thesis, Cambridge University, 1959. The specific reference here is p. 151.

36. Thomas Fowell Buxton, *The African Slave Trade and Its Remedy* ([1839] London: Dawsons, 1968), 512–513.
37. Howard Temperley, *White Dreams, Black Africa: The Antislavery Expedition to the Niger, 1841–1842* (London: Yale University Press, 1991).
38. I take this directly from Lloyd, *Navy and the Slave Trade*, 106.
39. Instructions to Captain Trotter of Niger expedition, January 1841, C.O. 2/21.
40. Palmerston to Grey, 11 December 1849, copy, F.O. 84/780.
41. Quoted, Lloyd, *Navy and the Slave Trade*, 110.
42. Palmerston's instructions to Beecroft, 21 February 1851, F.O. 84/858. Also, Ronald Hyam, *Britain's Imperial Century, 1815–1914: A Study of Empire and Expansion* (New York: Barnes and Noble, 1976), 23.
43. Grey to N.M. Macdonald, 7 November 1848, C.O. 268/4. See also Colin Newbury, ed., *British Policy towards West Africa: Select Documents, 1786–1874* (Oxford: Clarendon, 1965).
44. Mbaeyi, *British Military and Naval Forces*, 131.
45. "Papers Relative to the Reduction of Lagos...", *Parliamentary Papers*, 1852, LIV. See also W.B.R., "Lagos 1851", *Naval Review*, August 1851, 271–277, which lists all vessels and promotions.
46. K. Onwuka Dike, *Trade and Politics in the Niger Delta, 1830–1885: An Introduction to the Economic and Political History of Nigeria* (Oxford, 1956), 175; see also Newbury, *British Policy towards West Africa*, 120.
47. Quoted in John Darwin, *Unfinished Empire: The Global Expansion of Britain* (London: Penguin, 2013), 61.
48. *Parliamentary Papers, 1867–1868* [167], vol. xlv, 638–639; Bartlett, "Mid-Victorian Reappraisal of Naval Policy", 193.
49. A.P. Eardley-Wilmot to Admiralty, 19 December 1865, Adm. 123/184, sec.1, no. 4A.
50. Addington minute, 23 February 1853, F.O. 101/34; Gavin, "Palmerston's Policy", 195.
51. Brock, dossier on HMS *Rocket*, Maritime Museum of British Columbia.
52. Leslie Gardiner, *The British Admiralty* (Edinburgh: Blackwood, 1968), 218.
53. Slave importations to Brazil dropped: 42,000 in 1839, 14,000 in 1841, 17,000 in 1842, and indication that the Navy's net was not as effective as might be imagined. Figures from Gavin, "Palmerston's Policy", 140. Foote's report is noted in Admiralty to Foreign Office, 23 November 1842, F.O. 84/445.
54. Quoted in Bartlett, "Mid-Victorian Reappraisal of Naval Policy", 193.
55. ["Wacelet"] *Cox and the JuJu Coast: A Journal Kept Aboard HMS "Fly" 1868/9 by John George Cox* (St. Helier, Ellison, n.d.), passim.
56. Ibid., xxv.
57. Commodore Dowell's guidance for Senior Officers West Coast Africa, 14 July 1870, C.O. 267/308/7722. This came in consequence of the importunate Sir Arthur Kennedy, governor of Sierra Leone, and his demands for protection, plus his complaint against the inaction of HMS *Rocket*, under Captain Walshe, who refused to "punish" offenders. Kennedy to C.O. 23 May 1870, C.O. 267/305/6320.
58. Roger Anstey, *The Atlantic Slave Trade and British Abolition, 1760–1810* (London: Macmillan, 1975).
59. Chapelle, *Search for Speed Under Sail*, 319. This lists four vessels. There were many such, with the ex-slaver *Bella Josephina*, renamed *Adelaide*; *Henriquetta*, renamed *Black Joke*; *Dos Amigos*, renamed *Fair Rosamond*; and *Caroline*, renamed *Fawn* among the

principal ones. *Black Joke* and *Fair Rosamond* were built at Baltimore and had long naval service as slave-catchers. See further particulars in Howard I. Chapelle, *The History of American Sailing Ships* (New York: Bonanza Books, 1985), 156–164; see David Lyon and Rif Winfield, *The Sail & Steam Naval List: All the Ships of the Royal Navy 1815–1889* (London: Chatham, 2004), 134–135, notes at least eight schooners that were wrecked on reefs, keys, coasts of the West Indies and Caribbean, 1826–1835, and most of these were ex-pirate or ex-slave vessels taken into imperial service. More complete surveys were needed, sailing directions, buoys and lighthouses too; but these were stormy waters, subject to heavy weather (notably gales and hurricanes).

60. Laird Clowes, *Royal Navy: A History*, 6, 234.
61. Hugh Thomas, *The Slave Trade: The Story of the Atlantic Slave Trade, 1440–1870* (New York: Simon & Shuster, 1997), 749–785; David R. Murray, *Odious Commerce: Britain, Spain, and the Abolition of the Cuban Slave Trade* (New York: Cambridge University Press, 1980) recounts the difficult diplomatic issues.
62. Leslie Bethell, *The Abolition of the Brazilian Slave Trade: Britain, Brazil and the Slave Trade Question* (Cambridge: Cambridge University Press, 1970). For an epitome, see the same author's account in Leslie Bethell, ed., *The Cambridge History of Latin America, Volume III: From Independence to c. 1870* (Cambridge: Cambridge University Press, 1985), 728–737. See also, George Francis Dow, *Slave Ships and Slaving* (Salem, MA:: Marine Research Society, 1927), 250.
63. Bethell, *Abolition of the Brazilian Slave Trade*, 327–363; also, Robert Conrad, *The Destruction of Brazilian Slave Trade, 1850–1888* (Berkeley and Los Angeles: University of California Press, 1972), 23.
64. David Eltis, *Economic Growth and the Ending of the Transatlantic Slave Trade* (Oxford: Oxford University Press, 1987), 82, 92–94, 101.
65. Ibid., 82.
66. Bernard Semmel, *Jamaican Blood and Victorian Conscience: The Governor Eyre Controversy* (Boston: Houghton Mifflin, 1963).

11 Treaty-Making and Dhow-Chasing in the Indian Ocean

1. Grace Fox, *British Admirals and Chinese Pirates, 1832–1869* (London: Kegan Paul, Trench, Trubner and Co., 1940), 147; see also G. A. Wood, "Pax Britannica: The Royal Navy around 1860," in G.A. Wood and P.S. O'Connor, eds., *W.P. Morrell, a Tribute* (Dunedin: University of Otago Press, 1978).
2. As will be seen in this chapter and that following it, the British public (and Parliament) were not alerted to the horrors and extent of the slave traffic of East Africa until David Livingstone (amplified by others) brought it to their attention. In addition, these seas were the commercial dominion of the East India Company, which did not seek to police slavery and slave-trading though it was concerned about damage to its seaborne commerce attributable to piracy. As a subject for historians, too, the study of the East African trade came well in the wake of those works that dealt with West Africa. A partial explanation is that the West African trade was linked to the Americas and was therefore more visible as a problem to be addressed by "the Saints" and others in Britain, but of primary importance is the fact that the trade of East Africa (other than in slaves) was of a petty and unimportant sort to European interests, and the Portuguese seemed largely indifferent to the slave trade there until Livingstone brought the horrors of it to the attention of the British public, when,

perhaps naturally, the Portuguese complained mightily. In short, East Africa was a commercial backwater to British interests at that time. Later, missionary and corporate frontiers supplanted the influence brought there by the Navy, all part of the scramble for Africa and its partition that marked the last two decades of the century. German press agitation played a role in British responses, but, until Kruger threatened intervention at the time of the Anglo-Boer War, it was not a place of security concern. For the change in British attitudes after 1885 and especially after 1895, see Robinson and Gallagher, *Africa and the Victorians*, 420–449.

3. In the "cold shower" department regarding piracy, see Peter Earle, *The Pirate Wars* (New York: St Martins, 2006).
4. In 1846, Captain Belcher in the *Sammarang*, surveying the Moluccas, was preyed upon by a horde of Dyaks. He carried out extensive reprisals and claimed nearly £12,000 for himself and the ship's company. After review by the Privy Council, the award was granted. However, a governmental review followed and in 1850 the measure was modified.
5. For an example of this, see Sherard Osborn, *Quedah; or Stray Leaves from a Journal in Malayan Waters* (new ed; London: Routledge, 1865). The first edition was published in 1857.
6. Raymond C. Howell, *The Royal Navy and the Slave Trade* (New York: St. Martin's Press, 1987), v.
7. Colomb, *Slave Catching*, 22.
8. Quoted, Hyam, *Britain's Imperial Century*, 44.
9. Malcolm, *Sketches in Persia*, 1: 27–28; also, Gerald S. Graham, *Great Britain in the Indian Ocean* (Oxford: Clarendon, 1967), 237–242.
10. For further particulars, see Graham, *Great Britain in the Indian Ocean*, 246–250.
11. Ibid., 246, 456. The security of Napoleon was the first charge of the commander-in-chief on the Cape station. The story of Napoleon's jailers may be followed, in part, in Frank Giles, *Napoleon Bonaparte: England's Prisoner* (London: Constable, 2001).
12. Neville Thompson, *Earl Bathurst and the British Empire* (Barnsley: Leo Cooper, 1999); Hugh Johnston, *British Emigration Policy, 1815–1830: Shovelling Out Paupers* (Oxford: Clarendon, 1972).
13. Eric A. Walker, ed., *The Cambridge History of the British Empire: Volume VIII: South Africa, Rhodesia and the High Commission Territories* (Cambridge: Cambridge University Press, 1963), 239–247.
14. On Somerset, Albany and the Cape, see Thompson, *Earl Bathurst and the British Empire*, 196–210; see also Johnston, *British Emigration Policy, 1815–1830*, Chapter 3.
15. W. Keith Hancock, *Survey of British Commonwealth Affairs*, 2, pt. 1 (1942), 13.
16. Memorandum by Edward Fairfield, 4 August 1885, C.O. 879/23/304.
17. Raymond W. Beachey, *The Slave Trade of Eastern Africa* (New York: Barnes & Noble, 1976), 38–39.
18. W. Wilberforce to F. Moresby, 28 May 1822, printed in Moresby, *Two Admirals*, 26–27.
19. Moresby's further role can be followed in his letter to the Admiralty, 9 June 1822, Adm. 1/2188. For more detail on the Moresby Treaty and others, and the deviance of various peoples to get round them, see Beachey, *Slave Trade of East Africa*, 42–50; see also Graham, *Great Britain in the Indian Ocean*, 198–202, 211–213.
20. For a discussion of anti-slavery and anti-slave trade decrees and treaties, see R.W. Beachey, ed., *A Collection of Documents on the Slave Trade of Eastern Africa* (London: Rex Collings, 1976), 103–133; Also, Arnold T. Wilson, *Persian Gulf*...(Oxford: Clarendon, 1928), 216.
21. Beachey, *Slave Trade of East Africa*, 39.

22. Reginald Coupland, *Exploitation of East Africa 1856–1890: The Slave Trade and the Scramble* (2nd. ed.; London: Faber and Faber, 1968), 1.
23. Rear-Admiral James Dacres, Instructions to SNO Mauritius, 9 October 1847, Adm. 123/1, 17–22.
24. Commodore J. Norse to J.W. Croker, 5 January 1823, in George Theal, ed., *Records of South-Eastern Africa, Volume 9* (reprint, Cape Town: C. Struik, 1964), 20.
25. See Sick Return for 30 November 1822, Adm. 1/2268, Cap O 14, and Owen to Secretary of the Admiralty, [?] May 1823, Adm.1/2269, Cap O 18; see also Thomas Boteler, *Narrative of a Voyage of Discovery to Africa and Arabia 1821 to 1826* (2 vols. London: R. Bentley, 1835).
26. See Correspondence Relating to Aden, *Parliamentary Papers*, 1839, vol. XL, no. 37; see also Robert J. Gavin, "Palmerston's Policy towards East and West Africa, 1830–1865", PhD thesis, University of Cambridge, 88–86.
27. Richmond, *Statesmen and Sea Power*, 269.
28. Boyd Cable, A *Hundred Year History of the P. & O. Peninsular and Oriental Steam Navigation Company, 1837–1937* (London: Ivor Nicholson and Watson, 1937), 4.
29. Coupland, *Exploitation of East Africa*, 81–85.
30. This draws on *British and Foreign State Papers, 1839–1840*, vol. 28 (1857), 1259–1260.
31. Additional treaties, discussed in ibid., 1260.
32. Memorandum by Palmerston, 6 December 1846, F.O. 84/647; J.B. Kelly, *Britain and the Persian Gulf, 1795–1880* (Oxford: Clarendon, 1968), 583.
33. C.U. Aitchison, *A Collection of. Treaties, Engagements and Sanads Relating to India and Neighbouring Countries*, vol. XII, no. 909, gives the assorted agreements with sheiks and native chiefs. The literature on this subject is impressive; see, in particular, Graham, *Great Britain in the Indian Ocean* and, of specific value to the location in question and for a longer epoch, J.B. Kelly, *Britain and the Persian Gulf*. The story may be traced into the more modern period in Wilson, *The Persian Gulf*, especially Chapter 28; see also T.J. Bennett, "The Past and Present Connection of England with the Persian Gulf", *Journal Society of the Arts*, June 1902; see also C.J. Low, *History of the Indian Navy (1613–1863)* (2 vols.; London, 1877).
34. Quoted in James Morris, *Farewell the Trumpets: An Imperial Retreat* ([1978] Harmondsworth: Penguin, 1979), 111–112.
35. Frank Broeze, "The Shipowner of Asia since 1815", paper read at the National Maritime Museum, Greenwich, September 1984, 3.
36. Coupland, *Exploitation of East Africa*, 82.
37. Quoted in preface, R.H. Crofton, *The Old Consulate at Zanzibar* (London: Oxford University Press, 1935).
38. Ibid., 23.
39. Ibid., 28.
40. Ibid., 53; also, Murray, *Ships and South Africa*, 57.
41. Colomb, *Slave Catching*, 21–23.
42. R.F. Burton, Commanding East African Expedition, on board HEIC Sloop of War *Elphinstone*, to Royal Geographical Society, 15 December 1856, in Richard Burton, *The Source of the Nile: The Lake Regions of Central Africa* ([1860] London: Folio Society, 1993), 559–565.
43. See correspondence printed in Appendix to ibid., 567–577.
44. On trade in East Africa, see *Cambridge History of the British Empire*, 3: 66–67.
45. Disraeli to Hamerton, 1841, in Reginald Coupland, *East Africa and Its Invaders* (*London*: 1938), 517–519. Resolution of 28 March 1861; quoted in Coupland, *The Exploitation of East Africa*, 151.

46. Friendly, *Beaufort of the Admiralty*, 330.
47. Thomas, *Slave Trade*, 789.
48. Letter to Dr Tidman, 23 May 1856, in W. Garden Blaikie ed., *The Personal Life of David Livingstone* (New York: Fleming H. Revell, n.d.), 501–502.
49. E. Marjorie Moore, *Adventure in the Royal Navy: The Life and Letters of Admiral Sir Arthur William Moore, 1847–1934* (Liverpool, C. Tinling, 1964).
50. William Laird Clowes, *The Royal Navy: A History*, vol. 7 (London, 1903), 386–391.
51. Colomb, *Slave Catching.*
52. Howell, *The Royal Navy and the Slave Trade*, 51.
53. Report of Select Committee on East Africa Slave Trade, *Parliamentary Papers*, 1871, vol. 12.
54. Moore, *Adventures in the Royal Navy*, 38.
55. Ibid., 147–48.
56. Coupland, *Exploitation of East Africa*, 143; see also Rear Admiral C.R. Hillyar, evidence to 1871 Committee on East Africa Slave Trade, Q.1164.
57. Marcia Wright, "East Africa, 1870–1905," in J.D. Fage and Roland Oliver, eds., *The Cambridge History of Africa, Volume 6, from 1870 to 1905* (Cambridge: Cambridge University Press, 1985), 546–557.
58. Moore, *Adventures in the Royal Navy*, 38.
59. Colomb, *Slave Catching* 396–402; W.C. Devereux, *A Cruise in the 'Gorgon'* ([1869] reprint, with introduction by Donald Simpson, London, 1868), 105; and George Sulivan, *Dhow Chasing in Zanzibar Waters* ([1873], reprint, with introduction by Donald Simpson, London: 1968), 253–254. The observations of these naval officers speak of their strong anti-slavery views as well as their powers of description and dedication to task.
60. Hamerton to Secretary, Bombay Government, 13 July 1841 and 3 January 1842, Zanzibar Archives, E.4; Graham, *Great Britain in the Indian Ocean*, 160–161.
61. Quoted, Howell, *Royal Navy and the Slave Trade*, 168. This fine work discusses the episode at length; see also Laird Clowes, *Royal Navy: A History*, 7: 386–387, Hansard, 266: 679; *The Times*, 6 and 12 December 1881.
62. Based on Captain Robert Woodward's report of proceedings; *Parliamentary Papers* [5428] Slave Trade, No. 1, 1888, cited in Laird Clowes, *Royal Navy: A History*, 7: 387–388.
63. Devereaux, 84. Quoted, Graham, *Great Britain in the Indian Ocean*, 136.
64. Ibid.
65. On this theme generally, see Leland H. Jenks, *The Migration of British Capital to 1875* (new ed.; London: Nelson, 1963).
66. John Morley, *The Life of William Ewart Gladstone* (3 vols. London: Macmillan, 1903), 3: 119; see also Macdonagh, "Anti-Imperialism of Free Trade," 165–166.
67. Ronald Robinson and John Gallagher with Alice Denny, *Africa and the Victorians: The Climax of Imperialism* (New York: Anchor, 1968), 48.
68. Quoted, ibid. 49.

12 Darkening Horizons

1. For army matters, see Kenneth Bourne, *Britain and the Balance of Power in North America, 1815–1908* (London: Longmans, Green, 1967); for naval ones, see Barry

Gough, *The Royal Navy and the Northwest Coast of North America, 1810–1914: A Study of British Maritime Ascendancy* (Vancouver: UBC Press, 1971).

2. C.R. Fay, "Movement towards Free Trade, 1820–1853," in J. Holland Rose, A.P. Newton and E.A. Benians, eds., *Cambridge History of the British Empire, Volume 2: The Growth of the New Empire, 1783–1870* (Cambridge: Cambridge University Press, 1961), 408–409.
3. For this and other views, see Bernard Semmell, *The Rise of Free Trade Imperialism* (Cambridge: Cambridge University Press, 1970), 155, and for a discussion, see Brown, *Economics of Imperialism*, 106–107.
4. Duke of Somerset to W.E. Gladstone, 12 and 15 October 1859, British Library, Gladstone papers, Add. MS. 44,304, fols. 13–14 and 17–18.
5. A.J.P. Taylor in Stephen W. Sears, ed., *The Horizon History of the British Empire* (n.p.; American Heritage Publishing, 1973), 498.
6. A.P. Thornton, *The Imperial Idea and Its Enemies: A Study in British Power* (2nd ed. London: Macmillan, 1985), xxix–xxx.
7. Charles P. Stacey, *Canada and the British Army, 1846–71* (rev. ed.; Toronto: University of Toronto Press, 1963); see also, by the same, "Myth of the Unguarded Frontier, 1815–1971," *American Historical Review*, 56 (October 1950), 1–18.
8. William Fox, *The War in New Zealand* (London: Smith Elder, 1866); John Belich, "Colonization and History in New Zealand," in Winks ed., *Oxford History of the British Empire, 5: Historiography*, 183; Also, among numerous histories of the wars, see John Belich, *New Zealand Wars and the Victorian Interpretation of Racial Conflict* (Auckland: University of Auckland Press, 1986).
9. Dilke and Wilkinson, *Imperial Defence*, 33–34.
10. Morris, *Heaven's Command*, p. 535.
11. Nicholas Mansergh, *Commonwealth Experience* (New York: Praeger, 1969), 127.
12. Ibid., 129–130.
13. Mansergh, *Commonwealth Experience*, 124–125; see Donald Schurman, *Imperial Defence, 1868–1887*, John Beeler, ed. (London: Frank Cass, 2000), 100–125, and Brian Tunstall, "Imperial Defence, 1870–1897", *Cambridge History of the British Empire*, 3: 230–254.
14. Schurman, *Imperial Defence*, 117.
15. Memo by Percy Lake, "Colonial Defence: Reinforcements for War", confidential, 12 April 1889, quoting the Admiralty's dictum as given to the Colonial Office, 8 November 1881, Naval Intelligence Papers, No. 4, copy, Adm.1/7322 (B3605).
16. "Report of a Conference, held at the Colonial Office, on the Subject of the Conveyance of Reinforcements to our Colonial Garrisons in the Event of War with a Maritime Power", secret, 19 December 1889, copy in ibid.
17. William Johnston, William G.P. Rawling, Richard Gimblett, and John MacFarlane, *The Seabound Coast: The Official History of the Royal Canadian Navy, 1867–1939, Volume 1* (Toronto: Dundurn, 2010).
18. C.E. Callwell, *Effect of Maritime Command on Land Campaigns Since Waterloo* (Edinburgh: William Blackwood, 1898), 328–331.
19. G.A. Sanderson, "The European Partition of Africa: Origins and Dynamics", in Fage and Oliver eds., *Cambridge History of Africa, Volume 6*, 97.
20. Carnarvon to Sir Bartle Frere, 12 December 1876, Carnarvon Papers, PRO 30/6/34; cited in ibid., 100.
21. For naval actions and Zanzibar, see Laird Clowes, *Royal Navy: A History*, 7, 435–439, and L.W. Hollingsworth, *Zanzibar under the Foreign Office, 1890–1913* ([1953] Westport: Greenwood, 1975), 119–30.

22. Laird Clowes, *Royal Navy: A History*, 7: 413–414.
23. Edward Grey, *Twenty-Five Years, 1892–1916* (2 vols. New York: Stokes, 1925), 1:12–15.
24. Laird Clowes, *Royal Navy: A History*, 7: 336–374.
25. Robinson, "Non-European Foundations of European Imperialism", 131.
26. Thomas, *Slave Trade*, 790.
27. Quoted, Stanley Bonnett, *The Price of Admiralty: An Indictment of the Royal Navy, 1805–1966* (London: Robert Hale, 1968), 160.
28. See Roger Parkinson, *The Late Victorian Navy: The Pre-dreadnought Era and the Origins of the First World War* (Woodbridge: Boydell, 2008), 89–92.
29. Quoted, Bonnett, *Price of Admiralty*, 162.
30. It is clear that these episodes marked a unique phase of the nineteenth century, perhaps a turning point in British awareness of the difficulties. "In Britain," writes Kennedy, "...one could detect such a groundswell of opinion, occasioned in part by a growing pride in an empire whose significance was only now being explained by Froude, Dilke and Seeley (of whom the two latter were Liberals), and even more by an appreciation of the rising challenges to Britain's world position." Kennedy, *Rise of Anglo-German Antagonism*, 150.
31. *Nineteenth Century*, February 1889, quoted in Richmond, *Statesmen and Sea Power*, 273.
32. For the various possibilities of how an imperial federation might be governed, see Richard Jebb, *The Britannic Question: A Survey of Alternatives* (London: Longmans, Green, 1913).
33. A.D. Elliott, *The Life of George Joachim Goschen, First Viscount Goschen 1831–1907* (2 vols London: Longmans Green, 1911), 2: 206–208.
34. Eric Grove, ed., *Great Battles of the Royal Navy* (Annapolis: Naval Institute Press, 1994), 236.
35. Chamberlain, Birmingham speech, 13 May 1898, *The Times*, 14 May 1898.
36. Ibid.
37. Briton C. Busch, *Britain and the Persian Gulf, 1894–1914* (Berkeley and Los Angeles: University of California Press, 1967).

13 The Lion and the Eagle

1. J.C. Wylie, "Mahan: Then and Now," in John B. Hattendorf, ed., *The Influence of History on Mahan* (Newport, R.I.: Naval War College Press, 1991), 37.
2. Roger Willock, "Gunboat Diplomacy: Operations of the North America and West Indies Squadron, 1875–1915," *American Neptune*, 28 (1968), 103.
3. Willock, *Bulwark of Empire*, 130–150.
4. Admiral Sir Anthony Hopkins to J.A. Fisher, 27 August 1897, FISR 1/1, 30, Churchill Archives Centre, Cambridge.
5. Fisher to Secretary of the Admiralty, 18 September 1897, Adm. 1/7329.
6. Ruddock F. Mackay, *Fisher of Kilverstone* (Oxford: Clarendon, 1973), 212–13; see also Oscar Parkes, *British Battleships* (London: Seeley Service, 1957), 370.
7. Arthur J. Marder, ed., *Fear God and Dread Nought: The Correspondence of Admiral of the Fleet Lord Fisher of Kilverstone* (3 vols.; London: Jonathan Cape, 1956–1960), 1: 101.
8. Clements Markham, *Life of Admiral Sir Leopold McClintock* (London: John Murray, 1909), 292; David Murphy, *The Arctic Fox: Francis Leopold McClintock, Discover of the Fate of Franklin* (Toronto: Dundurn, 204), 166–167.

9. See A.T. Mahan, *Interest of America in Sea Power, Present and Future* (Boston: Little, Brown, 1897).
10. Lieutenant Bingham's letter is printed in Reginald Bacon, *Life of Lord Fisher of Kilverstone, Admiral of the Fleet* (2 vols: London: Hodder and Stoughton, 1929), 1: 116; quoted, Richard Hough, *First Sea Lord: An Authorized Biography of Admiral Lord Fisher* (London: George Allen and Unwin, 1980), 109.
11. Lewis Bayly, *Pull Together! The Memoirs of Admiral Sir Lewis Bayly* (London: George G. Harrap, 1939), 82–85.
12. This is to be found in Ian Marshall's book, a copy of which I have so far been unable to locate. I owe this reference to Kenneth Hagan.
13. Admiral of the Fleet Lord Fisher, *Memories* (London: Hodder and Stoughton, 1919), 225. The story has often been retold as in Taprell Dorling, *Men o' War* (London: Philip Allan, 1929), 228.
14. Alan Wescott, "William Thomas Sampson," *Dictionary of American Biography*, 16 (1938), 321–323.
15. Ibid., 323.
16. See, in particular, Commodore Bourke to Fisher, 27 February 1898, Adm.1/7340A.
17. Captain W.H. Pigott (Captain in Charge, Bermuda) to Fisher, 9 January 1898, Adm. 1/7339B. Fisher was in touch with the governors of Bermuda and Canada on this matter. Fisher to Admiralty, 17 January 1898, ibid. Whether this force was destined for St. Pierre to occupy or for Devil's Island to spring Dreyfus is not revealed in the documents; the answer is unlikely ever to be known.
18. Fisher to James R. Thursfield, 10 November 1898, Halifax, Marder, *Fear God and Dread Nought*, 1: 139. For a discussion of Fisher's war plans and opinions of Admiral Sir William Henderson, then commodore in Jamaica, and of Reginald Bacon, Fisher's biographer, see ibid., 348–349, n. 80; Also, Bacon, *Fisher*, 1:119–20.
19. Fisher to Mrs Reginald Neeld, 23 March 1898, Bermuda, ibid., 1:139.
20. The discussions began in 1880, and may be followed (particularly Sir J. Pauncefote's memo of 9 May 1881) in Kenneth Bourne and Donald C. Watt, eds., *British Documents on Foreign Policy* (multiple volumes; London, 1990), I, C, 9:73–118.
21. Winston Churchill, *Great Contemporaries*, ed. James W. Muller ([1937} Wilmington, Delaware: ISI Books, 2012), 245.
22. Director of Military Intelligence, Memorandum respecting the Clayton–Bulwer Treaty, 9 December 1898, F.O. 55/392; see also Charles S. Campbell, Jr., *Anglo-American Understanding. 1898–1903* (Baltimore: Johns Hopkins Press, 1957, 353–356.
23. George O. Squier, "The Influence of Submarine Cables upon Military and Naval Supremacy," *National Geographic*, 12, 1 (January 1901), 1–12.
24. P.H. Colomb, *Naval Warfare, Its Ruling Principles and Practice Historically Treated* (3rd ed. London: W.H. Allen, 1898), Appendix. Colomb's aim was to provide a scientific analysis of naval history, its benefit to show rules or principles of naval warfare. The work was novel and was an attempt to sweep aside the old works glorifying the deeds of British sea warriors. So arid was the work that it may have had the opposite effect in the literary circles of the age. It contained no Mahanian deductions, though it did point out that rapid long-range gunnery would be more effective than the great big gun. That was a lesson that the Royal Navy did not learn. The fallacy of the great weapon continued to dominate British naval thought (and therefore hull design).
25. Squier, "Influence of Submarine Cables upon Military and Naval Supremacy," 3.

26. Algernon Aspinall, *Pocket Guide to the West Indies: British Guiana, British Honduras, Bermuda, the Spanish Main, Surinam and the Panama Canal* (London: Sifton, Praed, 1936), 280.
27. See Samuel F. Wells, Jr., "British Strategic Withdrawal from the Western Hemisphere, 1904–1906," *Canadian Historical Review*, 49, 4 (December 1968), 335–356.
28. James Ford Rhodes, *The McKinley and Roosevelt Administrations, 1898–1909* (New York: Macmillan, 1922), 252.
29. Michael T. McMaster and Kenneth J. Hagan, " 'His Remarks Reverberated from Berlin to Washington,' " *US Naval Institute Proceedings*, 136, 12 (December 2010), 66–71.
30. *The Times*, 6 May 1919; *Christian Science Monitor*, 8 May 1919; and, for Daniels's telling of it, E. David Cronin, ed., *The Cabinet Diaries of Josephus Daniels, 1913–1921* (Lincoln: University of Nebraska Press, 1963), 407.

14 The Trident Bearers: The Navy as Britannia's Instrument

1. Nicholas A. Lambert, *Planning Armageddon: British Economic Warfare and the First World* War (Cambridge, MA: Harvard University Press, 2012), 1–184.
2. Selborne letter 31 October 1901, in Bryce, *Crisis of British Power*, 136.
3. Admiralty Memorandum on imperial defence presented to the Colonial Conference 1902, dated June 1902 (revised April 1903), in Arthur B. Keith, ed., *Speeches and Documents on British Colonial Policy, 1763–1917* (2 vols in one; Oxford: Oxford University Press, 1966), 2: 230–237.
4. See the full particulars in the memorandum by Langdale Ottley, 27 February 1907, in Nicholas Tracy, ed., *The Collective Naval Defence of the Empire, 1900–1940* (Aldershot: Navy Records Society, 1997), 68–72.
5. Matthew S. Seligmann, *The Royal Navy and the German Threat 1901–1914: Admiralty Plans to Protect British Trade in a War Against Germany* (Oxford: Oxford University Press, 2012).
6. Paul Kennedy, *The Rise of the Anglo-German Antagonism, 1860–1914* ([1980] London: Ashfield, 1987).
7. Humphrey H. Smith, *A Yellow Admiral Remembers* (London: Edward Arnold, 1932), 54.
8. Leslie Gardiner, *The British Admiralty* (Edinburgh: William Blackwood, 1968), 294–295.
9. Arthur J. Marder, The *Anatomy of British Sea Power: A History of British Naval Policy in the Pre-Dreadnought Era, 1880–1905* (New York: Alfred A. Knopf, 1940), 16.
10. Ibid., 16–17.
11. Admiral Fisher's essential documents, written or collected by him as C-in C Portsmouth and as First Sea Lord, were gathered together as three privately printed volumes *Naval Necessities*. The essential first two were published, respectively, in Peter Kemp, ed., *The Papers of Admiral Sir John Fisher, Volume I* (London: Navy Records Society, 1960) and Peter Kemp, ed., *The Papers of Sir John Fisher, Volume II* (London: Navy Records Society, 1964)., 1: 22 and 2: 125–136, quoted ibid.
12. Marquess of Crewe, *Lord Rosebery* (2 vols.: Toronto: Macmillan of Canada, 1931), 2: 426.
13. Fisher to Esher, 8 April 1910, in Lord Fisher, *Memories* (London: Hodder and Stoughton, 1919), 197.

14. B.M. Chambers, "Some Considerations as to the Factors Which Govern the Limit of Size in Battleships", *Naval Review*, 17 (1929), 450.
15. Peter Worsley, *The Trumpet Shall Sound: A Study of "Cargo" Cults in Melanesia* (2nd ed.; New York: Schockan Books, 1970), 178–179; *Pacific Islands Monthly*, October 1947, 71.
16. Robert L. Davison, *The Challenges of Command: The Royal Navy's Executive Branch Officers, 1880–1919* (Farnham: Ashgate, 2011).
17. Winston Churchill, *The World Crisis* (London: Thornton Butterworth, 1923–31), 5 vols. in 6), 1: 93.
18. This is the view of one historian. John Bach, *The Australia Station: A History of the Royal Navy in the South West Pacific, 1821–1913* (Kensington, NSW: New South Wales University Press, 1986), 2.
19. Arthur Marder, ed., *Fear God and Dread Nought: The Correspondence of Admiral of the Fleet Lord Fisher of Kilverstone* (3 vols.; London: Jonathan Cape, 1952–), 1: 147. This is the general theme in Marder, *From the Dreadnought to Scapa Flow: The Royal Navy in the Fisher Era, 1904–1919; Volume 1: The Road to War, 1904–1914* ([1961] Barnsley: Seaforth, 2013).
20. Stephen Roskill, *Hankey: Man of Secrets* (3 vols. London: Collins, 1970–1974), 1: 40, also (for Hankey's observations) 39.
21. M. Hankey to Mrs Robert Hankey, 3 January 1899, in ibid., 39.
22. Maurice Hankey, *The Supreme Command 1914–1918* (2 vols.: London: Allen & Unwin, 1961), 1: 13–14.
23. Roskill, *Hankey: Man of Secrets*, 1: 40.
24. HMAS *Australia* (1911), a battle-cruiser, was laid down at John Brown shipyard, Clydebank.
25. *Colonial Conference of 1902, Summary of Proceedings* (Ottawa: King's Printer, 1902), 4, 31–32; O.D. Skelton, *Life and Letters of Sir Wilfrid Laurier* (2 vols. Toronto: Oxford University Press, 1921), 2: 294.
26. I take this line of reasoning from Nicholas Mansergh, *The Coming of the First World War: A Study in the European Balance, 1878–1914* (London: Longmans, Green, 1949).
27. Laird Clowes, *Royal Navy: A History*, 7: 76.
28. Charles Repington, "The Military Defence of the Empire", by our Military Correspondent, *The Times*, 24 May 1909, 43.

15 Recessional: The End of *Pax Britannica* and the American Inheritance

1. Augustus Agar, *Showing the Flag* (London: Evans, 1962), 25–27.
2. A.E.M[?], "HMS *Wistaria,*" ms., copy in Maritime Command Museum, Admiralty House, Halifax, N.S.
3. Nicholas Mansergh, *Survey of British Commonwealth Affairs: Problems of External Policy, 1931–1939* (London: Oxford University Press, 1952), 52–56.
4. Barry Hunt, " Road to Washington: Canada and Empire Naval Defence, 1918–1921", in James Boutilier, ed., *The RCN in Retrospect, 1910–1968* (Vancouver: UBC Press, 1982), 44–61, 350–352.
5. Woodcock, *British in the Far East*, 221.
6. Ian H. Nish, *The Anglo-Japanese Alliance* (London: Athlone, 1968), 231.
7. John Keay, *Empire's End: A History of the Far East from High Colonialism to Hong Kong* (New York: Scribner, 1997), 74–84.
8. Quoted, Marder, *Old Friends, New Enemies*, 3.

9. Lloyd, *Nation and the Navy*, 267.
10. Jon Tetsuro Sumida, *Inventing Grand Strategy and Teaching Command: The Classic Works of Alfred Thayer Mahan Reconsidered* (Washington, DC: Woodrow Wilson Center Press, and Baltimore: Johns Hopkins University Press, 1997).
11. For an introduction, see Jerry W. Jones, *U.S. Battleship Operations in World War I* (Annapolis: Naval Institute Press, 1998); for discussions, see David Trask, *Captains and Cabinets: Anglo-American Naval Relations, 1917–1918* (Columbia: University of Missouri Press, 1972).
12. See Baily, *Pull Together!* especially foreword by Franklin Delano Roosevelt.
13. Ibid., 35.
14. Quoted, Joseph P., Lash, *Roosevelt and Churchill 1939–1941: The Partnership that Saved the West* (New York: W.W. Norton, 1976), 34–35.
15. Speech of 5 September 1940. Quoted in Winston S. Churchill, *The Second World War, Volume 2: Their Finest Hour* (London: Cassell, 1949), 362.
16. Speech, 5 September 1940, ibid, 367.
17. Ibid., 212.
18. Ibid., 213–214.
19. W. Roger Louis, *British Strategy in the Far East, 1919–1939* (Oxford: Oxford University Press, 1971), 260–267.
20. R. Backhouse to J. Sommerville, 5 December 1938, Adm. 1/9767. See also Stephen Roskill, *Naval Policy between the Wars: Volume 2: The Period of Reluctant Rearmament* (Annapolis: Naval Institute Press, 1976), 432.
21. David Hobbs, *The British Pacific Fleet: The Royal Navy's Most Powerful Strike Force* (Barnsley: Seaforth, 2011).
22. Stephen Roskill, *The War at Sea, Vol. 3, Part 2* (London: HMSO, 1961), 383; G. Hermon Gill, *Royal Australian Navy, 1942–1945* (Canberra: Australian War Memorial, 1968), 682–683.
23. Malcolm M. Murfett, *Hostage on the Yangtze: Britain, China, and the Amethyst Crisis of 1949* (1991). In 1957 the story was told in the British film *Yangtze Incident* (issued in the United States as *Battle Hill, Escape of the Amethyst* and *This Greatest Glory*) with Richard Todd playing Lieutenant Commander Kerans.
24. Coxswain Leslie Frank's ms. diary of the episode, copy in author's possession.
25. Ibid.
26. Lieutenant Commander Kearns, Memorandum, Yangtze Incident, 18 December 1949, included in ibid.
27. Gregory Haines, *Gunboats on the Great River* (London: Macdonald and Jane's, 1976), 48. The episode involving the loss of *Peterel* is given at 156–159. Re; standing orders, as of 1932, see ibid., 46–47.
28. "Economic strength, not imperial power, should now be the goal – although it needed no trained Marxist to point out (as the chorus of voices from Asia and Africa did point out) that these were the two sides of a single coin." Thornton, *For the File on Empire*, 372.
29. Ibid., 373.
30. Winston S. Churchill, *Lord Randolph Churchill* (new ed. London: Odhams, 1952), 12.
31. Simon Winchester, *Outposts: Journeys to the Surviving Relics of the British Empire* (new ed., New York: Harper Perennial, 2004), 340–341.
32. Jeremi Suri, "America the Overcommitted," *International Herald Tribune*, 15–16 October 2011, 10.
33. Lewis, *Navy in Transition;* quoted, *Naval Review*, 55 (January 1966): 71.

34. F.A. Voight, *Pax Britannica* (London: Constable, 1949), 544–547. The author was former editor of the influential journal *The Nineteenth Century and After.*
35. Paul Kennedy, The *Rise and Fall of the Great Powers: Economic Change and Military Conflict from 1500 to 2000* (London: Unwin Hyman, 1988), 359.
36. W.W. Rostow, "Beware of Historians Bearing False Analogies", *Foreign Affairs* (Spring 1988), 863–868 (quotation, 868); and Kennedy's reply: "Pointers from the Past", *Foreign Affairs* (Summer 1966), 1008–1111; see further, Kennedy's "Fin-de-Siècle America", *New York Review of Books*, 37, 11 (28 June 1990), 31–40.
37. Clark G. Reynolds, *Command of the Sea: The History and Strategy of Maritime Empires* (new ed. 2 vols: Malabar, Fla: Krieger, 1985), 2: 546–547.
38. Wm. Roger Louis and Ronald Robinson, "The Imperialism of Decolonization", *Journal of Imperial and Commonwealth History,* 22, 3 (September 1994), 462–511; see also Louis, "Dissolution of the British Empire", *Oxford History of the British Empire,* 4 (1999): 330–331.

Notes on the Historical Materials

Chapter 1: Defining *Pax Britannica*

Literature on the history of the Royal Navy is vast and discursive. Even in noting general works on the subject that relate to the years of *Pax Britannica*, 1815–1914, the historian is struck with the mass of materials. I have been guided by Eugene L. Rasor, *British Naval History Since 1815: A Guide to the Literature* (New York: Garland, 1990). Many general histories of the Navy have been written that bear on this period, including Michael Lewis, *The Navy of Britain: A Historical Portrait* (London: George Allen and Unwin, 1948), to my way of thinking one of the most perceptive works of the age, even if dated. The reader learns much about the style of the Navy, and also its traditions and sense of individuality. John Winton, *An Illustrated History of the Royal Navy*, published in association with the Royal Naval Museum, Portsmouth (London: Salamander, 2000), bears the official seal but is entirely accurate as to its subject, and its intention to discuss the changing times and circumstances of the Navy, from the early days of anti-piracy to the nuclear age. It is fabulously illustrated (and the Navy was fabulously prone to being illustrated). It lacks a bibliography. For an accurate treatise of the more modern era, one can do no better than consulting Anthony J. Watts, *The Royal Navy: An Illustrated History* (Annapolis: Naval Institute Pres, 1994), which contains 14 chapters that take the story of *Pax Britannica* up to 1914. A work with a heavy textual base, it is worth attention, though again it lacks a bibliography. An equally fine profile of the age is in J.R. Hill, ed., *Oxford Illustrated History of the Royal Navy* (Oxford: Oxford University Press, 1996), which has a bibliography. A more specialized work for the latter decades is Peter Padfield, *Rule Britannia: the Victorian and Edwardian Navy* (London: Routledge & Kegan Paul, 1981). Based on a sound appreciation of naval memoirs, this is an important introduction to naval studies of the era. Of specific value, though dated, is W. Laird Clowes, *The Royal Navy: A History* (7 vols. [1897–1913] London: Chatham, 1997). See also Paul Kennedy, *Rise and Fall of British Naval Mastery* (London: Allen Lane, 1976 and later editions).

Because *Pax Britannica* belongs to that important 100 years of unbridled British influence on and over the seas, certain works under the heading of "Imperial history" command our attention. The best way to deal with this is to consult Volume 3 of the *Oxford History of the British Empire*, ed. Andrew Porter (Oxford University Press, 1999). This contains an important chapter on imperial defence by Peter Burroughs, and discussion of the same issue in many another chapter. Volume 5 of the same series, *Historiography*, edited by Robin Winks, contains various chapters on the historical literature of the West Indies (B.H. Higman), Australia (Stuart Macintyre), New Zealand (James Belich) and three of particular relevance: "Exploration and Empire" (Robert A. Stafford), "The Royal Navy and the British Empire" (Barry M. Gough) and "Imperial Defence" (David Killingray), plus concluding chapters by A.P. Thornton and Robin Winks that are worth the consideration of any serious student. *Cambridge History of the British Empire*, E.A. Benians, J. Holland Rose et al. (9 volumes, to 1959) contains discussions of early histories of enduring merit, which form a guide to documents (some in print) in British repositories. Of particular use to the student are lists of *Parliamentary Papers* of the British Government, a corporate public distillation of official correspondence and statistical data that provides a useful framework for any imperial and colonial history. Ronald Hyam's *Britain's Imperial Century, 1815–1914: A Study of Empire and Expansion* (New York: Barnes and Noble, 1974) asks many fine questions and provides an overall coverage of the epoch. The subthemes of profit and power are demonstrated in P.J. Cain and A.G. Hopkins, *British Imperialism, 1688–2000* (2nd ed. London: Pearson, 2002). For a discussion, see Raymond E. Dumett, *Gentlemanly Capitalism and British Imperialism: The New Debate on Empire* (London: Longman, 1999).

That the British were informed by the classical world of the Greeks and Romans has been laid open clearly by Christopher Hagerman in his *Britain's Imperial Muse* (Palgrave Macmillan, 2013). Attempts to formulate the basics of *Pax Britannica* begin with Gerald S. Graham, *The Politics of Naval Supremacy: Studies in British Maritime Ascendancy* (Cambridge: University Press, 1965). C.J. Bartlett, *Great Britain and Sea Power, 1815–1853* ([1963] Aldershot: Gregg Revivals, 1993) is indispensable to the eve of the Crimean War and is richly based on an array of documentary sources. On the Admiralty, see N.A.M. Rodger, *The Admiralty* (Lavenham: T. Dalton, 1979). Worth close study is the perceptive Stanley Bonnett, *The Price of Admiralty: An Indictment of the Royal Navy, 1805–1966* (London: Hale, 1966). The most recent study is that of C.I. Hamilton, *The Making of the Modern Admiralty: British Naval Policy-Making, 1805–1927* (New York: Cambridge University Press, 2011); see also his *Anglo-French Naval Rivalry, 1840–1870* (Oxford: Clarendon, 1993).

Chapter 2: Empire of the Seas

For an introduction, see Brian Lavery, *Empire of the Seas: How the Navy Forged the Modern World* (London: Anova Books, 2009). For an analysis of specific challenges in the 1830s and 1840s, see Rebecca Berens Matzke, *Deterrence through Strength: British Naval Power and Foreign Policy under the Pax Britannica* (Lincoln: University of Nebraska Press, 2011). On ships, see Andrew D. Lambert, *The Last Sailing Battlefleet: Maintaining Naval Mastery 1815–1850* (London: 1991), and for later years, see D.K. Brown, *From Warrior to Dreadnought: Warship Development, 1906–1922* (London: Chatham, 2002). On social aspects, see John Wells, *The Royal Navy: An Illustrated Social History, 1870–1982* (Stroud: Sutton, 1994); Robert L. Davison, *The Challenges of Command: The Royal Navy's Executive Branch Officers, 1880–1919* (Farnham: Ashgate, 2011). For the lower deck, see John Winton, *Hurrah For the Life of a Sailor: Life on the Lower Deck in the Victorian Navy* (London: Michael Joseph, 1977). For the state of navies and construction on the eve of the First World War, see Viscount Hythe, ed., *The Naval Annual, 1913* ([1913] Newton Abbot: David & Charles, 1970).

Chapter 3: Anchors of Empire

Jonathan G. Coad, *The Royal Dockyards, 1690–1850: Architecture and Engineering Works of the Sailing Navy* (Aldershot: Scolar, 1989). Among many books on Bermuda, I have consulted, and recommend, Ian Stranack, *The Andrew and the Onions: The Story of the Royal Navy in Bermuda, 1795–1975* (2nd ed. Old Dockyard Bermuda: Bermuda Maritime Museum Association, 1990); Edward Harris, *Great Guns of Bermuda* (Mangrove Bay: Bermuda Maritime Museum Association, 1992); Roger Willock, *Bulwark of Empire: Bermuda's Fortified Naval Base, 1860–1920* (2nd ed. Old Royal Navy Dockyard: Bermuda Maritime Museum Press, 1988).

Chapter 4: Surveying the Seas, Expanding the Empire of Science

Fergus Fleming's *Barrow Boys* (New York: Atlantic Monthly Press, 1998) provides a fresh introduction to Barrow and his various schemes. Christopher Lloyd, *Mr Barrow of the*

Admiralty (London: Collins, 1980), if dated, remains the essential study of a great traveller and personality of the age. More generally, Alfred Friendly's *Beaufort of the Admiralty* (London: Hutchinson, 1977) repays close study, and serves as a model for what might be done with George Henry Richards or John Washington. I have relied repeatedly on George Ritchie, *The Admiralty Chart: British Naval Hydrography in the Nineteenth Century, with an Introductory Essay by Andrew David* (new edition; Edinburgh: Pentland, 1995), a work of erudition and wide compass.

Chapter 5: Informal and Formal Empires in the Americas

These are the key scholarly monographs covering the Western Hemisphere during *Pax*: Kenneth Bourne, *Britain and the Balance of Power in North America, 1815–1908* (London: Longman, 1967); Charles Maier, "Managing Discord in the Americas: Great Britain and the United States, 1886–1896", PhD thesis, Royal Military College of Canada, 2010; Rory Miller, *Britain and Latin America in the Nineteenth and Twentieth Centuries* (London, 1993); Barry Gough, *The Royal Navy and the Northwest Coast of North America, 1810–1914: A Study of British Maritime Ascendancy* (Vancouver: UBC Press, 1971). For the Falklands, see Barry Gough, *The Falkland Islands/Malvinas: The Contest for Empire in the South Atlantic* (London: Athlone, 1992).

Chapter 6: Challenges of Europe, the Mediterranean and the Black Sea

H.L. Hoskins, *British Routes to India* ([1928] New York: Octagon, 1966) is useful for this chapter and for the next. See also Andrew Lambert, *The Crimean War: British Grand Strategy against Russia, 1853–1856* (Manchester: Manchester University Press, 1990). See also my notes and suggestions for Chapters 1 and 2.

Chapter 7: The Indian Ocean, Singapore and the China Seas

On rivalry with the Dutch, Nicholas Tarling, *Anglo-Dutch Rivalry in the Malay World, 1780–1824* (Cambridge: Cambridge University Press, 1962) is the classic account. For the spread of British imperial interests and naval actions beyond the Cape of Good Hope, I have used Gerald S. Graham, *Great Britain in the Indian Ocean: A Study of Maritime Enterprise, 1810–1850* (Oxford: Clarendon, 1967), based on Admiralty papers. On anti-piracy, see Nicholas Tarling, *Piracy and Politics in the Malay World: A Study of British Imperialism in Nineteenth-Century South-East Asia* (Melbourne and Canberra: F.W. Cheshire, 1963); Kathleen Harland, *The Royal Navy in Hong Kong* (Liskeard, 1985).

Chapter 8: The Imperial Web in the South Pacific

John Bach, *The Australia Station: A History of the Royal Navy in the South West Pacific, 1821–1913* (Kensington: New South Wales University Press, 1986) and Jane Samson, *Imperial Benevolence: Making British Authority in the Pacific Islands* (Honolulu: University of Hawaii Press, 1998) are outstanding studies of naval difficulties and actions. Of key importance are John M. Ward's *British Policy in the South Pacific, 1783–1893: A Study in British Policy towards the South Pacific Islands Prior to the Establishment of Governments by Great Powers* (Sydney: Australasian Publishing Company, 1948) and W.P. Morrell, *Great Britain in the Pacific Islands* (Oxford: Clarendon, 1960). See also Alan Frost and Jane Samson, *Pacific*

Empires: Essays in Honour of Glyndwr Williams (Carleton South: Melbourne, 1999) and Jane Samson, ed., *British Imperial Strategies in the Pacific, 1750–1900* (Aldershot: Ashgate, 2003).

Chapter 9: Send a Gunboat!

This chapter rests heavily on Barry Gough's *Gunboat Frontier: British Maritime Authority and Northwest Coast Indians, 1846–1890* (Vancouver: UBC Press, 1984), where the "politics" of naval intervention are examined more closely and the interpretation of such actions are analysed more generally. With regard to gunboats themselves, still reliable is Anthony Preston and John Major's *Send a Gunboat: 150 Years of the British Gunboat* (rev. ed.; Annapolis, MD: Naval Institute Press, 2006).

Chapter 10: Anti-Slavery: West Africa and the Americas

Charles Davies, *The Blood Red Arab Flag: An Investigation into Qasimi Piracy, 1797–1820* (Exeter: University of Exeter Press, 1997). Essential still is Christopher Lloyd's *The Navy and the Slave Trade* (London: Longmans, 1949), which is useful in its guidance to the *Parliamentary Papers* that form the essential documentation for any such study. Supplementary to this is W.E.F. Ward's *The Royal Navy and the Slavers* (London: Allen & Unwin, 1969). Hugh Thomas, *The Slave Trade: the Story of the Atlantic Slave Trade, 1440–1870* (New York: Simon & Schuster, 1997) provides a useful beginning point for the non-specialist and contains many useful leads to printed and primary, chiefly British, sources. Roger Anstey provides essential British background in *Atlantic Slave Trade and British Abolition, 1760–1810* (London: Macmillan, 1975). For Brazil, see Leslie Bethell's *The Abolition of the Brazilian Slave Trade* (Cambridge: Cambridge University Press, 1970) and also Peter Conrad, *The Destruction of Brazilian Slavery* (Berkeley and Los Angeles: University of California Press, 1972), which examines Brazilian accounts.

Chapter 11: Treaty-Making and Dhow-Chasing in the Indian Ocean

Raymond Howell, *The Royal Navy and the Slave Trade* (New York: St. Martin's, 1987) is the standard study, based on primary sources, of how the Navy was directed to eastern seas, round the Cape of Good Hope. His study of the Navy's "spider's web" is brilliant. Other works, by Lloyd and Ward, noted for the previous chapter, have some coverage of these broader seas, but Howell remains the basic source. For the earlier era, and the treaties signed for the Red Sea and the Arabian Gulf, I have relied on Graham, *Great Britain in the Indian Ocean*, cited in Chapter 7, above; see also, J.B. Kelly, *Britain and the Persian Gulf* (Oxford: Clarendon, 1968). Essential, too, is R.W. Beachey's *A Collection of Documents on the Slave Trade of Eastern Africa* (New York: Barnes & Noble, 1976).

Chapter 12: Darkening Horizons

This is not the neglected "dark age" of British naval history, as is so often claimed. The essential work is John F. Beeler, *British Naval Policy in the Gladstone-Disraeli Era, 1866–1880* (Stanford: Stanford University Press, 1997). Colin White, *Victoria's Navy: The End of the Sailing Navy* (Havant, Hants.: Kenneth Mason, 1981) is a useful study of the change and its implications. Bryan Ranft, ed., *Technical Change and British Naval Policy, 1860–1939* (London: Hodder and Stoughton, 1977). Donald Schurman, *The Education of a Navy: The Development of British Naval Strategic Thought, 1867–1914* (London: Cassell, 1965) repays close study. See also my notes and suggestions for Chapter 14.

Chapter 13: The Lion and the Eagle

Admiral Fisher's time in North American and West Indies waters has been underrated, even by his champion, Arthur Marder, and slavishly followed by others since. But some useful correspondence (apart from the Adm. 1 and Adm. 128 [Station] files cited) is printed in Marder, ed., *Fear God and Dread Nought: The Correspondence of Admiral of the Fleet Lord Fisher of Kilverstone, Volume 1* (London: Jonathan Cape, 1952). Among other studies, see A.E. Campbell, *Great Britain and the United States, 1895–1903* ([1960] Westport, CT: Greenwood, 1974); George W. Monger, *The End of Isolation: British Foreign Policy, 1900–1907* (London, T. Nelson, 1963); Mary Williams, *Anglo-American Isthmian Diplomacy, 1815–1915* (Washington, DC: American Historical Association, 1916).

Chapter 14: The Trident Bearers: The Navy as Britannia's Instrument

For an introduction to the overarching themes, see Bernard Semmel, *Liberalism & Naval Strategy: Ideology, Interest, and Sea Power during the Pax Britannica* (Boston: Allen & Unwin, 1986). Arthur J. Marder, *The Anatomy of British Sea Power, 1880–1905* (New York: Alfred Knopf, 1940), though dated, has been my guide here on the "politics" of naval paramountcy with useful side glances at imperial rivalries, noticeably in the Far East and foreign policy. Roger Parkinson, *The Late Victorian Navy: The Pre-Dreadnought Era and the Origins of the First World War* (New York: Boydell, 2008), is a new look at the material covered by Marder, with benefit, though the conclusions are essentially the same. Jon Sumida, *In Defence of Naval Supremacy: Finance, technology, and British Naval Policy, 1889–1914* (Boston: Unwin Hyman, 1989, and other printings), Nicholas Lambert, *Sir John Fisher's Naval Revolution* (Columbia: University of South Carolina Press, 1999) and Arthur Marder, *From the Dreadnought to Scapa Flow, Volume 1* ([1960] Barnsley: Seaforth, 2013) remain essential in the historical literature. For background material I consulted Miriam Hood's *Gunboat Diplomacy, 1895–1905: Great Power Pressure in Venezuela* (London: George Allen & Unwin, 1983), based on Foreign Office materials. See also Peter Padfield, *Rule Britannia: The Victorian and Edwardian Navy* (London: Routledge & Kegan Paul, 1981).

Chapter 15: Recessional: The End of *Pax Britannica* and the American Inheritance

For consequences of dominion autonomy for British external policy, the best introduction remains Nicholas Mansergh's *Survey of British Commonwealth Affairs: Problems of External Policy, 1931–1939* (London: Oxford University Press, 1952). This work addresses a far larger timespan than is suggested by the title. For naval matters more specifically, see Stephen Roskill, *Naval Policy Between the Wars* (2 vols.; London, Collins, 1968, 1976). Paul Kennedy, *The Rise and Fall of the Great Powers: Economic Change and Military Conflict from 1500 to 2000* (London: Unwin Hyman, 1988) provides the basic beginning for retrospectives on *Pax Britannica*. William Roger Louis, *British Strategy in the Far East, 1919–1939* (Oxford: Oxford University Press, 1971) provides the essential policy analysis. More generally, see Ann Trotter, *Britain and East Asia, 1933–1937* (Cambridge: Cambridge University Press, 1975). Several chapters in Brown and Louis, *Oxford History of the British Empire, Volume 4: The Twentieth Century* address these concerns; see especially those by John Darwin, Anthony Clayton, Robert Holland, and Roger Louis. See also William Roger Louis, *Imperialism at Bay, 1941–1945: The United States and Decolonization of the British Empire* (Oxford: Oxford University Press, 1977) on the subject of ideological differences expressed by the United States, making all the more difficult Britain's attempts to sustain the British Empire during the Second World War; the same foreshadowed differences in worldwide influence by both powers in subsequent years.

Index of Ships

Note: All are British warships except where noted. Locators followed by the letter 'n' refer to notes.

Subject Index

Note: Locators followed by the letter 'n' refer to notes.

Printed and bound by CPI Group (UK) Ltd, Croydon, CR0 4YY